Settlement and Society: aspects of West European prehistory in the first millennium B.C.

edited by T. C. Champion and J. V. S. Megaw

Leicester University Press 1985

First published in 1985 by Leicester University Press
First published in the United States of America in 1985 by
St. Martin's Press, Inc.

Designed by Arthur Lockwood
Set in Linotron 202 Sabon and Univers
by Wyvern Typesetting Limited, Bristol
Printed and bound in Great Britain
at the University Press, Cambridge

British Library Cataloguing in Publication Data

Settlement and society: aspects of West European
prehistory in the first millennium B.C.
1. Iron age – Europe
I. Champion, T. C. II. Megaw, J. V. S.
936 GN780.2.A1

ISBN 0–7185–1232–4
ISBN 0–7185–1256–1 Pbk

Contents

Illustrations

Frontispiece: detail of handle mount of bronze flagon from Waldalgesheim, Kr. Kreuznach (Rhein. Landesmuseum Bonn; photo J. V. S. Megaw)

Abbreviations

Note: Places of publication are given only for works published outside the United Kingdom. Commonly accepted abbreviations such as *J.* for *Journal, Rev.* for *Review* etc. have been used in journal titles; other abbreviations are listed below.

Ant. J.	*Antiquaries Journal*
Arch. Korr.	*Archäologisches Korrespondenzblatt*
Bonner Jahrb.	*Bonner Jahrbücher*
BAR	British Archaeological Reports
Bull. Inst. Archaeol. Univ. London	*Bulletin of the Institute of Archaeology, University of London*
Hamburger Beiträge zur Archäol.	*Hamburger Beiträge zur Archaölogie*
Jahrbuch RGZM	*Jahrbuch des Römisch-Germanischen Zentralmuseums, Mainz*
Procs. Prehist. Soc.	*Proceedings of the Prehistoric Society*
Procs. Royal Irish Acad.	*Proceedings of the Royal Irish Academy*
Procs. Soc. Ant. Scotland	*Proceedings of the Society of Antiquaries of Scotland*
RG Forsch.	Römisch-Germanisch Forschungen
World Archaeol.	*World Archaeology*

For the three S's

Foreword

Like many collections of essays such as those in the pages that follow, this volume has its inspiration rather than final form rooted in a conference.

With three exceptions, the papers assembled here were originally given at a conference entitled 'European societies in the first millennium B.C.' organized in London by the Prehistoric Society at Easter 1981 and at a related research seminar on specialization of production held in Oxford immediately afterwards. Both at the conference and in this volume it was thought best to focus on a limited number of themes and areas at the cost of leaving many topics of interest untouched. Only one paper deals with non-Celtic 'barbarian' society, while subsistence economy, ideology, technological innovation and mortuary analysis, which, with the growing evidence particularly for settlement archaeology could all have been included at greater length, are discussed largely incidentally. Also, a deliberate decision was made to exclude the Late La Tène period, though considerable advances have been made in recent years in our knowledge of economy and political organization in this final phase of the pre-Roman Iron Age. Possible long-term trends in social organization are not ignored, however, and at least two papers (Lorenz and Nash) represent bold attempts to move beyond the details of the data to a reconstruction of the changing nature of Iron Age society and politics.

As Editors, we owe apologies to all our readers and – almost – all our contributors for the delays which have ensued since this volume was first conceived. The logistics of coordinating across two hemispheres and three continents are only part of the story, and it is but their due that we should express our thanks for actually bringing this book into physical being to Sara Champion who translated as well as composed, Sue Semmens who proved that the title 'Research Assistant' is simply a synonym for *Mädchen für Alles*, and Sue Martin who has endured with ruthless equanimity the fate of editing one of the Editors for the third time.

Guy Fawkes Night 1983

TCC
JVSM

Introduction: approaches to the study of Iron Age settlement and society

T. C. Champion and J. V. S. Megaw

Of all the periods of European prehistory, the Iron Age is the most plentifully endowed with material evidence. The years from the first explorations in the cemeteries around the Hallstatt salt-mines in 1824 to the rectification of the Jura waterways in 1868 and the subsequent major discoveries and excavations at La Tène, marked an epoch of major discoveries. Most striking of course were the early excavations in the *Fürstengräber* zones of eastern France, the Rhineland and southern Germany – although it must be noted that many key finds still await adequate study more than a century after their initial publication. The continuing wealth of material recovered from the Dürrnberg bei Hallein, where the first recorded finds date to A.D. 1577, shows that the age of discovery is by no means over. Over the years dispersement of material into collections both private and public has certainly raised practical problems, both of research and in the politics of the restitution of cultural property. Thus to study adequately the discoveries made in 1882 at the Duchcov (Dux) spring in north-west Bohemia or the grand Carniolan depredations of Grand Duchess Paul Friedrich of Mecklenburg, one must travel not only to the capitals of the old Austro-Hungarian Empire but to the British Isles, the United States and even Australia.

In more recent years intensive work by scholars in the south of France, northern Italy, Hungary and Romania, to name four regions hardly touched on in these pages, have vastly increased our knowledge of the development of Celtic society – particularly in zones where it impinged on and intermingled with that of other contemporary cultural groups. Of course the work of synthesis began early, as evidenced by Otto Tischler's first chronological ordering of the Hallstatt and La Tène periods, in 1881 and 1885 respectively, while the first extensive review of pre-Roman Celtic art – alas never published – was presented by Sir Arthur Evans as the 1898 Rhind Lectures of the Society of Antiquaries of Scotland. In effect, by the beginning of the twentieth century the broad outlines of the chronological sequence and the regional variations in the Iron Age had been established, and though there have been some modifications to those ideas and much progress towards their more precise definition, they have not been as substantially transformed by later research, as, for instance, is the case with the Neolithic and earlier Bronze Age. It is something of a surprise to find that not only do we lack an up-to-date overview of the period but that despite the comparatively plentiful and well-established body of archaeological data, the discussion of its interpretation in terms of the development of prehistoric society has been virtually neglected. By comparison with some other periods, even the Palaeolithic, the examination of such topics as social organization, exchange, subsistence economy, political structure and ideology in the Iron Age has lagged rather behind, and indeed in some areas has scarcely begun.

An explanation for this might be found in the sheer abundance of the material: we cannot see the cultural wood for the typological trees, or (more cynically) it is easier to theorize when you have little evidence to refute your theories. It is true that it can be very difficult to stand back from the data and think more generally, but it is doubtful if this is the whole answer. Archaeology has, on the whole, adopted a broadly uniform interpretative approach to the Iron Age throughout Europe, one which has been conditioned by modern European perceptions of the past. For, once the general chronological pattern of the first millennium had been fixed, it was clear that the material of the Iron Age belonged to groups directly ancestral to modern societies who exercised their interest in their past through the medium of history. This has had a number of effects. Firstly, there has been a very different pattern in the development of Iron Age studies in different parts of Europe: in the Mediterranean region it has evolved as classical archaeology, which has seen archaeology largely as the hand-maiden of history, used to give details to a picture formed primarily from the written records. In neighbouring regions a similar approach has prevailed, as the concepts of *Protohistoire* and *Frühgeschichte* show, even though the historical documentation is less good; only in northern Europe, far from the Mediterranean, has the Iron Age been regarded as properly prehistoric. The intellectual dominance of history in modern European thinking as *the* discipline for the study of past societies, especially the past of one's own society, has meant that in many cases a ready framework for the interpretation of Iron Age material has been found to hand in the seemingly relevant written sources, however meagre and difficult of interpretation they may have been – a point argued further in this volume by T. C. Champion and Ludwig Pauli. Here is a problem of particular relevance for those concerned to reconstruct not only the framework of Iron Age society but its beliefs and the development of its artistic manifestations.

A second consequence has been a greater degree of regional fragmentation of archaeological studies than in any earlier period. Not only has the bulk of the material made it natural for archaeologists to concentrate on the archaeology of their own home regions, but the historical approach to its interpretation has imposed a certain partitioning on modern cultural, ethnic or nationalistic lines. For just as modern states are concerned with their own historic past, so by extension that ideological interest reaches out to the protohistoric and later prehistoric periods. Since at least the time of Napoleon III, active encouragement has been given to archaeological research by many states, and this has in various ways affected the interpretation of the archaeological record: pre-Roman Celts and Thracians, early Germans and Slavs among others have all been used, with varying degrees of subtlety, to promote modern political interests, a field most interestingly and recently reviewed by Karel Sklenář (1983). Though the cruder cases are obvious, the more subtle consequences of this approach include a general reluctance to view matters from a broad geographical perspective or to adopt a more independent explanatory approach.

One of the papers in this volume arises out of a concern with the existence of a historical record for the Iron Age which has been largely taken as the foundation on which an interpretation of the archaeological record should be built. T. C. Champion argues that the explicitly historical approach which has been adopted to this evidence fails to exploit its true value. There is much of incidental interest for archaeologists in this historical record, but if the whole of the written evidence is taken with the undoubted wealth of the surviving material remains, then there is a body of data possibly without parallel for the exploration and testing of ideas about the growth of complex societies.

In view of the wealth – one might say, almost imbalance – of data and the prevailingly historical approach to the Iron Age, it is perhaps surprising that more work has not been done to the analysis of mortuary evidence. None of the papers in this volume is directly concerned with the social interpretation of such evidence, though its importance is implicitly acknowledged in many papers, not least those of Nash, Pauli and Sara Champion, and Lorenz both reviews the work of central European scholars in this area and provides a detailed discussion of the complex patterns to be seen in the archaeological record even of one small area. The study of prehistoric social organization through mortuary data has been one of the major growth points of archaeological research in the last 15 years, and the European Iron Age, with its well-known – or to some people, infamous – predominance of data derived from funerary contexts, would have seemed on the surface to be an ideal field for such investigation (Bergonzi 1983). It would appear to have all the advantages that an archaeologist could ask for: there are comparatively large cemeteries, many of the burials are inhumations, many are well furnished and the chronology of the period is comparatively well established. Despite some salutary warnings (e.g. Hodson 1979), very little attempt has been made to exploit the wealth of this evidence for the investigation of Iron Age society, and it may be possible to offer some reasons for this. One is undoubtedly the intellectual gulf that exists between the traditional practice of archaeology in much of Europe and the practitioners of the innovative approaches of recent years, still tediously referred to as the 'new archaeology'. This has had, until recently, very little impact in Europe except in Britain and Scandinavia. On the one hand, archaeologists familiar with the European Iron Age data, if aware of the new approaches, have by and large not been prepared to experiment with them, while those looking for data on which to use their new methods have been largely ignorant of later European prehistory and often guilty of building their theoretical houses of cards on an all too flimsy foundation of poorly recorded, and frequently misrecorded, find material.

Another reason may lie in the nature of the evidence itself, at first sight so attractive. On closer inspection, much of it turns out to be less good. Though cemeteries are still being investigated, remarkably few modern large-scale excavations have actually appeared in print; this seems to be particularly true of the La Tène period, especially in central and western Europe. Indeed, many of the recent works containing extensive burial evidence are in fact publications of material excavated many years ago, for example Münsingen (Hodson 1968; Bergonzi 1983), Jenišův Újezd (Waldhauser 1978), Magdalenska gora (Hencken 1978), Stična (Wells 1981) and of course Hallstatt (Kromer 1959) and the Dürrnberg (esp. Pauli 1978; Bergonzi 1983). These old excavations, even when made accessible through modern republication, always pose questions of the fullness and reliability of the sources; anthropological identifications are frequently lacking, the finds themselves may have disappeared and the standards of observation and documentation that prevailed in the original excavation may be hard to assess. Even in the case of an excavation with apparently good documentation and preservation, a rigorous *Quellenkritik* is necessary to establish a firm basis of usable evidence, as Barth and Hodson (1976) have shown for Hallstatt itself.

Despite these problems, some progress has been made. Hodson (1979) has provided a useful summary of some recent work: attempts are now being made to face the comparatively simple problems of differentiation in burial on the basis of age and sex (e.g. Hodson 1977, Dušek 1966), and a variety of organizing principles can be recognized in Iron Age cemeteries. Hodson, in his 1979 paper, has distinguished four such types of cemetery organization: cemeteries exclusively for one small segment of society, in particular high-status adult males; cemeteries with an important central burial and lower-status peripheral burials; cemeteries with the burials organized spatially into family groups; and cemeteries with the burials segregated spatially on the basis of age and sex. In an interesting study of the cemeteries of northern France, Demoule (1982) also notes the last two of these patterns and suggests a chronological trend from sexual segregation to family groups.

Another, rather bolder, approach to the mortuary data has been an attempt to discern the nature of the hierarchical structure of the living society, a topic briefly reviewed elsewhere (Megaw 1982, 221f.). Kilian-Dirlmeier (1970), for instance, has used the variation in grave 'wealth' in Alsace to suggest a markedly hierarchical structure of late Hallstatt society. Similar methods, but with a statistical underpinning through the use of correlation coefficients, have been used (in addition to those cited by Lorenz in his contribution to this volume) by Dušek (1977) on the 'Thracian' cemetery of Chotín and by Bujna (1982) on La Tène cemeteries in eastern Europe (compare Martin-Kilcher 1981). Pauli (1972), in an article exploring in detail some of the ideas upon which he expands here, offers a complex reconstruction of social organization in one small region of southern Germany. On the whole, though, the opportunities offered by this line of enquiry have not been anything like totally exploited.

In contrast to the cemetery evidence, that for settlements, in many areas at least, is sparse or non-existent (Duval and Kruta 1972). Some regions, it is true, such as Britain and Scandinavia, have a tradition of settlement excavation, but it is only in recent years that even there the scale of investigation has grown to what would currently be regarded as appropriate. Elsewhere, the intensive study of settlements before the late La Tène period has been sadly neglected, with the occasional notable exception of some major sites of which the Heuneburg is one of the most extensively examined and the best known through both detailed and summary publications (Kimmig 1983a). It is not that smaller settlements did not exist or that they cannot be identified, for they can, as a glance at any of the many regional surveys of Iron Age material or at the regular reports of new finds, particularly in central European periodicals, will show; features belonging to settlements are continually being observed, especially the larger ones such as pits or the sunken-floored structures of central Europe. Such observations could offer a valuable source of information for archaeological research, but again this is an area which has not so far been adequately appreciated or utilized.

There are, however, some signs that this imbalance is beginning to be corrected and this volume contains two papers specifically devoted to questions of settlement archaeology. Sternquist explores some of the theoretical problems involved in the analysis of settlement patterns, while Demoule and Ilett report on the results of one research programme in France. Both in the Aisne valley and on the Aldenhoven plateau in western Germany rescue archaeology in advance of quarrying has been focussed in particular on the Neolithic, but in both areas our knowledge of other periods, not least the Iron Age, has also benefited. Clearly, it is only through such research programmes which combine extensive survey with excavation that a proper understanding of settlements and settlement patterns is going to be gained, and through it an insight into other matters such as the organization of the subsistence economy.

One topic that has received a lot of attention is trade, especially long-distance trade between the more developed Mediterranean societies and their northern neighbours. There is now an extensive and well-known literature, though again it is only in the last decade that attention has moved on from the types of objects exchanged and the routes by which they travelled to the nature of the broader social, economic and political relationships in which they figured (Fischer 1973; Frankenstein and Rowlands 1978; Wells 1980; Hedaeger 1978; most recently Kimmig 1983b). Two of the papers presented here take up this topic, though with rather different conclusions. Wells argues for a significant role played by trade with the Mediterranean in the transformation of Early Iron Age society, while Fulford is inclined to question the importance usually attached by archaeologists to the trade between the Roman Empire and its neighbours.

By contrast, exchange at the local level has attracted little research. This may in part be due to the scarcity of artefacts other than pottery which are susceptible to scientific characterization for the determination of source. Peacock's pioneering studies of ceramic petrology (1968; 1969) were carried out on English Iron Age pottery, and Waldhauser's study of the distribution of rotary quern stones (1981) shows the potential of this approach, but it is not an area that has yet been widely explored, though particularly in the fields of ceramic studies some important research awaits publication (see p. 176 below). In the comparative absence of scientific analytical data, the determination of source must rest on stylistic criteria, and the question of the possibility of recognizing the products of one craftsman or one school has exercised Iron Age archaeologists for a considerable time.

With particular relation to the 'art' of the La Tène Iron Age there has been a recent upsurge in interest in these problems as they reflect not only the west but the key regions of central and eastern Europe as well. From earlier work (e.g. Megaw 1970; 1973; Frey and Schwappach 1973) to more detailed studies of the later phases of La Tène art in the latter areas (see Kruta in Duval and Kruta 1982 for a most useful bibliography), there have been attempts to refine the all-too-simple tripartite divisions of Paul Jacobsthal's still indispensible 1944 survey. Again, in contrast to what some have seen as the inappropriate influence of conventional art-historical approaches – and in particular those of the classical archaeologist – several writers have attempted to analyse what exactly constitutes the 'Celticness' of Celtic art. Following Duval's beautifully illustrated survey of 1979, one awaits with interest publication of the second series of Rhind Lectures to be delivered on a European Iron Age theme, those given by Otto-Herman Frey in 1978, two generations after Evans, under the title of 'Pre-Roman Celtic Art'. Certainly one of the most pressing points, and one which is the most difficult of solution, is the need to define 'the nature of the distinctions or transformations of [borrowed motifs in Iron Age art] adequately using conventional art-historical methods of analysis and description' (Castriota 1982: 18). There is indeed a pressing need to establish not only a fixed terminology but a conceptual basis for the study of La Tène art, as has been quite correctly pointed out in a number of reviews of one no-longer-so-new review of the material (e.g. Schwappach 1975); the question remains, however, of how to achieve those admirable aims.

These and related problems are considered in three of the papers here. Sara Champion is concerned with both the theoretical problems of defining products of a single source and the substantive conclusions to be drawn from a study of certain well-defined groups of material. Welbourn, working from a general ethnoarchaeological viewpoint, takes a more pessimistic view about the possibility of archaeology to answer such questions, while Megaw muses on his current views as to the reconstruction not only of the nature and meaning of art within Iron Age society but also the role of the producers of such art.

As indicated at the outset, this is a partial view of part of the area and content of a period of prehistory which, despite a somewhat deceptive appearance of plentiful material evidence, has remained seemingly intractible of analysis and interpretation. As editors we are all too aware that our own knowledge – let alone, we suspect, that of many of our hoped-for readership – is likely to be partial indeed of much interesting work which has been undertaken in more recent years, for example by Russian scholars (e.g. Kukharenko 1959; Bidzilya 1971; Kasparova 1981; see also the useful summary by Sulimirski 1976). Notwithstanding, it is our hope that in this collection of contributions by archaeologists, anthropologists and art historians, we may be able to demonstrate that Iron Age studies, like culture itself, is by no means in a terrible state of stasis.

Bibliography

Barth, F. E. and Hodson, F. R., 1976.'The Hallstatt cemetery and its documentation: some new evidence', *Ant. J. 46:* 159–76.

Bergonzi, G., 1983. 'Münsingen-Rain (Svizzera) e Dürrnberg presso Hallein (Austria): alcuine osservazione sulla struttura sociale nel La Tène antico', in E. Arslan (ed.), *Popoli e facies culturali celtiche a nord e a sud delle Alpi dal V al I secolo a.C.: Atti del Colloquio Internazionale: Milano 14–16 Novembre 1980* (Milan): 49–58.

Bidzilya, V. I., 1971. *Istoriya Kultury Zakarpattya* (Kiev).

Bujna, J., 1982. 'Spiegelung der Sozialstruktur auf Latènezeitlichen Gräberfeldern im Karpatenbecken', *Památky Archeologické 73:* 312–431.

Castriota, D., 1982. *Continuity and innovation in Celtic and Mediterranean ornament* (Doctoral thesis, Columbia University; University Microfilms Int., Ann Arbor, MI/ London).

Demoule, J-P., 1982. 'L'Analyse archéologique des cimetières et l'exemple des nécropoles celtiques'. In G. Gigoli and J-P. Vernant (eds.), *La Mort, les Morts dans les sociétés anciennes* (Cambridge and Paris): 319–27.

Dušek, M., 1966. *Thrakisches Gräberfeld der Hallstattzeit in Chotín*, Arch. Slovaca Fontes VI (Bratislava).

Dušek, S., 1977. 'Zur chronologischen und soziologischen Auswertung der Gräberfelder von Chotín', *Slovenská Archaeológia 25:* 11–46.

Duval, P-M., 1979. *Les Celtes* (2 edn, Paris).

Duval, P-M. and Kruta, V. (eds.), 1972. *L'Habitat et la nécropole à l'ãge, du fer en Europe occidentale et orientale*, École Pratique des Hautes Etudes, IVe section 323.

Duval, P-M. and Kruta, V. (eds.), 1982. *L'Art celtique de la période d'expansion: IVe et IIIe siècles avant notre ère*, École Pratique des Hautes Études, IVe section III. 13.

Fischer, F., 1973. 'KEIMHΛIA. Bemerkungen zur kulturgeschichtlichen Interpretation des sogenannten Südimports in der späten Hallstatt- und frühen Latène-kultur des westlichen Mitteleuropa', *Germania 51:* 436–59.

Frankenstein, S. and Rowlands, M. J., 1978. 'The internal structure and regional context of early Iron Age society in south-western Germany', *Bull. Inst. Archaeol. Univ. London 15:* 73–112.

Frey, O-H. and Schwappach, F., 1973. 'Studies in early Celtic design', *World Archaeol. 4. 3:* 339–56.

Hedaeger, L., 1978. 'A quantitative analysis of Roman imports north of the Limes (0–400 AD) and the question of Roman-Germanic exchange.' In K. Kristiansen and C. Paludan-Müller (eds.), *New Directions in Scandinavian Archaeology* (Copenhagen): 191–216.

Hencken, H., 1978. *The Iron Age Cemetery of Magdalenska gora, Slovenia*, American School of Prehistoric Research, Bull. 32, Peabody Museum, Harvard University (Cambridge, Mass.).

Hodson, F. R., 1968. *The La Tène Cemetery at Münsingen-Rain,* Acta Bernensia V (Berne).

Hodson, F. R., 1977. 'Quantifying Hallstatt: some initial results', *American Antiquity 42:* 394–412.

Hodson, F. R., 1979. 'Inferring status from burials in Iron Age Europe: some recent attempts.' In B. C. Burnham and J. Kingsbury (eds.), *Space, Hierarchy and Society* (BAR IS 59): 23–30.

Kasparova, K. V., 1981. 'The formation of the Zarubintsy Culture and its south-western links' [in Russian], *Sovetskaya Arkh.* 1981(2): 57–79.

Kilian-Dirlmeier, I., 1970. 'Bemerkungen zur jüngeren Hallstattzeit im Elsass', *Jahrbuch RGZM 17:* 84–93.

Kimmig, W., 1983a. *Die Heuneburg an der oberen Donau = Führer zu arch. Denkmälern in Baden-Württemberg,* I (2nd edn, Stuttgart).

Kimmig, W., 1983b. 'Die griechische Kolonisation im westlichen Mittelmeergebiet und ihre Wirkung auf die Landschaften des westlichen Mitteleuropa', *Jahrbuch RGZM 30:* 3–78.

Kromer, R., 1959. *Das Gräberfeld von Hallstatt* (Florence).

Kukharenko, I. V., 1959. 'La diffusion des objets laténiens sur le territoire de l'Europe orientale' [in Russian], *Sovetskaya Arkh.* 1959(1): 31–51.

Martin-Kilcher, S., 1981. 'Das keltische Gräberfeld von Vevey VD', *Jahrbuch der Schweizerischen Gesellschaft für Urgeschichte 64:* 107–56.

Megaw, J. V. S., 1970. *Art of the European Iron Age: a study of the Elusive Image.*

Megaw, J. V. S., 1972. 'Style and style-analysis in continental Early La Tène art', *World Archaeol. 3.3:* 276–92.

Megaw, J. V. S., 1973. 'The decorated sword-scabbard from Cernon-sur-Coole (Marne) and Drňa, Rimavska Sobota (Slovakia)', *Hamburger Beiträge zur Archäol. 3.2:* 119–37.

Megaw, J. V. S., 1982. 'Finding purposeful patterns: further notes towards a methodology of Pre-Roman Celtic art'. In Duval and Kruta 1982: 213–29.

Pauli, L., 1972. 'Untersuchungen zur Späthallstattkultur in Nordwürttemberg. Analyse eines Kleinraumes im Grenzbereich zweier Kulturen', *Hamburger Beiträge zur Archäol. 2.1:* 1–166.

Pauli, L., 1978. *Der Dürrnberg bei Hallein* III, Münchner Beiträge zur Vor- und Frühgeschichte 18 (Munich).

Peacock, D. P. S., 1968. 'A petrological study of certain Iron Age pottery from western England', *Procs. Prehist. Soc. 34:* 414–27.

Peacock, D. P. S., 1969. 'A contribution to the study of Glastonbury ware from south-western Britain', *Ant. J. 49:* 41–61.

Schwappach, F., 1975. Review of Megaw 1970, *Germania 53: 226–36.*

Sklenář, K., 1983. *Archaeology in Central Europe: the First 500 Years.*

Sulimirski, T., 1976. 'The Celts in eastern Europe', in J. V. S. Megaw (ed.), *To Illustrate the Monuments: Essays on Archaeology presented to Stuart Piggott:* 181–90.

Tischler, O., 1881. 'Gliederung der vorrömischen Metallzeit', *Korr. für Deutsche Geschichte, Anthropologie, Ethnologie und Urgeschichte, 12:* 121–7.

Tischler, O., 1885. 'Über die Gliederung der La-Tène-Periode und über die Dekorirung der Eisenwaffen in dieser Zeit', *Korr. für Deutsche Geschichte, Anthropologie, Ethnologie und Urgeschichte, 16:* 157–61.

Waldhauser, J., 1978. *Das keltische Gräberfeld bei Jenišův Újezd in Böhmen=Arch. Výzkum v Severních Čehách 6–7* (published 1980).

Waldhauser, J., 1981. 'Keltské rotačno mlýny v Čechách', *Památky Archeologické 72:* 183–221.

Wells, P. S., 1980. *Culture Contact and Culture Change: Early Iron Age central Europe and the Mediterranean world.*

Wells, P. S., 1981. *The emergence of an Iron Age Economy: The Mecklenburg grave groups from Hallstatt and Stična* (American School of Prehistoric Research, Bull. 33, Peabody Museum, Harvard University, Cambridge, Mass.).

1

Written sources and the study of the European Iron Age

T. C. Champion

During the first millennium B.C. many areas of Europe came firmly within the sphere of written records. There had, of course, been the Linear A and more especially Linear B inscriptions of the Minoan and Mycenean world in the previous millennium, and the Achaeans and possibly other Europeans had figured in the royal archives of the Near East, particularly in those of the Hittites, but the region of Europe to which these documents refer is largely restricted to Greece, and the value of their contents, though important, is limited. By the end of the first millennium, however, most areas of Europe were to some extent within the field covered by contemporary written records. The sources for our study of the period are thus augmented, and it is incumbent on us as archaeologists to take note of and to exploit this new evidence. Hawkes (1951:9) proposed what he called a 'Cognitional System of Nomenclature' to describe the various stages of historicity between the truly unhistoric, that is before the beginning of written records anywhere, and the fully historic; the scheme of intermediary stages, comprising telehistoric, parahistoric, penehistoric and protohistoric, seems too complicated for regular use, but does serve to make the important point that regions differ greatly in the degree and nature of the documentation available, not least in the critical question of whether the documentation springs from within the society itself, or from some other external society.

One question which has not been greatly discussed, and which cannot be pursued at any length here, concerns the reasons for the introduction of writing and its long-term consequences. It is true that there has been some debate over the purposes of the earliest Greek writing (e.g. Snodgrass 1980:78–84), and the suggestion has been made of a connection with the promotion of epic poetry, which was itself part of the process of the emergence of the new social order of the Greek *polis*. What is less clear, however, is why the actual writing down of hitherto oral poetry should have been thought useful or, in more general terms, what any society perceived at a specific point to be the advantage of adopting a written script. It is indeed difficult in such questions to avoid the assumptions and expectations of our own highly literate society in which the transmission of material in writing is so normal a part of everyday life. These assumptions have in fact been one of the long-term consequences of the success of writing in western civilization; its presence or absence forms an obvious criterion on which to divide other societies into two classes. Similarly, the study of written records – that is, history – forms the normal method of investigating past societies, whether our own or not.

The distinction between prehistory and history, whether ancient or medieval, is thus one that stems naturally from the conditions of our own society, even if its effects are to obscure essential points of comparability between literate and illiterate societies with which all who are interested in the human past, whether historians, archaeologists or anthropologists, should be greatly concerned. Nor does the introduction of transitional phases, such as Protohistory, *Protohistoire* or *Frühgeschichte*, help, since such concepts serve only to perpetuate the role attached to written records in the investigation of such periods as the Iron Age or post-Roman Europe, and to history as the appropriate mode of thought for their study.

One obvious example of this modern attitude of mind is the separation of classical archaeology from the archaeology of earlier periods in the Mediterranean and of contemporary periods in other areas of Europe (though the archaeology of the Minoan and Mycenean periods and of the Etruscans hover rather awkwardly between the two traditions). The Greek and Roman worlds are so well supplied with documentation about themselves that the approach to the study of their past has been predominantly a historical one, in which archaeology has played a large but subordinate role and anthropology, at least until recently (e.g. Humphreys 1978), an almost negligible one. It is not part of my intention here to discuss these societies in any further detail, but I will return later to the artificiality of our own modern disciplinary boundaries and the advantages to be gained for European archaeology by crossing them.

The sources for temperate and northern Europe are only minimally internal. By the end of the Iron Age some parts at least of central and western Europe were literate, at least for certain bureaucratic purposes: as Jacobi (1974) has argued, the evidence of Caesar concerning the records that he found among the baggage of the Helvetii (*Gallic Wars,* i.29) and the use of writing among the Druids (*Gallic Wars,* vi.14), and the surviving fragments of styli and writing tablets, to which one might also add the recognition of papyrus in southern Britain, albeit in the process of coin production (Allen 1971; Wild 1966), clearly demonstrate the geographically widespread literacy of the La Tène III period, confined though it was to the areas of urban development and possibly to only certain sections of society in those areas. With the exception of coins and some monumental inscriptions and the Coligny calendar, nothing has survived – unfortunately, papyrus burns and wax tablets, unlike clay, tend to melt rather than harden when exposed to fire.

The only other internal material potentially applicable to the first millennium B.C. is the earliest statum of Irish literature, the Ulster Cycle, which Jackson (1964) argued offers us a window on the Iron Age. The true position is perhaps more complex and some of his conclusions need further discussion and modification. As Mallory (1981) has shown, some of the technical details of the swords seem more relevant to the weapons of the Early Christian period than to the Iron Age, and we may also wonder if the obvious Homeric parallels do not in fact owe more to the conscious imitation of Homer in early Christian times than to the innate similarities of Homeric and Iron Age Irish society. On the other hand, if we accept the general picture of social and political organization offered by the Ulster Cycle, there now seems little reason to follow Jackson's (1964:50–2) arguments for a *terminus post quem* fixed by the introduction of La Tène culture to Ireland in the second century B.C. The correct date could be much earlier, and in any case it is not necessary to restrict the pattern of Iron Age society shown in the Ulster Cycle to the La Tène period, whatever its dates; it could well be applicable for some centuries earlier. The problems in using this material have not yet been solved, and though they will be cited on occasion, the main concentration will be on the sources external to temperate Europe.

The range of sources

It is possible to distinguish five groups of sources for the European Iron Age, two of major importance, three of minor, but worth considering for the sake of completeness. The Greek and Latin authors clearly represent two major groups of sources, but less well known are the Assyrian and Chinese historical records and some passages of the Old Testament. These last concern predominantly the Scythian and Cimmerian peoples of south Russia, and in the case of the Bible also the Phoenicians. The expansion of the Cimmerians and the Scythians brought them into contact with the Assyrians and the Chinese (Phillips 1972; there is no full treatment of all these sources, but for the Scythians in particular, see works cited by Hrala 1980). The most detailed records are the Assyrian inscriptions and letters which tell of the migration of these peoples southwards into Asia Minor and the Near East from the late eighth century B.C. onwards, leading to a temporary establishment of Scythian domination to the north of Assyria at the end of the seventh century. Though the records are primarily relevant to the political and military history of the Near East, they do have an importance further afield and give detail and chronological precision to the account of the Scythians in Herodotus (iv.1–144). They document the emigration of Cimmerian people from south Russia – apparently whole communities of men, women and children; and the very different Scythian expansion, in which bands of horse-riding young men set out for military conquest. They pose questions about the nature of the society and its circumstances which necessitated such emigration and stimulated such adventures; and they provide a context for the Scytho-Assyrian connections at a time immediately prior to the appearance of Assyrian-inspired motifs in the decoration found in the fabulously wealthy graves of the sixth-century Scythian aristocracy.

The relevant references in the Bible are less well known. Apart from those concerning the Cimmerians cited by Phillips (1972), the main topic is Phoenicia. The character of Phoenician trade is described particularly in Ezekiel 27; Asiatic manufactured goods were exported in exchange for minerals, and there was also a trade with the hinterland in foodstuffs and raw materials (cf. also 1 Kings 5:9). The importance of the slave trade is shown in a number of references (e.g. Joel 3:4; Amos 1:6). It is difficult to assess the area affected by these trading activities, but they demonstrate the background to the Phoenician colonization of the central and western Mediterranean that was to play so great a part in the transformation of the Mediterranean world in the early Iron Age.

Of much the greatest importance, however, for their number, variety of content, and geographical and chronological range are the Greek and Latin sources. This body of literature is, of course, far too large to synthesize here: there are certainly well over 100 authors whose works contain some material of relevance, and indeed some parts of it have already been treated in detail by earlier writers. The discussion of the Celts by Posidonius in Book 23 of his *Histories*, surviving only in quotations from him by other writers, has been reviewed by Tierney (1960) and more recently by Nash (1976a). Thompson (1965) has gathered together the material relevant to the early Germans, and Piggott (1968) has quarried a rich vein of references to the Druids; there are also other discussions of smaller topics such as the Celtic migration to south-eastern Europe by Nachtergael (1977), or of specific regions such as the central Balkans by Papazoglu (1978). Through the work of these and other modern authors, much of this classical literature is now well known, but there has been no modern discussion of it as a whole, and little attempt to assess it against the archaeology, or to use it as an independent source of evidence to set beside the archaeology in a study of the first millennium B.C. I believe that the value of this material is much greater than has hitherto been realized, and hope to show here ways in which that value can be exploited.

One of the main advantages for us is that the tradition of historical writing that prevailed through much of the relevant period of classical literature did not make a clear distinction between what we regard as the separate disciplines of history, geography and ethnography; hence there are in many authors of overtly historical works long passages of geographical or ethnographic writing. Even when a more distinct notion of geography was developed, the subject remained heavily ethnographic in its orientation. It is in the richness and variety of this ethnographic material, as well as in the more purely historical and geographical, that the value of these sources to archaeology lies.

Problems in interpretation

The use that has been made of the sources, however, has concentrated on the historical and geographical, despite enormous problems of correlation with archaeology. Much of the geographical writing is concerned only with physical features such as mountains and rivers, and its main interest lies in the evidence for the improvement of the classical world's knowledge of its neighbouring lands. There are, however, also references to the people, in particular lists of tribal names, for example in Strabo, sometimes augmented as in Ptolemy by lists of the names of important sites. These latter can sometimes be given tentative or even reasonably certain identifications with archaeologically known sites, but attempts to recognize such tribes archaeologically are mostly doomed. Our theoretical understanding of the nature of such tribal groups, and their possible correlation with the patterning of material culture elements or settlement systems, has not yet reached the stage (if it ever can) where such identifications would be regularly possible; discussion of, for instance, whether the Scordisci or the Eraviscae were responsible for certain burials is at present largely futile. Only rarely can such identifications be made, for instance in parts of central France at the end of the Iron Age, where the patterning of settlement systems and of coin distributions, but seldom of other cultural features, can be used to define political boundaries (e.g. Nash 1976b:122–5).

If static social patterns are so difficult to recognize in the archaeological record, one might expect that unique historical events would be even more so. This has not deterred archaeologists from trying, and the prevailing interpretation of the archaeological record has been a historical rather than an anthropological one. Naturally, one prevailing theme in the literature was the threat to Greece and Rome of invasion from the north, and numerous attempts have been made to provide archaeological evidence for these migrations or invasions. These identifications have always been based on an over-simplistic view of the relationship between social groups and material culture, and have frequently caused more problems than they have solved. For example, in the case of the historically known migration of Celts from central Europe into Italy, the archaeology of those areas attributable to the tribes of non-Celtic origin in northern Italy is generally no less influenced by central European La Tène fashions and artefacts than is that of the tribes of Celtic origin; again, Caesar's reference to settlers from Belgium in southern England (*Gallic Wars*, v.12) has led to a fruitless search for their archaeological manifestation and on occasions to gross distortion of the archaeological record (Hachmann 1976; Champion 1979:416 and n.43). Many other examples could be quoted, such as the problems of correlating the eastward spread of La Tène burial rites, art styles and ornamental fashions with the historically recorded Celtic migrations, or attempts to identify archaeologically the known migrations of the Cimbri and Teutones. It may well be possible ultimately to identify such historical events in the archaeological record on a regular basis, but it has not yet been done very satisfactorily, and too little thought has been given to the theoretical problems of how historical and archaeological categories might be correlated.

Of much greater importance and interest to the archaeologist is the more specifically ethnographic element in the classical writers, and yet it has never been systematically studied. Before it is possible to go on to demonstrate the value of these sources for this purpose, it is necessary to consider some of the problems involved in using them.

In the first place, there are problems that arise from the very nature of the texts, their transmission and survival. They comprise many substantial works, such as Strabo's *Geography* or Tacitus's *Germania*, others in which there are considerable passages of interest, such as Herodotus's *History* or Caesar's *Gallic Wars*, but also many scattered references in other writers, some of whom survive only fragmentarily. Some major works have been lost entirely, others such as Posidonius's Celtic ethnography (Book 23 of his *Histories*) survive only in quotations in other writers. Where they do survive, many texts, even some of the most important and substantial, have received little critical attention. Herodotus and Tacitus, to be sure, have had their fair share or more, but Strabo in particular has been scandalously neglected – there is no modern edition of or commentary on his *Geography*. The same is true of other authors such as Ptolemy and Pomponius Mela, with the addition that they have not even been translated into English. These, however, are mere practical difficulties; though they may help to explain why some of the authors are neglected by archaeologists, they do not themselves present any serious problem in using the content of the texts as a source for prehistoric Europe.

More serious are problems that arise from the content of that written record, and from a consideration of its reliability. These can be grouped under three headings; problems arising from factual error, misinformation or misunderstanding by the authors or their sources; problems arising from the philosophical viewpoint of the authors; and those which stem from the literary conventions within which the authors worked.

Problems of factual error or misunderstanding can frequently be recognized if the resulting text is internally illogical, or if there is an obvious means of verification. Livy (v.33–6), for instance, describes the Celtic migrations over the Alps as coming from an area that was fertile and well populated; this offers no explanation for the migration, though Livy clearly intended it to, and he has apparently misunderstood a source describing over-population in Gaul, as is confirmed by an alternative version of the same account in Justin (xxiv.4). Strabo (vii.2.1), on the other hand, could not understand a source which seems to have referred to marine inundation in northern Europe, and expresses surprise at people fleeing from such a commonplace phenomenon as a tide. Frequently, however, especially where there is no logical inconsistency or obvious means of verification, possible factual errors will go unnoticed or unproved, even if suspected. There is no means of solving this problem, though a general estimate of an author's sense and reliability may be formed; some may indeed deserve Macaulay's description of Diodorus Siculus as 'that stupid, credulous, prosing old ass' or the dismissal of much of Curtius Rufus as 'miserable rubbish', but many do not.

No writer can help being influenced by the prevailing view of the world and his own philosophical inclinations, and indeed many of our authors specifically announce their own views: Posidonius, for instance, was a Stoic, and Stoics believed in the necessity of returning to a state of prehistoric innocence, which was reflected in the contemporary barbarian societies (though Posidonius was also influenced by other conflicting views). Stuart Piggott (1968) has analysed, in the specific context of the Druids, the two main traditions current in the classical world of attitudes towards the less civilized peoples with whom they came into contact. A 'hard' primitivism, shared by Posidonius (despite his Stoic beliefs) and others, regarded these barbarians in a realistic and unflattering way; a 'soft' primitivism idealized them and emphasized their desirable qualities. The same conflict can be seen in classical portrayals of barbarians in sculpture, for instance on triumphal arches or tombstones or in the highly idealized noble savage seen in the sculptures of the Dying Gaul, and also in the ambivalence of words such as 'primitive' or 'barbaric' in our own language.

This polarization of attitudes was reflected in a parallel conflict with regard to the development of classical society, seen either as a rise from primitive barbarism or as a decline from a primal Golden Age. It was commonly believed that this original state, whether perceived favourably or unfavourably, was mirrored in the contemporary societies of the uncivilized world; hence geographically remote peoples could be invested with all the qualities, good or bad, of chronologically remote ones. The Golden Age, and equally the ultimate barbarism, could be located in the mists of time or the mists of northern Europe.

These attitudes have undeniably coloured much, if not all, that was written about the northern neighbours of the classical world, but I would argue that the record is not thereby invalidated. The contrast between classical and barbarian was predominantly this: either the simple, noble, honest savage set against the corruptions of the urban world, or the shameless, untrustworthy, uncultured barbarian against the culture, manners and justice of civilization. This moral contrast is seldom augmented by any notion of different values attached to differences in technology, material culture or social organization. It may be wise, therefore, to ignore assessments of the morality of barbarian peoples, but this should not seriously undermine our belief in other assertions about them.

It is interesting to note that, just as there is no serious discussion, or perhaps even no realistic perception, of synchronic contrasts in the fundamental organization of geographically remote societies and the classical world, so also there is little, if any, conception of diachronic change in technology, material culture or social organization within either the classical or the barbarian world. The classical perception of society was essentially a static one, and cultural change as a phenomenon requiring discussion and explanation was not within that society's conceptualization of the human condition. Occasionally, of course, contrasts in material culture obtruded so markedly that comment was essential. The Etruscans and their culture, for example, seemed so different and were so near at hand that some explanation was called for: at least from the time of Herodotus (i.94) this explanation, with scarcely a dissenting view, was in terms of some version of migration from the eastern Mediterranean. Likewise many of the cultural changes of the post-Mycenean period in Greece could be explained in the literary tradition by reference to Dorian invaders or the return of the Heraclids. Recently many authors (e.g. Tritsch 1974:237; Hooker 1979) have been inclined to treat these stories with increasing scepticism. If we are not dealing with origin myths actually promoted by the new elites of archaic Greece, then we are seeing the first attempts of a later literary tradition to come to grips with the problem of explaining social and political change in post-Mycenean Greece; the results are of interest for a history of literary and sociological thinking in the Greek world, but this early espousal of the invasion hypothesis does not inform us meaningfully about the realities of change in the first half of the first millennium B.C.

There was also a failure to conceive of the possibility that interaction between the classical world and the barbarian could itself be the cause of change in the culture or social organization of either side. Many writers were of course quite well aware of the economic dependence of the classical world on exchange with neighbouring societies, and that fashions in jewellery or hair-styles might be borrowed, but there was no realization that these relationships might themselves stimulate more important social changes.

These shortcomings in the conceptual tool-kit of the classical writers do not necessarily invalidate what they wrote, but it is essential to consider carefully the context in which they wrote, the sources they had available and the period to which those sources refer. The lack of any concept of social change meant that descriptions of other societies were essentially timeless, and hence could be copied by a much later author; by which time the society could have changed in fundamental ways. This is of the greatest importance, since, as I shall argue below, the non-classical societies were far from static at the time of the relevant records, possibly even as a direct result of their closer interaction with the complex societies of the classical world, and the lack of awareness in the writers of such time depth and such change should not blind us to their existence.

There is, moreover, one further problem to be considered, one that arises not from the philosophical inclination of the authors but from the literary conventions that governed them. The German scholar Norden in his study of early Germany and Tacitus's *Germania* (1959) developed the idea of the *Wandermotiv*, or migratory motif, to account for some of the stranger assertions about the early Germans which found parallels in other writers' accounts of other societies. The principle is well described by Goodyear (1970:9): 'Physical or sociological characteristics which one writer ascribes to a remote people are borrowed by a later writer and transferred to another people altogether and this may happen many times until there grows up a stock of commonplaces, descriptive and characterising traits which may be applied indifferently to any people which is being described. Even words and phrases are borrowed.' Literary critics are thus armed with a powerful tool for reducing the information content of any text to nothing at a stroke, and even Norden himself was moved to protest at the use to which his original theory (developed in the specific context of the school of Greek rhetorical writing on geography) had been put. This view still finds supporters today, especially among literary critics who find themselves ranged against historians and archaeologists who have an interest in maximizing the factual value of the texts. In a recent paper on Ireland in the classical sources, for instance, Killeen (1976) invokes the theory to dismiss Strabo's account of endocannibalism; he quoted with approval Thomson's (1948:153) description of Caesar's reference to polyandry in northern Britain as 'a bad rumour', to be dismissed because similar practices were recorded elsewhere by Herodotus (iv.104; iv.172; iv.180); and he likewise rejects Pomponius Mela's account of the rich pastures of Ireland causing cattle to swell and burst, first as a fairy tale and second because Curtius Rufus (v.1.12) says the same of cattle in Babylonia – but this is just the result of allowing cattle to feed on too rich a diet of some crops such as clover, and is no less real for occurring, and being commented on, in different regions. Herein lies the crux of the problem, for how are we to distinguish between mere literary artifice and genuine records of geographically widespread phenomena which might strike either the classical or the modern mind as unusual? Much will undoubtedly depend on one's assessment of any particular author, but there is surely a limit to literary imitation.

There are undoubtedly problems in interpreting the sources. To add to those already mentioned, the Greek rhetorical school of geographical writing also placed great emphasis on recording θαύμαστα καὶ παράδοξα, the weird and wonderful, and we are frequently given an anecdotal account of exotic or unusual features rather than a full description. The testimony of even these writers can be used with care, and there are others who wrote in a different literary tradition – Herodotus, Thucydides, Polybius, Caesar, Tacitus among others. This is not the place to prolong the arguments in favour of treating them as trustworthy sources, but we should note the working principle enunciated by Thompson (1965:vii): 'The explicit assertions of Caesar and Tacitus are credible unless they are self-evidently erroneous (which they rarely are) or unless there is archaeological or other evidence (and there rarely is) with which they cannot reasonably be reconciled.' With due caution when dealing with authors of a different stamp, this principle should form the basis of our approach to the written sources for the Iron Age.

The content of the sources

After this somewhat lengthy justification of the usefulness of the sources, it is now possible to turn to their substantive content. I believe that, despite all the problems of access, assessment and interpretation, they represent a worthwhile body of data, the true value of which has not yet been realized. This value lies partly in the enormous richness and variety of content, partly in the wide geographical scope covered, and partly (perhaps most importantly) in the fact that a considerable time-range is represented. To take the most obvious examples, Polybius and Posidonius describe the Celts (or some part of them) in the third and second centuries B.C., while Caesar's account of them refers to the mid-first century B.C.; there is similarly a gap of a century and a half between the accounts of the Germans given by Caesar and Tacitus. Parts of south-eastern Europe on the northern fringes of the Greek world were continuously within the orbit of Greek historical writing from the fifth century B.C. onwards. This time-range is enormously important, since it permits us to discuss social and cultural change through time. It is clearly impossible to analyse all the available sources here, but it is possible to give examples of their value to archaeologists. Some are already well known – the works of Tierney and Nash on the Celts and of Thompson on the early Germans have been cited above – but these studies have been restricted to specific groups or areas, and have not tried a more thematic approach or a more generalized account of non-classical European societies, or to use the full range of sources to elucidate the themes of recent archaeological enquiry.

To take the theme of subsistence first, there are numerous references which are too unspecific to be of much value, and others which contain anecdotal oddities, though many of these are of interest: spring and winter sown crops in Britain (Diodorus Siculus ii.47), underground storage of crops in Britain (Diodorus Siculus v.21.5) and Germany (Tacitus, *Germania* xvi.4), and numerous references to a diet more reliant on meat and milk than would have been common in the Mediterranean region. We hear of sheep whose wool is plucked rather than shorn (Pliny, *Nat. Hist.* viii.191), which may account for the lack of recognizable sheep-shears in prehistoric Europe; and of the dependence of cattle on salt, presumably as a means of supplementing the supply of minerals; for without it the cattle died (Pseudo-Aristotle, *De ausc. mir.* 138). There are also accounts of the specific hazards of agriculture in some areas; for instance, the Balearic islands were threatened by a plague of rabbits (Strabo iii.2.6; iii.5.3; Pliny, *Nat. Hist.* viii.217), which undermined houses and destroyed crops; after seriously contemplating mass emigration, the inhabitants eventually imported ferrets from north Africa. It would be interesting to speculate on the archaeological correlates of both the problem and the solution.

We also have more detailed accounts of the adaptation of certain societies to particular environments. Strabo, for instance, describes the life of the inhabitants of the upland regions of northern Spain (iii.3.3–8) and of nomadic pastoralists of the Russian steppe (vii.3.17–18).

There are numerous references to metallurgy: to tin from Cornwall and elsewhere (Strabo iii.2.9), to gold in France (Strabo iv.1.13) and around Aquilea and in the eastern Alps (Strabo iv.6.12; v.1.8), to the rich metal deposits of Spain (e.g. Strabo iii.2.8); descriptions of silver mining and processing in Spain (Strabo iii.2.8–10), and references to the high quality of iron production in Noricum (Strabo v.i.8).

One of the most difficult problems in prehistory is to reach reasonable estimates for population figures, but here also the texts can be of some value. Figures quoted, for example, for the migrating Cimbri and Teutones may or may not be reliable, but they are of minimal use since we do not know anything of the area to which they refer. With the Helvetii, however, we are on firmer ground: Caesar's figure of 263,000 with 105,000 others (*Gallic Wars,* i.29) may be plausible since it derives from records discovered in their baggage – though it must be admitted that figures in other authors vary from 157,000 (Orosius vi.7.5) to 480,000 (Strabo iv.3.3). The territory of the Helvetii in western Switzerland is known, and the resulting estimated density, which approximates to likely figures for the late medieval period, might be used with due caution for central Europe in the Late La Tène.

Population pressure on available subsistence resources is also documented. The Triballi, for instance, were forced into mass raids on their neighbours in Thrace through famine (Diodorus xv.36.1–4). All the major migrations, Celts into Italy, Celts into south-eastern Europe, Cimbri and Teutones from north Germany, together with other groups including the Tigurini, one of the *pagi* of the Helvetii, the Helvetii themselves from Switzerland, are all explained as reactions to such imbalance between population and resources and the desire for new land (Champion 1980). Clearly from at least the fifth, and possibly the sixth, century B.C. some parts of central Europe were subject to considerable pressure of population on the available land, for which the seemingly drastic solution of mass emigration was regularly adopted.

Settlements are frequently referred to, but seldom in much detail; Xenophon's account of a Thracian village (*Anabasis* vii.3), for instance, and Caesar's descriptions of the hill-forts he attacked (Rivet 1971) are among the exceptions. The existence of a settlement hierarchy is vouchsafed by Caesar's classification of Helvetic settlement as towns, villages and individual houses (*Gallic Wars*, i.5); his figure of twelve towns to four hundred villages abandoned by them at the time of their migration corresponds reasonably well with the figure of twenty-four villages dependent on the urban centre of Nemausus (Nîmes) in the Rhone valley (Strabo iv.1.12).

Naturally exchange figures prominently. Strabo gives details, for example, of trade through Aquilea (v.1.8: slaves, cattle and hides) and of the exports (grain, cattle, gold, iron, silver, hides, slaves and hunting dogs) and imports (ivory, amber, glass) of Britain (iv.5.2). Trade in foodstuffs was particularly common: Spain, for example, exported corn, oil, wine, honey and salted fish as well as wax, pitch, vermilion and vegetable dyes (Strabo iii.2.6).

These examples have been chosen more or less at random, and the effect is somewhat anecdotal, but they do serve to demonstrate the wealth of factual detail available. Other topics of interest to archaeologists are also covered: warfare, for example fighting methods among the tribes of Spain (Strabo iii.3.6); the slave trade (discussed with references by Nash in this volume); and burial, for instance Herodotus's (iv.71) description of the ritual of a Scythian royal burial and the symbolic meaning attached to it, which deserves an honoured place as our best approach to appreciating the social context of such ceremonies.

Iron Age society as seen in the sources

The references in the previous section show the potential interest of the written sources for many different themes of investigation in prehistoric Europe, but no mention has yet been made of what is perhaps the most valuable feature of the texts, the record they provide for social and political organization during a prolonged contact phase which saw rapid social change in many parts of Europe. Though fragmentary, it is an ethnohistorical account of chiefdom societies and early states which is without parallel for its time-span.

The descriptions of Celtic society in Posidonius and Caesar, and of Germanic society in Caesar and Tacitus, are well known, but they are merely the most detailed and most studied accounts. From more fragmentary references elsewhere, it is possible to suggest that there were certain features that were widespread, if not universal, in the social organization of later prehistoric Europe; the general pattern revealed may indeed have its origins very much earlier (Rowlands 1980).

Power and status depended largely on the individual's ability to recruit followers within his society and allies outside it, through the institutions of clientage and marriage alliances. A client offered his support to his patron in return for the promise of prestige, protection and subsistence; a patron could recruit more clients through success in warfare or by conspicuous generosity to his existing clients. The classic example of this system at work in Celtic society is Orgetorix, who assembled ten thousand clients when he was in danger of being put on trial for his life (*Gallic Wars*, i.4). Similar institutions are also recorded in Spain (Strabo iii.4.18: 'it is an Iberian custom to devote their lives to whomever they attach themselves to, even to the point of dying for them'; Val. Max. ii.2.11; Plutarch, *Sertorius* 14), and in Ireland (Jackson 1964:9–10). Athenaeus (vi.49) used the term παράσιτος, which might be translated 'parasite, hanger-on, follower', but has the same root meaning as Latin *comes*, Irish *ceili* and English 'companion' – that is, someone who eats with someone.

At the highest level an individual who was able to establish dominance over all his rivals might be recognized as a king, but he too would have his immediate set of clients. In the Macedonian court, for example, the ἑταῖροι were totally dependent upon the favour of the king for their position and they formed a body of military commanders and administrators to put the king's rule into practice (Hammond and Griffith 1979:395–404). Similar institutions are also recorded in Epirus (Hammond 1967: 572–93) and in Noricum (Alföldy 1974: 42–4), where Livy (xliii.5.8) records the presence of *comites* in the court.

Externally status was promoted by forging marriage alliances with powerful lineages in other communities. Caesar describes the system very clearly with reference to Dumnorix of the Aedui (*Gallic Wars*, i.18): 'his power was extensive not only in his own state but also in the neighbouring ones. To secure this power he had given his mother in marriage to the noblest and most powerful man among the Bituriges, he has himself taken a wife from the Helvetii, and had married his half-sister and his female relations to men of other states'. The same principle can be seen at work, for example, in the Macedonian royal family, who were connected in complicated ways with neighbouring dynasties, such as that of Epirus. Voccio, king of Noricum, gave his sister in marriage to Ariovistus, king of the Suebi in eastern France 600km away (*Gallic Wars*, i.53).

Various strategies were adopted to maintain and foster these connections and to consolidate power within the community. Royal dynasties were frequently polygamous; this is recorded for the Macedonians (Justin ix.8.3), Epirus (Plutarch, *Pyrrhus* 4 and 9) and Illyria (Dio xii.53.1). This allowed the ruling lineage to establish a variety of external alliances and possibly also to ensure a sufficient set of children from whom an heir could emerge. On the other hand it enhanced the possibility of competition between surviving sons, and sibling rivalry was a common feature. Dumnorix and Diviciacus, though brothers, were rivals for the premier status among the Aedui and leaders of opposed factions (*Gallic Wars*, i.18–20). Gentius, a king of Illyria in the second century B.C., was afraid that his brother Plator's proposed marriage to a Dardanian princess would strengthen his position too much; he therefore had his brother and his leading supporters killed, and married the princess himself (Polybius xxix.13; Livy xliv.30.4).

One important mechanism for consolidating vertical integration within the society was the institution of fosterage. Young men of noble families were sent to live in the household of a superior or the king, to be brought up and trained there. This established ties between foster-father and foster-son and between foster-brothers which cut across kinship lines; it also provided the king with hostages from all the most powerful families to deter any attempts at revolt. Such fosterage can be seen in the 'royal pages' of the Macedonian court (Hammond and Griffith 1979:401–2), said to have been instituted by Philip II (Arrian, *Anabasis* iv.13.1), and in Ireland (Jackson 1964:10).

An understanding of this social structure will help to explain the archaeological record, for it does have material correlates. The web of alliances formed by the elites of different societies provided a set of pathways along which ideas could be transmitted and innovations widely shared. The competitive nature of relationships within society demanded methods to demonstrate status. The royal family of Macedonia marked the emergence of its power by the creation of a courtly culture in which hunting, lavish royal burials and the worship of Herakles were all important elements (Hammond and Griffith 1979:152–8); they also claimed descent from the rulers of Argos (Thucydides ii.99), and under Alexander I began to imitate Greek ways. As Macedonia became incorporated into the Greek world, and ultimately came to dominate it, so the process continued further north and west. In Epirus the height of Pyrrhus's power was marked by a phase of monumental building at Phoinike, Dodona and Ambracia (Hammond 1967:572–93). In Thrace to the north the short-lived revival of the Odrysian state under Seuthes III was symbolized in the construction of Seuthopolis, aping Greek architecture and Macedonian styles of urban nomenclature (Dimitrov and Cicikova 1978).

These examples have barely scratched the surface of the data, and have scarcely begun to explore the correlation with the archaeological record. They have, however, demonstrated the potential of this period for the examination of general problems in the emergence of states and in the relationships between complex societies and their less complex neighbours.

Bibliography

Alföldy, G., 1974. *Noricum.*

Allen, D. F., 1971. 'British potin coins: a review', in M. Jesson and D. Hill (eds.), *The Iron Age and its Hill-forts:* 127–54.

Champion, T. C., 1979. 'The iron age (c.600 BC–AD 200)', in J. V. S. Megaw and D. D. A. Simpson (eds.), *Introduction to British Prehistory:* 344–432.

Champion, T. C., 1980. 'Mass migration in later prehistoric Europe', in P. Sörbom (ed.), *Transport Technology and Social Change* (Stockholm): 31–42.

Dimitrov, D. P. and Čičikova, M., 1978. *The Thracian City of Seuthopolis* (BAR S38).

Goodyear, F. R. D., 1970. *Tacitus.*

Hachmann, R., 1976. 'The problem of the Belgae seen from the continent', *Bull. Inst. Archaeol. Univ. London 13:* 117–37.

Hammond, N. G. L., 1967. *Epirus.*

Hammond, N. G. L. and Griffith, G. T., 1979. *A History of Macedonia,* II.

Hawkes, C. F. C., 1951. 'British prehistory half-way through the century', *Procs. Prehist. Soc. 17:* 1–15.

Hooker, J. T., 1979. 'New reflections on the Dorian invasion', *Klio 61:* 353–60.
Hrala, J., 1980. 'Pohledy do soucane skythologie' [in Czech with German summary: Einblick in die gegenwärtige Skythologie], *Památky Archeologické 71:* 267–307.
Humphreys, S. C., 1978. *Anthropology and the Greeks.*
Jackson, K. H., 1964. *The Oldest Irish Tradition: a window on the Iron Age.*
Jacobi, G., 1974. 'Zum Schriftgebrauch in der keltischen Oppida nördlich der Alpen', *Hamburger Beiträge zur Archäol. 4:* 171–81.
Killeen, J. F., 1976. 'Ireland in the Greek and Roman writers', *Procs. Royal Irish Acad. 76 C:* 207–15.
Mallory, J. P., 1981. 'The sword of the Ulster Cycle', in B. G. Scott (ed.), *Studies on Early Ireland: Essays in honour of M. V. Duignan:* 99–114.
Nachtergael, G., 1977. *Les Galates en Grèce et les Sôtéria de Delphes* (Brussels).
Nash, D., 1976a. 'Reconstructing Poseidonios' Celtic ethnography', *Britannia 7:* 111–26.
Nash, D., 1976b. 'The growth of urban society in France', in B. W. Cunliffe and R. T. Rowley (eds.), *Oppida: the Beginnings of Urbanisation in Barbarian Europe* (BAR S11): 95–133.
Norden, E., 1959. *Die germanische Urgeschichte und Tacitus Germania* (4th edn).
Papazoglu, F., 1978. *The Central Balkan Tribes in Pre-Roman Times* (Amsterdam).
Phillips, E. D., 1972. 'The Scythian domination in western Asia: its record in history, scripture and archaeology', *World Archaeol. 4:* 129–38.
Piggott, S., 1968. *The Druids.*
Rivet, A. L. F., 1971. 'Hill-forts in action', in M. Jesson and D. Hill (eds.), *The Iron Age and its Hill-forts:* 189–202.
Rowlands, M. J., 1980. 'Kinship, alliance and exchange in the European Bronze Age', in J. Barrett and R. J. Bradley (eds.), *Settlement and Society in the British Later Bronze Age* (BAR 83): 15–55.
Snodgrass, A. M., 1980. *Archaic Greece.*
Thompson, E. A., 1965. *The Early Germans.*
Thomson, J. O., 1948. *History of Ancient Geography.*
Tierney, J. J., 1960. 'The Celtic ethnography of Posidonius', *Procs. Royal Irish Acad. 60 C:* 189–275.
Tritsch, F. J., 1974. 'The "Sackers of Cities" and the "movement of populations" ', in R. A. Crossland and A. Birchall (eds.), *Bronze Age Migrations in the Aegean:* 233–9.
Wild, J. P., 1966. 'Papyrus in pre-Roman Britain?', *Antiquity 40:* 139–42.

2

Early Celtic society: two centuries of wealth and turmoil in central Europe

Ludwig Pauli*

For the Romans, 18 July 387 B.C. was always the *dies ater*, but almost 2,400 years later for today's archaeologist it is a red-letter day. It is, after all, one of the very few fixed points in early Celtic history. It was then that on the River Allia the Celtic hordes inflicted an annihilating defeat on the Romans, who were at that time trying to impose themselves on the Etruscans. All the critical developments which led to the Celtic migrations to the south of the Alps and the Balkans had in fact taken place before that date.

The information yielded by Roman historians on the background to the Celtic migrations is so scanty that the most important passages can be cited here in full.

Pliny the Elder, a native of Como, gives a short but significant account (Köves-Zulauf 1977):

> Produnt Alpibus coercitas ut tum inexuperabili munimento Gallias hanc primum habuisse causam superfundendi se Italiae, quod Helico ex Helvetiis civis earum fabrilem ob artem Romae commoratus ficum siccam et uvam oleique ac vini praemissa remeans secum tulisset; quapropter haec vel bello quaesisse venia sit. (Naturalis Historia xii.2.5.)

> It is stated that the Gauls, imprisoned as they were by the Alps as by a then insuperable bulwark, first found a motive for overflowing into Italy from the circumstance that a Gallic citizen from Switzerland named Helico, who had sojourned at Rome on account of his skill as an artificer, had brought with him when he came back some dried figs and grapes and some samples of oil and wine; and consequently we may pardon them for having sought to obtain these things even by means of war.[1]

Pompeius Trogus came from Gallia Narbonensis; his work *Historiae Philippicae* survives only in the quotations comprising about 10 per cent of the original by Justin. The Celtic migration is mentioned in two places:

* trans. Sara Champion.

2 Early Celtic society: two centuries of wealth and turmoil in central Europe

Ludwig Pauli

His autem Gallis causa in Italiam veniendi sedesque novas quaerendı intestina discordia et adsiduae domi dissensiones fuere, quarum taedio cum in Italiam venissent, sedibus Tuscos expulerunt et Mediolanum, Comum, Brixiam, Veronam, Bergomum, Tridentum, Vincentiam condiderunt. (xx.5.7–8.)

Namque Galli abundante multitudine, cum eos non caperent terrae, quae genuerant, CCC milia hominum ad sedes novas quaerendas velut ver sacrum miserunt. Ex his portio in Italia consedit, quae et urbem Romanam captam incendit, et portio Illyricos sinus ducibus avibus (nam augurandi studio Galli praeter ceteros callent) per strages barbarorum penetravit et in Pannonia consedit. (xxiv.4.1–3.)

For these Gauls, however, the reason for their coming to Italy and seeking new lands was internal discord and bitter dissension at home; when, wearying of this, they had come into Italy, they expelled the Etruscans from their lands and founded Milan, Como, Brescia, Verona, Bergamo, Trento and Vicenza.

For when their native lands could no longer contain the Gauls with their swelling numbers, they sent 300,000 men to seek new territories, like an offering of the first fruits of spring. Some of these settled in Italy, where they captured and burned even the city of Rome; some, led by the birds (for the Gauls are experienced above others in the study of augury), spread through the head of the Adriatic and settled in Pannonia.[2]

Livy (born in Padua) is rather more detailed in his historical account. First he offers a version from a southern viewpoint:

Eam gentem traditur fama dulcedine frugum maximeque vini nova tum voluptate captam Alpes transisse agrosque ab Etruscis ante cultos possedisse; et invexisse in Galliam vinum inliciendae gentis causa Arruntem Clusinum ira corruptae uxoris ab Lucumone cui tutor ipse fuerat, praepotente iuvene et a quo expeti poena, nisi externa vis quaesita esset, nequiret; hunc transeuntibus Alpes ducem auctoremque Clusium oppugnandi fuisse. Equidem haud abnuerim Clusium Gallos an Arrunte seu quo alio Clusino adductos; sed eos qui oppugnaverint Clusium non fuisse qui primi Alpes transierint satis constat. Ducentis quippe annis ante quam Clusium oppugnarent urbemque Romam caperent, in Italiam Galli transcendere; nec cum his primum Etruscorum sed multo ante cum iis qui inter Appenninum Alpesque incolebant saepe exercitus Gallici pugnavere. (v.33.2–6.)

The story runs that this race, allured by the delicious fruits and especially the wine – then a novel luxury – had crossed the Alps and possessed themselves of lands that had before been tilled by the Etruscans; and that wine had been imported into Gaul expressly to entice them, by Arruns of Clusium, in his anger at the seduction of his wife by Lucumo. This youth, whose guardian he had been, was so powerful that he could not have

> chastised him without calling in a foreign force. He it was who is said to have guided the Gauls across the Alps, and to have suggested the attack on Clusium. Now I would not deny that Arruns or some other citizen brought the Gauls to Clusium, but that those who besieged Clusium were not the first who had passed the Alps is generally agreed. Indeed it was two hundred years before the attack on Clusium and the capture of Rome, that the Gauls first crossed over into Italy; neither were the Clusini the first of the Etruscans with whom they fought; but long before that the Gallic armies had often given battle to those who dwelt between the Appennines and the Alps.

In the following chapter he seems instead to be using a Celtic source, for here he describes particulars of the procedure for the sending out of the hordes:

> De transitu in Italiam Gallorum haec accepimus: Prisco Tarquinio Romae regnante, Celtarum quae pars Galliae tertia et penes Bituriges summa imperii fuit; ii regem Celtico dabant. Ambigatus is fuit, virtute fortunaque cum sua, tum publica praepollens, quod in imperio eius Gallia adeo frugum hominumque fertilis fuit ut abundans multitudo vix regi videretur posse. Hic magno natu ipse iam exonerare praegravante turba regnum cupiens, Bellovesum ac Segovesum sororis filios impigros iuvenes missurum se esse in quas di dedissent auguriis sedes ostendit; quatum ipsi vellent numerum hominum excirent ne qua gens arcere advenientes posset. Tum Segoveso sortibus dati Hercynei saltus; Belloveso haud paulo laetiorem in Italiam viam di dabant. (v.34.1–4.)

> Concerning the migration of the Gauls into Italy we are told as follows: While Tarquinius Priscus reigned at Rome, the Celts, who make up one of the three divisions of Gaul, were under the domination of the Bituriges, and this tribe supplied the Celtic nation with a king. Ambigatus was then the man, and his talents, together with his own and the general good fortune, had brought him great distinction; for Gaul under his sway grew so rich in corn and so populous, that it seemed hardly possible to govern so great a multitude. The king, who was now an old man and wished to relieve his kingdom of a burdensome throng, announced that he meant to send Bellovesus and Segovesus, his sister's sons, two enterprising young men, to find such homes as the gods might assign to them by augury; and promised them that they should head as large a number of emigrants as they themselves desired, so that no tribe might be able to prevent their settlement. Whereupon to Segovesus were by lot assigned the Hercynian highlands; but to Bellovesus the gods proposed a far pleasanter road, into Italy.[3]

The thesis which appears twice explicitly in Livy, that a good '200 years' before the sack of Rome 'in the time of King Tarquinius Priscus' there was a prior Celtic migration to Italy seems to me to be more of a misunderstanding than a memory of particularly intensive Transalpine relationships in the sixth century B.C. This is shown by recent studies on the basis of philology (Sordi

1976/77; Grilli 1980) as well as archaeological evidence (Frey 1971a; Negroni Catacchio 1978). Also C. de Simone's attempt (1979) to adopt Livy's chronology, again with the derivation of some Etruscan family names from Celtic, goes beyond historical reality. J-J. Hatt's attempt (1960) to effect a compromise between Livy and the archaeological dates on the basis of the theory of a confusion between Tarquinius Priscus and Tarquinius Superbus is likewise totally without credence.

According to literary tradition, therefore, the following clues as to the causes of the Celtic migrations – at least as the Romans (and their partly Greek sources) saw them – are offered: overpopulation; internal disputes; the temptations of the South; Etruscan search for military assistance. It is immediately obvious that we are dealing with the stock themes which constantly reappear in written history and which are quoted with differing emphases from the Celtic migrations through the Germanic folk movements to the colonization of north America and the Russian invasion into Afghanistan (Vajda 1973/4). One can only note them and investigate what in each specific case could actually have lain behind these themes.

So what was wrong on the eve of the Celtic migrations? In order to find out the answer, we must first do away with the unfortunate break which has conventionally been placed between the Hallstatt and La Tène periods. As a result of this division phenomena have divorced which topographically, culturally and historically belong wholly together. This is particularly regrettable in the case of especially important areas like south-west Germany (Zürn 1941; Aufdermauer 1966; Liebschwager 1972; Nellissen 1975; Fischer, F. 1967), southern Bavaria (Kossack 1959) and the Oberpfalz (Torbrügge 1979; Uenze 1964). Only in the middle Rhine does the continuity between the Hallstatt and La Tène cultures obtrude so strongly that the period divisions have been set at the actual point when the cemeteries that had been in use for centuries went out of use (Engels 1967; Joachim 1968; Haffner 1976; also Polenz 1973). Only in small areas like the Hagenau forest (Schaeffer 1930; Kimmig 1979) or north Württemberg with its new finds (Zürn 1970; Pauli 1972), and for individual outstanding sites like the Dürrnberg bei Hallein (Penninger 1972; Moosleitner *et al.* 1974; Pauli 1978) and the Heuneburg on the upper Danube (Kimmig 1983a; Mansfeld 1973; Lang 1974; Dämmer 1978) has all the comparable material which bridges the chronological 'culture boundary' been dealt with together.

The grounds for challenging the phase boundaries are that they frequently do less than justice to historical reality. The critical question is this: from what point in time can and should we be speaking of 'Celts'? Which historical situation is to be causally linked with it? There have been many answers to this question which I have briefly summarized elsewhere (Pauli 1980). I offer here four definitions with supporting arguments.

1. *A Celt is one who speaks Celtic.*
To a large extent this sort of definition is suitable only for the Roman and post-Roman period, when there is a sufficient flow of epigraphic and historical sources. Ultimately it goes back to the question of when the institutionalization

of nation states first began, especially in central Europe. For earlier periods it is hardly useful, for no-one knows how far back the later recognized language groups go, and how great the differences were between neighbouring languages and dialects. This does not mean that I underestimate the role of language as an important means of communication, and would deny the relationship between language areas and social or trade areas which form the basis of cultural areas. However, the traditional attempts of linguists to trace back 'Celtic' or even 'Indo-European' through the millennia as the common early languages seem to be endowed with even less conviction (Pisani 1953; Pulgram 1958). Antiquated ideas, whether of the genealogical tree of language in the Darwinian sense (cf. Schmid 1978) or of the character of folk movements (Vajda 1973/4), fit well with the equally antiquated ideas of archaeologists of previous generations who work from the equation culture=race=language (for early German history already fully rectified by Wenskus 1961). Quite apart from this, the linguistically useful sources for this early period are decidedly meagre (Wagner 1969; 1970).

Nevertheless there is one example of the fruitful collaboration between linguists and archaeologists, and for the especially important early period. In 1962 Giacomo Devoto brought together the collected references in earlier works with new evidence for a 'Lepontic language' and expounded his view that it in fact tended towards Celtic rather than Italian (Devoto 1962). His evidence, inscriptions and place-names, is distributed in the area of the southern Swiss and Lombard-Piedmont lakes as well as in the southern bordering part of the Po valley as far as Milan. Devoto also concludes that this evidence for language must be earlier than the historically documented Celtic migrations around 400 B.C. The linguistic and archaeological evidence correspond closely. Before the Celtic migrations around 400 B.C. there is in fact only one possibility of demonstrating a horizon of foreign types and customs in the same area to such a degree that it is possible to suggest the invasion of largish groups of people (Pauli 1971a:48). This is the 'Canegrate facies' which first emerged as an independent culture through the publication of the cemeteries at Canegrate (Lombardy) and Ascona (Kt. Ticino). According to currently accepted chronology it begins in the thirteenth century B.C. and then gradually mixes in with indigenous traditions (Proto-Golasecca B and C). Archaeological analysis suggests that these people must have come from the area on the far side of the northern arc of the Alps. Eastern France, northern Switzerland and south-west Germany are also related regions.

Among linguists today there seems to be no doubt that Lepontic is to be thought of as a Celtic language (Lejeune 1971; Schmidt 1977). This means that already in the thirteenth century B.C. the specific individuality of Celtic was very strongly marked. Strongly enough, in any case, for one to be able to distinguish the remains of this early phase after 800 years of 'Italianization' in the Golasecca region very clearly from that of the new Celtic incursions around 400 B.C. Nevertheless, we must not deceive ourselves: no-one knows what unusual dialect was spoken by the Golasecca people around 500 B.C. However, the basic facts of the case are acknowledged by even so sceptical a scholar as Fischer (1981:58).

From this we may conclude that although the early stages of the Celtic language stretch back a long way, a correlation with the assertions of the ancient sources on the living areas of the Celts is not directly possible. Of early Celtic history we know just about nothing apart from the fact that there were groups who were repeatedly on the move.

2. *Celts lived where the earliest written sources suggest they did.*
This point can be dealt with easily. Herodotus had basically not the slightest idea where they lived (Fischer 1972), and the famous passage in Hecataeus of Miletus was first recorded by Stephen of Byzantium over 1,000 years later. The statement that the *keltike* lay in the Massilia hinterland could therefore be a more recently acquired fact (Duval 1971:176). Nevertheless, it emerges from Herodotus that there was a people in Europe who at that time were known by the name of 'Celts'. And the Danube – here *Danuvios*, not *Istros* – also had something to do with it; moreover, they seem at his time not yet to have been settled in Upper Italy.

3. *The Celts can be traced back archaeologically into the grey mists of antiquity.*
This view contradicts everything that we know of the antecedents of Europe's present ethnic population, including the early Germans (Wenskus 1961). Peoples are communities who over the centuries can come together and who can similarly break apart. Certainly language plays a role, but no less important are political relationships. Who would think of searching for the first Germans, the first Austrians, the first French and the first English?

The starting point for such attempts to work backwards were observations based on historically documented and archaeologically recognizable folk movements, particularly those by the Germans at the transition from late antiquity to the early Middle Ages. Thus Gabriel de Mortillet already in 1871 ventured to localize the area of origin in west central Europe of the migrating tribes according to the written sources on the basis of 'Celtic' finds in northern Italy. This procedure can still be seen as legitimate today, for we are here dealing with a restricted local variation of a cultural phenomenon within a short period which, at least in this case, cannot be explained in any other way than by actual migration (Champion, T. C. 1980).

It is, however, a different case with attempts to trace back historical phenomena within a more or less unchanging region. Here the doors are open to the arbitrary weighting of individual factors. The real question is, if the Celts were settled in central Europe in the fifth century B.C., how long had they already been there and what evidence can be used to trace them? The multitude of answers to this question that have been offered over the last century shows at best that no agreement will be reached by this route (Pauli 1980).

The problem must be approached in a different way. The relationships of the late Bronze Age, the Hallstatt period and the La Tène period in the areas of politics, social structure, art and religion must be analysed, all these being components which can be at least partly treated by archaeological means. The question always to be kept in mind is from when the Celts felt themselves to be a coherent group, a group which perceived itself as distinct from other people, having developed an individual self-awareness.

In this sense I propose as a thesis:

4. *'Celts' is an idea endowed with a socio-psychic background and is firmly established in a real historical situation.*

The description of this situation, which must have largely determined the future destiny of central Europe and the neighbouring region, is the aim of the following paragraphs.

Facts

Everyone engaged in research on the Late Bronze Age and Iron Age in central Europe is in the habit of showing that in this period there was a reversal in the area's relationship with the Mediterranean region. After the wide-ranging network of interactions in the thirteenth to twelfth centuries B.C. which even today has to be partly explained in terms of population movements – the Dorian migration, for example – Urnfield cultures became widespread. This is basically a similar phenomenon to the one we are describing here, though it has been much less extensively studied. Between themselves they supported no more than the usual contacts; cultural and technical innovations appear mainly to have come from the north Balkans (von Merhart 1969). Equally involved are central Europe and upper and even central Italy. The Alps were no hindrance to these contacts (Primas 1975), so that all in all a Mediterranean influence on central Europe cannot be denied (Pauli 1971b).

This is first really true for the Hallstatt C period, as a new thrust of innovation reached the West from the Balkans, though only as far as Bohemia and Bavaria with a few isolated examples further west (Fischer U. 1979:115). The evidence is above all in the form of rich male graves which also contain wagons and horse-gear (Kossack 1954b). The warriors have their sword with them in the grave; it is no longer, as in the latest Bronze Age, deposited predominantly as an offering in rivers or in 'hoards' (Torbrügge 1965:88). The indications here, therefore, are of a warrior aristocracy in eastern central Europe who cannot renounce their status symbol even in the grave. The social position of these warriors within society and in relation to each other is not easy to define (Kossack 1970:139). It would seem that we are dealing with chiefs of relatively small bands of apparently equal status. Larger concentrations of power are unlikely, for in this particular period, in the seventh century B.C., there are no defended hill-top settlements compared with those of the late Bronze Age (Hallstatt B) and the sixth to fifth centuries B.C. (Härke 1979). Only in the eastern Alpine area, in Steiermark, Carniola and Slovenia, did a stronger social differentiation emerge, and that on the basis of wealth accrued through iron (Gabrovec 1966; Pauli 1984:24).

This situation changed fundamentally and surprisingly quickly in the decade after 600 B.C. It was then that Greek Massalia and neighbouring colonies were founded; Bologna and Este developed into centres which were almost city-like in character. Central Europe came into direct contact with the south, which no longer retained cultural superiority (Kimmig 1974; 1983b).

These contacts are naturally most obviously manifested in the long-known Mediterranean imports, which are also important for the chronology (Dehn and Frey 1979). They range from splendid pieces only transportable by river, like the Vix krater, to the adoption from northern Italy of safety-pin brooch fashions; even a southern fan found its way to the north (Spindler 1980b). Also, bronze cauldrons for great feasts were manufactured after Etruscan prototypes (Hawkes and Smith 1957). So we are not only dealing with imports in the strict sense, or even with 'trade' in exotic valuables (coral, for example: Champion S. 1976); much more important is the fact that in many regions the southern prototypes stimulated imitations.

An outstanding example is the mud-brick wall at the Heuneburg (Kimmig 1975; 1983a), built by an architect who must have seen the southern prototypes with his own eyes. The same goes for the warrior *stele* from the Hirschlanden tumulus (Zürn 1964; 1970; Beeser 1983) and the wheeled couch from the recently uncovered chieftain's grave at Hochdorf near Ludwigsburg (Biel 1980; 1981; 1982). These examples date to the sixth century B.C., and are in an area which on the basis of its rich finds would appear (along with Burgundy) to be the centre of the western Hallstatt culture, that is, Baden-Württemberg. What we can see there is a phase of sumptuous gifts (Fischer F. 1973) and of imitations of southern manners by the indigenous chiefs.

The feudal structure of society is unmistakeable (Frankenstein and Rowlands 1978). The powerful families dug themselves in behind wall and ditch: on the Heuneburg, Hohenasperg, Mont Lassois (Joffroy 1979), Château-sur-Salins (Piroutet 1936), Châtillon-sur-Glâne (Ramseyer 1983; Schwab 1983), Breisach (Bender *et al.* 1976), to name only the most important and as yet partly examined sites (Kimmig 1969). However, the enemy against whom they dug themselves in is also noteworthy: on the one hand it was against jealous neighbours and relations, on the other against their own subjects who were drawn into all kinds of compulsory service – building walls, raising enormous tumuli (Spindler 1980a:143), effecting transportation, supplying natural produce.

Perhaps a brief comment on the question of weaponry may be added. The Hallstatt D period interrupts in a hitherto puzzling manner the tradition of the sword (at least in the grave). This weapon had been known since the Bronze Age, and from La Tène A became again the typical weapon of the Celtic warrior. Only in Hallstatt D is the short dagger the almost totally predominant thrusting weapon in the western Hallstatt region (on the few 'swords' see Spindler 1980c). During the first part of this period a relatively large number of male graves contained these weapons, but in the developed Hallstatt D phase they were almost entirely limited to the richest graves (Sievers 1980; 1982:57ff.). The main weapon in normal warrior graves, on the other hand, is the spear, often in twos or even threes. On analogy with much later situations one might conclude that the dagger was not a true weapon but served as a status symbol for the leader, whose subordinates did the killing. And the more power was concentrated in the hands of a few potentates, so the more limited to this small circle was the wearing and the placing in graves of valuable daggers.

This also means that the exercise of power in the daily life of the individual was ever more strongly restricted (naturally not in war, when spears in the sense of hoplite weaponry played a most important role; Frey 1973), and was the monopoly of the small aristocratic group. In this can also be perceived an indicator for the further development of an early 'high culture' with the beginnings of a primitive state system. A further indication of 'feudalization' consists incidentally in the rich 'chieftain's graves' from now on being geographically separated from the ordinary cemeteries, a feature also to be observed in the early Middle Ages (Christlein 1973:160).

In this sense the dagger offers a good possibility for delineating the region in which far-reaching changes are involved (Kimmig 1976:393 Abb.85; Sievers 1980:Abb.1). It comprises the western Hallstatt region between Champagne and the Salzburg area, between the German Mittelgebirge and the fringe of the Alps. The real border to the east must have been the River Inn, as a comparison with the Roman period suggests, when it served as the border between the provinces of Raetia and Noricum (Pauli 1978:409). Hallstatt itself occupied a special position outside this zone (Frey 1971c; Egg 1980). The same area stands out in the distribution of Hallstatt gold finds (Kimmig and Rest 1954:215 fig.7; Piggott 1965:188 fig.105).

This feudal Hallstatt world came to a violent end. The final destruction is proved at the Heuneburg and is to be presumed for the other major sites. Not one of them has finds in any appreciable number which can be ascribed to the Early La Tène period, taken solely typologically. This, however, is exactly the point around which revolve all the discussions concerning the relationship between the Late Hallstatt and Early La Tène cultures. In brief, it concerns to what extent these two cultures overlap chronologically (Zürn 1952; Pauli 1972; Mansfeld 1973:64; Lang 1974:59; Gersbach 1981). Interpretations are widely divergent; they range between a ten-year overlap in the sense of a normal transition horizon (Dämmer 1978:62) and almost a century with the concept of historical overlap implying a long contemporaneity of two life-styles. This is not the place for a full discussion of the opposing opinions (cf. Pauli 1973; 1974b; 1981b). I would like to summarize here my conception of the problem (Pauli 1972; 1978:411). It is based on the thesis that a better understanding can be achieved if Hallstatt D3 (the horizon marked by *Fusszier* fibulae and *Stangengliederketten*) and La Tène A existed contemporaneously.

During the fifth century B.C. many fundamental changes took place in central Europe.

a. The destruction of the defended *Fürstensitze* corresponds with a break in the practice of burying the dead in tumuli to be observed from Burgundy to Bohemia. The old tradition of local burial places is suddenly broken, either with the graves of Hallstatt D3 (particularly in Baden-Württemberg) or with those of La Tène A (Switzerland, north Bavaria, Bohemia). The rite of inhumation burial in flat graves appears first in Champagne (Les Jogasses and other cemeteries) and in western Switzerland (for example at Münsingen) (Lorenz 1978:33 and this volume). Nowhere is there a regional continuity with former cemeteries, and in southern Germany in particular we are only dealing with small groups of graves which were themselves abandoned after a short time (Krämer 1964:20; Fischer F. 1967).

b. In the area of the Hunsrück-Eifel culture which up until now had only been sparsely settled, we suddenly find *Fürstengräber* (Fischer F. 1981:fig.16) as well as many cemeteries with less richly equipped burials (Joachim 1968; Haffner 1976:148). Without doubt this area experienced a remarkable prosperity which can only have been based on economic factors (Driehaus 1965). There is much to suggest that valuable iron ore was discovered and smelted. The knowledge for this complex process appears to have come from the Etruscans who themselves in Populonia were smelting the similar iron ore from Elba (Witter 1942).

c. The so-called 'chieftains' graves' of the Hunsrück-Eifel culture are basically different from those of the region with Hallstatt D sites. There may be only a superficial difference between the Hallstatt wagon with four wheels, the last vehicle for the *Ekphora*, or journey to the grave, and the two-wheeled battle cart (Harbison 1969), an innovation which is after all derived from Italo-Etruscan prototypes (cf. Sesto Calende in the Golasecca culture: Pauli 1971a:110; de Marinis 1975). More important is the fact that these 'chieftains' graves' contain jewellery and ritual objects decorated in an entirely new style, the Early Celtic style of the Early La Tène culture (Jacobsthal 1944; Megaw 1970; Frey and Schwappach 1973). In spite of assertions to the contrary (see most recently Kimmig 1981) this has no real precursor in the centres of late Hallstatt culture. So here there is a qualitative difference. An independent and permanent transformation of an original model is something different from more or less able copies of isolated forms and motifs.

d. If we analyse the true novelties in La Tène art, four points stand out as important. First, Graeco-Etruscan palmettes and other fancy motifs were the favourite models, but Early La Tène Celts altered them at will and put them together in new ways (Frey 1971b; 1980). Second, the high number of oriental motifs is more surprising. If they were transmitted to the north secondarily through the Greeks and Etruscans then they attest an 'orientalizing phase' for central Europe with a corresponding chronological displacement (Sandars 1971; 1976; Megaw 1975). Because this phenomenon already has certain precursors and parallels in south-east Alpine and Venetic situla art of the sixth to fifth centuries B.C. (di Filippo 1967; Boardman 1971; di Filippo Balestrazzi 1980) there is no chronological gap: the people confronted with it were clearly ready to take it up. Third, particularly Celtic is the association with circle constructions, which are often very well disguised and can only be extracted by means of the most scrupulous analysis. This sort of concealment was wholly foreign to Mediterranean people (Lenerz-de Wilde 1977). Finally, at the same time Late Bronze Age and Hallstatt symbols, like sun-discs, water birds and horses (Kossack 1954a) almost completely disappear. Some elements live on in some areas (Pauli 1975:202–3), but they can be easily recognized as isolated survivals from the past.

e. It may be concluded from all this that a new art of this kind cannot be interpreted simply as a superficial adaptation of foreign prototypes, as Megaw emphasizes in his contribution to this volume. As in Greece and Etruria, an influence from Oriental art must also be recognized in central Europe, to the extent that the new elements within a short time completely replaced or at least outnumbered the old. But with the motifs the religious content too must have found its way west, although changed and weakened. Thus central Europe itself possessed its 'orientalizing phase'. Even when from the third century B.C. Italic-Hellenistic influences gained the upper hand, these oriental motifs for their part continued though by archaeologically untraceable traditions: examples are sword stamps (Wyss 1954; Pauli 1984:128, fig. 75) and wooden sculpture in a holy place (Planck 1980; 1982; Bittel 1981:Abb. 45–6).

f. In the early history of central Europe there are three periods when men wore favoured amulets and gave them to the dead in the grave: the Early Bronze Age, Late Hallstatt/Early La Tène and the early Middle Ages (Pauli 1975). Belief in the efficacy of amulets was especially common in periods of internal and external unrest, of personal danger and of revolution in current norms of thought and behaviour (Hansmann and Kriss-Rettenbeck 1966:232; Pauli 1975:199).

g. At such a time too the sanctity of graves was broken. A majority of the Hallstatt chieftains' graves had already been robbed in antiquity, many of them very soon after deposition (the Hohmichele, Grafenbühl, Üetliberg). Although not exactly comparable, the Early Bronze Age and early medieval periods can be further cited as periods of intensive grave robbing in central Europe (Pauli 1981a). As with the belief in amulets, this shows that the old norms were being set aside. The graves of the 'chiefs' were no longer inviolable, and grave goods were stolen on account of their intrinsic value. The dissolution of traditional ideas, and the mental and physical ability to ignore them, cannot be denied.

The model

If all observations based on fact are taken into account, it does not seem to be exaggerating to speak of a fifth-century B.C. crisis. It develops in a logical, if not inevitable, way from the intensified southern contacts in central Europe from the sixth century B.C. The correlations that are made and interpreted certainly go beyond the facts and can only be presented in the form of a model. Such a model becomes more plausible if it can be considered alongside other periods and areas with comparable precursors and better evidence.

The fascination of the south and its desirable goods – especially luxury ritual vessels and wine – must have been a very important factor in the feudalization of early Celtic society. Possibly, too, the slave trade contributed to an intensified power organization, for central Europe could not offer much else in exchange. Raiding and skirmishing between local chieftains who themselves stayed in their fortified settlements must have led the farmers in need of protection into greater dependence. So by turning towards the south the Celtic aristocracy simultaneously brought on their own destruction. For the contacts were not limited to the exchange of goods; there must also have been an active exchange of people. Such exchanges did not only bring technical know-how, but also beliefs and ideas in the realms of art, religion and politics.

Let us not forget that in the Mediterranean world also much was changing. Around 510 B.C. tyranny was overthrown in Athens, and democracy was gradually established. Similar events – though somewhat later, after the sack of Cumae in 474 B.C. – occurred in the still minor city of Rome and perhaps in some other cities in Etruria, such as Chiusi. From around 540 B.C. Greek expansion in the west came to an end because of the restriction of their sea power at the hands of the Carthaginians. Thus the colonies on the southern French coast turned markedly to the hinterland, and not simply on account of the already renewed interest in the land route for Cornish tin. On the other hand, Etruria became even more strongly oriented to the north as its expansion southward was decisively halted by the Greeks following the sack of Cumae. In the intellectual field Pythagoras was an important figure, his theories having close links with Orphism which itself came from the Thraco-Balkan region. These teachings became popular, particularly with the lower orders of the Greek world (Thomson 1961:195); was this a counteraction to the superficial fascination of the upper strata of northern border peoples with the ostentation of the overpowerful south in many regions?

Nowhere can we better identify the penetrating power of new ideas from the south than in early Celtic art. But it is even more surprising that it is almost totally absent from the old centres of Late Hallstatt culture, and is as much seen in the form of the ostentatious products of talented goldsmiths and bronze-casters as it is in the stock of decorations for the unspectacular things of daily life like rings, belthooks and fibulas (cf. Kimmig 1979:134 map 4). This is not altered by the lengthened period of a few 'Early La Tène chieftains' graves', for example the secondary burial in the giant tumulus of Klein Aspergle near Ludwigsburg (Paret 1943/8). The new finds from the chieftain's grave at Üetliberg near Zurich (unfortunately previously robbed), comprising two disc brooches decorated in Early La Tène style (Drack 1981), only corroborate the fact that this art was also certainly known in south-west Germany and northern Switzerland (Drack 1966) but was only in exceptional cases accepted by the upper class. The way out, which is to class these two graves as the latest, already 'La Tène-ized' examples of chieftains' graves, is as much a matter of opinion as my own interpretation. There is, however, no objective evidence.

Such a remarkable split is evident between La Tène art and the old west Hallstatt area that its roots must lie very deep. Because there is also a shift northwards in the economic emphasis (to Champagne, and the Hunsrück-Eifel culture) we must also presume quite genuine political and social structures. I have developed for this a model in imitation of the sixteenth and seventeenth centuries A.D. – the period of the Reformation, the Thirty Years' War, the first bourgeois revolutions in the Netherlands and England, the transition to absolutism, the shift of industrial potential – which attempts for the fifth century B.C. to bring the different facts into at least a partly logical and historically possible relationship. Important starting points for my interpretation have obviously already appeared in some earlier works (Kahrstedt 1937/8; Filip 1973; 1977).

One starting point is, as has already been noted, the indisputable fact that the feudal Hallstatt world from Burgundy to Bohemia came to a sudden and violent end. It was replaced by the La Tène B culture which, at least archaeologically, is fundamentally different from what preceded it: no more 'chiefly residences' but farms and hamlets, at best simple enclosures; no more 'chiefly graves' but an egalitarian basic range of grave goods placed in simple burials dug into the ground (Lorenz 1978). No one denies that there were still both rich and poor, but wealth was apparently not institutionalized as power and was not put in the grave for show. A further starting point is the fact that shortly before 387/6 B.C., at the latest, there was an exodus of people – whole families and their relations – from central Europe to the south and south-east: the Celtic migration (Contzen 1861). People do not leave their homeland without reason (Krüger 1977). Only when unendurable strains occur there do men and their wives and children seek their salvation in foreign lands (Kahrstedt 1937/8).

If we then bring the religious background of early Celtic art into the equation, and the economic revolutions besides, there can be no doubt that early Celtic society is an extremely interesting subject for historical and sociological study. Late Hallstatt society was so fascinated by the south that it got into a blind alley at the end of which self-destruction was waiting. The time was not ripe for a balance between the wishful thinking of the upper class and the minimal needs of the lower orders of the tribe. Tyranny as a system had to break down – though on other grounds than in Greece, Etruria and Rome. The infrastructure could not support it.

For the time being the conflict that broke out in late Hallstatt society seems to have been resolved. In any case the sudden flowering of the northern fringe area is attributed to a real influx of people (Haffner 1976:156; Thénot 1976:91). Whether only the economic attraction, particularly the postulated iron boom in the Middle Rhine, is responsible remains in question. The new beginning is only intelligible if we consider the obviously new religious components in Early La Tène art. It is then possible to see, particularly in those people who moved north, a removal on religious, political and perhaps also economic grounds. This phenomenon played an important part in the turmoil of the sixteenth and seventeenth centuries A.D. (Trevor-Roper 1967:13 and 55). Perhaps in the fifth century B.C. the emigrants were similar: economic interests showed them the direction, but religious motives gave the impetus (Trevor-Roper 1967:32–3). Of course this ought not to be seen mechanistically, as again the sixteenth century shows: 'Regional research shows clearly that similar political and social structures in two areas or states in no way produces the same attitudes in the inhabitants towards the Reformation and the peasants' revolt. Individual personalities like priests and peasant leaders, the local psychological situation, the human climate, the influence of agitation from other areas could have played a decisive role' (Bosl and Weis 1976:190).

At the same time this means that in the fifth century B.C. also this spread of new ideas, fashions and way of life need not have been due only to the movement of large groups of people. The best example is provided by the Dürrnberg bei Hallein (Pauli 1978:486). There the persistence of an indigenous people with their strong relationships with the inner Alps cannot be doubted, yet nevertheless the centre was willingly and very quickly opened up to new influences from the west. The Dürrnberg developed into one of the most important centres of the eastern La Tène culture. That there was at this period a real population increase can now be established because of cemeteries positioned in the low-lying areas which had apparently not been previously settled – seen above all in the recent excavations of 1981 in areas which up until now had not produced a single grave. According to the analyses possible so far the Dürrnberg graves contain no immigrants from a really recognizable region buried abroad, despite Megaw's suggestion to the contrary (see p. 173 below). The range of forms, apart from the ubiquitous novelties of the Early La Tène culture, remains so strongly within the local tradition that only immigrants from the immediate vicinity can be suggested. This conclusion is based, of course, on the hypothesis that one can separate at least the first generation of immigrants sufficiently well archaeologically from the indigenous inhabitants. The situation in the period of the later Germanic migrations strongly favours this, but in the light of new and extensive excavations a deeper analysis will perhaps reveal striking differences.

Because in this period, which is contemporary with La Tène A, the old structures were not completely dismantled – the 'chieftains' graves' from Champagne to Bohemia and the Dürrnberg being evidence of the existence of a wealthy and ostentatious upper class following the old Hallstatt model (Fischer F. 1981:Abb. 16; Pauli 1974a) – the first phase in the shift of power must have been initiated through the relations of the upper class and their adherents. The same is the case everywhere for the first phase of Greek colonization too (Hasebroek 1931:110; Kahrstedt 1937/8:40). An important adjustment with the lower levels has indeed taken place, for in contrast to the Hallstatt D3 area, in the Moselle and the middle Rhine the rite of chiefly burial does not end around 400 B.C. at the transition from La Tène A to B, but about two generations later (Reinheim, Waldalgesheim), and the tumulus cemeteries in this region end early in the third century B.C. (Haffner 1976:159). With this is linked a clearer, if only temporary, decline in population. Can we see in this the evidence for participation in the later phases of Celtic migration?

Migration to more distant and hardly known areas was the second reaction of people in central Europe coping with the new situation. It was more radical, and the people in Italy, the Balkans and even Asia Minor experienced the results. Whether in fact 'overpopulation' was responsible has not to date been archaeologically proven. On the contrary, 'overpopulation' is a very subjective term, for spiritual and political constraints in the homeland can also lead to migration.

To what extent the destruction of the hated princely residences and the actual exodus occurred simultaneously cannot be determined as long as our chronological system remains so insecure and can be so variously interpreted (Dämmer 1978:62; Gersbach 1981; Spindler 1981; Pauli 1981b). Central Europe was not left completely without people, but the early Celtic world had completely disappeared.

In these enterprises the upper-class families played an important role, just as they did much later, as 'insurrections of the early modern period can only be successful when they are based on the cooperation of the lower levels of the population with part of the leading group' (Haan 1981:105; Forster and Greene 1970:14). To the eyes of the Romans the situation appeared quite different; they saw it as a colonizing expedition in which the *rex* Ambigatus sent two large hordes under the leadership of close relatives in search of land.

In this connection Livy transmits a detail whose use has been hitherto overlooked, and with it I return to the beginning of my discussion. He reports explicitly that Ambigatus had appointed the son of his sister to the leadership of the emigrants. It may be that he had no son of his own that he could trust with this important task, but one thing still remains surprising: the passing of rank, power and wealth from mother's brother to sister's son is seen as one of the characteristics of a matrilinear society (Schneider and Gough 1961). This observation can be archaeologically confirmed, for the analysis of Late Hallstatt cemeteries in north Württemberg provides evidence for just such a family structure (Pauli 1972:39ff.;114ff.). In the Mühlacker cemetery, which is endowed with particularly good evidence for such difficult research, it can be established that for the first time there is an observable difference in the women's and girls' wear which can at least be construed in terms of a distinction between married and unmarried women. Also in the central burial of one of the tumuli laid out according to the normal pattern there lies what may thus be termed a 'married' woman together with her husband and unmarried dead children. On the death of the married daughter of the heir a new tumulus was constructed in which were buried all the dead members of the next generation. That at least is my interpretation of the archaeological facts, and from them it can be concluded that in the case of the female, this was the ruler of the local court, this was the person on whom family tradition was based.

This should not be surprising, for in the succession of the Roman kings also (in part an Etruscan development) the female line played a decisive role, with son-in-law following father-in-law (Frazer 1920:229ff.; Pauli 1972:122ff.). I will not continue here with this theme of 'matrilinear descent' or even 'matriarchy' (Weisweiler 1940), but it should be carefully noted that sometimes results can be gained by archaeological means which in unexpected ways suddenly confirm old traditions or at least allow them to appear in a different light.

The same goes also for the story of Helico, who allegedly incited the Celts to migrate through the temptations of the south (Köves-Zulauf 1977). Certainly this factor must not be underrated, but one detail seems to me to be just as important. Helico was explicitly characterized as a *faber*, a craftsman in the widest sense certainly but doubtless also comparable to a 'smith', who worked widely in 'Rome'; he was also active in Etruria. There could be encapsulated in this a legendary tradition from another period, that capable craftsmen were exchanged between central Europe and Italy and southern France (as on the Heuneburg, or with Hirschlanden) and the iron industry in the Hunsrück-Eifel area received an unsuspected stimulus based on new – possibly Etruscan – specialist knowledge.

Helico, according to the legend, returned to his native land, but other Celts appear to have remained in the south. This is at least suggested by the family names in Etruria and Liguria which in origin may go back to Celtic personal names (de Simone 1979; 1980). The inscriptions certainly date to the period before traditional Celtic migrations. Even if it is not linguistically impossible that those persons could have come only from northern Italy, from the area of the Golasecca culture with its partly 'Celtic' speaking peoples, it is tempting to see in these names a slight echo of toing and froing over the Alps (cf. Frey 1971a) that influenced so permanently the social and cultural development in central Europe in the early Celtic period. In the end there were always those who made history and those who suffered from it.

Notes

1. Translation taken from H. Rackham (ed.), *Plinius: Naturalis Historia* (London and Cambridge, Mass., 1960).
2. Translation T. C. Champion.
3. Translations taken from R. M. Ogilvie (ed.), *Livy: Histories* (1974).

Bibliography

Aufdermauer, J., 1966. *Die Hallstattkultur in Südbaden* (unpublished dissertation, Universität Freiburg).
Beeser, J., 1983. 'Der kouro-keltos von Hirschlanden', *Fundberichte aus Baden-Württemberg 8:* 21–46.
Bender, H., Dehn, R. and Stork, I., 1976. 'Neuere Untersuchungen auf dem Münsterberg in Breisach (1966–1975): 'Die vorrömische Zeit', *Arch. Korr. 6:* 213–24.
Biel, J., 1980. 'Das Grab von Hochdorf', in Lessing 1980: 49–54.
Biel, J., 1981. 'The late Hallstatt chieftain's grave at Hochdorf', *Antiquity 55:* 16–18.
Biel, J., 1982. 'Ein Fürstengrabhügel der späten Hallstattzeit bei Eberdingen-Hochdorf, Kr. Ludwigsburg (Baden-Württemberg). Vorbericht', *Germania 60:* 61–104.
Bittel, K., 1981. 'Religion und Kult', in K. Bittel, W. Kimmig and S. Schiek (eds.), *Die Kelten in Baden-Württemberg* (Stuttgart): 85–117.
Boardman, J., 1971. 'A southern view of Situla Art', in J. Boardman, M. A. Brown and T. G. E. Powell (eds.), *The European Community in Later Prehistory. Studies in honour of C. F. C. Hawkes:* 121–140.
Bosl, K. and Weis, E., 1976. *Die Gesellschaft in Deutschland 1: von der fränkischen Zeit bis 1848* (Munich).
Champion, S., 1976. 'Coral in Europe: commerce and Celtic ornament', in P.-M. Duval and C. F. C. Hawkes (eds.), *Celtic Art in Ancient Europe: Five Protohistoric Centuries:* 29–37.
Champion, T. C., 1980. 'Mass migration in later prehistoric Europe', in P. Sörbom (ed.), *Transport Technology and Social Change* (Stockholm): 31–42.
Christlein, R., 1973. 'Besitzabstufungen zur Merowingerzeit im Spiegel reicher Grabfunde aus West- und Süddeutschland', *Jahrbuch des Römisch-Germanischen Zentralmuseums 20:* 147–80.
Contzen, L., 1861. *Die Wanderungen der Kelten* (repr. Wiesbaden, 1968).
Dämmer, H-W., 1978. *Die bemalte Keramik der Heuneburg*, RG Forsch. 37 (Mainz).
Dehn, W. and Frey, O-H., 1979. 'Southern imports and the Hallstatt and early La Tène chronology of central Europe', in D. and F. R. Ridgway (eds.), *Italy before the Romans:* 489–511.
Devoto, G., 1962. 'Pour l'histoire de l'indoeuropéanisation de l'Italie septentrionale:

quelques étymologies lépontiques', *Revue de Philologie,* 3rd ser. *36:* 197–208.

Drack, W., 1966. 'Gürtelhaken mit Zierblech der Stufe Hallstatt D3 aus dem Jura und dem Waadt', in *Helvetia Antiqua. Festschrift E. Vogt* (Zurich): 126–36.

Drack, W., 1981. 'Der frühlatènezeitliche Fürstengrabhügel auf dem Üetliberg (Gemeinde Uitikon, Kanton Zürich)', *Zeitschrift für Schweiz. Archäol. und Kunstgeschichte 38:* 1–28.

Driehaus, J., 1965. ' "Fürstengräber" und Eisenerze zwischen Mittelrhein, Mosel und Saar', *Germania 43:* 32–49.

Duval, P-M., 1971. *La Gaule jusqu'au milieu du Ve siècle* (Paris).

Egg, M., 1980. 'Fremdlinge', in Lessing 1980: 85–7.

Engels, H-J., 1967. *Die Hallstatt- und Latènekultur in der Pfalz* (Speyer).

Filip, J., 1973. 'Le problème de la double origine des Celtes en Europe centrale', *Études Celtiques 13:* 583–93.

Filip, J., 1977. *Celtic Civilisation and its Heritage* (2nd edn).

di Filippo, E., 1967. 'Rapporti iconografici di alcuni monumenti dell'arte delle situle', in *Venetia. Studi miscellanei di Archeologia delle Venezie 1* (Padua): 97–200.

di Filippo Balestrazzi, E., 1980. 'Nuovi confronti iconografici e un'ipotesi sui rapporti fra l'area delle situle e il mondo orientale', in *Este e la civiltà paleoveneta a cento anni dalle prime scoperte,* Atti dell'XI convegno di studi etruschi e italici, Este-Padova 1976 (Florence): 153–70.

Fischer, F., 1967. 'Alte und neue Funde der Latène-Periode aus Württemberg', *Fundberichte aus Schwaben, N.F. 18/1:* 61–106.

Fischer, F., 1972. 'Die Kelten bei Herodot. Bemerkungen zu einigen geographischen und ethnographischen Problemen', *Madrider Mitteilungen 13:* 109–24.

Fischer, F., 1973. 'KEIMHΛIA. Bemerkungen zur kulturgeschichtlichen Interpretation des sogenannten Südimports in der späten Hallstatt- und frühen Latène-Kultur des westlichen Mitteleuropa', *Germania 51:* 436–59.

Fischer, F., 1981. 'Die Kelten und ihre Geschichte', in K. Bittel, W. Kimmig and S. Schiek (eds.), *Die Kelten in Baden-Württemberg* (Stuttgart): 45–76.

Fischer, U., 1979. *Ein Grabhügel der Bronze- und Eisenzeit im Frankfurter Stadtwald* (Frankfurt).

Forster, R. and Greene, J. P., 1970. *Preconditions of Revolution in Early Modern Europe* (Baltimore, Md).

Frankenstein, S. and Rowlands, M. R., 1978. 'The internal structure and regional context of Early Iron Age society in south-western Germany', *Bull. Inst. Archaeol. Univ. London 15:* 73–112.

Frazer, J. G., 1920. *The Magical Origin of Kings* (reprint 1968).

Frey, O-H., 1971a. 'Fibeln vom westhallstättischen Typus aus dem Gebiet südlich der Alpen. Zum Problem der keltische Wanderung', in *Oblatio. Raccolta di studi di antichità ed arte in onore di Aristide Calderini* (Como): 355–86.

Frey, O-H., 1971b. 'Die Goldschale von Schwarzenbach', *Hamburger Beiträge zur Archäol. 1:* 85–100.

Frey, O-H., 1971c. 'Hallstatt und die Hallstattkultur'. *Mitteilungen d. österreichischen Arbeitsgemeinschaft für Ur- und Frühgeschichte 22:* 110–4.

Frey, O-H., 1973. 'Bemerkungen zur hallstättischen Bewaffnung im Südostalpenraum', *Arheološki Vestnik 24:* 621–36.

Frey, O-H., 1980. 'Die Keltische Kunst', in *Die Kelten in Mitteleuropa* (Salzburger Landesausstellung im Keltenmuseum Hallein, Österreich): 76–92.

Frey, O-H. and Schwappach, F., 1973. 'Studies in early Celtic design', *World Archaeol. 4:* 339–56.

Gabrovec, S., 1966. 'Zur Hallstattzeit in Slowenien', *Germania 44:* 1–48.

Gersbach, E., 1981. 'Die Paukenfibeln und die Chronologie der Heuneburg bei Hundersingen/Donau', *Fundberichte aus Baden-Württemberg 6:* 213–23.

Grilli, A., 1980. 'La migrazione dei Galli in Livio', in *Studi in onore di F. Rittatore Vonwiller II* (Como): 183–92.

Haan, H., 1981. 'Prosperität und Dreissigjähriger Kreig', *Geschichte und Gesellschaft 7:* 91–118.

Haffner, A., 1976. *Die westliche Hunsrück-Eifel-Kultur,* RG Forsch. 36 (Berlin).

Hansmann, L. and Kriss-Rettenbeck, L., 1966. *Amulett und Talisman. Erscheinungsform und Geschichte* (Munich).

Harbison, P., 1969. 'The chariot of Celtic funerary tradition', in *Marburger Beitrage zur Archaologie der Kelten. Festschrift für W. Dehn,* Fundberichte aus Hessen, Beiheft 1 (Bonn): 34–58.

Härke, H., 1979. *Settlement Types and Settlement Patterns in the West Hallstatt Province* (BAR Int. S57).

Hasebroek, J., 1931. *Griechische Wirtschafts- und Gesellschaftsgeschichte* (Tübingen; repr. 1966).

Hatt, J-J., 1960. 'Les invasions celtiques en Italie du Nord – leur chronologie', *Bull. Soc. Préhistorique Française 57:* 362–72.

Hawkes, C. F. C. and Smith, M. A., 1957. 'On some buckets and cauldrons of the Bronze and Early Iron Ages', *Ant. J. 37:* 131–98.

Jacobsthal, P., 1934. 'Einige Werke keltische Kunst', *Die Antike 10:* 17–45.

Jacobsthal, P., 1944. *Early Celtic Art* (repr. 1969).

Jankuhn, H., Nehlsen, H. and Roth, H. (eds.), 1978. *Zum Grabfrevel in vor- und frühgeschichtlicher Zeit. Untersuchungen zu Grabraub und 'haugbrot' in Mittel- und Nordeuropa,* Abhandlungen der Akademie der Wissenschaften in Göttingen, phil.-hist. Klasse, Dritte Folge, 113.

Joachim, H.-E., 1968. *Die Hunsrück-Eifel-Kultur am Mittelrhein, Bonner Jahrbücher,* Beiheft 29 (Cologne and Graz).

Joffroy, R., 1979. *Vix et ses Trésors* (Paris).

Kahrstedt, U., 1937/8. 'Eine historische Betrachtung zu einem prähistorischen Problem', *Prähist. Zeitschrift 28–9:* 401–5.

Kimmig, W., 1969. 'Zum Problem späthallstättischer Adelssitze', in K.-H. Otto and J. Herrmann (eds.), *Siedlung, Burg und Stadt. Studien zu ihren Anfängen* (Berlin): 95–113.

Kimmig, W., 1974. 'Zum Fragment eines Este-Gefässes von der Heuneburg an der oberen Donau', *Hamburger Beiträge zur Archäol. 4:* 33–96.

Kimmig, W., 1975. 'Die Heuneburg an der oberen Donau', in *Ausgrabungen in Deutschland I* (Mainz): 192–211.

Kimmig, W., 1976. 'Spätbronzezeit' and 'Hallstattzeit' in article 'Bewaffnung', in H. Beck, H. Jankuhn, K. Ranke and R. Wenskus (eds.), *Reallexikon der Germanischen Altertumskunde,* II (Berlin and New York): 376–409.

Kimmig, W., 1979. 'Les tertres funéraires préhistoriques dans la forêt de Haguenau: Rück- und Ausblick', *Prähist. Zeitschrift 54:* 47–176.

Kimmig, W., 1981. 'Keltische Kunst', in K. Bittel, W. Kimmig and S. Schiek (eds.), *Die Kelten in Baden-Württemberg* (Stuttgart): 160–203.

Kimmig, W., 1983a. *Die Heuneburg an der oberen Donau.* Führer zu vor- und frühgeschichtlichen Denkmälern in Württemberg und Hohenzollern 1 (2nd edn, Stuttgart).

Kimmig, W., 1983b. 'Die griechische Kolonisation im westlichen Mittelmeergebiet und ihre Wirkung auf die Landschaften des westlichen Mitteleuropa', *Jahrbuch RGZM 30:* 5–78.

Kimmig, W. and Rest, W., 1954. 'Ein Fürstengrab der späten Hallstattzeit von Kappel am Rhein', *Jahrbuch RGZM 1:* 179–216.

Kossack, G., 1954a. *Studien zum Symbolgut der Urnenfelder- und Hallstattzeit Mitteleuropas,* RG Forsch. 20 (Berlin).

Kossack, G., 1954b. 'Pferdegeschirr aus Gräbern der älteren Hallstattzeit Bayerns', *Jahrbuch RGZM 1:* 111–78.

Kossack, G., 1959. *Südbayern während der Hallstattzeit,* RG Forsch. 24 (Berlin).

Kossack, G., 1970. *Gräberfelder der Hallstattzeit an Main und Fränkischer Saale* (Kallmünz).

Kossack, G., 1981. 'Gedanken zur Periodisierung der Hallstattkultur', in *Die Hallstattkultur. Symposium Steyr 1980*, ed. Land Oberösterreich (Linz): 35–46.
Köves-Zulauf, T., 1977. 'Helico, Führer der gallischen Wanderung', *Latomus 36:* 40–92.
Krämer, W., 1964. *Das keltische Gräberfeld von Nebringen (Kreis Böblingen)* (Stuttgart).
Krüger, B., 1977. 'Zum Problem germanischer Wanderungen', in J. Herrmann (ed.), *Archäologie als Geschichtswissenschaft* (Berlin): 225–33.
Lang, A., 1974. *Die geriefte Drehscheibenkeramik der Heuneburg 1950–1970 und verwandte Gruppen*, RG Forsch. 34 (Berlin).
Lejeune, M., 1971. *Lepontica* (Paris)= 'Documents gaulois et para-gaulois de Cisalpine', *Études Celtiques 12:* 357–500.
Lenerz-de Wilde, M., 1977. *Zirkelornamentik in der Kunst der Latènezeit,* Münchner Beiträge zur Vor- und Frühgeschichte 25 (Munich).
Lessing, E., 1980. *Hallstatt – Bilder aus der Frühzeit*, ed. U. Schaaff (Munich and Vienna).
Liebschwager, C., 1972. 'Zur Frühlatènekultur in Baden-Württemberg', *Arch. Korr. 2:* 143–8.
Lorenz, H., 1978. 'Totenbrauch und Tracht. Untersuchungen zur regionalen Gliederung in der frühen Latènezeit', *Bericht der Römisch-Germanischen Kommission 59:* 1–380.
Mansfeld, G., 1973. *Die Fibeln der Heuneburg 1950–1970,* RG Forsch. 33 (Berlin).
de Marinis, R., 1975. 'Le tombe di guerriero di Sesto Calende e le spade e i pugnali hallstattiani scoperti nell'Italia nord-occidentale', in *Archaeologica. Scritti in onore di A. Neppi Modona* (Florence): 213–69.
Megaw, J. V. S., 1970. *Art of the European Iron Age.*
Megaw, J. V. S., 1975. 'The orientalising theme in Early Celtic art: East or West?'. In J. Fitz (ed.), *The Celts in Central Europe. Papers of the II Pannonia Conference, Székesfehérvár 1974=Alba Regia 14:* 15–33.
Meid, W., 1968. *Indogermanisch und Keltisch,* Innsbrucker Beiträge zur Kulturwissenschaft, Sonderheft 25.
von Merhart, G., 1969. *Hallstatt und Italien. Gesammelte Aufsätze zur frühen Eisenzeit in Italien und Mitteleuropa,* ed. G. Kossack (Mainz).
Moosleitner, F., Pauli, L. and Penninger, E., 1974. *Der Dürrnberg bei Hallein II. Katalog der Grabfunde aus der Hallstatt- und Latènezeit, Zweiter Teil,* Münchner Beiträge zur Vor- und Frühgeschichte 17 (Munich).
Negroni Catacchio, N., 1978. 'I Celti in Transpadana dal periodo delle invasioni al III sec. a. Cr.'. In *I Galli e l'Italia,* ed. Soprintendenza archeologica di Roma: 76–80.
Nellissen, H., 1975. *Hallstattzeitliche Funde aus Nordbaden* (Bonn).
Paret, O., 1943/8. 'Das Kleinaspergle', *Jahrbuch für prähist. und ethnographische Kunst 17:* 47–51.
Pauli, L., 1971a. *Studien zur Golasecca-Kultur* (Heidelberg).
Pauli, L., 1971b. 'Die Golasecca-Kultur und Mitteleuropa. Ein Beitrag zur Geschichte des Handels über die Alpen', *Hamburger Beiträge zur Archäol. 1:* 1–83.
Pauli, L., 1972. 'Untersuchungen zur Späthallstattkultur in Nordwürttemberg. Analyse eines Kleinraumes im Grenzbereich zweier Kulturen', *Hamburger Beiträge zur Archäol. 2:* 1–166.
Pauli, L., 1973. Review of Mansfeld 1973, *Bonner Jahrb. 173:* 506–18.
Pauli, L., 1974a. 'Der goldene Steig. Wirtschaftsgeographisch-archäologische Untersuchungen im östlichen Mitteleuropa', in *Studien zur vor- und frühgeschichtlichen Archäologie. Festschrift für J. Werner* (Munich): 155–39.
Pauli, L., 1974b. Review of Lang 1974, *Bonner Jahrb. 174:* 682–7.
Pauli, L., 1975. *Keltischer Volksglaube. Amulette- und Sonderbestattungen am Dürrnberg bei Hallein und im eisenzeitlichen Mitteleuropa,* Münchner Beiträge zur Vor- und Frühgeschichte 28 (Munich).

Pauli, L., 1978. *Der Dürrnberg bei Hallein III. Auswertung der Grabfunde,* Münchner Beiträge zur Vor- und Frühgeschichte 18 (Munich).
Pauli, L., 1980. 'Die Herkunft der Kelten. Sinn und Unsinn einer alten Frage', in *Die Kelten in Mitteleuropa* (Salzburger Landesausstellung im Keltenmuseum Hallein, Österreich): 16–24.
Pauli, L., 1981a. Review of Jankuhn *et al.* 1978, *Germania 59:* 467–75.
Pauli, L., 1981b. Review of Dämmer 1978, *Bonner Jahrb. 181:* 630–8.
Pauli, L., 1984. *The Alps. Archaeology and Early History.*
Penninger, E., 1972. *Der Dürrnberg bei Hallein I. Katalog der Grabfunde aus der Hallstatt- und Latènezeit, Erster Teil,* Münchner Beiträge zur Vor- und Frühgeschichte 16 (Munich).
Piggott, S., 1965. *Ancient Europe.*
Piroutet, M., 1936. 'La Tène A ou La Tène Ia – leur date et les fouilles de Château-sur-Salins (Jura)', in *XIIe Congrès préhistorique de France* (Toulouse/Foix): 832–41.
Pisani, V., 1953. 'Allgemeine und vergleichende Sprachwissenschaft – Indogermanistik', in K. Honn (ed.), *Wissenschaftliche Forschungsberichte, Geisteswissenschaftliche Reihe* II (Bern): 3–93.
Planck, D., 1980. 'Die abschliessende Untersuchung in der spätkeltischen Viereckschanze von Fellbach-Schmiden, Rems-Murr-Kreis', *Archäol. Ausgrabungen 1980,* ed. Gesellschaft für Vor- und Frühgeschichte in Württemberg und Hohenzollern (Stuttgart): 50–9.
Planck, D., 1982. 'Eine neuentdeckte keltische Viereckschanze in Fellbach-Schmiden, Rems-Murr-Kreis; *Germania 60:* 105–72.
Polenz, H., 1973. 'Zu den Grabfunden der Späthallstattzeit im Rhein-Main-Gebiet', *Bericht der Römisch-Germanischen Kommission 54:* 107–202.
Primas, M., 1975. 'Zur Interpretation weiträumig verbreiteter Kulturelemente in Norditalien und dem alpinen Gebiet während der Jungbronzezeit', *Jahresbericht des Instituts für Vorgeschichte der Univ. Frankfurt a. M. 1975:* 46–56.
Pulgram, E., 1958. 'Indo-European and "Indo-Europeans" ', in *The Tongues of Italy* (Cambridge, Mass.): 139–56.
Ramseyer, D., 1980. 'Châtillon-sur-Glâne – un centre commercial du premier âge du fer en Suisse', *Archéologia 146:* 64–71.
Sandars, N., 1971. 'Orient and Orientalising in early Celtic art', *Antiquity 45:* 103–12.
Sandars, N., 1976. 'Orient and orientalising: recent thoughts reviewed, in P.-M. Duval and C. F. C. Hawkes (eds.), *Celtic Art in Ancient Europe. Five Protohistoric Centuries:* 41–55.
Schaeffer, F. A., 1930. *Les Tertres funeraires préhistoriques dans la forêt de Haguenau II. Les Tumulus de l'âge du fer* (Haguenau).
Schmid, W. P., 1978. *Indogermanistische Modelle und ost-europäische Frühgeschichte* (Abhandlungen der geistes- und sozialwissenschaftlichen Klasse, Akademie der Wissenschaften und der Literatur, Mainz).
Schmidt, K. H., 1977. *Die festlandkeltischen Sprachen,* Innsbrucker Beiträge zur Sprachwissenschaft, Vorträge 18.
Schneider, D. M. and Gough, K. (eds.), 1961. *Matrilineal Kinship* (Berkeley, Cal.).
Schwab, H., 1983. 'Châtillon-sur-Glâne. Bilanz der ersten Sondiergrabungen', *Germania 61:* 405–58.
Schwappach, F., 1972. 'Floral decorations and arc-designs in the Early Style of Celtic art', *Études Celtiques 13:* 710–32.
Schwappach, F., 1973. 'Frühkeltisches Ornament zwischen Marne, Rhein und Moldau', *Bonner Jahrb. 173:* 53–111.
Sievers, S., 1980. *Die mitteleuropäischen Hallstattdolche. Ein Beitrag zur Waffenbeigabe im Westhallstattkreis,* Kleine Schriften aus dem Vorgeschichtlichen Seminar Marburg, Heft 7.
Sievers, S., 1982. *Die mitteleuropäischen Hallstattdolche,* Prähistorische Bronzefunde VI, 6 (Munich).

de Simone, C., 1979. 'Un nuovo gentilizio etrusco di Orvieto (Katacina) e la cronologia della penetrazione celtica (gallica) in Italia', *Parola del Passato 182:* 370–95.
de Simone, C., 1980. 'Gallisch Nemetios – etruskisch Nemetie', *Zeitschrift für vergleichende Sprachforschung 94:* 198–202.
Sordi, M., 1976/77. 'La leggenda di Arrunte chiusino e la prima invasione gallica in Italia', *Rivista di Storia Antica 6/7:* 111–17.
Spindler, K., 1980a. *Magdalenenberg VI* (Villingen-Schwenningen).
Spindler, K., 1980b. 'Zur Elfenbeinscheibe aus dem hallstattzeitlichen Fürstengrab vom Grafenbühl', *Arch. Korr. 10:* 239–48.
Spindler, K., 1980c. 'Das Eisenschwert von Möhrendorf, Lkr. Erlangen-Höchstadt – Ein Beitrag zu den Hallstatt D-Schwertern', in K. Spindler (ed.), *Vorzeit zwischen Main und Donau* (Erlangen): 206–26.
Spindler, K., 1981. 'Zur absoluten Chronologie der Hallstattkultur', in *Die Hallstattkultur. Symposium Steyr 1980*, ed. Land Oberösterreich (Linz): 47–64.
Thénot, A., 1976. 'Le passage du Hallstatt à La Tène dans le quart Nord-Est de la France', in *Le Passage du 1er au 2e âge du fer en Europe*, Colloque XXIX du IXe Congres de l'UISPP, 1976 (Nice): 71–93.
Thomson, G., 1961. *Studies in Ancient Greek Society II. The First Philosophers.*
Torbrügge, W., 1965. 'Vollgriffschwerter der Urnenfelderzeit. Zur methodischen Darstellung einer Denkmälergruppe', *Bayerische Vorgeschichtsblätter 30:* 71–105.
Torbrügge, W., 1979. *Die Hallstattzeit in der Oberpfalz I. Auswertung und Gesamtkatalog,* Materialhefte zur Bayerischen Vorgeschichte 39 (Kallmünz).
Trevor-Roper, H., 1965. 'The general crisis of the seventeenth century', in T. Aston (ed.), *Crisis in Europe 1560–1660: 59–96.*
Trevor-Roper, H., 1967. *Religion, the Reformation and Social Change.*
Uenze, H. P., 1964. 'Zur Frühlatènezeit in der Oberpfalz', *Bayerische Vorgeschichtsblätter 29:* 77–118.
Vajda, L., 1973/4. 'Zur Frage der Völkerwanderungen', *Paideuma. Mitteilungen zur Kulturkunde 19/20: 5–53.*
Wagner, H., 1969. 'The origin of the Celts in the light of linguistic geography', *Trans. Philological Soc.:* 203–50.
Wagner, H., 1970. 'Studies in the origins of early Celtic civilisation', *Zeitschrift für celtische Philologie 31:* 1–45.
Weisweiler, J., 1940. 'Die Stellung der Frau bei den Kelten und das Problem des keltischen "Mutterrechts" ', *Zeitschrift für celtische Philologie 21:* 205–79.
Wenskus, R., 1961. *Stammesbildung und Verfassung. Das Werden der frühmittelalterlichen gentes* (Cologne and Graz).
Witter, W., 1942. 'Über Metallgewinnung bei den Etruskern', *Bericht der Römisch-Germanischen Kommission 32:* 1–19.
Wyss, R., 1954. 'Das Schwert des Korisios. Zur Entdeckung einer griechischen Inschrift', *Jahrbuch des Bernischen Historischen Museums 34:* 201–22.
Zürn, H., 1941. *Die Hallstattzeit in Württemberg: Die Grabfunde* (unpublished diss., Universität Tübingen).
Zürn, H., 1952. 'Zum Übergang von Späthallstatt zu Latène A im südwestdeutschen Raum', *Germania 30:* 38–45.
Zürn, H., 1964. 'Eine hallstattzeitliche Stele von Hirschlanden, Kr. Leonberg (Württbg.)', *Germania 42:* 27–36.
Zürn, H., 1970. *Hallstattforschungen in Nordwürttemberg,* Veröffentlichungen des staatlichen Amtes für Denkmalpflege Stuttgart, Reihe A, 16 (Stuttgart).

3

Celtic territorial expansion and the Mediterranean world

Daphne Nash

There are two dimensions to political expansion in most ancient societies.[1] One is their internal development within a defined territory from less to more complex political forms, associated with increasingly efficient exploitation of their human and natural resources. The second is territorial expansion. This might take the form either of progressive encroachment by an expanding heartland into adjacent social territories, or of emigrant colonization in more distant regions geographically unconnected with the parent society.

The forces which governed each society's expansion were generally internal to it in origin, inherent in the very structure of its social and political relationships. Each undoubtedly possessed social conventions and legal codes designed to minimize the danger that ambitious individuals or strong political groups might upset its prevailing political equilibrium and precipitate an unwelcome transformation in its internal structure. This danger was most acute in periods of close and rewarding contact with a much stronger society, which gave these groups and individuals access to wealth, military power and political prestige on a scale which made it difficult or impossible to contain their activities within the existing framework of their society. I should like to argue that external conditions, particularly in the Mediterranean region, were normally responsible for the timing and extent of social change in Celtic Europe.

Territorial expansion was one way in which a society might release the internal tensions associated with political expansion without resorting to substantial change in the organization of its social relationships. In an expansionary period, therefore, most Celtic societies undoubtedly spread territorially within their own region, usually by forming tributary border dependencies and gradually absorbing the closest of them into their metropolitan core. I shall argue that migratory expansion was a widespread response to the internal problems experienced in a period of advanced political expansion, and was particularly characteristic of one form of Celtic society, the warrior societies of the Rhineland, Seine Basin, and central Europe. This was because of their unusually demanding need for agricultural land, their military relations with the outside world, and their peculiar difficulties in containing internal political stress.[2]

Celtic warrior societies

The Celtic societies which launched the great migrations may be described as warrior societies to distinguish them from those Celtic societies, such as the West Hallstatt chiefdoms described below, which adopted other modes of social organization and were more sedentary in their habits, even in a period of advanced political expansion. In many respects, all early Celtic class societies were alike.[3] Political and military leadership were the exclusive preserve of an equestrian nobility, among whom weaker nobles paid allegiance and tribute to stronger chiefs or kings, in return for the benefits of association with their greater prestige, access to their craftsmen, and a guarantee of diplomatic and legal protection. In its most complex form, the political hierarchy might be unified under a single king to whom even district chiefs paid personal homage of this sort.[4] In these societies, it seems probable that nobles and rich peasants alike were landowners. Freeholding peasants performed military service as heavy-armed infantry, and were closely associated politically and culturally with the nobility. The principal occupation of the peasant class as a whole, and the exclusive activity of its landless sections was, however, agriculture, and this was the bedrock of every Celtic economy.

The key feature which distinguished a warrior society from others was the direct use of peasants' labour as servants and warriors to supply the wealth needed to satisfy the ambitions of the nobility. Peasants' agricultural production enabled such a society to subsist, but was not the mainstay of its expansion, as was the case in other types of agrarian society. Instead, their harvest as warriors performed this function at the expense of external societies, in the form of plunder, ransom, indemnities and tribute secured from communities whose very defeat was itself a contribution to political expansion.

Some of the fruits of warriors' labour, notably livestock, metalwork and arms, were directly employed within the captors' own economy. Of the rest, much was sold profitably to stronger societies, for luxury goods which included wine and fine metalwork. These goods were essential for the conduct of noble rivalries within the warrior society itself. Among the plunder sold in this way, human captives were pre-eminently important. Finally, and most profitably of all, a noble might enter into a contract with a stronger overlord and provide him with the services of a mercenary army under his own leadership. For this, he and his soldiers were paid, while any spoils they might capture in the course of wars between wealthy opponents were themselves a handsome reward for their labours. To be paid to plunder in a stronger region was the most lucrative of all external relationships into which a warrior society might enter.[5]

The revenues required to sustain noble competition in any expanding society were therefore, in warrior societies, exacted from peasants chiefly in their capacity as soldiers. It may be predicted that in these societies military mobilization was maintained at a very high level, and that this had a number of consequences which influenced their territorial expansion.[6]

Territorial expansion in a warrior society

In the first place, the demands of arable agriculture were not compatible with a high level of peasant mobilization as soldiers in an expanding society. Many Celtic warrior societies seem consequently to have had an abnormally large pastoral component in their subsistence economy, and this tendency was reinforced by their use of cattle to articulate military relationships at every social level. Contractual ties both between peasants and nobles, and between weaker and stronger nobles themselves, were therefore probably sealed by a grant of cattle made by patron to dependant, who then rendered his patron services and a rent or tribute appropriate to his social standing.[7] A society with inflated herds of cattle required a larger territory than one which relied more heavily upon arable agriculture for its livelihood, and this consequently influenced the speed and extent of a warrior society's territorial expansion. Both nobles and armed peasants were, moreover, landowners, and an armed peasantry on whom the nobility was dependent for the pursuit of its ambitions was in a good position to press its territorial needs upon its leaders. In a society such as this, there was a perennial need for fresh land to sustain the free status of nobles and peasants alike. Territorial expansion in either form was, therefore, unusually extensive in these societies.

In the second place, warfare itself was a necessary activity, not simply for the conduct of noble rivalries, but for the sake of the essential revenues it yielded. Warfare and raiding were therefore regular occurrences during the summer months, and the most rewarding forms of warfare – slave raiding into peripheral areas and mercenary service in stronger regions – constantly led war bands of Celts far from their home communities in search of their fortunes. Colonial emigrants might often choose to settle in remote areas with which such contact had previously been made.[8]

It is likely, furthermore, that Celtic societies organized in this way had peculiar difficulties in containing internal political tensions. A numerous and militarily successful nobility inevitably engendered violent rivalries, and made precarious subordinates. Enforcement of political control over them was difficult, particularly when they were individually in receipt of the rewards of gainful warfare, and could command substantial followings of warriors.[9] One widely adopted solution to the political tensions characteristic of a period of successful foreign warfare was therefore to export this problem periodically, by organizing irrevocable emigrations under strong noble leadership.[10] This served the dual purpose of ridding a territory of factious nobles and potentially troublesome warrior-peasants, and of setting up a colony which might, at least in principle, serve as home from home in alien territory, and as a base from which yet more distant enterprises might be organized.

Finally, it seems probable that most Celtic warrior societies attempted to keep significantly gainful contact with foreigners outside their frontiers. Productive warfare was, of course, by definition an extra-territorial activity, but profitable trade seems also to have been kept at a safe geographical distance. Foreign traders, particularly from a stronger region, might therefore be positively repelled, like all other alien intruders, if they attempted to approach a warrior territory.[11] Instead, representatives of warrior societies preferred to travel themselves to the markets where they sold their plunder and produce, and there to select the goods they wanted in exchange. In so doing, they might travel colossal distances, exploiting their equestrian skills.[12]

Excluding foreigners from a social territory in this way was at once a display of prestige and a useful defensive manoeuvre. It made intruders easy to identify and eliminate, and it meant that returning compatriots were remote from potential sources of outside support or refuge. Those whose exploits were perceived as threatening could therefore more easily be subjected to whatever means of social control their community had at its disposal. It also gave the warrior society a large uninhabited border territory into which it could expand its heartland without interference.[13]

Celtic warrior societies' use of their territory therefore had a number of characteristics which not only affected their territorial expansion but ought also in principle to be identifiable in the surviving archaeological record. Firstly, they had well-defined frontiers, which were especially clear-cut where they served to separate a warrior region from an adjacent alien society. Their exclusion of most foreigners from their territory, and their highly developed sense of their peculiar social identity, reinforced any cultural differences they might have from neighbouring agrarian societies, even Celtic ones. Where such frontiers survived for substantial periods they may be recognized in a stark discontinuity in the cultural record on either side. Such a frontier may, I believe, be seen very clearly in the seventh and sixth centuries, dividing the warrior communities of the Seine Basin from the agrarian Celts of Berry and Burgundy.[14]

Secondly, the economic structure of a warrior society was such that internal exchange played a negligible role in the accumulation of wealth. Most agricultural surplus and domestic manufactured goods were therefore consumed within their district of origin, while luxury goods were mainly distributed through transactions dependent upon contractual relations among the nobility and armed warriors, rather than by market exchange. In such a society, the landowning classes might select locations for their most significant settlements which show scant regard for control of long-range transport routes, and their territories yield no evidence whatever for the formation of settlements with what might be interpreted as marketing or bulk storage functions. Warrior nobilities seem to have been more interested in inland waterways as adjuncts to cattle pasture or as territorial boundaries than as essential facilities for the transportation of produce.[15]

Finally, periods of conspicuous military success associated with access to profitable external markets for plunder and mercenary labour were signalled in warrior societies by rapid territorial expansion not only in their own region but far beyond it, continually extending the geographical reach of their predatory activity. Land to annexe, and the lure of productive raiding, led to the colonization of peripheral areas. As weaker societies withdrew from their advance, the colonial frontier pushed forward until it had reached the ends of the inhabited world in Ireland, or the barrier of resistant societies in Germany and central Europe.[16] At the same time, the attraction of markets for their plunder and the opportunity for mercenary service, which was often rewarded with land to settle as a resident garrison, prompted colonization of stronger regions, ultimately as far east as Asia Minor. Colonies on the fringe of stronger regions might, if successful at all, become very strong, ultimately eclipsing and finally peripheralizing the societies which had originally launched them.[17]

The sixth and fifth centuries were a period of rapid expansion by the Celtic societies of northern France and southern Germany. This was only one of several expansionary episodes in the history of Celtic Europe in the Iron Age, but is adequately documented both by ancient textual accounts and by archaeological material. It will therefore serve to illustrate the principal characteristics of these societies in a phase of territorial expansion. In what follows, I shall concentrate upon the expansion of the warrior societies, since they display these characteristics most clearly, and are best illustrated in the surviving material.

Celtic expansion in the sixth century (fig. 3.1)

There were two primary centres of Celtic warrior expansion, in the Hunsrück–Eifel region in the middle Rhineland, and in Champagne in northern France. Each was associated with one of the two strongest late West Hallstatt chiefdoms: the Hunsrück–Eifel nobility with the Hohenasperg complex in Germany, and that of Champagne with the Mont Lassois complex in eastern France.[18] I should like to argue that the warrior societies in question developed in the periphery of the great West Hallstatt chiefdoms to form interdependent cores of two adjacent warrior regions that were radically separate socially and politically from the West Hallstatt chiefdoms, but were nonetheless profoundly dependent upon them until the end of the sixth century. The social and political development of the West Hallstatt zone and the Celtic warrior regions must therefore be regarded as separate though complementary aspects of the same historical process, linked by their participation in a single system of long-range contact with the Mediterranean world.[19]

I would suggest, therefore, that the Celtic society of the West Hallstatt world differed in a number of key respects from that of the Hunsrück–Eifel area and Champagne, and that the frontier which separated them had the diplomatic and military functions sketched above. By contrast with the warrior societies across this frontier, I shall argue that the expansion of the West Hallstatt chiefdoms was fuelled by external relations of a diplomatic rather than a military character, supported by long-range trade with northern Italy and above all with Massalia. The very location of the centres of power in these societies as they grew in complexity demonstrates the importance which their nobility attached to the control of long-distance transport routes and supply systems within their own territory.[20] What distinguished the political economy of these societies from their warrior cousins was almost certainly that their peasant population was exploited predominantly through its produce rather than through its military labour. Surplus was therefore converted into more valuable forms of wealth mainly by exchange, and the consequences of this for their internal development is reflected in their precocious formation of settlements which possess what may be construed as storage and marketing functions.[21]

In such a society, moreover, there were two strong disincentives to allowing a high level of warrior mobilization among the peasant population. In the first place, in so far as agricultural labour and military service made incompatible demands upon able-bodied men, it was more in these societies' interest to encourage the former. Secondly, the political benefits of maintaining a largely disarmed and therefore politically inert peasant class were considerable, since it served to keep noble ambitions within manageable limits and thus to contain internal violence. Chiefs and kings might therefore often prefer to employ foreign mercenaries than to mobilize compatriot peasants in times of stress. This prompted a substantial degree of military dependence upon neighbouring societies able to supply alternative military forces.[22] The interdependence of the two principal forms of Celtic society was undoubtedly based upon their provision of complementary services for one another – the wealthier agrarian societies supplying wealth and opportunities for warfare, and the weaker warrior societies supplying military labour, slaves and raw materials.

The ultimate basis of the wealth of the leaders of the West Hallstatt chiefdoms was therefore the surplus produce of their own territories, augmented in value by trade with foreign societies. In order for this type of economy to expand successfully, however, it required profitable relations both with weaker peripheral societies and with strong partners in regions nearer to the Mediterranean, forming a chain of three mutually alien societies which it served to link into a single system. The West Hallstatt chiefdoms of the sixth century seem to have performed this function between the warrior Celts in their periphery to the west and north, and the Etruscans and Greeks to the south, especially at Massalia. What they sent south undoubtedly consisted of their own produce, together with goods they obtained cheaply from their peripheral partners; they used the rewards of their external dealings to extend their influence within their own region, a process which undoubtedly required at least intermittent use of

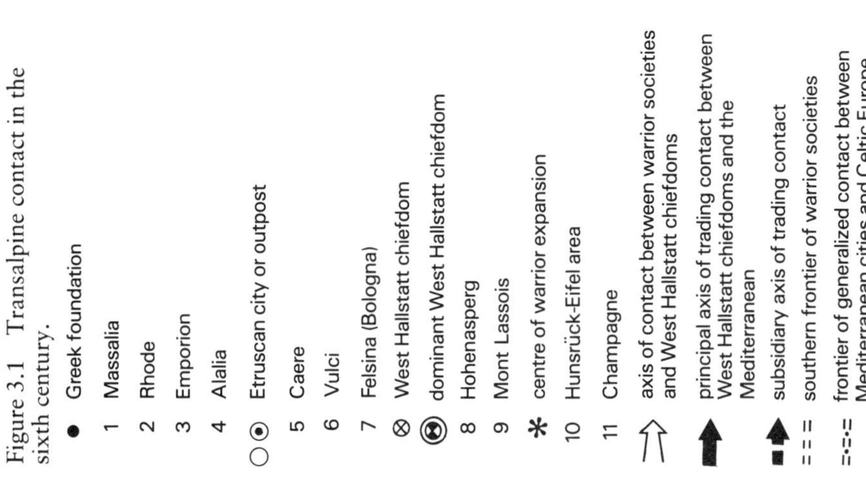

Figure 3.1 Transalpine contact in the sixth century.

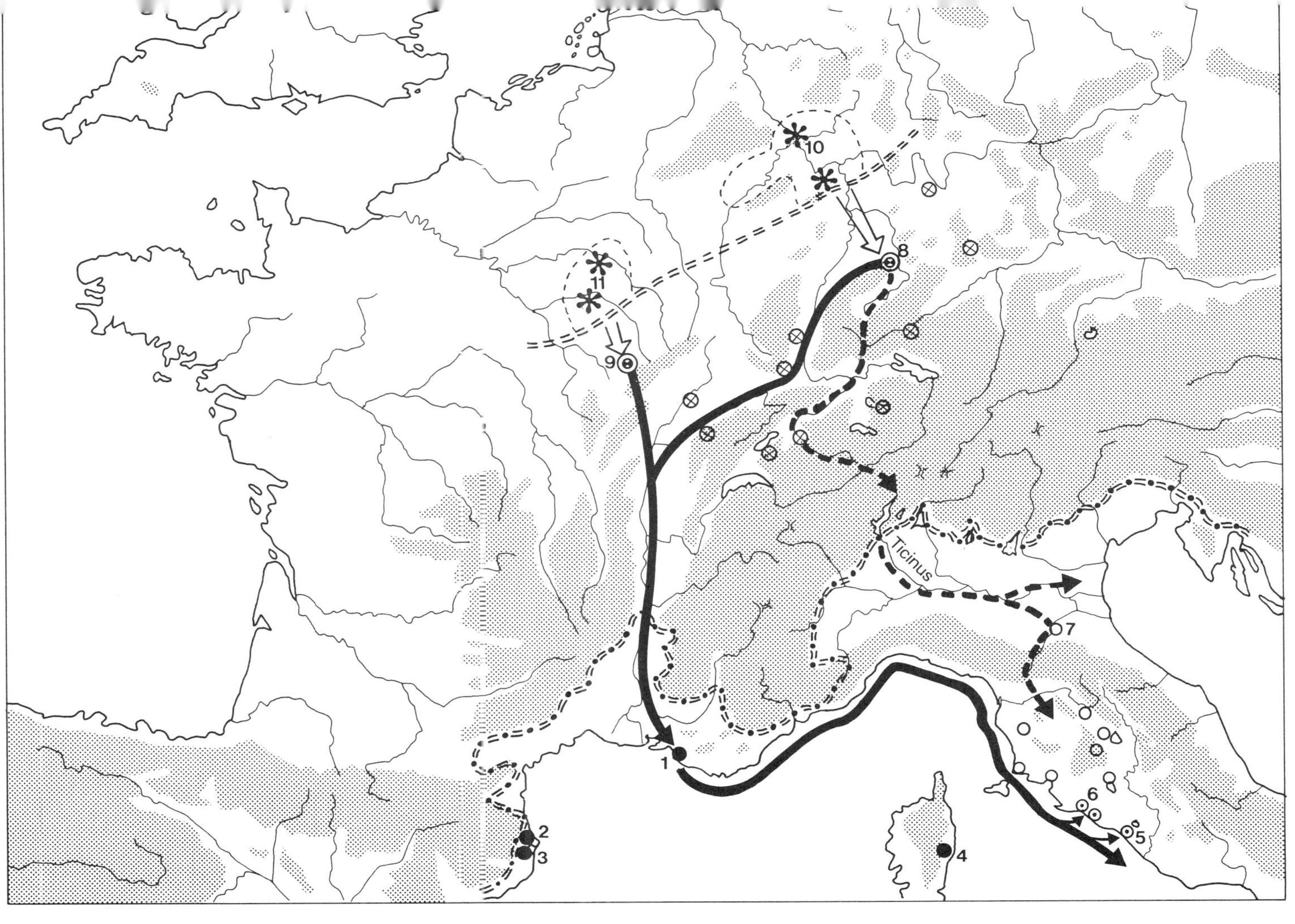

10
8
11
9
Ticinus
7
1
2
3
4
6
5

armies, perhaps often hired from the warrior societies with which they were in most regular contact. Since the expansion of the warrior societies was a product of their relationship with the West Hallstatt chiefdoms, the basis of the wealth of these societies requires closer examination at both ends of the system of long-range contact which linked them.

Massalia and the Celtic world

The relationship between the West Hallstatt centres and Massalia was almost certainly based upon Massalia's capacity to provide a rewarding market for the goods which the West Hallstatt Celts brought south. Otherwise the journey would have been impossibly costly and its fruits incapable of sustaining the conspicuous power of the Celtic chiefdoms. Massalia in her turn shipped goods to markets in Italy and the eastern Mediterranean, and provided a harbour and market at which foreign sea traders could acquire goods of northern origin. This provision of harbour and marketing facilities was undoubtedly the mainstay of Massalia's long-term prosperity.

Massalia had two landwards supply systems for her markets. The most important and enduring was her immediate hinterland in the lower Rhône valley as far north as the Isère, and in adjacent northern Italy and the Alps. This hinterland supplied her with most of her subsistence requirements, the ship-building materials she needed for her outstanding fleet, and trade goods which included such commodities as salt, herbs and silver.[23] It also gave access to Ligurian slaves and mercenary soldiers. The other, more precarious and less essential, system was that which linked her with the remoter Celtic world. Massalia's prosperity during the Hellenistic period, when this link was severed, demonstrates her capacity to flourish without it, but its importance during the seventh and sixth centuries is reflected not only in the strength of the West Hallstatt chiefdoms which seem to have provided it, but in the expense of the diplomatic gifts apparently presented by Massalia or her allies to the dominant West Hallstatt chiefs to guarantee its continuance.[24]

The material basis of this long-range contact between the Celtic world and Massalia remains a matter for speculation, but four types of commodity may be identified as candidates: foodstuffs and raw materials, metals, miscellaneous exotica, and slaves. All were probably conveyed south in varying proportions, but their importance for the existence of such a costly and diplomatically complex system of long-range contact almost certainly differed enormously.

Foodstuffs such as, for instance, salt pork, and raw materials such as hides or furs probably played a part in this southwards trade, but are unlikely to have been as important to Massalia and her customers as her own more immediate and much cheaper sources of much the same goods. Alone, therefore, they are most unlikely to have accounted for the success of the contact between the West Hallstatt Celts and Massalia, and they probably played no more than an auxiliary role in supporting a system whose primary function was more specialized.

Metals, likewise, probably played no more than a supporting role in this trade.[25] Massalia could obtain most of the silver she needed from Italy, Languedoc and Spain, and her copper and tin undoubtedly came principally from Languedoc. Only gold and iron might have come in significant quantities from Celtic sources, and there is no reason to suspect that either was conveyed south in proportions sufficient to account for the importance of this trading contact with the Celts. Neither seems likely to account for the role which the Celtic warrior societies played in the development of the system. Similarly, exotica such as amber and furs were certainly conveyed to the Mediterranean world through Celtic Europe, and probably contributed usefully to the profits of West Hallstatt trade with Massalia, but are unlikely to have been the mainstay of their relationship. Mediterranean demand for them was not adequate to provide support for an entire regional system of strong chiefdoms whose wealth was dependent upon their long-range trading activities with the Mediterranean south, and their relationship with the warrior societies of their Celtic periphery.

I should like to propose, instead, that the staple commodity in this system which linked the Celtic world with Massalia and Etruscan Italy was slaves, captured by warrior societies and sold to the West Hallstatt chiefdoms, whose representatives brought them south to Massalia. There they were either shipped by Massalia herself to more distant markets, or sold to visiting merchants. For the present discussion, the most important of these were almost certainly Etruscans from the coastal cities, perhaps especially Caere, with the Carthaginians in second place. In support of this hypothesis, it may be noted that the Phocaeans, who founded Massalia, and the Etruscans who preceded them in western waters, had a widespread reputation in antiquity as pirates and slave dealers.[26]

The West Hallstatt chiefdoms and the warrior Celts

To pursue this argument, however, it is necessary to look more closely at the basis of relations between the developing Celtic warrior societies and their associates in the West Hallstatt zone. It seems highly probable that the West Hallstatt chiefdoms were the first strong external markets at which the emergent warrior nobility exchanged what they had to offer for more coveted forms of wealth.[27] There were three principal types of commodity which the warrior societies could supply: animals and animal products, plunder, and mercenary soldiers.

Animals and animal products, especially in the form of horses and hides, had undoubtedly been important as staple items in exchange with stronger societies from time immemorial.[28] It is most unlikely, however, that the profits of this type of exchange were ever adequate to support political expansion on the scale experienced by the warrior societies in the middle Rhineland and Champagne in the sixth century. Such expansion was almost certainly based instead upon a more specialized relationship with a stronger society, which the expanding peripheral partner could exploit to its own advantage at the expense of its own regional neighbours and its remoter peripheral associates. Where the warrior societies of Celtic Europe are concerned, I would suggest that the twin bases of such relationships were always the sale of plunder and of warrior services. A strong and therefore militarily successful warrior society could supply both more abundantly than its weaker rivals, while at the same time their provision served to develop its military capabilities, thus contributing strongly to its increasing dominance within its own region.

Plunder from peripheral wars and raids was by definition an essential source of revenue for any warrior society, and among such plunder, human captives undoubtedly always took pride of place, since they could be sold back to their own societies for a ransom, or sold to stronger markets for the most valuable types of luxury goods.[29] The continuous demand for slaves in all ancient European societies, and above all in the Mediterranean world, ensured that this rewarding outlet for plunder was always open, and it played an important role in Celtic expansion whenever regular contact was established with a particularly eager market for their captives. Such, I would propose, were the West Hallstatt chiefdoms, whose strength was premissed upon their ability to supply slaves, together with other miscellaneous commodities, to Mediterranean markets in northern Italy and especially at Massalia. The sale of human plunder, whose capture was itself a by-product of Celtic warrior expansion, was surely the single most enduring feature in the long-term relationship between the warrior societies of northern Celtic Europe and the Mediterranean cities and states, articulated during the sixth century by the intermediary role of the West Hallstatt chiefdoms.

Finally, warrior societies had their services as mercenary soldiers to sell, both to the neighbouring chiefdoms at whose markets they sold most of their plunder, and to remoter societies as well. As a source of revenue, mercenary employment was exceptionally rewarding, and was probably always much sought after, even at very great geographical distances. Mercenary employment had three important consequences for the society which supplied such armies. It gave them access to the wealth they needed for conspicuous expansion. It developed their military capacities, by enabling large armies to be assembled, and by giving them experience of the military disciplines and techniques necessary for successful conflict with more complex and technically sophisticated societies.[30] Finally, mercenary service for foreign overlords often held out the prospect of long-term or permanent settlement abroad, as resident garrisons or military colonies from which subsequent generations of recruits might be drawn. This prospect assisted the process of territorial expansion, and the permanent export of unmanageable tensions from the parent society.

While, therefore, slave raiding drew a warrior society into its peripheral hinterland, mercenary service attracted it into stronger regions. This process probably began for the Celtic warrior societies of northern France and the middle Rhineland during the late seventh and sixth centuries, when small groups of warriors could enter into contractual relationships with the nascent chiefdoms of the upper Rhineland and eastern France, and with other employers closer to the Mediterranean. It probably reached critical proportions, however, during the second half of the sixth century, when the military needs of the West Hallstatt chiefdoms were at their highest, and at the same time regular independent contact with Etruscan markets and employers was being established in northern Italy.

Celtic expansion in the fifth century (fig. 3.2)

The decades around the end of the sixth century were therefore a turning-point in the development of the Celtic warrior societies of western Europe, as they emancipated themselves from their traditional dependence upon the chiefdoms of the West Hallstatt zone and instead secured direct and independent access to the wealth they needed from the Mediterranean world. Unprecedentedly strong warrior chiefdoms, often colonial in origin, then began to form along the frontiers of the Mediterranean states, soon eclipsing the remote inland societies that had originally launched them, and quickly depriving the West Hallstatt chiefdoms of the basis of their livelihood. Within a couple of generations from their first appearance in the early fifth century, the colonial warrior chiefdoms had achieved a dominance over their northern compatriots that was to last until the early second century.[31]

Once it had begun in earnest, therefore, Celtic warrior expansion gathered a momentum which led to a cultural and political dominance within temperate Europe that was to last until it was destroyed by the consequences of Roman expansion. The vital role played by the Etruscans in the early stages of this process was soon assumed instead by the Greeks, contributing vastly to the scale of Celtic expansion. By the early fifth century the West Hallstatt chiefdoms had lost their traditional function of mediating between the slave-producing warrior societies of the north and the markets of the Mediterranean. They therefore also lost the rewards of this role which had sustained them in power, and as a result experienced rapid political contraction. Instead, the expanding warrior chiefdoms in their periphery formed independent and far more profitable relationships with the Mediterranean world, which served to draw their territorial expansion south and east, towards their most reliable markets and employers.

A complex sequence of events around the end of the sixth century inaugurated this change in the relations between Celtic Europe and the Mediterranean, the most important of which were the disuse of the specialized system of long-distance trade which had linked the West Hallstatt chiefdoms and Massalia, and the colonization of northern Italy by Celtic warrior communities. The chief victims of the first event were the West Hallstatt chiefdoms themselves and the coastal cities of Etruria, because of their mutual dependence upon the trade through Massalia. The chief beneficiaries of the second were the warrior Celts, and the cities of inland Etruria and the wider Hellenistic world who employed their plunder and military labour to fuel their own expansion. The formative events in this process may provisionally be traced at both ends of the chain of contact between Celtic Europe and the Mediterranean.

Changes in Mediterranean contact with the Celts

At the southern end, therefore, changes in the structure of economic and political relations among the Mediterranean cities themselves served to disrupt established patterns of contact between the western and eastern Mediterranean, and this had serious repercussions in their European hinterland. Three related developments in the early fifth century were particularly important in effecting these changes.

The first was a significant episode in the process of western Greek expansion at the expense of the coastal Etruscan cities, which began during the sixth century and was completed during the fifth. The Phocaean colony of Alalia in Corsica, founded in the mid-sixth century opposite the coast of Etruria, could give Greek ships access to Massalia without putting in to Etruscan ports. It therefore challenged the Etruscans' traditional dominance in the coastal carrying trade between southern Gaul and the Greek ports of southern Italy, a function which was of central importance to Etruscan prosperity. The Phocaeans, moreover, rivalled the Etruscans as pirates, capturing slaves and other plunder from coastal settlements in the western Mediterranean. Alalia was a point from which Etruria itself was in danger.[32] A sharp conflict in 539–535 between the Etruscans with their Carthaginian allies, and the colonists at Alalia, drove the Phocaeans from their colony, but the victory gave the Etruscans little long-term satisfaction, since it almost certainly ruptured diplomatic relations between the Etruscan coastal cities and Massalia. I suggest that the chief short-term consequence of the struggle over Alalia was the exclusion of Etruscan ships from the harbour and market facilities at Massalia, and that this exclusion, even if it was only partially successful and of short duration, had important long-term repercussions in Celtic Europe because of its consequences for the Etruscan cities themselves.

Such an event dealt a serious blow to the economic position of these cities, whose relationship with one of their most important western markets was in jeopardy. Their ships were obliged to travel further, past hostile waters, to acquire what they needed in Languedoc and Spain instead.[33] It was, therefore, at this juncture, between 535 and 525, that some of the coastal cities of Etruria, and Vulci in particular, seem to have begun to develop landwards contact with

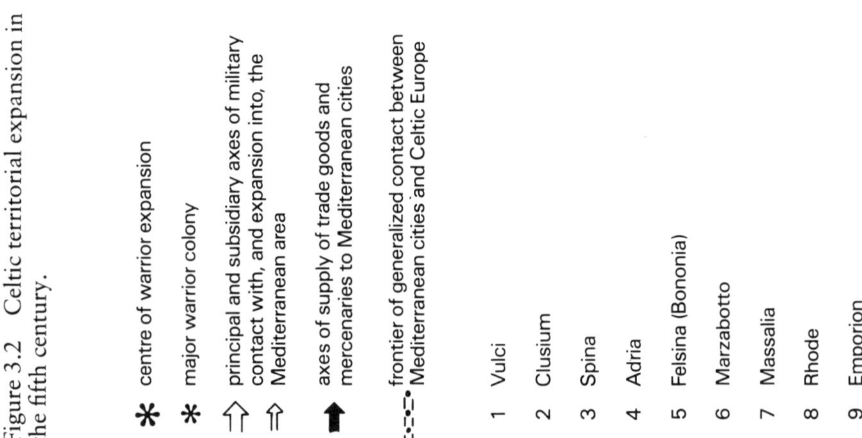

Figure 3.2 Celtic territorial expansion in the fifth century.

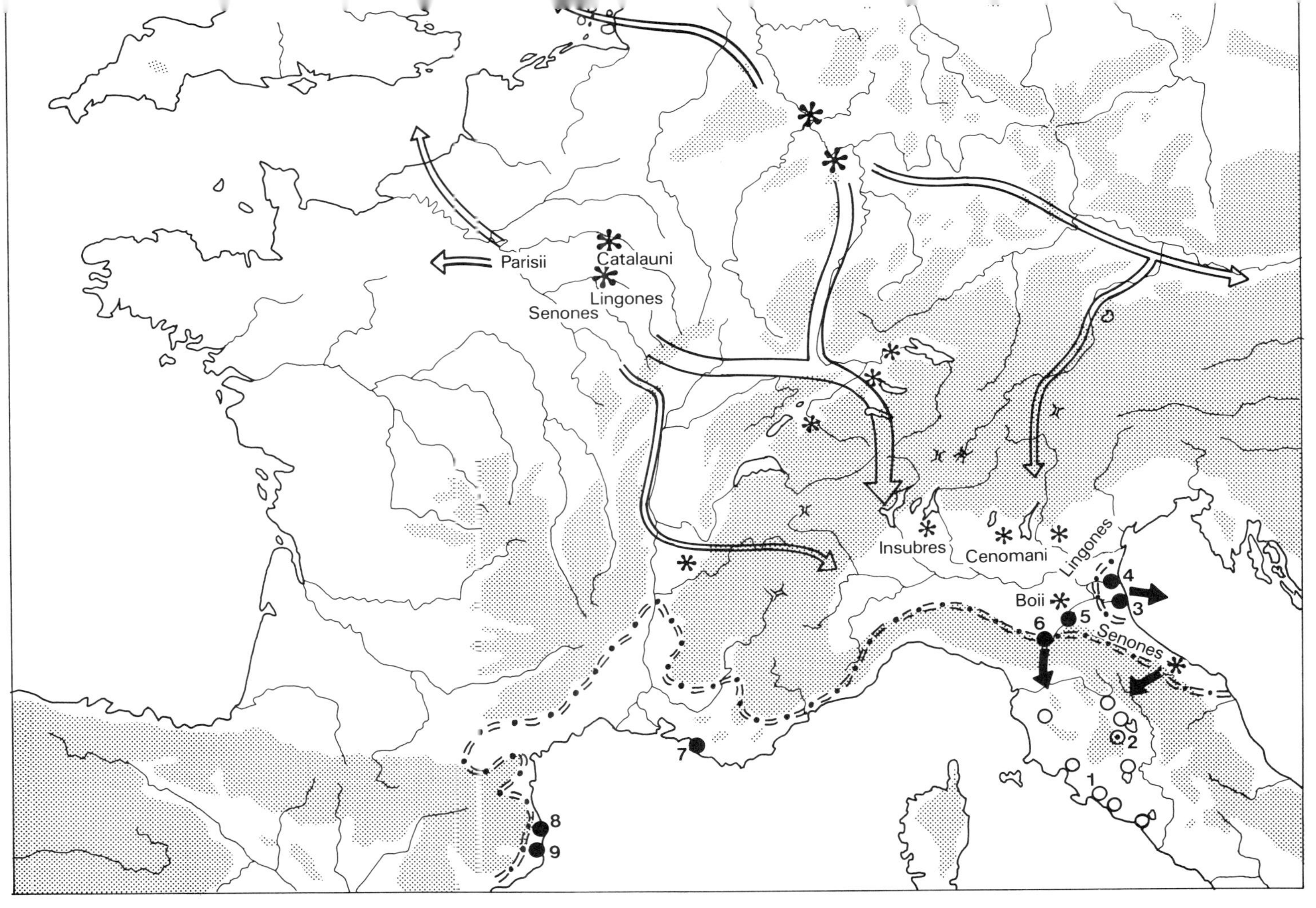
Parisii
Catalauni
Lingones
Senones
Insubres
Cenomani
Lingones
Boii
Senones
1
2
3
4
5
6
7
8
9

Celtic Europe by providing markets for Transalpine visitors in the north Italian plain, and to rely more heavily than before upon the Adriatic ports of Spina and Adria for access to the eastern Mediterranean. The long-term consequences of these developments were, however, to promote the growth of the inland cities of Etruria at the expense of the cities of the coast (see below), and to foster the expansion of the warrior Celts at the expense of their West Hallstatt associates.

Massalia itself, by contrast, lost little from its frosty diplomatic relations with the Etruscans, since its contact with the expanding Greek cities of Sicily and Italy, and its independent trading activity in the wider Mediterranean, ensured its prosperity even without the specialized custom of the coastal Etruscan cities. I suggest, therefore, that it was the process of Greek expansion in the western Mediterranean at the expense of the Etruscans that was ultimately responsible for initiating the changes which occurred around the end of the sixth century in Celtic Europe.

The second important sequence of events in this period were, then, those which fuelled Greek expansion in the western Mediterranean. A decisive phase in this process began in the eastern Mediterranean with the Ionian revolt against Persia in 499, the Persian capture of the principal Greek cities of Asia Minor in the late 490s, and the Persian advance on mainland Greece in 480. This led to the expansion of Athens within Aegean Greece, and a consequent revision of the political and economic structure of the eastern Mediterranean, which inaugurated over a century of struggle among its leading states. These events absorbed most of the political energies of the cities of metropolitan Greece, and altered the basis of their relations with their western colonies and outposts. This in turn gave the latter the space in which to constitute themselves as the core of a strong western Mediterranean region, dominated by the Greek cities of southern Italy and Sicily at the interface of what were now two major Mediterranean regions.

The third and, for Celtic Europe, decisive development was the rising dominance of the Greek cities of Sicily and southern Italy, which possessed the best harbours at this key position in the central Mediterranean, and controlled the Straits of Messina. These cities could exclude unwelcome shipping, particularly from Punic and Etruscan cities, thus safeguarding Greek interests in articulating seaborne relations between the western and eastern Mediterranean. Anaxilas of Rhegion effectively shut the Straits of Messina to Etruscan shipping in the 470s, and in 474 Etruscan fleets were twice defeated in major naval battles with the Greeks off Himera and Cumae. Thus the coastal cities of Etruria, sandwiched between Massalia and Magna Graecia, suffered worst from western Greek expansion, as they were deprived of their traditional role in long-range shipping in the Mediterranean. Although some, notably Vulci, seem to have found satisfactory landward sources of revenue, they were never to regain their once dominant position in the north-western Mediterranean.[34]

One of the immediate consequences of the setbacks to the Etruscans in the 470s appears to have been the demise of the specialized system of contact which had previously linked Massalia with the West Hallstatt chiefdoms. This seems to have flourished for about a generation after the events at Alalia, perhaps increasingly serving Greek rather than Etruscan and Punic customers at Massalia, but it came to an end during the 470s, when Greek and Etruscan imports seem to disappear from the archaeological record of the West Hallstatt chiefdoms.[35] The reasons for the termination of their accustomed relationship with the Mediterranean south were undoubtedly both political and economic in character. The diplomatic and economic cost of the relationship undoubtedly increased as the Celtic chiefdoms expanded and required ever greater revenues of Mediterranean origin to sustain their power, with disastrous consequences in a period when demand for their merchandise at Massalia was changing as a result of the increasing exclusion of the Etruscans from their accustomed sea-trading activities. Etruscan traders could ill afford to raise the prices they paid at Massalia. For Greek traders, however, Massalia was only one market among many for what must by any standards have been unskilled slaves, and they too would have resisted paying rising prices for them. No Greek city, even Massalia itself, shared the Etruscan coastal cities' severe economic dependence upon the markets of the north-western Mediterranean seaboard as a staple source of their livelihood.

As Etruscan demand fell, in step with their progessive exclusion from their traditional trading activities, Massalia itself could therefore well afford to allow its increasingly costly commitment to maintaining diplomatic and trading contact with the West Hallstatt chiefdoms to lapse. The attractions of the contact faded as its expense increased, since Massaslia had plentiful alternative sources of cheap slaves and a prosperous livelihood. Massalia's own needs and those of its regular fifth-century customers could instead be satisfied cheaply and adequately from its own hinterland and from pirate activity along the Mediterranean coastlines.

Changes in Celtic Europe

At the northern end of the system, therefore, two convergent processes brought the West Hallstatt chiefdoms to the end of their period of dominance and inaugurated the ascendency of the warrior societies in their hinterland. The first was the suggested change in demand for Celtic merchandise at Massalia, since the West Hallstatt chiefdoms had nothing to offer which could substitute for their lost revenues from slaves. If, even for a few years, Massaliote markets were unable to absorb the slaves they brought, or to offer an adequate price for them, the West Hallstatt chiefs themselves would be unwilling or unable to purchase captives from neighbouring warrior societies. Their loss of Mediterranean revenues, moreover, made it difficult for them to maintain their political power over their subordinates, or to sustain their prestige with neighbouring regions. Under these circumstances, the warrior societies which traditionally relied upon them for markets for their plunder and for mercenary employment would be attracted instead to exploit more distant but more rewarding markets, whose attractiveness was enhanced by the impending failure of the West Hallstatt chiefdoms. They therefore switched their attention increasingly to the development of their long-standing contact with the Etruscans in northern Italy, which had previously taken second place in importance to their contact with the chiefs of the West Hallstatt zone, but had been gaining in importance since the 520s.[36] This hastened the contraction of the West Hallstatt chiefdoms by withdrawing from them their most important peripheral sources of revenue.

At the same time, the political violence of a period of imminent crisis in the West Hallstatt chiefdoms meant that their need for Celtic soldiers rose, fuelling the momentum of warrior expansion. Incautious employment of mercenaries probably attracted warrior settlement in West Hallstatt territories, helping to form a continuous chain of contact between the heartlands of warrior expansion in northern France and the middle Rhineland, and pastures new in northern Italy.[37] As relations with Etruscan markets proliferated in the north Italian plain and on the Adriatic, Celtic colonial settlement in northern Italy gathered pace. The expanding warrior societies now no longer needed the patronage of their West Hallstatt neighbours. With their livelihood destroyed, the complex chiefdoms of the late sixth century dissolved and seem eventually to have come under the dominance of the strongest of the new warrior chiefdoms in their vicinity, as tributary dependencies.[38]

Events in Etruria itself accelerated this process. The cities of the western coast had entered a period of economic decline, and by the end of the fifth century even Vulci provided much reduced support for Celtic expansion. Those inland, however, and especially Clusium, experienced a marked improvement in their fortunes, associated with trans-Apennine contact with the Celts, and their access to the ports of Spina and Adria, which gave them an outlet to the eastern Mediterranean which bypassed the Greeks of Sicily and southern Italy. I suggest that these inland Etruscan cities played a role in the fifth century expansion of the warrior Celts comparable with that of the coastal cities in the expansion of the West Hallstatt chiefdoms of the sixth.[39]

The inland Etruscan cities had a different economic structure from those on the coast. Agriculture played a more important role in their prosperity, and it is probable that, like the agrarian chiefdoms and states of Celtic Europe itself, they needed rather a lot of slaves, and had a tendency to employ mercenaries when they needed to supplement their compatriot armies of heavy-armed infantry, so as to avoid the risks of arming the normally non-combatant sections of their peasantry. In northern Italy, therefore, the Celts found expanding Etruscan markets for their traditional produce, and could in addition sell their services to cities locked in the upheavals attendant upon a major shift in the internal political structure of Italy.[40]

During the fifth century, relations with the Etruscans in northern Italy was without doubt the mainstay of Celtic warrior expansion, but this relationship had run its course by the early fourth century, which saw the final contraction of Etruscan power in Italy, and brought the Celts into still more rewarding contact with the cities of the Greek Mediterranean. By the 390s Celts were serving as mercenaries for Dionysius I of Syracuse, and for 200 years they proceeded to play a crucial role in the formation of the Hellenistic world in the service of Greek and Punic employers. The fruits of these military relationships, which supplemented the rewards of the perennial sale of produce and slaves, gave the warrior societies which established themselves on the margins of the Hellenistic world an unprecedented dominance within temperate Europe.

Their dominance lasted, however, only so long as their military services were required in the Mediterranean region. When the Roman conquest of the Hellenistic states put an end to this source of external revenues, the Celts were left only with the profits of exchange to supply their needs for Mediterranean wealth. This forced the dominant warrior chiefdoms along the margins of the Mediterranean to adapt to their altered external conditions in ways which effectively destroyed their traditional economic structure. Those which succeeded in effecting this transformation prospered, and continued to expand, forming a virtually continuous belt of strong agrarian kingdoms and states beyond the frontier of the Roman empire. When this occurred, the centres of warrior expansion returned to their historic heartlands, as Belgic and German warrior societies supplied slaves and mercenary soldiers once more to stronger Celtic agrarian societies further south. As a by-product of Roman expansion in Massalia's hinterland, the Rhône valley was re-established at the end of the second century as an arterial corridor connecting Celtic Europe with the slave markets of the Mediterranean, precipitating under new historical conditions a pattern of warrior expansion which was structurally very similar to that of the sixth century.

Postscript (1984): the foundation date of Massalia

The text above was written in 1982, and is based upon what was then the generally accepted chronology for Greek activity in the western Mediterranean. This placed the foundation of Massalia in c.600, and ascribed dates in the seventh and sixth centuries to the emergent Celtic chiefdoms further north, on the basis of the imported Mediterranean goods found in burials and on settlement sites. Recent work by E. D. Francis and Michael Vickers has, however, called into question the dating currently placed upon the archaic Mediterranean metalwork and pottery on which depends the historical interpretation of archaeological sites throughout the Mediterranean and its hinterland.[41] This has important consequences for the Etruscans and the Celts, since it alters the absolute historical context to which the observed archaeological record of both societies belongs.

Where the Celtic west is concerned, goods such as 'Rhodian' bronze oinochoai and types of Ionian and Corinthian pottery previously dated to the late seventh or early sixth centuries may well be lowered in date by some 60 years, thereby severing the connection between the appearance of much early Greek material in France, and a Massalia founded in c.600. The chronology of Attic pottery is also substantially lowered. Black Figure ware, which determines the chronology of the major late West Hallstatt societies, is placed in the late sixth to early fifth century, while orientalizing metalwork and Attic Red Figure pottery, which was previously held to have originated in the 530s, is seen now to belong to a period immediately following the first major Greek victories in the Persian Wars, not before 480. This affects the chronology of the decline of the

West Hallstatt chiefdoms and the explosive expansion of the warrior societies of the Hünruck–Eifel and Champagne, whose noble paraphernalia was greatly inspired by this orientalizing Greek material. The discrepancy between the traditional chronology for Greek manufactured goods and that proposed by Francis and Vickers narrows after 480 to close completely in the 450s. This revised chronology has the merit of giving much more emphasis than before to the tremendous surge of Greek economic activity between c.480 and 450. This was reflected both in new initiatives in artistic and technical achievement, and in the accelerated political growth throughout the Greek world that attracted the attention, and roused the curiosity, of the ancient historical writers.

While I am convinced of the validity of the Francis–Vickers chronology, I have only recently become aware of it, and have not yet been able to examine its ramifications in depth. I have therefore chosen to leave the text written in 1982 as it stands, in order to show how the issues dealt with may be related to the traditional chronology, rather than to make hasty alterations to it as it goes to press. Instead, I would like to take this opportunity to outline some of the consequences for my argument of one of the most important changes which the revised chronology brings about. This concerns the foundation date of Massalia.

There are two discrepant ancient traditions concerning the foundation of Massalia. One places it around the year 600.[42] This date has been widely accepted as authentic because of its apparent correspondence with the appearance in southern France of Greek material traditionally dated to around that period. The other tradition places the foundation in around 540.[43] This date accords remarkably well with the Francis–Vickers chronology for the leading types of Greek archaic material found in France, whose appearance can still very reasonably be associated with the foundation of Massalia.

The early date need not, however, be abandoned altogether. We are not in fact obliged to choose between 600 and 540 as though these dates were mutually exclusive alternatives. There is a little very early Mediterranean material in the coastal zone of France ascribable on the revised chronology to the first half of the sixth century, and it is very probable that there was indeed an early sixth century Phocaean trading outpost at or near the site of Massalia, perhaps to be identified with Saint-Blaise. This settlement was in all likelihood founded on precisely the sort of small-scale diplomatic basis described by the local writer Trogus Pompeius (*apud* Justin xliii.3–4) who says its inhabitants subsisted on fishing, trade, and above all the piracy for which the Phocaeans were renowned. The major Phocaean colonial city of Massalia is surely a separate foundation belonging to the period of Persian harassment of Ionia in the mid-sixth century which also prompted the emigration of Phocaean refugees to Alalia, itself founded from Phocaea 20 years previously on the advice of an oracle (Herodotus i.165.1). It was the aggressive behaviour of these new Phocaean colonists which provoked the retaliation of Caere and Carthage five years after their arrival.

If the foundation of Massalia occurred around 540, it would clarify its otherwise somewhat puzzling absence from the story of Alalia as recounted above. On the prevailing chronology, Massalia must have been a thriving city of two generations' standing at the time of the battle of Alalia. Such a city might be expected to have taken an interest in the survival of a compatriot foundation in Corsica which provided a useful port of call on the way to Italy. Yet Massalia seemingly stood aloof from the conflict between the combined Etruscan and Carthaginian fleets and the colonists at Alalia. This apparent difficulty disappears, however, if Alalia represented the first mid-sixth century Phocaean attempt to found a city in Etruscan-dominated waters. The conflict over Alalia in 539–535 would then have occurred very shortly after the foundation of Massalia, an event which is likely to have been perceived as threatening to Etruscan and Carthaginian interests in the north-western Mediterranean because it presaged the formation of a chain of important Phocaean trading colonies. The destruction of Alalia will then have been an attempt to abort this development. In the mid-sixth century political environment which now emerges into view, the Phocaeans from Alalia retreated quite naturally to Italy after their defeat, where their future among established Greek cities might seem more secure than on the Gallic coastline where the colony of Massalia was as yet a fresh and speculative venture.[44]

The revised chronology, then, would envisage that during the first half of the sixth century, Greek settlement of the Gallic coastline was confined to a few comparatively modest trading outposts and pirate stations mainly around the Rhône delta. This means that Greek and Etruscan dealings with the Celts to the north of the Rhône were, during this period, on a rather similar footing, and that, in combination, they promoted the early development of the West Hallstatt chiefdoms. The foundation of Massalia in c.540 by fresh colonists from Phocaea then marked an important turning-point in these relationships, because it set up the privileged marketing arrangements described above, which channelled Etruscan and Carthaginian trade through the port of Massalia, which could now afford to protect its interests with a strong fleet. It would therefore now be to the period between 540 and c.480 that the final flowering of the West Hallstatt chiefdoms properly belongs. The close connection which I have proposed between the fortunes of the coastal Etruscan cities and the development of the Celtic slave-supplying societies remains, I believe, as I have outlined it above, but now in a different historical setting. Thus, the eclipse of the Etruscan coastal cities and the accompanying shift in the internal political structure of Etruria in the fifth century, and the collapse of the West Hallstatt chiefdoms which coincided with the great expansion of the warrior societies of the Hünsruck–Eifel and Champagne, can now no longer be regarded as indirect consequences of the battle of Alalia, but instead as related aspects in the north-western Mediterranean of the more general and far-reaching upheavals that attended the Greek victories over the Persians in the first half of the fifth century. These gave rise to a rapid growth in the economy of the leading Greek cities in both spheres of the Mediterranean at the expense of their foreign competitors, with the sort of results that can be observed in the events outlined above.

Notes

1. The arguments presented in this paper will be developed more fully in my *Lineage, Class and State in Celtic Europe c.600 BC–AD 43*, which is in preparation. Political expansion is here used both to describe the legitimate and illicit advancement of strong groups and individuals at the expense of weaker members of their own society, and to describe the advancement of an entire society at the expense of its weaker neighbours.
2. I shall refer to the other type of Celtic society as 'agrarian'. The origin of the distinction between the two principal forms of Celtic society cannot be discussed here. Under the appropriate external conditions, however, it is clear that societies might shift from one form to the other. The warrior form was the less stable of the two, being radically dependent upon certain specialized types of relationship with stronger agrarian societies for its survival.
3. The discussion in this paper concerns neither lineage societies nor states, whose expansion was governed by different principles.
4. The political structure of such a society has been analysed, for instance, by Frankenstein and Rowlands 1978, whose conclusions I largely accept.
5. When, for example, in 231 B.C. the Cisalpine Insubres and Boii wanted to hire Transalpine mercenaries (Gaesatae) for an attack on Rome, they attracted them with 'a large sum of gold . . . and the vast wealth that would be theirs if they were victorious' (Polybius ii.22.2).
6. This proposition cannot be defended in detail here. Its consequences are reflected, for instance, in the high proportion of weapon burials in warrior areas, and in the apparent political structure of areas such as the Hunsrück–Eifel (Wells 1980:116) or the first century Helvetii, a state with an illustrious warrior past (Caesar, *Gallic Wars*:i.2.4–5).
7. Use of cattle in this way is implied for instance by Polybius (ii.17.9–12,cf.ii.26.5) describing the earliest Transalpine warrior immigrants to northern Italy.
8. Slaves were taken as plunder wherever the Celts made war, even in Italy (Polybius ii.26.5). For the importance of warfare in warrior societies see e.g. Caesar, *Gallic Wars*:i.1.4 (Helvetii), i.1.3 (Belgae), vi.21.3 (Germani). Caesar reported that the Belgae first came to Britain to raid, and then to settle (v.12.2). Celtic agrarian societies, of course, followed more peaceable lines of contact, probably leading to limited settlement in the Rhône valley and in Italy adjacent to the Alps during the sixth century (cf. Livy v.34, whose earliest stratum I believe can be shown to belong to the sixth century, and the West Hallstatt world).
9. Hence the somewhat disingenuous remark made by Ambiorix, a chief of the first-century warrior Eburones, that his warriors had as much power over him as he had over them (Caesar, *Gallic Wars*:v.27.3). A strong noble's armed following would consist of his permanent personal retinue of young nobles, compatriot peasant warriors under contract to him, and foreign mercenaries on special occasions.
10. Thus emigrants are often referred to as exiles by outsiders (e.g. Polybius ii.7.6).
11. E.g. Belgae (especially Nervii): Caesar, *Gallic Wars*:i.1.3, ii.15.4. Excessive proximity to a much stronger region, without the option of military service in it, in fact made it impossible for a warrior society to maintain itself as such.
12. Their practice of visiting distant markets was recognized by Wells (1980:136ff.), who correctly stresses their employment as mercenaries. I do not believe the Celts obtained significant Italian revenues from such peaceable activities as those he proposed on p.139. Filip (1960:58) recognized the importance of slave trading in this contact. For fifth-century contact with Italy see e.g. Wells (1980:133ff.). For sixth-century contact with Mediterranean France see Taffanel 1962, and Livy's tradition of mercenary contact with Massalia around 600 (v.34.8).
13. Cf. Caesar, *Gallic Wars*:vi.23.1 (Germani).
14. See e.g. Freidin (1982:207ff., burial record). A similar frontier later separated the

warrior south-east of Britain from what I believe were the agrarian chiefdoms of Armorican type in the south-west (Nash 1984).

15. This is most marked in Champagne, but can also be detected in the Hunsrück–Eifel area (e.g. Wells 1980:117). The specialized manufacturing functions of the largest settlements in the most advanced warrior kingdoms – such as Manching or Camulodunum – have nothing to do with market exchange. The goods made at such places under noble patronage (e.g. coins, weapons, metalwork) were instead almost certainly distributed through contractual and especially military relationships among the senior nobility. For rivers as boundaries see Caesar, *Gallic Wars*:v.11.8 (Thames), i.1.2 (Marne), or Irish epics, which abound with demarcation disputes among the nobility conducted at fords. Rivers as a source of revenue for agrarian societies: Strabo iv.3.2.
16. This expansion is reflected e.g. in the spread of the ethnic names of warrior groups into their periphery: Cenomani to eastern Armorica and (probably) East Anglia (Iceni); Parisii to Yorkshire (Paris); Catalauni probably to Essex and Hertfordshire (Catuvellauni). Outlying colonies were often defeated or absorbed into their new cultural environment: Caesar, *Gallic Wars*:vi.24.3–6 (Volcae).
17. This is how the Germani were lured into agrarian eastern France in the first century B.C. (Caesar, *Gallic Wars*:i.31.4).
18. For the West Hallstatt zone see Härke 1979, Frankenstein and Rowlands 1978 and Wells 1980. For the warrior societies see Bretz-Mahler 1971, Freidin 1982, Frankenstein and Rowlands 1978 and Wells 1980. These provide full documentation. The interdependence of the two groups of Celtic societies is not only demonstrable from cultural material, but is also apparent from their geographical association and the timing of their development.
19. I therefore disagree with the view that the early La Tène warrior societies were in any way linear descendants of the West Hallstatt chiefdoms. Such continuity is expressed, e.g. by Filip (1960:47ff.). Both are nonetheless Celtic, in the sense in which both Dorians (or Spartans) and Ionians (or Athenians) were Greeks.
20. This has been argued convincingly, e.g. by Frankenstein and Rowlands 1978, Härke 1979 and Wells 1980; it requires no further defence here.
21. By marketing functions I mean distribution of goods from their places of manufacture or assembly by direct exchanges between producers and customers, whose primary objective was the exchange itself; this contrasts with customary transactions such as gift or payment whose primary function was social or political in nature.
22. This dependence was later repeated in the relationship between the eastern Gallic (agrarian) states, and sources of Transrhenan (warrior) mercenaries (cf. n.17 above).
23. For produce of Massalia's hinterland see Benoît 1965. For that involved in trade between the West Hallstatt zone and Massalia see Wells (1980:70), although I would disagree with the assertion that the trade was not dependent upon any specialized resource, even if it included a wide range of auxiliary goods.
24. For discussion of diplomatic gifts see Frankenstein and Rowlands 1978 and Wells 1980:72ff.
25. Wells (1980:39ff.) has a useful and well-documented discussion of the potential contribution of metals and miscellaneous exotica to this contact.
26. During the seventh and sixth centuries, slave markets were vigorous in the eastern Mediterranean. This is a complex subject which cannot be dealt with here in any detail. For the reputation of the Etruscans 'who more than any other people ravaged the Mediterranean' see Strabo x.4.9; Vergil, *Aeneid*:viii.481ff. (Caere); for that of the Phocaeans see Herodotus vi.17; Justin xliii.3.5, and for Ionians in general Ezekiel 27:13.
27. The geographical location of the West Hallstatt chiefdoms, on this interpretation, therefore define the eastern fringe of contact with Celtic warrior societies (fig. 3.1).
28. Hides are often mentioned as staple commodities in exchange with warrior societies

and nomads: Strabo xi.2.3 (of Tanais on the Black Sea – 'slaves, hides and such other things as nomads possess'); v.1.8 (of Aquileia on the Adriatic 'slaves, cattle, hides'); iv.5.2 (of Britain – 'hides, slaves, dogs, grain, cattle, gold, silver and iron).

29. Ransom farms captives as a long-term resource, to be captured again another time. Slaves are commonly mentioned in exchanges with barbarians (n.28 above). Their inclusion in a long list of trade goods obscures their importance to the society which captured them. Wine may have been the principal commodity exchanged for them, as at Aquileia (Strabo v.1.8) and in southern Gaul (Diodorus Siculus v.25.3). Wells (1980:64ff.) rightly stresses the importance of wine in relations between Massalia and the Celtic north. Livy v.33.2 identifies wine as an important focus of Celtic interest in Italy.
30. Cf. adoption of phalanx tactics (e.g. Caesar, *Gallic Wars*:i.24.4) and other Mediterranean military techniques (iii.23.5, vii.30.4).
31. Their material culture is what is properly known as La Tène II.
32. Alalia: Herodotus i.166.
33. Etruscan contact with Languedoc continued, although increasingly rivalled by Massoliote and Greek trade. These western markets had always been important, but were now awkward to get at. See e.g. Arnal *et al.* 1974; Hodson and Rowlett 1974.
34. For Vulci as origin of most metalwork acquired by the Transalpine Celts, see e.g. Wells (1980:119ff.). Carthage survived western Greek expansion because of her control of the south-western Mediterranean. Contraction of Etruscan shipping on the Mediterranean coasts of Gaul is reflected in the profiles of imports at such sites as Lattes (Arnal *et al.* 1974).
35. E.g. Wells 1980:102.
36. *Ibid.*:130.
37. Garrisons may be the origin of some of the warrior communities which occasionally appear near West Hallstatt settlements, for instance at Le Pègue (Hatt 1970:92). The centre of gravity of warrior expansion to northern Italy was the Seine basin (Lingones, Senones, Cenomani, Boii). The sheer expense of hiring mercenaries may have hastened the decline of the West Hallstatt chiefdoms, as revenues were taken out of their economy by returning warriors.
38. Dominance of the warrior chiefdoms of Switzerland during the fourth to second centuries is reflected in their increasing influence upon the material culture of adjacent areas of eastern France, previously within the West Hallstatt zone.
39. The influence of the Etruscans upon the warrior Celts is undoubted: two-wheeled chariots, their Etruscanized script (Lepontic alphabet and ultimately ogam), miscellaneous decorative motifs and of course the imported metalwork. Cf. Livy v.33.
40. Upheavals at this time involved not only the Etruscans, of course, but the entire Italian peninsula, in a three-way struggle among the Etruscans, Greeks and Italians (particularly Rome).
41. E. D. Francis and M. Vickers (1983, 1985); M. Vickers (forthcoming). I am greatly indebted to Michael Vickers for bringing this new work to my attention, and am most grateful for the time he has spared me to discuss its immediate implications for the history of the western Celts. Naturally, the views I express here are my own responsibility.
42. Timaeus *apud* Scymnius Chius, Müller *Geographici Graeci Minores* I, 204, II. 201–4; Livy v.34.1,8; Justin xliii.3.4 links it with *a* Tarquin (either Priscus, c.616–579 B.C., or Superbus, c.535–509 B.C.).
43. Isocrates vi.84.1; Pausanias x.8.6; and, apparently, Thucydides i.13.6.
44. Ammianus Marcellinus xv.7 actually associates the Phocaean foundation of Massalia with that of Velia, in the time of Harpagus the Mede (540 B.C.).

Bibliography

Arnal, J., Majurel, R. and Pradès, H., 1974. *Le Port de Lattara (Lattes, Hérault)* (Bordighera/Montpellier).

Benoît, F., 1965. *Recherches sur l'Hellénisation du midi de la Gaule* (Aix-en-Provence).

Bretz-Mahler, D., 1971. *La Civilisation de la Tène I en Champagne* (*Gallia* suppl. XXIII: Paris).

Filip, J., 1960. *Celtic Civilisation and its Heritage* (Prague).

Francis, E. D. and Vickers, M., 1983. '*Signa priscae artis*: Eretria and Siphnos', *J. Hellenic Studies 103:* 49–67.

Francis, E. D. and Vickers, M., forthcoming. 'Geometric pottery at Hama and its implications for Near Eastern Chronology', *Levant 27* (forthcoming 1985).

Frankenstein, S. and Rowlands, M. J., 1978. 'The internal structure and regional context of early Iron Age society in south-western Germany', *Bull. Inst. Archaeol. Univ. London 15:* 73–112.

Freidin, N. P. J., 1982. *The Early Iron Age in the Paris Basin* (BAR S131).

Haffner, A., 1976. *Die westliche Hunsrück–Eifel Kultur* (Berlin).

Härke, H. G. H., 1979. *Settlement Types and Patterns in the West Hallstatt Province* (BAR IS57).

Hatt, J-J., 1970. *Celts and Gallo-Romans.*

Hodson, F. R. and Rowlett, R. M., 1974. 'From 600 BC to the Roman Conquest'. In S. Piggott, G. Daniel and C. McBurney (eds.), *France Before the Romans:* 157–191.

Nash, D., 1984. 'The basis of contact between Britain and Gaul in the late pre-Roman Iron Age'. In S. Macready and F. H. Thompson (eds.), *Cross-Channel Trade between Gaul and Britain in the pre-Roman Iron Age*: 92–107.

Taffanel, O. and J., 1962. 'Deux tombes de cavalier du 1er Age du Fer à Mailhac', *Gallia 20:* 3–32.

Vickers, M., forthcoming. 'Early Greek coinage, a reassessment', *Numismatic Chronicle.*

Wells, P. S., 1980. *Culture Contact and Culture Change: early Iron Age Central Europe and the Mediterranean World.*

4

Mediterranean trade and culture change in Early Iron Age central Europe

Peter S. Wells

The first half of the last millennium B.C. was a time of profound culture change in central Europe (see discussion in Peroni 1979). The first settlements which might be called 'towns' (Neustupný 1970; Hensel 1970) emerged at this time, providing evidence indicating specialized crafts industries, commerce in local and long-distance networks, populations substantially larger than those of settlements of earlier periods, and clear differences in wealth and status among members of the communities. These changes are most apparent in two regions of central Europe: one consists of modern south-west Germany, eastern France, and northern Switzerland, a region I shall call west-central Europe; the other is in the East Alpine lands of Austria and Slovenia, most particularly in the region of Lower Carniola in Slovenia. Slightly later, beginning around the middle of the last millennium B.C., similar changes occurred in other parts of central Europe, including the Marne valley, the Middle Rhineland, the Hallein area of Austria, and Bohemia, all in the context of the Early La Tène material culture (see Pauli 1980). This paper will confine itself to the earlier changes, associated with the Hallstatt material culture and more or less confined to west-central Europe and the south-east Alpine region. The development of substantial manufacturing and commercial centres in these two areas is the principal respect in which the societies of the Early Iron Age differed from those of preceding periods of European prehistory.

Another new phenomenon of the early Iron Age was the start of intensive trade relations between communities in these parts of Europe and societies of the Mediterranean world. Already during the Neolithic and Bronze Ages there is much archaeological evidence for trade between Mediterranean lands and interior Europe, but from the eighth century B.C. on, evidence for such trade increases greatly in quantity and changes in character.

This discussion will address the connection between trade with Mediterranean societies and cultural changes which happened in central Europe. My aim here is to draw attention to some of the issues concerning changes in these two early Iron Age contexts. In many respects the results of the changes were similar, but in one aspect in particular, that concerning the development of elites, there are important differences suggested by the archaeological evidence. I shall attempt to define these differences, as they appear in the present state of research, and suggest one tentative model which might, with further investigation and refinement, account for them. I offer no conclusions at this stage, since the evidence, particularly in the south-east Alpine region, is not yet abundant enough or of adequate quality to permit the drawing of conclusions. But I put forward at least a preliminary suggestion as to the reasons for the observed patterns, one which can be tested as more modern field research is carried out and published.

West-central Europe

Archaeological sites in this region yield abundant evidence for interaction with societies of the Mediterranean world, in particular with Greeks. Much of the evidence is reviewed in Wells 1980, and only a few aspects will be mentioned here again.

Black-figure Attic pottery has been recovered on at least nine settlements of the region and in several graves, most of it dated to the final third of the sixth century B.C. Ceramic amphorae from the Greek world, which probably carried wine and perhaps sometimes olive oil, are represented at many of the same settlements and in a few graves. Bronze vessels manufactured in Greek workshops have been found in a number of richly-outfitted burials, including such extraordinary objects as the huge krater at Vix (Joffroy 1954), the rod-tripod from Grafenbühl (Zürn 1970), and the cauldron from Hochdorf (Biel 1978). Other Greek products at Grafenbühl include two sphinxes, one carved of ivory and the other of bone and amber, and remains of furniture also carved of ivory, bone, and amber. Other imports from the Mediterranean area include silk textile found in the Hohmichele tumulus at the Heuneburg (Hundt 1969), and coral, which is well represented both on settlements and in graves (Champion 1976). Wine was being brought from the Mediterranean coast of France into central Europe, as indicated by sets of Attic vessels for serving and drinking the beverage and by the amphorae.

Other kinds of evidence also point to interactions between these communities and peoples of the Mediterranean. The clay-brick wall at the Heuneburg is unique in central Europe and was designed by someone familiar with such walls in the Mediterranean world (Kimmig 1968: 47–56). The Hirschlanden stele from northern Württemberg, which originally stood on top of a burial mound, betrays familiarity with Mediterranean sculptural traditions (Röder 1970).

The luxury imports began arriving in west-central Europe at the beginning of the sixth century B.C., and they stopped appearing in the course of the first half of the fifth century B.C. The products traded to the Greeks in exchange for these Mediterranean luxury goods do not survive in the archaeological record. But we can at least make educated guesses about them on the basis of Greek textual evidence concerning similar relations elsewhere on the borders of the Greek world and from later, Roman and medieval, data about commerce between

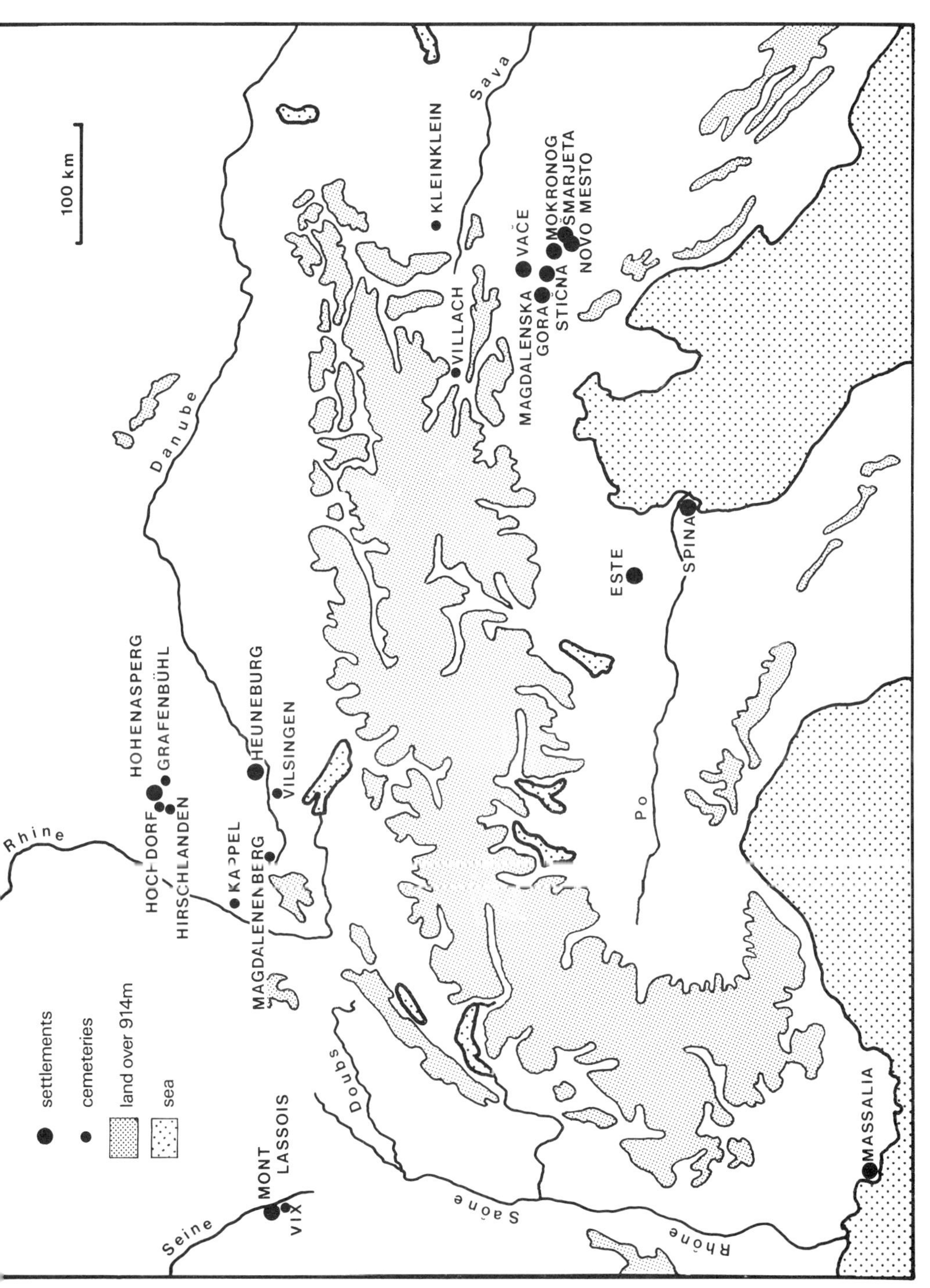

Figure 4.1 Map showing principal sites mentioned in the text.

west-central Europe and the Mediterranean. The products were probably mainly raw materials and partly-finished goods such as grains, salted meat, wool, honey, wax, pitch, hides, leather, and perhaps slaves.

At the same time that the Greek luxury imports were arriving, major changes in economic and social organization were taking place in central Europe. Before about 600 B.C. settlements throughout central Europe were principally isolated farmsteads and small hamlets; evidence from both settlements and cemeteries indicates that communities rarely had over 30 or 40 members (Kossack 1959:86). Little trade is represented in the archaeological record; only bronze metal was regularly passed between communities. Crafts were organized on a household basis, and there is little evidence for specialized manufacturing of any kind, except some limited metal-working. The small communities throughout central Europe were similar to one another in material wealth and in economic organization. With very few exceptions they were farming communities with subsistence economy based upon cultivation of millet, barley, wheat, and rye, along with a variety of garden crops; pigs, cattle, sheep, and goats were kept (Jankuhn 1969:71–81). The principal evidence for the limited status differentiation in cemeteries dating to the first part of the Early Iron Age (Hallstatt C) is the presence of one or two graves outfitted with a sword of bronze or iron, and often containing more ceramic vessels than the majority of graves. The persons buried in these graves can be viewed as leading individuals of small hamlet communities, perhaps senior males of extended family units. These graves are similar to one another in character, suggesting that no important status differences existed between the leaders of the various small communities (Kossack 1959; 1972).

After about 600 B.C. patterns began to change in west-central Europe, at about the same time that Ionian Greeks from the city of Phocaea on the west coast of Asia Minor established a trading colony at Massalia (modern Marseille), just east of the mouth of the Rhône river (Wackernagel 1930; Clavel-Lévêque 1974). At this time the Heuneburg and other hill-forts were established, and in the course of the sixth century B.C. they grew to become centres of population and of specialized craft industries and trade (Kimmig 1969; 1975). The number of inhabitants at these centres is difficult to estimate, but it was probably at least several hundred at such sites as the Heuneburg. Among the industries evident are iron production, bronze casting, pottery manufacture, and the working of such luxury materials as coral (imported), lignite, jet and gold. In addition to the trade with the Greek world, these centres carried on commerce with northern Europe for amber, with mining communities in the Swabian Jura for lignite and jet, and with miners and merchants who supplied copper and tin.

Important changes in social organization also took place. A series of graves dating from the first decades of the sixth century B.C. were found to be more richly outfitted than any of the previous period. They contain both luxury products of local industries, such as gold neckrings and bronze vessels, and also imported items of Mediterranean origin. The graves at Kappel (Kimmig and Rest 1954) and Vilsingen (Schiek 1954) both contained Greek (or possibly

Etruscan) bronze jugs as well as bronze vessels of local manufacture, wagons, and weapons. The grave at Kappel also had in it gold jewellery including a neckring and a bracelet. These graves stand out markedly from the majority of graves of the period, which contain one or several objects of bronze jewellery and one or two ceramic vessels.

This differentiation in burial equipment suggests that differences were developing in the amount of material wealth possessed by members of society. The grave at Vix, dating to the end of the sixth or beginning of the fifth century B.C., contained an ornate bronze krater standing over 1.5m high and weighing over 200kg, two Attic drinking cups, two Etruscan bronze basins, an Etruscan bronze jug, a Greek silver bowl with a gold omphalos, a local bronze basin, a four-wheeled wagon, a gold neckring probably of Greek origin, amber beads, and local bronze and iron jewellery including fibulae with coral inlay (Joffroy 1954). The objects in the central burial at Grafenbühl, of about the same date, are similar in their exceptional character (Zürn 1970). It appears that throughout the sixth century B.C. a continuous process of social differentiation was taking place in west-central Europe, as a result of which commanding individuals came to control large amounts of material wealth, and presumably also power, represented by the number and variety of exceptional luxury objects in their graves (Frankenstein and Rowlands 1978).

About 40 rich graves are known from west-central Europe dating to this century, and so it is possible to trace these changes in some detail over time. Throughout this period the great majority of graves continues to be outfitted with small numbers of bronze jewellery objects and other ornaments such as beads. The rich graves are distinguished from other burials in three major respects. First, they have larger quantities of grave goods than do the majority, both in numbers of individual objects and in numbers of categories of objects. This difference is clear when we compare the inventories of rich graves with those of poorer graves in tumuli which were excavated under well-controlled conditions. In the Hohmichele tumulus at the Heuneburg (Riek 1962), Graves I and VI contained vastly greater quantities of grave goods than did the others. Similarly, the central grave at Grafenbühl was much more richly outfitted than the other burials around it (Zürn 1970). Second, the rich graves contain many kinds of objects which never occur in plain graves. Gold neckrings occur only in graves containing other exceptional wealth. The regularity of gold neckrings in rich graves, and their stylistic similarity to one another (Paret 1942), would suggest that they represented a badge of status or rank. Exotic luxury imports, such as the Vix krater and ring, the Grafenbühl tripod and sphinxes, and the Hochdorf cauldron, also occur only in otherwise wealthy graves. Third, the rich graves are distinguished topographically from the rest of the burials in a cemetery. They are usually situated at the centre and base of large burial mounds, with other graves arranged at the sides and higher up. The situation at the Magdalenenberg near Villingen is illustrated here (fig. 4.2), with the central burial in a wooden chamber and the other, much more modest, graves arranged concentrically around it. Other examples of this pattern include the Hohmichele tumulus (Riek 1962:7 fig. 2) and Grafenbühl (Zürn 1970). The rich central

4 Mediterranean trade and culture change in Early Iron Age central Europe

Peter S. Wells

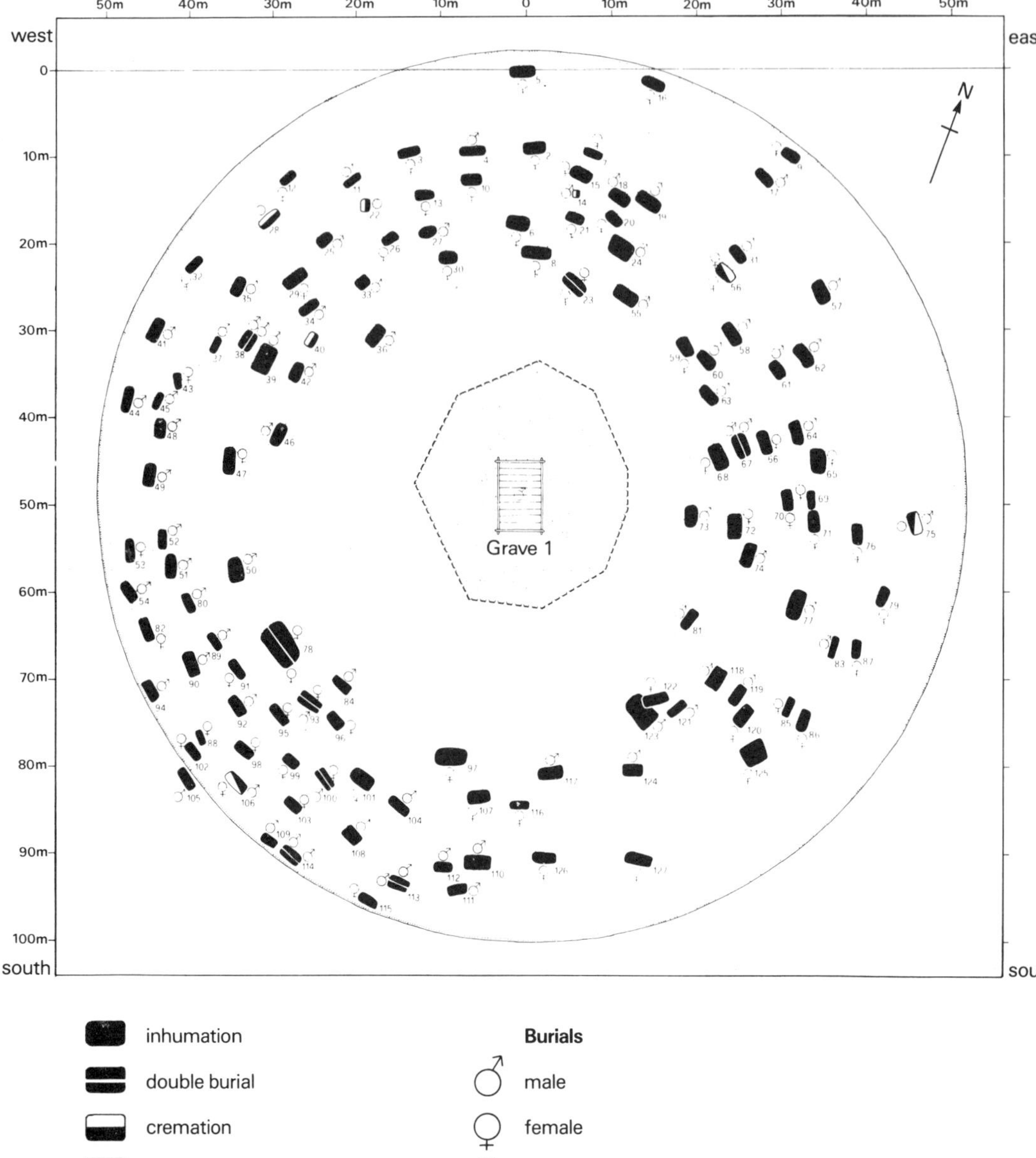

Figure 4.2 Plan of the Magdalenenberg tumulus showing the central chamber burial and 126 graves around it. (Reproduced with permission from K. Spindler, 'Grabfunde der Hallstattzeit vom Magdalenenberg bei Villingen im Schwarzwald,' in *Ausgrabungen in Deutschland 1950–1975*, I, 232, fig. 36: Römisch-Germanisches Zentralmuseum, Mainz, 1975).

graves often have carefully constructed burial chambers of hewn planks, as at Grafenbühl (Zürn 1970:12 fig. 5) and Hochdorf (Schiek 1981:123 fig. 52).

Sometime between about 500 and 450 B.C. the special developments of the sixth century B.C. came to an end (Wells and Bonfante 1979). The import trade in Greek luxury goods stopped, and settlements such as the Heuneburg and Mont Lassois ceased to function as centres of industry and trade. No more graves were equipped with the great wealth of Vix and Grafenbühl (except Kleinaspergle, which is a special case), and the specialized craft industries which had been producing luxury products of bronze and gold declined in activity, as did both local and long-distance trade systems.

South-east Alpine region

My discussion will centre on Lower Carniola, the region of the Yugoslav Republic of Slovenia which extends south-east from Ljubljana in the direction of the Croatian border. In Lower Carniola there is clear evidence for the development of economic centres similar in many respects to those of west-central Europe (Gabrovec *et al.* 1970; Frey 1974; Wells 1981), and for intensive trade relations with surrounding peoples, paticularly those of the Italian peninsula (Frey 1969). Again, the most apparent evidence for interaction is that of imports. In Lower Carniola the imported objects originated principally in different parts of Italy, instead of in the Greek world.

A bronze tripod from a grave at Novo mesto (Gabrovec 1968; fig. 4.3), at least two bronze figurines from different parts of Slovenia (Starè 1975a), and several carved amber ornaments (e.g. Wells 1981:112) are among probable imports from Etruria. Ceramic oinochoai and so-called 'Apulian' kraters (fig. 4.4) manufactured in southern Italy are represented in a series of graves (Frey 1969:76–7), as are other kinds of pottery found at different sites in Lower Carniola and neighbouring areas (Frey 1969:84 n.20).

Evidence is particularly abundant of interactions between communities of Lower Carniola and those of north-east Italy, the Veneti centred at Este. Most obvious is the development of the situla art in the two areas, with the exchange of actual objects and movement of individual craftsmen between the regions (Frey 1969; 1970). The products of sheet bronze bearing situla art include buckets, helmets, shield bosses, belt plates, and earrings (Kastelic 1965). A wide range of other objects which are very similar in the two regions, including pottery, fibulae, dress pins, and dagger-knives, also point to regular interactions (Frey 1969; Frey and Gabrovec 1971).

As in the case of west-central Europe, here too the objects which survive archaeologically represent only a small portion of the trade which was being carried on. On the basis of statements by classical writers, particularly Strabo, concerning trade in these regions during the Early Iron Age (see Šašel 1977) and later, we can make reasonable guesses about the trade. Iron was probably a principal export product from the south-east Alpine region to Italy (Šašel 1977; for a summary of the arguments see Wells 1981:113); other exports included such items as cattle and dairy products, hides and leather, amber from the north,

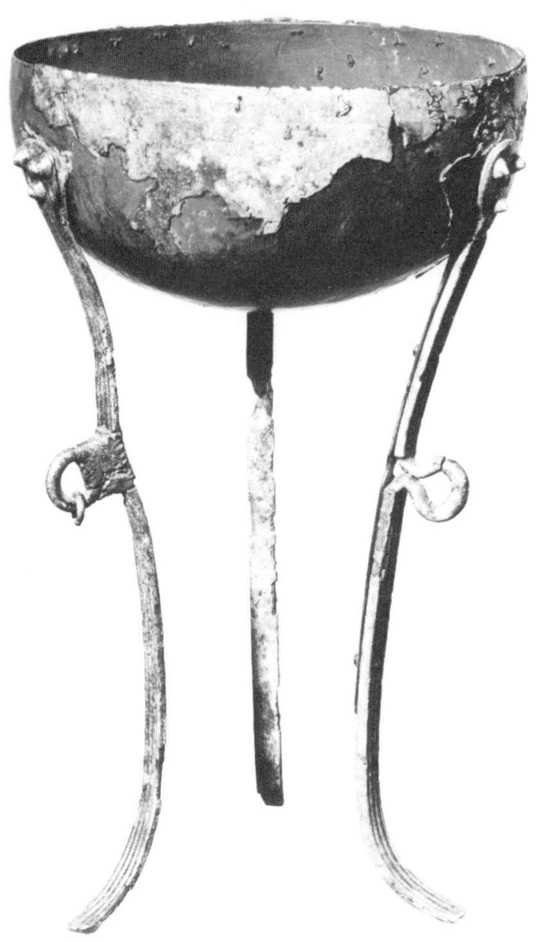

Figure 4.3 Bronze tripod from Novo mesto. Height about 42cm. (Photograph courtesy Stane Gabrovec, Narodni muzej, Ljubljana; originally published in Gabrovec 1968, fig. 2.)

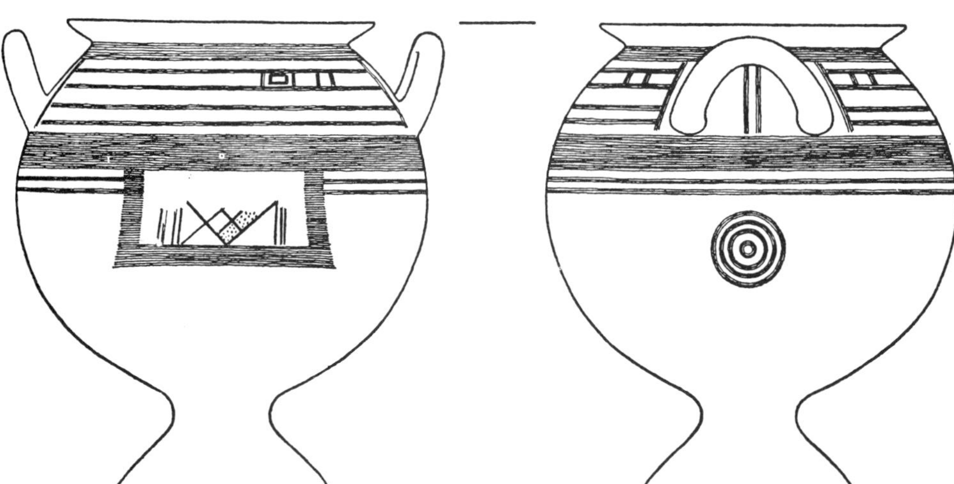

Figure 4.4 Ceramic 'Apulian' krater from Črnomelj, representative of all of the vessels of the group. Height about 25cm. (Reproduced with permission from O.-H. Frey, *Die Entstehung der Situlenkunst:* Walter de Gruyter, Berlin, 1969, 79, fig. 47.5.)

and honey. Goods traded from Italy included primarily wine, and also olive oil and other such luxury foodstuffs, as well as bronze and pottery objects.

The changes which occurred in Lower Carniola in conjunction with the growth of these trade relations are generally similar to those that occurred in west-central Europe. In the south-east Alpine region the communities of the Late Bronze Age were also small in size and carried on only limited specialized crafts and trade (Wells 1981:101–9). The subsistence economy was similar to that of west-central Europe, based on the same cereal grains, garden crops, and domesticated animals (references in Wells 1981:96–7). During the eighth century B.C., at the same time that iron was first being extracted and worked on a relatively large scale (Müllner 1908; Rieth 1942), hill-top settlements with substantial defensive walls were established at such sites as Stična, Magdalenska gora, Vače, Novo mesto, Šmarjeta, and Mokronog (Gabrovec 1973:372). Extensive cemeteries of tumulus graves (and in some cases flat graves, as at Vače) were begun around the new hill-forts (fig. 4.5). Manufacturing and commercial activity at these centres increased over a period of time, reaching their highest point during the sixth and fifth centuries B.C. These hill-fort communities also maintained specialized industries in iron, bronze, glass, gold, and other substances (Wells 1981:101–9).

Iron workers were producing large numbers of fine objects from the abundant and easily-accessible local hematite and limonite ores. Vast slag deposits at the early Iron Age hill-forts, together with slag chunks in a number of graves of the period, attest to the industrial activity (Müllner 1908). The iron objects best represented in the graves include knives, spearheads, axes, fibulae, and rings (see catalogues cited in Wells 1981). Bronze smiths were producing, from imported copper and tin, a wide range of jewellery items, including belt plates, earrings, bracelets, leg rings, and fibulae; bronze vessels of different forms (fig. 4.6); and defensive weaponry such as helmets and cuirasses. The quantities of bronze objects being manufactured and placed in graves were much larger than during the Late Bronze Age, and new technical processes were being developed such as methods for producing large objects of sheet bronze and the use of the lathe.

A flourishing industry in glass beads made Slovenia the principal centre of bead production in early Iron Age Europe. Both the numbers of beads and the range of colours and forms represented in the graves are much greater than elsewhere in central Europe (Haevernick 1974; fig. 4.7), and beads were being exported from the production sites to other parts of Europe, including the trade centres of west-central Europe discussed above (Reim 1981:218). The quantities of gold present in graves in Slovenia are much smaller than those in the graves of west-central Europe, but do indicate at least a limited craft industry in that precious metal (Knez 1974), whereas copper was being imported on a large scale, and the mining areas in the Tirol and Land Salzburg appear to have been among the principal sources (Moosleitner 1977:117). For tin, we are unfortunately poorly informed as to source areas (Muhly 1973). The evidence in the graves indicates that the quantities of copper and tin being brought in, and of bronze objects being made, increased greatly between the Late Bronze and Early Iron Ages (Wells 1981:110–11). Amber was being imported from northern

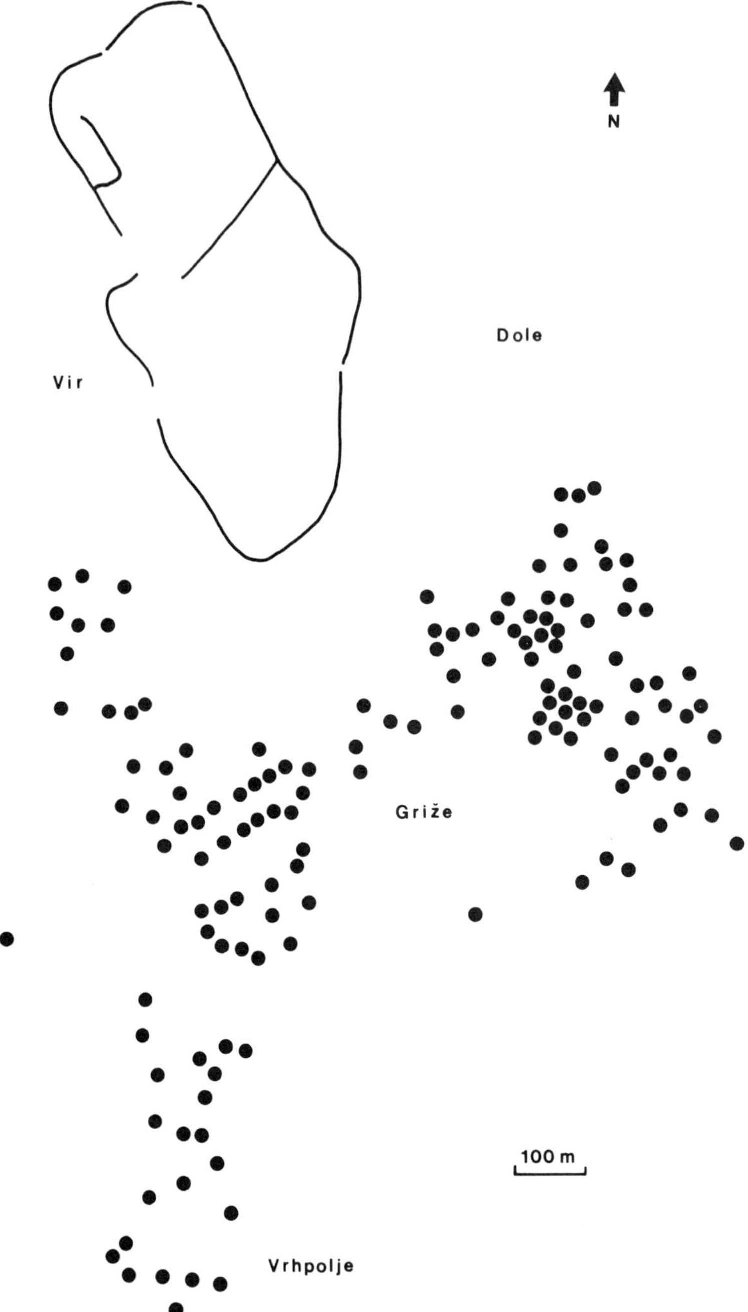

Figure 4.5 Plan showing the walls of the hill-fort at Stična and the tumuli now visible around it. (Based on a plan by O.-H. Frey and reproduced with permission from P. S. Wells, *The Emergence of an Iron Age Economy: The Mecklenburg Grave Groups from Hallstatt and Stična*: Peabody Museum, Harvard University, 1981, 46, fig. 23.)

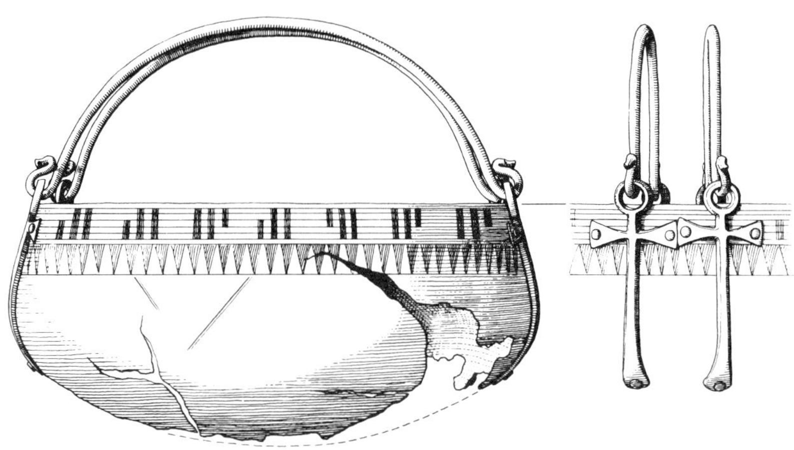

Figure 4.6 Cauldron of sheet bronze with cast handles and handle attachments, from Mecklenburg Grave 3 in Tumulus II at Stična. Diameter at rim about 25cm. (From Wells 1981, 153, fig. 37a.)

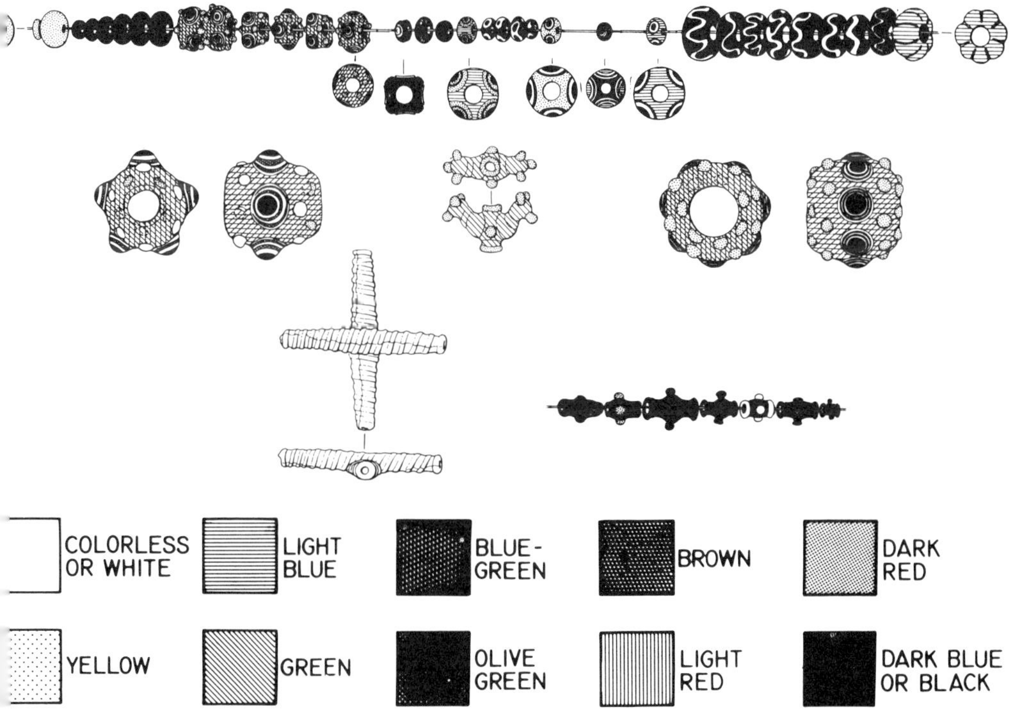

COLORLESS OR WHITE
LIGHT BLUE
BLUE-GREEN
BROWN
DARK RED
YELLOW
GREEN
OLIVE GREEN
LIGHT RED
DARK BLUE OR BLACK

Figure 4.7 Glass beads from Mecklenburg Grave 2 in Tumulus V at Stična, illustrating some of the range in shape and colour of the beads being produced at the large settlements in Lower Carniola. The vertical cylinder of the cross-shaped bead is 5cm long. (From Wells 1981, 190, fig. 114.)

Europe into Slovenia in sizeable quantities, and the graves at the centres contain large numbers of amber beads, most often as necklaces and bracelets (fig. 4.8). Besides being buried with the dead, amber was re-exported from the commercial centres in Lower Carniola to Italy (Bohnsack 1976). Another well-represented import is graphite, used to ornament ceramic vessels, which was being mined from a variety of Alpine deposits (e.g. Kossack 1959:71).

Social changes accompanied the economic ones in Lower Carniola, as they did in the other region. Here too series of graves more richly equipped than the majority appeared at about the same time as the changes in settlement systems and economy. The burial pattern of the Late Bronze Age was one of little differentiation of wealth in the graves. Many cemeteries of the period have been excavated in Lower Carniola and other parts of Slovenia (e.g. Knez 1966; Puš 1971; Gabrovec 1973; Starè 1975b), and they consistently show modest grave inventories with relatively little differentiation in wealth of goods. During the eighth century B.C., at the same time that evidence for trade and other interaction with groups in Italy and in other regions increases in quantity and the principal hill-fort centres were established, clear differentiation appears in burial equipment. Among the graves which exemplify this new pattern are those containing cuirasses at Stična (Gabrovec 1966:10–13) and at Novo mesto (Gabrovec 1960). These graves, like others of the same period reflecting the same economic and social changes at Villach (Müller-Karpe 1952) and Kleinklein (Schmid 1933; Dobiat 1980) on the southern edge of the Alps in Austria, are characterized particularly by the presence of large weapons (swords, spears, cuirasses, helmets) and elaborate, sometimes imported, bronze vessels.

The rich graves of Early Iron Age Slovenia have in common with those of west-central Europe a large number of grave goods which often occur together as characteristic of these special burials (large weapons, bronze vessels). But they differ from the rich graves of west-central Europe in two important respects. Those in Lower Carniola and neighbouring regions do not contain objects

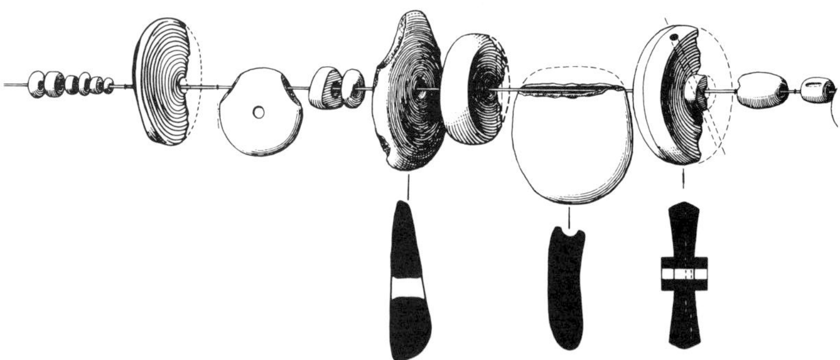

Figure 4.8 Amber beads from Mecklenburg Grave 16 in Tumulus VI at Stična, illustrating some forms current during the Early Iron Age. The large bead in the centre is 3cm wide. (From Wells 1981, 206, fig. 147c.)

which *never* occur in plainer graves. Bronze cuirasses, helmets, and vessels tend to occur in graves wealthier than average, as do ornaments of sheet gold, but none of these objects is restricted to the richer graves (examples at Stična cited in Wells 1981:118). There is no apparent badge of status which survives in the majority of richer graves but not in others, comparable to the gold neckrings of west-central Europe. Nor do the graves in Lower Carniola contain elaborate luxury products imported from outside, comparable to the Vix krater and ring, the Grafenbühl tripod and sphinxes, or the Hochdorf cauldron, or even more modest ones such as the bronze jugs from Kappel and Vilsingen. During the sixth and especially fifth centuries B.C. luxury imports such as Attic painted pottery and Etruscan bronze vessels occur in abundance at such north-east Italian centres as Bologna and Spina (Aurigemma 1960), yet to judge by the material known to date very few found their way to Lower Carniola or adjacent areas (Kimmig 1974:69–70). The imports in the richer graves in Lower Carniola are much plainer objects, usually everyday items in their societies of origin, such as single ceramic vessels (fig. 4.4) and in one case a small bronze bowl (Gabrovec 1966:11 Fig. 5.4). Rarely is more than a single import present in a grave, compared to nine imported luxury objects in the grave at Vix and four still remaining in the plundered central grave at Grafenbühl. Many of the richest burials of Lower Carniola do not contain any imported products from Mediterranean lands (e.g. Knez 1978), in sharp distinction to the contemporaneous rich graves of west-central Europe.

Also unlike the rich graves in that other region, those in Lower Carniola are generally not distinguished topographically from the others. Rather than forming the central grave in a mound, the richest burials are often arranged along with all the others, concentrically around the centre, which is often empty. One example of a recently excavated tumulus is illustrated here, Tumulus IV of the Kandija cemetery at Novo mesto (fig. 4.9). Similar is the plan of the Great Tumulus at Stična with its 183 graves (Gabrovec 1974:168–9, plan 1).

Although the number of scientifically excavated tumuli is still small and far-reaching conclusions are impossible, the differences in the positioning of the richer graves relative to other graves in the two regions appear to be significant. In west-central Europe, the pattern suggests that the individual in the centrally-situated rich grave was far above the others buried around him/her in status (not to mention in wealth, reflected in the grave goods). In Lower Carniola, the location of rich graves in the same position in the tumuli as the others suggests that such a substantial status difference did not exist there. Thus both the evidence of the wealth and character of the grave goods and that of the relative positions of wealthy and plain graves suggest that the individuals buried in wealthy graves in west-central Europe were of considerably greater status and wealth relative to the other members of their communities than their counterparts in Lower Carniola.

As noted, the number of controlled studies of burial mounds in Lower Carniola is still very small, and the patterns noted here may well change as the evidence grows. Working with what we have now available, what hypothesis can be proposed to account for this suggested difference in relative status of the

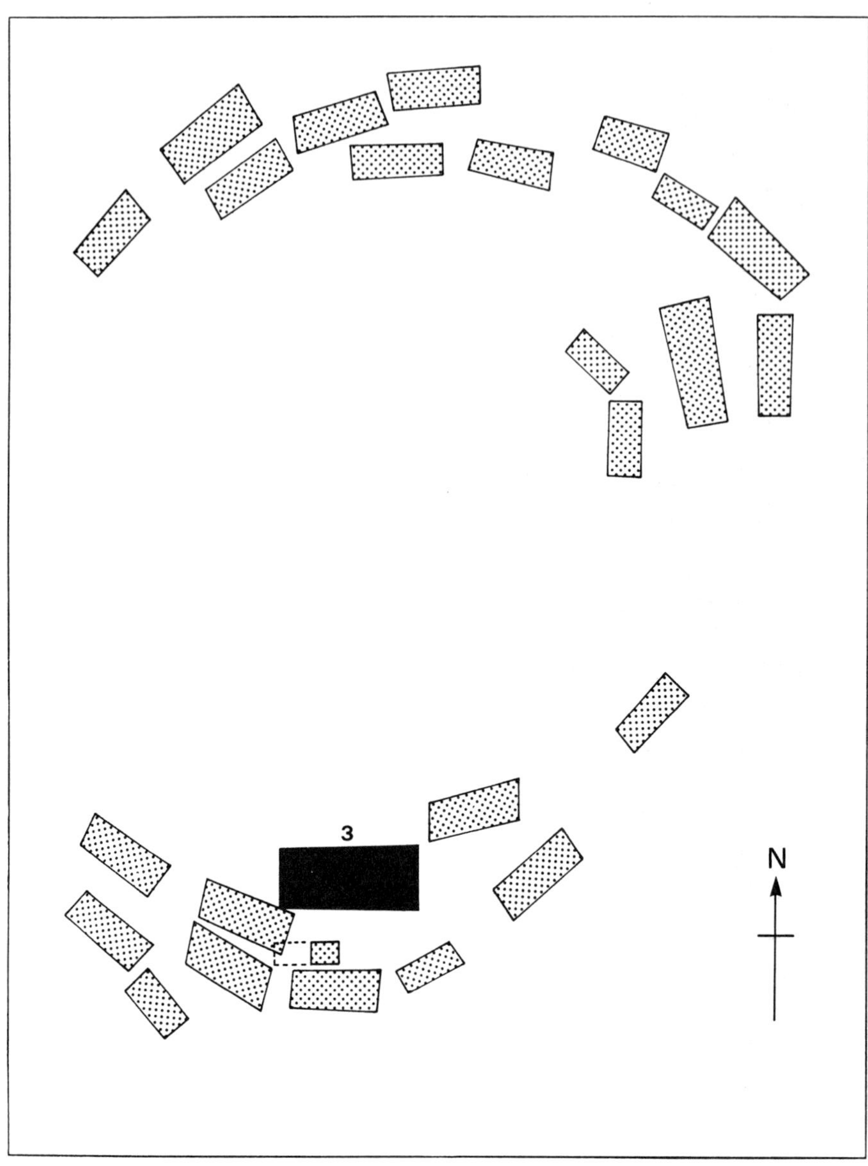

Figure 4.9 Plan of Tumulus IV in the Kandija cemetery at Novo mesto, showing the location of the richly outfitted Grave 3 among the other burials arranged concentrically around the centre. Scale 1:2000m. (Reproduced with permission from T. Knez, 'Ein späthallstattzeitliches Fürstengrab von Novo mesto in Slowenien', *Germania 56*, 1978, 127, fig. 1: Römisch-Germanische Kommission.)

'elite' individuals in the two contexts, based upon the observed differences in their burial patterns?

Mechanisms and models

In trying to understand the nature of these changes which occurred in the Early Iron Age, I have examined a wide range of historically and ethnographically documented instances of interaction between societies. Patterns of human behaviour have regularities, as many anthropologists have demonstrated; cultures change in specific ways as a result of particular kinds of stimuli (Kroeber 1948; Barnett 1953). We have no reason to believe that human groups living in Iron Age Europe behaved substantially differently from those of the more recent past and present. Thus mechanisms of culture change which can be identified in apparently similar situations in more modern contexts are likely to shed light on processes of change in the past.

In examining well-documented cases of interaction between societies, I have looked particularly at the nature of interactions and the reasons for them; material components of the interactions (what was being traded); and effects of interaction on the societies involved. I have found, as others have, that regularities can be identified in both the mechanisms of interaction between societies and in the kinds of changes effected by those interactions. These regularities can be used to develop models for application to prehistoric contexts. Application of such models does not provide any 'right answer' to interpretation, but it does allow us to judge the archaeological evidence in terms of processes of change demonstrated in living societies. Such models have two important uses for our study of the past: first, they enable us to suggest a coherent explanation for changes apparent in the archaeological record; and second, they help point up other kinds of information which we can try to recover in future investigations.

Often in contact situations, such as those summarized above, societies reorganize their economic activities in order to produce larger quantities of goods sought by another society. This economic reorganization is stimulated by the desire to acquire luxury goods available through exchange. Reorganization of a community's economy brings a whole series of other changes along with it. Often, larger numbers of individuals devote more time and energy to producing goods for export, and larger communities develop for more efficient production. Since individuals generating trade goods need others to produce their basic necessities such as food, clothing, and shelter, these latter persons are also added to the ranks of the growing communities. Another direct result of these changes is the strengthening of authority, and increase in wealth and status, of those persons, usually community heads, who interact directly with the representatives (often merchants) of the other society. Since they occupy central roles in the coordinating of the economic system, their power and wealth increase as the economic system grows in productivity and the community grows in size (see Gall and Saxe 1977).

These general patterns of change identifiable in hundreds of contexts of contact and trade (e.g. Herskovits 1938; Foster 1962; Walker 1972) can be applied to the Early Iron Age contexts. In west-central Europe, the Greek demand for a variety of natural and partly-processed goods and Greek ability to offer attractive luxury products including Attic painted pottery, bronze vessels and wine, are likely to have stimulated central European communities to produce larger surplus quantities of the sought-after goods. Such economic reorientation can account for the development out of a background of isolated farmsteads and small hamlets of manufacturing and commercial centres such as the Heuneburg and Mont Lassois, shortly after 600 B.C. when Phocaean Greeks established their trading colony at Massalia. The Kappel and Vilsingen jugs and the Grächwil hydria may well represent the early stages of interaction between Greek merchants and leaders of small central European communities. These leaders may have encouraged the members of their communities to produce greater quantities of goods for trade to Greek merchants, and in so doing begun a process leading to the development of larger centres for collection and production. The appearance of the rich graves can be viewed in terms of increase in the wealth, status, and power of the heads of these producing communities. In the course of the sixth century B.C. some of these communities grew to a size of several hundred persons and the craftsmen and merchants at them were generating substantial quantities of goods for export. The status, wealth, and power of the community leaders grew along with growth in the economic activity.

The same general kinds of changes are apparent in Lower Carniola and neighbouring regions of south-east Alpine Europe. There, centres of production developed, beginning in the eighth century B.C., probably particularly for the smelting and forging of iron for trade to groups in Italy. The principal difference between the results of the changes brought about by such economic reorganization in west-central Europe and in Lower Carniola is in the character of the social differentiation of the elites apparent in the burial patterns. (We are considering here only the emergence of elites, and not changes in status and wealth among other groups in the societies.) How can we account for these differences?

One important factor worthy of consideration and further examination is that of the natural and cultural geography of the interactions in each case. (I shall offer a hypothesis along these lines for future testing as more data become available from Lower Carniola.) West-central Europe is a considerable distance from the Greek port of Massalia, very roughly some 600km. Goods had to be transported over this distance, and through territories occupied by many other groups (on these groups, see Arcelin 1976; Millotte 1976; Nicolas 1976). Considerable manpower and organization were probably required to carry out successful commercial expeditions. For bulk goods, such as most of the export items from west-central Europe probably were, individual entrepreneurs might have had difficulty making the journey with any substantial quantities, and they would have faced the possibility of attack and plunder by local groups in the lands through which they were passing. Much more likely would have been highly organized and relatively large-scale expeditions set up by the principal individuals at the growing communities of central Europe; such expeditions would have been supported by the political power and military force needed to secure safe passage of goods to the Mediterranean coast. The organization and investment required to launch such expeditions meant that the individual or group sponsoring them could gain an effective monopoly on the trade, thus controlling both the flow of goods out of and into the central European communities and the internal distribution of the Mediterranean goods obtained in exchange. By controlling the distribution of imported luxury products in his own society, a potentate could control the production of goods for export as well (Wells 1980:97–9).

In the case of south-east Alpine Europe, the proximity of the two interacting societies in Lower Carniola and north-east Italy would have lessened the likelihood that such monopolies would develop. No foreign culture-area intervened between Lower Carniola and the Este region of north-east Italy, and no substantial centres of population or of political power are apparent between them. It is less likely that small-scale trading expeditions would have had difficulties in this context. Thus monopolies in the control of a few politically and militarily powerful individuals would not be as likely to have developed here.

This model of different organizational requirements for trading expeditions in the two regions would also help explain why many more centres of population and economic activity developed in Lower Carniola than in west-central Europe, relative to the sizes of the areas involved. In west-central Europe, the leading individuals at the centres who controlled the trade extended their influence far into the countryside, drawing resources from outlying settlements for trade south to the Mediterranean (Frankenstein and Rowlands 1978; Wells 1980:93 fig. 4.3). With extensive territories bound up in the commercial system operating at single centres, new centres could not easily develop within these regions (not to mention probable political and military intervention if any should try). In Lower Carniola such large-scale and centralized control of the trade did not develop and the result was the growth of a whole series of centres, each apparently carrying on its own activities of collection and production for trade to north-east Italy (Gabrovec *et al.* 1970:13 fig. 1).

Thus it may have been largely a result of different conditions of natural and especially cultural geography that the elites which emerged in each case expressed their eliteness to very different degrees. In west-central Europe, the advantage of organizing large-scale, protected expeditions would have favoured the emergence of individuals able to organize the manpower to outfit such ventures. If the trade systems developing during the sixth century B.C. were as important in the cultural changes as I believe (see also Renfrew 1975), those individuals organizing the trade would have acquired considerable prestige, status, and power. This exceptional status is reflected in their graves: at the centres of large tumuli, surrounded by those of other members of their communities, often in well-crafted wooden chambers, and accompanied by a series of burial goods of both local and foreign manufacture, at least some of which were unavailable to most members of the society.

In Lower Carniola the situation was different. The distance to north-east Italy and Este and, later, to Adria and Spina, was much less than that between west-central Europe and Massalia. More importantly, the peoples of Lower Carniola and the Venetic region had in common a great deal of material culture, and probably non-material as well, and they were not separated by other cultural groups. The close connections between the peoples of the two regions is apparent in many different kinds of objects, including those bearing situla art (Frey 1966; 1969; Peroni 1973; Guidi 1977; see Clarke 1968:306 fig. 58). Thus merchants did not have as far to transport goods, and the passage was probably much safer than in the other situation. Hence the natural and cultural geographical circumstances of the trade did not favour the emergence of powerful individuals to the same extent that it did in the other context. The trade still played an important part in cultural changes. Centres of commerce, industry and population developed from the eighth century B.C. onwards where none had existed before. Social differentiation is much more apparent in the graves from the eighth century B.C. on than before that time. But the individuals buried in the richest graves are not distinguished by separate locations at the centres of tumuli, nor by the elaborate burial chambers, nor by large numbers of imported luxury goods, nor even by local luxury products which are restricted to them.

The impression one gets from considering only these factors of elite burial discussed here is that the emerging high-status individuals in Lower Carniola remained much closer in status and wealth to the other members of their communities than did their counterparts in west-central Europe. As the database grows, it will be interesting to compare the burial patterns of the other individuals in communities in west-central Europe and Lower Carniola, to see whether changes which occurred among the rest of the societies paralleled those experienced by the new elite individuals.

I reiterate that the interpretation of the evidence offered here is a tentative one, pending both new discoveries and new analyses of materials already in museums. I expect it to be substantially refined and revised, and offer it here principally as a stimulus to further study of the patterns of change in these two dynamic regions of Early Iron Age Europe.

Bibliography

Arcelin, P., 1976. 'Les Civilisations de l'Âge du Fer en Provence'. In J. Guilaine (ed.), *La Préhistoire française* (Paris), II: 657–75.

Aurigemma, S., 1960. *La necropoli di Spina in Valle Trebba* (Rome).

Barnett, H. G., 1953. *Innovation: the Basis of Cultural Change* (New York).

Biel, Jörg, 1978. 'Das frühkeltische Fürstengrab von Eberdingen-Hochdorf, Landkreis Ludwigsburg', *Denkmalpflege in Baden-Württemberg 7:* 168–75.

Bohnsack, D., 1976. 'Bernstein und Bernsteinhandel'. In J. Hoops (ed.), *Reallexikon der germanischen Altertumskunde* (Berlin, 2nd edn), II: 290–2.

Champion, S., 1976. 'Coral in Europe: commerce and Celtic ornament'. In P-M. Duval and C. Hawkes (eds.), *Celtic Art in Ancient Europe:* 29–37.

Clarke, David L., 1968. *Analytical Archaeology.*

Clavel-Lévêque, M., 1974. 'Das griechische Marseille: Entwicklungs-stufen und

Dynamik einer Handelsmacht'. In E. C. Welskopf (ed.), *Hellenische Poleis* (Berlin), II: 855–969.
Dobiat, C., 1980. *Das hallstattzeitliche Gräberfeld von Kleinklein und seine Keramik* (Graz).
Foster, G. M., 1962. *Traditional Cultures and the Impact of Technological Change.*
Frankenstein, S. and Rowlands, M. J., 1978. 'The internal structure and regional context of Early Iron Age society in southwestern Germany', *Bull. Inst. Archaeol. Univ. London 15:* 73–112.
Frey, O-H., 1966. 'Der Ostalpenraum und die antike Welt in der frühen Eisenzeit', *Germania 44:* 48–66.
Frey, O-H., 1969. *Die Entstehung der Situlenkunst* (Berlin).
Frey, O-H., 1970. 'Figürlich verzierte Bronzeblecharbeiten aus Hallstatt und dem Südostalpengebeit'. In *Krieger und Salzherren* (Mainz): 82–95.
Frey, O-H., 1974. 'Bericht über die Ausgrabungen im Ringwall von Stična (Slowenien)'. In *Symposium zu Problemen der jungeren Hallstattzeit in Mitteleuropa* (Bratislava): 151–62.
Frey, O-H. and Gabrovec, S., 1971. 'Zur Chronologie der Hallstattzeit im Ostalpenraum'. In *Actes du VIIIe Congrès International des Sciences Préhistoriques et Protohistoriques* (Belgrade), I: 193–218.
Gabrovec, S., 1960. 'Grob z oklepom iz Novega mesta' [Panzergrab von Novo mesto], *Situla 1:* 27–79.
Gabrovec, S., 1966. 'Zur Hallstattzeit in Slowenien', *Germania 44:* 1–48.
Gabrovec, S., 1968. 'Grob s trinožnikom iz Novega mesta' [Das Dreifussgrab aus Novo mesto], *Arheološki Vestnik 19:* 157–88.
Gabrovec, S., 1973. 'Začetek halštatskega obdobje v Sloveniji' [Der Beginn der Hallstattzeit in Slowenien], *Arheološki Vestnik 24:* 338–5.
Gabrovec, S., 1974. 'Die Ausgrabungen in Stična und ihre Bedeutung für die südostalpine Hallstattkultur'. In *Symposium zu Problemen der jüngeren Hallstattzeit in Mitteleuropa* (Bratislava): 163–87.
Gabrovec, S., Frey, O-H. and Foltiny, S., 1970. 'Erster Vorbericht über die Ausgrabungen im Ringwall von Stična (Slowenien)', *Germania 48:* 12–33.
Gall, P. L. and Saxe, A. A., 1977. 'The ecological evolution of culture'. In T. K. Earle and J. E. Ericson (eds.), *Exchange Systems in Prehistory* (New York): 255–68.
Guidi, A., 1977. 'Precedenti della koinè adriatica nei rapporti tra l'area atestina e la Slovenia nell'VII e nel VIII secolo a.C.', *Rivista dell'Istituto di Studi Abruzzesi 15:* 1 23.
Haevernick, T. E., 1974. 'Zu den Glasperlen in Slowenien', *Situla 14–15:* 61–5.
Hensel, W., 1970. 'Remarques sur les origines des villes en Europe centrale'. In *Atti del convegno di studi sulla città etrusca e italica preromana* (Bologna) I: 323–8.
Herskovits, M. J., 1938. *Acculturation: The Study of Culture Contact* (New York).
Hundt, H.-J., 1969. 'Über vorgeschichtliche Seidenfunde', *Jahrbuch RGZM 16:* 59–71.
Jankuhn, H., 1969. *Vor- und Frühgeschichte vom Neolithikum bis zur Völkerwanderungszeit* (Stuttgart).
Joffroy, R., 1954. *Le Trésor de Vix* (*Côte-d'Or*) (Paris).
Kastelic, J., 1965. *Situla Art* (New York).
Kimmig, W., 1968. *Die Heuneburg an der oberen Donau* (Stuttgart).
Kimmig, W., 1969. 'Zum Problem späthallstättischer Adelssitze'. In *Siedlung, Burg und Stadt* (Berlin): 96–113.
Kimmig, W., 1974. 'Zum Fragment eines Este-Gefässes von der Heuneburg an der oberen Donau', *Hamburger Beiträge zur Archäol. 4:* 33–102.
Kimmig, W., 1975. 'Die Heuneburg an der oberen Donau'. In *Ausgrabungen in Deutschland 1950–1975* (Mainz), I: 192–211.
Kimmig, W. and Rest, W., 1954. 'Ein Fürstengrab der späten Hallstattzeit von Kappel am Rhein', *Jahrbuch RGZM 1:* 179–216.

Knez, T., 1966. 'Žarno grobišče v Novem mestu' [Das Urnengräberfeld in Novo mesto], *Arheološki Vestnik 17:* 51–101.
Knez, T., 1974. 'Halštatski zlati diadem iz Novega mesta' [Ein hallstattzeitliches Golddiadem aus Novo mesto], *Situla 14–15:* 115–18.
Knez, T., 1978. 'Ein späthallstattzeitliches Fürstengrab von Novo mesto in Slowenien', *Germania 56:* 125–49.
Kossack, G., 1959. *Südbayern während der Hallstattzeit* (Berlin).
Kossack, G., 1972. 'Hallstattzeit'. In O. Kunkel (ed.), *Vor- und frühgeschichtliche Archäologie in Bayern* (Munich): 85–100.
Kroeber, A., 1948. *Anthropology* (New York).
Millotte, J., 1976. 'Les Civilisations de l'Âge du Fer dans le Jura'. In J. Guilaine (ed.), *La Préhistoire française* (Paris), II: 724–33.
Moosleitner, F., 1977. 'Hallstattzeitliche Grabfunde aus Uttendorf im Pinzgau (Österreich)', *Arch. Korr. 7:* 115–19.
Müller-Karpe, H., 1952. 'Das Kriegergrab von Villach'. In *Festschrift R. Egger* (Klagenfurt), I: 104–13.
Müllner, A., 1908. *Geschichte des Eisens in Innerösterreich von der Urzeit bis zum Anfang des XIX Jahrhunderts* pt I: *Krain, Küstenland und Istrien* (Vienna).
Muhly, J. D., 1973. *Copper and Tin* (New Haven).
Neustupný, J., 1970. 'Essai d'explication de la fonction des stations préhistoriques fortifées en Europe centrale'. In *Atti del convegno di studi sulla città etrusca e italica preromana* (Bologna), I: 339–43.
Nicolas, A., 1976. 'Les Civilisations de l'Âge du Fer dans le sillon rhodanien'. In J. Guilaine (ed.), *La Préhistoire française* (Paris), II: 699–707.
Paret, O., 1942. 'Der Goldreichtum im hallstättischen Südwestdeutschland', *Jahrbuch für prähistorische und ethnografische Kunst* (Leipzig/Berlin), *15–16:* 76–85.
Pauli, L. (ed.), 1980. *Die Kelten in Mitteleuropa* (Salzburg).
Peroni, R., 1973. *Studi di cronologia hallstattiana* (Rome).
Peroni, R., 1979. 'From Bronze Age to Iron Age: economic, historical, and social considerations'. In D. and F. R. Ridgway (eds.), *Italy Before the Romans:* 7–30.
Puš, I., 1971. *Žarnogrobiščna nekropola na dvorišču SAZU v Ljubljani* (Nekropole der Urnenfelderkultur im Hof der Slowenischen Akademie der Wissenschaften und Künste in Ljubljana) (Ljubljana).
Reim, H., 1981. 'Handwerk und Technik'. In K. Bittel, W. Kimmig and S. Schiek (eds.), *Die Kelten in Baden-Württemberg* (Stuttgart): 204–27.
Renfrew, C., 1975. 'Trade as action at a distance: questions of integration and communication'. In J. A. Sabloff and C. C. Lamberg-Karlovsky (eds.), *Ancient Civilisation and Trade* (Albuquerque): 3–59.
Riek, G., 1962. *Der Hohmichele* (Berlin).
Rieth, A., 1942. *Die Eisentechnik der Hallstattzeit* (Leipzig).
Röder, J., 1970. 'Die Steintechnik der Stele'. In H. Zürn, *Hallstattforschungen in Nordwürttemberg* (Stuttgart): 69–72.
Šašel, J., 1977. 'Strabo, Ocra and archaeology'. In V. Markotic (ed.), *Ancient Europe and the Mediterranean:* 157–60.
Schiek, S., 1954. 'Das Hallstattgrab von Vilsingen'. In *Festschrift für Peter Goessler* (Stuttgart): 150–67.
Schiek, S., 1981. 'Bestattungsbräuche'. In K. Bittel, W. Kimmig and S. Schiek (eds.), *Die Kelten in Baden-Württemberg* (Stuttgart): 118–37.
Schmid, W., 1933. 'Die Fürstengräber von Klein Glein in Steiermark', *Praehistorische Zeitschrift 24:* 219–82.
Spindler, K., 1975. 'Grabfunde der Hallstattzeit vom Magdalenenberg bei Villingen im Schwarzwald'. In *Ausgrabungen in Deutschland 1950–1975* (Mainz), I: 221–42.
Starè, F., 1975a. *Etruscani in jugovzhodni predalpski prostor* [Die Etrusker und der südöstliche Voralpenraum] (Ljubljana).
Starè, F., 1975b. *Dobova* (Posavski Muzei, Brezice).

Wackernagel, H. G., 1930. 'Massalia'. In *Paulys Real-Encyclopädie der classischen Altertumswissenschaft* (Stuttgart), XXVIII: 2130–52.
Walker, D. E. (ed.), 1972. *The Emergent Native Americans: A Reader in Culture Contact* (Boston).
Wells, P. S., 1980. *Culture Contact and Culture Change: Early Iron Age Central Europe and the Mediterranean World.*
Wells, P. S., 1981. *The Emergence of an Iron Age Economy: The Mecklenburg Grave Groups from Hallstatt and Stična* (Cambridge, Mass.).
Wells, P. S. and Bonfante, L., 1979. 'West-central Europe and the Mediterranean: the decline in trade in the fifth century B.C.', *Expedition 21:* 18–24.
Zürn, H., 1970. *Hallstattforschungen in Nordwürttemberg,* Veröffentlichungen des staatlichen Amtes für Denkmalpflege Stuttgart, Reihe A, 16 (Stuttgart).

5

Roman material in barbarian society c.200 B.C.–c.A.D. 400

Michael G. Fulford

Introduction

The occurrence of Roman artefacts in regions that were not directly subject to the Roman state has long been a source of fascination. Since much of the material can be more closely dated than the native assemblages amongst which it is found, its potential for constructing chronologies of the indigenous material cultures discovered beyond the empire has long been appreciated. The methodical study of material towards that end has been tempered by various attempts to understand the mechanisms which brought the imported objects to their often remote destinations as well as the role that they played in the receiving society. To account for the movement of this material numerous explanations have been offered. These include such agencies as commercial trade, diplomacy, raiding, the return of mercenaries or auxiliaries, individual adventuring, and so on. The difficulties of interpreting distributions of Roman imports has been realized by many, notably Eggers (1951:72–7) and Wheeler in his classic synthesis *Rome Beyond the Imperial Frontiers* (1954) which adopted James Curle's notion of 'drift' (1932a) as a way of accounting for the trickle of imports from the Roman Empire to the barbarian world. Despite its vagueness – for it does not explain at all – this idea has continued to find acceptance with others (e.g. Robertson 1970) because it seems to embody a number of transfer-mechanisms other than commercial trade which could account for the relatively low volume of artefacts discovered. Wheeler did not consider commercial trade to have played a dominant role. However, archaeology has not yet developed the methodology for distinguishing in the material record the residues that might have resulted from the fruits of diplomacy rather than a barbarian raid; nor can a clear dividing line be drawn between the characterization of material residues as the result of commercial trade as opposed to any of a range of non-market systems. Understandably the date of the objects has led to the explanations that fit best with the scant historical record; considerations of the context of the imported material within the native society have tended to be overlooked. Thus, for example, the famous Hoby burial with its rich panoply of Roman imports has been widely interpreted as the grave of a chieftain in receipt of diplomatic gifts from the emperor Augustus (Wheeler 1954:38; Thompson 1965:53–4). Such an explanation is accommodated by the record of Tacitus who informs us of 'silver vessels which have been given to their [i.e. German] envoys and chiefs' (*Germania* 5). The presence of Roman imports in groups of richly furnished graves dated to the late third-early fourth century has been explained as the fruits of barbarian raiding, a persistent phenomenon of this period (Todd 1977:41–2). Only recently, and in the context of Mediterranean imports to Europe prior to Roman annexation, has any attempt been made to examine the relationship of such material to all the available evidence of settlement, burial and material culture of the receiving societies. Thus, on the one hand, following Frankenstein and Rowlands (1978), Wells (1980) has sought to explain the presence of Greek imports in southern Germany in settlements and burials in the later sixth century B.C. as the result of a complex exchange system linking that region with the Greek colony at Massilia; on the other hand, the presence of Etruscan bronzes, found only in burials, in the Saarland in the Early La Tène period, is explained in the context of mercenaries returning from service in Italy. But for the record of classical historians that Celtic mercenaries served in the Mediterranean (Griffith 1935) such a narrow interpretation of the material might not have been offered. The fact that the imports were of limited variety and were recorded only from burials favoured this interpretation (Wells 1980:136–7).

Whereas the pre-Roman imports of a Mediterranean origin in central Europe have now been considered in detail and in the context of the associated indigenous material as well, from both burials and settlement alike, the same kind of detailed treatment has not been given to Roman material beyond the frontiers between 200 B.C. and 400 A.D., largely because of the enormous quantity of finds and huge areas concerned. Nevertheless progress has been made in certain directions. Thus recently, Haselgrove (1976) and Nash (1976; 1978a), for example, have been concerned with the impact of Roman material on barbarian society in Britain and Gaul. They have tentatively explored the relationship of imported material with the development of social organization and urbanization. The Roman historian has also been interested in the extent of the material contact between Rome and barbarian society with a view to assessing the extent to which commercial interest influenced Roman foreign policy. There has, for example, been discussion over the extent to which the Claudian conquest of Britain was motivated by material interests (cf. Frere 1967:59; Webster 1980:84–5). Certainly even a superficial study of the material shows how substantial was the increase in trade to Britain after A.D. 43, only a fraction of which can be explained in terms of the supply of the invading army and administrators.

In general, Roman contact with barbarian societies is associated with the objects found in Europe beyond the frontier as established by Augustus. The monumental scholarship of Eggers (1951) has been the foundation of all recent study of the phenomenon. It has allowed for both the more detailed examination of smaller areas (e.g. Majewski 1960; Sakař 1970), and has allowed for the search for underlying trends and explanations (e.g. Hedeager 1977). Through a quantitative survey Hedeager has drawn attention to the phenomenon whereby certain classes of artefact, notably the more valuable items, tend to increase with distance from the frontier. She has also begun to analyse the impact of such goods in the later Iron Age society of Denmark (1980).

The study of Roman material has been hindered up to now in a number of respects. Firstly, an artificial barrier has been imposed between the study of material from those areas that were eventually incorporated within the empire and of that from areas beyond the mature frontier of Augustus and later. In order to appreciate the significance of Roman material at a regional level we must surely examine how Roman material behaves in the archaeological record across as wide a range of contexts in societies which shared between them independence from direct Roman control. Secondly, it is important that we should examine what happens to similar Roman artefacts *within* the Roman frontier in order to have a reference point for the exported material. Apart from providing evidence of date, consideration of Roman contexts is of vital importance to the discussion of the social and economic implications of Roman material beyond the empire. Finally, in an effort to broaden the enquiry, we should not omit to make comparisons between areas outside the frontier. The British and Irish evidence, for example, has been considered in isolation and needs to be reviewed in the light of what is understood of the continental material. The scope of this paper is, then, deliberately broad, in order that those issues which tend to be overlooked, when the geographical or chronological constraints are restricted, can be more fully discussed.

Before considering barbarian societies in receipt of Roman goods, whether subsequently annexed or not, it is worth reviewing the problems of recognizing the reciprocal movement of goods from barbarian societies into the Roman world, a factor which very much colours our view of the way in which Roman material travelled beyond the frontiers. Roman objects of trade are predominantly manufactured articles, such as personal jewellery or items connected with eating and drinking. Apart from clothing and wine which was often carried in amphorae, perishables or raw materials were seldom passed to barbarian societies, though the case of the restriction in trade with the Visigoths in the fourth century is surely rightly interpreted as interfering with food supplies and may not be unusual (Thompson 1966:14–20; Todd 1975:41). On the other hand, perishables or raw materials which are difficult to trace in the archaeological record were passed from barbarian societies into the Roman world (cf. Wild 1976:61). The trade in manufactured goods, though evidenced, appears to have been less widespread. In fact literary sources provide us with our best indication of the barbarian contribution. The example of Strabo's description of Britain's exports in the late first century B.C. will suffice. He lists grain, cattle, gold, silver, iron, hides, slaves and hounds (*Geography* iv.5,2). Typically for an ancient author no quantities are given. The remark of Strabo draws our attention to the problem of recognizing such exports in the archaeological record. Although metals do, of course, survive, there are enormous practical problems (of which the re-use of metal of varied origins is the best known) in determining their point of production. Thus, in any interpretation of Roman material and how it reached its destination, we must be aware of the near-invisibility of reciprocal exchanges where these might have existed. Only when pottery or metalwork was imported into the empire can we begin to recognize the presence of the native contribution to exchange.

As a starting date I have taken c.200 B.C., for it is from about this time that we can begin to recognize the presence of material in barbarian societies that may legitimately be described as Roman (by which is meant goods that either originated from the estates of Roman landowners or that were handled by Roman *mercatores* or *negotiatores*). From the beginning of the second century B.C. we may note, for example, the export of Italian wine (Dressel 1A) and table wares (Campanian A) as well as metalwork, much of it from Campanian estates and workshops.

The development of this trade in late Republican Italy after the end of the Second Punic War can be seen against the background of the growth in large slave-run estates in Italy (financed by the plunder of war) and the extrusion of local populations to Rome and overseas colonies, a process which Hopkins has recently brilliantly described (1978). The enlarged estates then proceeded to supply the expanding population of Rome and the new colonies with various goods, such as wine, and these also reached the barbarian world. It is reasonable to suppose that in gross terms the barbarian market was the least rewarding. Where organized trade was involved beyond the frontier, specific commodities such as Norican iron or Baltic amber were the objectives (Alföldy 1974:45–7; Pliny, *Natural History,* xxxvi.46).

It may seem curious that the first evidence of substantial long-distance trade should appear so late in the development of the Roman state. Partly this is a question of definition, i.e. when trade is Roman rather than south Italian or Etruscan, and partly it is a question of recognition. Much work needs to be done on Mediterranean assemblages of the fourth–second centuries B.C. in order to define the characteristics of, say, the amphorae and the tableware of that time, for during this period the city of Rome had already become dependent on the importation of corn from Sardinia and Sicily; thus important long-distance links of a particular kind did exist before the beginning of the second century B.C., if only between the city of Rome (and its supply ports) and the rest of the Mediterranean.

Roman trade with European societies later to become provinces

From c.200 B.C. we find Dressel 1A amphorae (as evidence of trade in wine), black-glazed pottery and metalwork among barbarian societies outside Rome's direct political control. In the case of Gaul we find a considerable degree of similarity with the distribution of earlier Greek and Etruscan imports, with the greatest number of finds occurring in the south and centre, particularly up the Rhône valley (Peacock 1971:fig. 36; Nash 1976: figs 8–9). We may suppose that Roman traders, whose presence is later documented by Caesar (e.g. *Gallic Wars* i.39; iv.2–3), were following old-established routes as well as perhaps being involved in existing exchange networks. This implies a considerable and perhaps unwarranted degree of continuity, although the character of the goods reaching barbarian societies continued to consist most notably of wine and a variety of feasting and drinking equipment, of metal, glass and pottery. Both in the sixth–fifth centuries B.C. and the later Republican period ceramics, notably amphorae and tableware, account for the majority of the finds.

Stratified examples are rare in the late Republican period and even where they are recorded, quantities are seldom noted (cf. Nash 1978b:329–35). An absence of conspicuous typological features, regarding amphorae in particular, combines with the lack of quantified data to frustrate a study of the pattern of importation over relatively short periods of time. Thus, in the case of Dressel 1 amphorae the distribution spans about two centuries. Although there is a typological change about the mid-first century B.C., the majority of finds are undistinguished body sherds. Without rims it is difficult to distinguish with confidence between pre- and post-Caesarian, let alone between late second- and early first-century B.C. examples.

Since many scholars believe that the access to Mediterranean trade had important consequences for the receiving society, to measure the changing rate of importation is of great importance. As Nash has written about pre-Caesarian Gaul, 'the additional, sudden and effectively unlimited availability of Mediterranean feasting wares from the mid-second century was [critical to society]' (1976:128). Leaving aside the question of whether the units of production were capable of unlimited expansion, it is extremely doubtful whether we could recognize in the archaeological record either sudden or dramatic changes in the pattern of importation. Nor is it certain that we have the means to even compare assemblages by the half-century (i.e. about two generations). The availability of imported goods becomes critical, Nash argues, when combined with mercenary redundancy following the Roman supremacy in the western Mediterranean – Gauls had been recruited to serve in the eastern Mediterranean and Sicily (Griffith 1935) – population increase (as measured by the increase in the number and size of settlements) and the emphasis on Celtic warrior achievement (deduced from her phase 2 Gallic coinage which she interprets as representing an increase in warrior payments) (Nash 1976:125–9). Following Terray (1974), she sees the advent of large-scale foreign trade resulting in major political change among the receiving societies, as ruling groups were forced to obtain more and more surplus from their subjects and enemies so as to attract trade and exchange with foreigners. The result was the establishment of strong coercive governments. In Central Gaul Nash argues for a sophisticated system of government comparable to that of archaic Greece and Italy. Arguments such as this rest on the assumption that imports suddenly became available in large quantities and that there was an awareness in contemporary society that such luxuries were indeed available in unlimited quantities. It is extremely doubtful whether in the pre-Caesarian period this was so, for one cannot envisage so rapid a transformation of Roman society and agriculture that would produce either the goods for trade or the means (traders, ships, etc.) by which they could reach Gaul. Gradual change following Roman supremacy in the western Mediterranean seems more reasonable, but in order to clarify that vital issue, it can all too readily be appreciated how urgent the necessity is of quantifying imports within as tight a chronological framework as possible.

If we look beyond Gaul we find that the impact of Rome on its European neighbours differed from region to region. In Noricum, for example, we find that Rome's relations were focussed on individual leaders such as Catmelus (from 178 B.C.) or his brother (?) Cincibilis (from 170 B.C.) who was described by Livy as *Rex Gallorum* (Alföldy 1974:31–2, 17–23). The development of these ties appears to have preceded the main influx of Roman goods, although, as we are informed, they were blessed by the exchange of rich gifts (Livy xliii.5, 8; xliv.4, 2). Central to the growth of contact between Rome and Noricum is the key site of the Magdalensberg with its attendant settlement of Roman traders. This site seems to have been the main point of contact between Romans and Noricans and it is our chief source for the nature of that relationship. The Augustan and Tiberian graffiti from the site suggest that goods for exchange were drawn from throughout the *Regnum Noricum* and may reflect a long-established organization (Alföldy 1974:73). The kingdom included at least the southern part of what later became the Roman province. The Romans applied the term *regnum* to *Noricum*, but it is not quite clear what precisely is meant by this. The native Norican coinage does not imply a single overlord, rather a number of *reguli* or princes, perhaps linked together in some federal arrangement whose centre lay at the Magdalensberg (Alföldy 1974:42–4; Mackensen 1975). Thus, in contrast to central Gaul where a kind of oligarchic rule emerged in the period leading up to Caesar's invasion, in Noricum, as in Britain and Dacia, a form of kingship developed. Altogether the evidence points to stable relations between Rome and the barbarian kingdom of Noricum; indeed it is difficult to recognize when it was subsumed into the empire.

Dacia provides a further point of comparison. Like Gaul she experienced a wide range of contacts with the Mediterranean – in this case the Greek world – from the fifth century B.C. when tableware pottery, wine-carrying amphorae and metalwork began to be imported (Glodariu 1976). The volume of trade in these luxury goods appears to increase from the late third century B.C., just as in Gaul. At this point luxuries of an Italian origin appear among the predominantly east Mediterranean imports. Once more the question arises, as it has done in the case of Gaul, whether the increase in importation was sufficient to promote social changes of the kind that have been suggested for Gaul.

In the first half of the first century B.C. a powerful, uniting leader, one Burebista, rose to prominence. Whether competition for Rome's trade was a factor in his emergence cannot be decided on present evidence. However, during his reign, Dacia (within the Carpathian ring) received what, superficially, seems wealth unparalleled for a barbarian European society from Italy and the east Mediterranean world. It has been estimated that about 25,000 denarii have been found in hoards in what approximates for ancient Dacia (Crawford 1977). This excludes other varieties of coin, such as the issues of Apollonia and Dyrrachium, which also reached Dacia. We should, however, be cautious about interpreting this phenomenon which, on such a scale, is unique to Dacia. We should consider very carefully whether the hoards do in fact point to unparalleled importation of silver, or whether they denote the results of unusual internal tensions within Dacian society. The closing dates of the hoards in question range from 80 B.C. to some time after Burebista's death in 44 B.C. Crawford (1977) suggested that the coinage represented payment for slaves after the traditional east Mediterranean sources had dried up following Pompey's success against the pirates in 67 B.C. Yet slaves could, presumably, be obtained throughout barbarian Europe, although no other area has produced anything which compares with this number of hoards. No interpretation of the mechanisms which introduced the silver to Dacia can satisfactorily explain why it was *hoarded*, rather than recycled or paid out again. The deposition of many hoards may have been occasioned during Burebista's reign or the critical period that followed it. Such was his power that Caesar contemplated campaigning against him shortly before his death (Strabo, *Geography* vii.3, 5). Concealment of the coin, we might suppose, was precipitated before the opportunity arose to re-use the silver in Dacian coin, jewellery and further trade. We surely cannot suppose that the coin was destined for *hoarding* immediately on receipt by the Dacian nobility. We could reasonably suggest that silver coin reached other parts of barbarian Europe on a comparable scale to the supplies to Dacia and that it was recycled or circulated back to the Mediterranean world. Indeed the proliferation of native coinages in gold and silver in areas where the natural mineral resources did not exist could very well be evidence of a greater inflow of Mediterranean bullion and coin than the surviving examples might suggest. In Dacia, we could argue, peculiar circumstances prevailed during the reign of Burebista which prevented trade and the re-use of the coin. The significance of the hoards thus takes on a greater social than economic meaning. After Burebista's death and the break-up of his kingdom (Strabo, *Geography* vii.3, 12) imports continued to reach Dacia – once again principally amphorae, table wares and other luxury metalwork. However Glodariu's (1976) research does not suggest that the rate of importation was appreciably higher during the period which ended with Trajan's wars of conquest. As with the Gallic finds, Glodariu's tables illustrate the problems of quantifying classes of broadly dated artefacts.

With the examples of Gaul, Noricum and Dacia, all of which eventually formed part of the Roman empire, we can see points of contrast as well as similarity. The range of imports seems to have been the same in all three areas, with an emphasis on wine, table wares and other luxury metalwork and glass. In the case of Dacia our attention is caught by the coin hoards. Generally, however, it is the ceramic evidence which, because of its survival factor, is the most abundant. This can be seen in the case of the Mediterranean imports in Gaul and Dacia. In Noricum finds seem to be confined to the Magdalensberg and this appears to offer a marked contrast with the Gallic and Dacian picture. While it is true that finds of Campanian and pre-Augustan amphorae are rare outside the Magdalensberg, this may partly reflect a difference in the character of goods reaching Noricum. In any case amphorae are not common at the Magdalensberg and this raises the possibility that wine was imported in skins or casks (Stöckli 1979:186–90; Christlein 1964:16–19). In this case there is then no possibility of making a straightforward comparison between Roman trade into Noricum and that into Central Gaul. During the period of importation we find that the social response is varied. Whereas a form of kingship emerged in Noricum and Dacia, an oligarchic form of government developed in central Gaul. Interestingly, and a point urging caution, it is only from Gaul, through Caesar's account of the Gallic wars, that we actually have some detailed information about social organization. The picture that we have of Norican and Dacian organization may be over-simplified. Regardless of this, it is noticeable that all three areas saw the emergence of large nucleated settlements, sometimes described as *oppida*, and increased craft specialization.

The difficulty of dating imports closely renders the task of evaluating the dynamics of pre-conquest trade and its effect on the receiving societies particularly difficult. If we consider briefly the case of Britain and its trade with the Mediterranean in the period before A.D. 43 (Cunliffe 1978a), it is useful to contrast the imports into southern Britain (from Cornwall to west Sussex) from the end of the second century B.C. with those in south-east Britain – north and south of the Thames estuary – which date partly from c.50 B.C., but very largely from the middle of the reign of Augustus, when the emperor's interests were concentrated on the development of Gaul and the Rhine frontier. The scale of the trade, perhaps mainly on a Rhine–Thames axis, was considerably greater than that to the south, which still continued, despite the shift in emphasis to the south-east. Most of the trade to the south seems to have been confined to ports, such as Hengistbury Head (Cunliffe 1978b) and inland finds are scarce. During the whole period of contact from c.100 B.C.–A.D. 43, it is difficult to identify any changes in settlement or social organization in south-west and central southern England. The territory of the Durotriges in particular is often selected as an area of conservatism at the time of the Claudian conquest, yet it had been in receipt of long-distance trade for at least 150 years. In contrast to the south coast we find from the later first century B.C. to north and south of the Thames, princely burials furnished with imported goods. Large numbers of imports, mostly ceramic and thus of comparatively little value, reached major centres like Camulodunum and Verulamium as well as minor settlements like the recently published site of Skeleton Green, Puckeridge, Herts. (Partridge 1981). After c.20 B.C. native currency began to bear legends which identify kings, some of whom can be recognized in the literary evidence. Suetonius, for example, describes Cunobelin as *Rex Britannorum* (*Caligula*, xliv.2). The growth of large settlement in valley bottom locations has been seen by some to be a response to the increased contact with the continent after Caesar. An important question to ask of the British evidence is why the contrast between the south/south-west and the south-east developed. One possibility is that, from a very early date, the elite in the south-east managed (by greater powers of coercion, perhaps) to obtain more goods to trade with the Continent. Alternatively we may see this as the casual result of a greater interest in Britain on the part of those who found the Thames the most convenient means of access to Britain. Such an expansion may well have arisen as a result of the growth of activity along the Rhine from

16 B.C. and may well have become essential to the maintenance of the Rhine army. Those who look for developments in Britain argue for increased crop production following a change in the agricultural regime with an increased exploitation of the heavier soils and leading to a shift in the pattern of settlement (Bradley 1978:126–9; Jones 1981). Although it may never be possible to distinguish cause and effect, it is clear that from the period when trade is archaeologically visible, combined with the burial evidence for a competitive elite there is evidence of new centres of population and specialization. In those areas of the south-east where most long-distance contact is evidenced it is difficult to be certain of the shift of settlement and its date, because these areas lack the classic hill-fort development of the Wessex chalk and the Welsh Marches. In the latest pre-Roman Iron Age our attention is directed towards certain expanding settlements, controlled by an already existing elite merely briefly illuminated through a short-lived phase of rich burial. Thus there is a sharp contrast with south-west and central southern England where imports continued to arrive, but where no other important developments, apart from the emergence of local coinages, can be set beside those visible in the south-east. It may be that the volume of trade between the two areas was different, and that it is the *scale* of trade which is the crucial factor in the promotion of change in the south-east. Consideration of the *volume* of trade may prove to be important in the assessment of change in other areas in contact with the Mediterranean. Finally, it needs to be stressed that, apart from the rich burials, the evidence of the trade between Britain and the Continent in the later Iron Age is based on the survival of comparatively low-value artefacts such as pottery and brooches. The source of the precious metals in the tribal coinages can only be guessed at. On analogy with the earlier Gallo-Belgic imports, imported gold from the continent is likely to have formed an important component, but difficult to prove (cf. Todd 1981:33). The British evidence then compares well with that of northern Gaul with its contrast between the rich burials and the comparatively humdrum quality of the imports in settlements (Collis 1977). The example of Britain also serves to draw attention to the problem of variation in the quantities of imports and the uneven effect that this may have had on the native society. This is highlighted by what happens in Britain after A.D. 43, when there was an unequivocal expansion of imports, despite the exigencies of the military occupation. The archaeological record reveals more imports for the period A.D. 43–c.70/80 than for any succeeding period. Although the army and the administration were partly responsible for this inflow, they were by no means entirely responsible and we may surely envisage a degree of breakdown in native society to allow more than just the tribal elite access to Roman and Gallic merchants. Simply on the basis of an increase in the number of findspots we can hazard greater interaction between merchant and native British society. The post-conquest expansion needs to be kept in mind when considering the likely effects of earlier contacts.

5 Roman material in barbarian society c.200 B.C.–c.A.D. 400

Michael G. Fulford

Roman trade with European societies never incorporated within the Empire

A useful perspective on trade and exchange between the Roman state and the regions later to be incorporated within the Empire can be gained by looking at trade between those provinces and the areas which *never* came directly under Roman rule for any length of time. With regard to the character of objects exported from the Roman world and the archaeological record, it is important to remind ourselves of the evidence of the provinces-to-be. From both Gaul and Britain, the bulk of our evidence consists of relatively low value artefacts, pottery sherds, fibulae, etc. There are higher value goods as well, such as bronze eating and drinking wares, but these are usually found in burials. Settlement finds far outnumber those from burials.

From beyond the Roman frontier when it was established along the Rhine and Danube, we have evidence of considerable numbers of Roman imports. The classic study of this remains Eggers' superb work (1951). More detailed regional surveys have followed, but Eggers' study remains the only survey for most of Europe. The main conclusions show that up to about 200km, and usually much less, from the Limes, there were finds of pottery, brooches and other relatively mundane items (such as querns and low-value bronze coins). These finds are explained in terms of short-distance trade ('buffer trade') with the Roman provinces. Beyond the 'buffer zone' are found more prestigious goods, such as bronzes, mostly vessels connected with eating and drinking, some precious metal, notably silver coin and glass ware. These finds extend up to 1000km from the frontier.

In the first century A.D. the source of the prestigious goods was mainly Italy and southern Gaul but, as provincial workshops developed, more and more objects originated from these. The prestigious items are found in graves or in hoards – often deposited in bogs – or as unassociated finds. In stark contrast the objects of the 'buffer trade' are usually found in settlements and their associated cemeteries. Altogether the range of finds from the 'buffer zone' is comparable to that from rural settlements *within* the Limes, although quantities may vary considerably. Hedeager (1977) has recently discussed the interesting phenomenon of the contrast between the generally low-value 'buffer zone' goods and the prestigious items found at greater distances from the frontier. She concluded that the rare presence of Roman luxury goods in graves within the 'buffer zone' implied different political conditions from the area beyond. She suggested that everyday Roman goods were exchanged on the fragments of the late Celtic social system, from which Roman influence had removed the upper echelons. Beyond the 'buffer zone' Roman luxury goods circulated at an elite level. Hedeager was puzzled by the fact that prestige goods seemed to increase rather than decrease with distance from the frontier, speculating on the kind of organization which could achieve this, while at the same time leaving the 'buffer zone' apparently without the luxuries which had, presumably, passed through its territory. An explanation for the lack of finds in the 'buffer zone' will be advanced below; but the apparent *increase* in finds with distance from the frontier may be deceptive. Hedeager assumes that the origin of all the imports were a number of points along the frontier system and makes no allowance, for example, for sea-voyages from the mouth of the Rhine to the Jutland peninsula and into the Baltic. Thus, rather than the Limes being the point of departure, harbours along the coastline from the Rhine to the eastern Baltic could have, in effect, served as the points of origin of the imports. Danzig bay, for example, shows a remarkable concentration of imports. Seaborne transport was much cheaper than carting goods by land and was clearly responsible for the distribution of the Westland cauldron (Eggers 1951:types 11–14, Karte 12). Knowledge of northern waters is implied by such works as Ptolemy's *Geography*.

To account for the lack of prestige objects in the 'buffer zone' we must turn to the provinces themselves. There we do not in general find material in a comparable state to that found beyond the 'buffer zone' outside the frontier. It is a curious irony that the catalogues of imports, such as the bronzes, form the basis for interpreting the all too common fragmentary remains from within the provinces. The rich central European finds often accompany burials, but the practice of furnishing graves becomes increasingly rare within the provinces. The persistence of the tradition of richly furnished burials may be noted in the provinces of Pannonia and Moesia which continued into the early third century (Möcsy 1974). Burials apart, one might have expected the towns and villas of the provinces to provide a rich array of the kind of objects which are found beyond the frontier, but this is not the case. Most finds are fragmentary. Silchester, a 40ha *civitas* capital, extensively excavated in the late nineteenth and early twentieth century, has produced only about five complete bronze vessels (Boon 1974). This pattern is paralleled at other major Roman sites in Britain, although none has been excavated to the same extent as Silchester. The paucity of finds from even substantial settlements does not, however, mean that metal vessels were rare. The hoard evidence from elsewhere in Britain suggests the reverse (Eggers 1966). Scarcity of finds may be explained by the fact that metal vessels, once discarded, were melted down and re-used. We can test this hypothesis by looking at Pompeii and Herculaneum where the entire artefact assemblage was preserved by the sudden disaster of A.D. 79. Bronzes, although far from being adequately catalogued, are fairly common. One example will suffice: in the study of Campanian bronze workshops Willers listed all known examples of makers' stamps. There were 36 examples of *one* particular bronze worker (P. Cibius Polybius). Of that number 25 per cent originated from Pompeii, while 50 per cent had been found beyond the Roman frontier (Willers 1907:85–91). Pompeii was a minor Italian town, but its assemblage of artefacts probably gives us a better idea of the *actual* assemblage of such an urban community, than the excavation of a settlement which had not been visited by any catastrophe which preserved its material assemblage. Such sites suggest that bronze and other metals were valued for their practical value and were constantly being recycled. Those societies which chose to bury their bronze vessels, etc. presumably esteemed these objects more for their social than their practical value.

It would be simplistic to divide barbarian societies between those that placed greater value on the material of Roman imports and those for whom the social value of the complete artefact was the greater. However, such an approach will help to explain the apparent anomaly of the 'buffer zone' where prestige goods are rare. Because of the presence of those goods beyond the 'buffer zone' it must be assumed that some at least passed through the border area by means of exchange transactions, etc. It would be stretching credibility too far to suppose that the people within the 'buffer zone' had no interest in such goods. What may reasonably be advanced is that similar processes operated in the 'buffer zone' as within the provinces themselves where, as we have seen, such prestige goods are rare as complete items. The problem still remains as to how we may gauge the impact of Rome beyond the frontier, in the awareness that the archaeological record of imports is likely to be flawed, reflecting different processes according to the degree of integration or interaction with the provinces themselves. It is surely more appropriate to consider the character of the whole material assemblage, including both Roman and native artefacts, on the assumption that, as far as re-usable materials are concerned, native objects of *re-used* Roman bronze are likely to be as important as intact Roman imports, which form only a minute proportion of the total (metal) goods exchanged.

Scotland may offer an illustration of this. Although it is difficult to isolate native from Roman, owing to the proximity of Roman forces in central and southern Scotland up to the early third century, it is generally true that objects that can be securely identified as imports are neither numerous, nor distinguished. From native settlements, therefore, the character of the Roman imports is of classic 'buffer zone' type with few rich finds. Richly furnished burials, typical of central Europe, are absent, but there are a number of hoard finds (Curle 1932b; Robertson 1970). However, to compensate for the lack of prestigious Roman goods in reliable native contexts, there is a distinguished native metalwork tradition whose floruit coincides with Roman occupation of Scotland, apparently fading out in the early third century. Distinguished metalwork of a prestigious kind can be isolated in the north-east, i.e. beyond the zone of direct military occupation, as well as in the lowlands, where were located workshops producing metalwork, such as the well-known button-and-loop fasteners and dragonesque brooches, which are also found in the lowland zone of southern Britain (Gillam 1958; Macgregor 1976; Stevenson 1966). It is of course a gross, but not unreasonable, assumption to see a connection between the metalwork tradition of Scotland in the first–second centuries A.D. and the general inflow of Roman goods. Conversely, it seems absurd to take the fragmentary evidence for Roman goods in Scotland completely at its face value. Consideration of the entire assemblage is essential.

Ireland, too, deserves reconsideration in this respect. Her Roman imports have been the subject of searching scrutiny and their presence has been seen more as a result of casual infiltration than regular contact (Bateson 1973; 1976; Warner 1976). Finds are interpreted as the debris of a few individuals, some perhaps auxiliaries who had served within the Roman army, rather than as the result of trade or loot. The number of finds is indeed small, especially when compared with Scotland, but given the latter's rich military occupation the comparison is not a fair one (cf. Mytum 1981). Ireland does share with Scotland a virtual absence of richly furnished burials. In the later Roman period, after the collapse of the Antonine frontier and the end of extensive campaigning in Scotland under Caracalla, there is a much greater degree of comparability between Ireland and Scotland. During this period there is not the same problem of distinguishing Roman from native as there was during the military occupation. In both countries in the later period, with the exception of the notable silver hoards in both areas, the material is mainly of low value goods, such as pottery, bronze coins and minor metalwork. Both countries can then be considered alongside other regions on the Continent outside the frontier which can be characterized by their Roman finds as part of the 'buffer zone'. Ireland, like Scotland, also supported flourishing traditions in metalwork, particularly bronze, during the Roman period. Some Irish objects certainly reached Britain (cf. Kilbride-Jones 1980). Once again, as with Scotland, we can only measure the impact of the proximity of the Roman Empire to Ireland by examining the development of settlement and material culture from before the Roman period and into the fifth century.

In assessing the impact of Rome on Ireland we should also not omit to compare the island with northern and western Britain generally, i.e. the area of the Roman province(s) outside the urbanized south-east. Fort sites excepted, finds of Roman material are not prolific, as a study of recent inventories and excavations shows (e.g. R.C.A.H.M., Anglesey, Caernarvonshire). Following Hopkins' (1980) suggestion that market trading was stimulated by the necessity of raising cash with which to pay tax, it has been suggested that in the non-urban regions taxes were raised in kind, thus obviating the need for markets where cash could be exchanged for produce (Fulford 1981). A system whereby taxation was raised in kind or as labour service could probably be paralleled in non-Roman Scotland and Ireland. Neither area has produced evidence of a native coinage which could have served a fiscal purpose. A common approach to exacting tribute or taxation may partly explain the low incidence of Roman finds in regions both inside and beyond the frontier. The comparison with western Britain once more serves to remind us of the dangers of interpreting Roman material beyond the frontier in isolation. One example illustrates the value to be gained by studying native sites in the context of their immediate neighbours within the frontier. Traprain Law – its silver hoard apart – stands out as a major site. Individually, the Roman imports seem of little importance, consisting of pottery, minor metalwork, etc. (Curle 1932b:354–62). Taking the assemblage as a whole, we find that Traprain has a remarkable collection which appears outstanding, in terms of the diversity and range of sources represented, in comparison with all native settlement (fort *vici* excluded) north of York.

Discussion

One of the major contrasts between societies in receipt of Roman goods beyond the mature frontiers of the empire and those receiving imports, but which were eventually incorporated within the empire, is the apparent stagnation of the former. Late Iron Age society in Gaul and Britain, as we have seen, is considered to have been in a state of rapid change. Part of the explanation for change, as evidenced by the growth of nucleated settlements, the development of coinage, the emergence of complex political organizations, etc., is laid at the door of the expanding Roman empire and the need to find essential resources in exchange for prestige goods from there. This may be an important factor, where the level of trade may have been the important trigger, but it has to be remembered that, over a period at least twice as long, no comparable development can be traced in barbarian Europe in the first–fourth centuries A.D. That there was social change east of the Rhine cannot be denied in the face of the literary evidence, so brilliantly expounded by Thompson (1965; 1966), but the overall developments in settlement and material culture cannot be compared with those of the late pre-Roman Iron Age in Britain, Dacia, Gaul, etc. That there were changes in the concentrations of Roman finds, from Bohemia in the early first century A.D. to Denmark and Scandinavia in the later Roman period, cannot be denied. In contrast those settlements in the 'buffer zone' where the evidence is best, such as the coastal region of Frisia and north Germany, while showing evidence of physical expansion and increasing craft specialization up to the fourth century A.D., do not show pronounced variation in the level of Roman contact as evidenced in the archaeological record from the first century A.D. (Todd 1975:95–133; Schmid 1978). Despite the length of time in which relations developed with the Roman provinces, there is no comparison with this region and either south-east Britain or central Gaul in the second–first centuries B.C. Thus if material contact does not seem as important a stimulant over four centuries to barbarian societies lying beyond the Limes, perhaps we should reconsider its role in the development of those societies that were assimilated into the Empire.

It may be that the overall volume of trade between the late Republic and the Empire of the second century A.D. had declined (cf. Hopkins 1980:105–6). Although it is difficult to quantify Roman material within close date ranges because of the variety of ways in which societies chose to eventually dispose of that material, Hedeager's study (1977) of Eggers' material does suggest that there was little difference in gross terms between the volume of Roman goods crossing the Limes in the early and late Empire. We must remember that Eggers' study concentrated on higher value goods and trends observed in this material may not be repeated with lower value artefacts. Indeed in Westphalia there does seem to have been a significant increase in minor Roman objects particularly in the fourth century in the settlements there (Beck 1970). Clearly we need a great deal more precise information on quantities of material. One of the assumptions of the late Republican trade to Gaul, Dacia, etc., is that it increased with time, although the nature of the material really militates against accurate quantification in close temporal units. Dacia has been studied in greater detail (Glodariu 1976). From the second/first century B.C. to the time of Trajan's conquest we can see increases in some classes of material, but as the evidence of silver coins so vividly demonstrates, not in all classes of material. Much more important is for us to consider developments in the entire material culture over the pre- and contact period. What is interesting about Dacia is that the period from Burebista (when the power of the Dacian kingdom seems to have been at its height) to the time of Decebalus is one when Dacia falls into some historical obscurity, yet it witnesses a measurable increase in imports (with the exception of coin). It will be interesting to compare this with the evidence of settlement from the mid-first century B.C. to the Roman conquest. Notwithstanding the increase in trade, the evidence for political organization up to the time of Decebalus does not hint at any development on the system of kingship established by the time of Burebista.

In seeking to broaden the discussion about Roman material found beyond the imperial frontier, I have attempted to include both these areas that received material before annexation and those that received imports but were never annexed. Attention has been paid to the way in which Roman artefacts appear in the archaeological record and how this varies inside and outside the frontier. One of the ways, for example, in which the finds from the provinces differ from finds well beyond the Limes, is in the comparative lack of rich grave furnishings, compensated by the rather undistinguished mass of material from settlements. It is interesting that the majority of the pre-annexation British, Gallic, Norican and Dacian finds are from settlements, stray finds and hoards. The practice of rich burial as evidenced by the North Gallic culture is not very widespread. Dacian coin-hoarding remains unexplained as perhaps a social, rather than a simple economic phenomenon.

Thus there is a greater degree of comparison among the areas that eventually became provinces than there is between these and the regions beyond the 'buffer zone'. It is most useful to see the 'buffer zone' along the frontier in the light of provincial finds where comparisons are closest; then the lack of rich burial finds becomes intelligible. We can at the same time gain insights in to the nature of the assimilation of Roman material culture in those areas within the empire, like much of northern and western Britain, where find densities compare with those in Ireland and Scotland.

The problem still remains as to why barbarian societies do not seem to have assimilated Roman material culture outside the mature Limes, to a comparable extent to their predecessors which were annexed. It is clear that in those areas the social value of imports retained a greater significance than did their practical value. The 'Celtic' world seems to have been more receptive to the absorption and integration of Roman culture. Increasing contact with the Celtic world has been demonstrated or suggested to an extent that is not visible in central Europe or Scandinavia in the first–fourth centuries A.D. It has been suggested that one of the objectives of the barbarian raids of the later Roman period was to take advantage of the comparative anarchy of the empire and seize more goods. Alternatively, the chaos of empire at certain times interrupted the supply of subsidies to barbarian tribes. Such is the relative crudeness with which we can date most Roman material – dating within a generation, whether manufacture or deposition, is virtually impossible unless there are very close historical constraints on the archaeological record (as with documented military campaigns) – that it is unrealistic to suppose that we will ever be in a position to generalize about the *immediate* causes lying behind some of the major barbarian movements. Long-term processes will be better understood by the integrated study of settlement and economy of societies beyond the Empire. It may be that central European barbarian societies did desire more material contact with the provinces, but were unable to produce goods of sufficient quantity or interest to the Roman world. Only the weakening of the frontier allowed an opportunity to exploit the riches of the Empire.

A broad study of this kind serves to highlight the problem of how far the exchange of material goods during this period affected the native social and political organizations. How far the amount of exchange and the ability for social organizations to obtain the necessary surplus will prove significant remains unclear. On the face of it there would appear to be a fundamental difference between the 'Celtic' world as absorbed into the empire and the areas that lay beyond the Limes.

In conclusion it is useful to recall the evidence for the late Saxon period in England when Hodges argues that trade (long-distance) declines immediately before the rise of towns (1977). Although this decline may be a trick of the archaeological record, the late Saxon case appears to reinforce the view derived from this study of the Roman period that by itself long-distance trade is not necessarily a stimulus to social change. However, there is likely to be a correlation between the volume of exchange and the degree of social change. At present it is not clear where the stimulus that produces visible evidence of change in the nature and volume of exchanges originated.

Conclusions

The evidence for Roman trade with European barbarian society c.200 B.C.–400 A.D. has been reviewed. A comparison has been made between societies in receipt of trade that were eventually annexed by Rome (*viz.* Britain, Dacia, Gaul and Noricum) with the aim of assessing the impact of trade on them. The consequence of trade is seen to be variable and may be connected with a varying volume of interchange from area to area. The evidence from the 'provinces-to-be' is then set against that from societies beyond the Rhine–Danube frontier of the imperial period. To help understand the significance of finds beyond the frontier it is important to see them in the light of contemporary provincial finds. Thus, the comparative lack of rich finds among 'buffer zone' societies becomes more intelligible. With distance from the frontier a great emphasis is placed on the social value of Roman imports and this occasions the increasing number of burial finds as opposed to the more numerous, but more mundane, finds from settlements closer to the frontier. In order to appreciate the native settlement and material culture of the 'buffer zone' it is necessary to study them in the context of their provincial counterparts. Consideration is given to the very different development of societies that were eventually incorporated within the Empire when compared with those societies in receipt of trade, but which remained outside the empire. It is suggested that if trade did have the impact on society that it is sometimes credited with, only appreciable differences (yet to be measured) in the volume of trade can explain the very variable response to that trade.*

Bibliography

Alföldy, G., 1974. *Noricum.*

Bateson, J. D., 1973. 'Roman material from Ireland: a reconsideration', *Procs. Royal Irish Acad. 73C:* 21–97.

Bateson, J. D., 1976. 'Further finds of Roman material from Ireland', *Procs. Royal Irish Acad. 76C:* 171–80.

Beck, H. (ed.), 1970. 'Spätkaiserzeitliche Funde in Westfalen', *Bodenaltertümer Westfalens 12* (Münster).

Boon, G. C., 1974. *Silchester: The Roman Town of Calleva.*

Bradley, R., 1978. *The Prehistoric Settlement of Britain.*

Christlein, R., 1964. 'Ein Bronzesiebfragment der Spätlatènezeit von Zugmantel', *Saalburg Jahrbuch 21* (1963/4): 16–19.

Collis, J., 1977. 'Pre-Roman burial rites in North-western Europe'. In R. Reece (ed.), *Burial in the Roman World:* 1–12.

Crawford, M. H., 1977. 'Republican denarii in Romania: the suppression of piracy and the slave trade', *J. Roman Studies 67:* 117–24.

Cunliffe, B. W., 1978a. *Iron Age Communities in Britain* (2nd edn).

Cunliffe, B. W., 1978b. *Hengistbury Head.*

Curle, J., 1932a. 'Roman drift in Caledonia', *J. Roman Studies 22:* 73–7.

Curle, J., 1932b. 'An inventory of objects of Roman and Provincial Roman origin found on sites in Scotland not definitely associated with Roman constructions', *Procs. Soc. Ant. Scotland 46:* 277–397.

Eggers, H. J., 1951. *Der römische Import im freien Germanien* (Hamburg).

Eggers, H. J., 1966. 'Römische Bronzegefässe in Britannien', *Jahrbuch RGZM 13:* 67–164.

Frankenstein, S. and Rowlands, M. J., 1978. 'The internal structure and regional context of Early Iron Age society in southwestern Germany', *Bull. Inst. Archaeol. Univ. London 15:* 73–112.

Frere, S. S., 1967. *Britannia: A History of Roman Britain.*

Fulford, M., 1981. 'Roman pottery: towards the investigation of economic and social change'. In H. Howard and E. L. Morris (eds.), *Production and Distribution. A Ceramic Viewpoint:* 195–208.

Gillam, J. P., 1958. 'Roman and native, A.D. 122–197'. In I. A. Richmond (ed.), *Roman and Native in North Britain:* 60–90.

Glodariu, I., 1976. *Dacian Trade with the Hellenistic and Roman World.*

Griffith, G. T., 1935. *Mercenaries of the Hellenistic World.*

Haselgrove, C., 1976. 'External trade as a stimulus to urbanisation'. In B. Cunliffe and T. Rowley (eds.), *Oppida in Barbarian Europe:* 25–49.

Hedeager, L., 1977. 'A quantitative analysis of Roman imports in Europe north of the Limes (0–400 AD), and the question of Roman–Germanic exchange'. In K. Kristiansen and C. Paludan-Müller (eds.), *New Directions in Scandinavian Archaeology,* Studies in Scandinavian Prehistory and Early History, I (Copenhagen): 191–216.

Hedeager, L., 1980. 'Besiedlung, soziale Struktur und politische Organisation in der alteren und jüngeren römischen Kaiserzeit Ostdänemarks', *Praehistorische Zeitschrift 55:* 38–109.

Hodges, R., 1977. 'Trade and urban origins in Dark Age England: an archaeological critique of the evidence', *Berichten van de Rijksdienst voor het Oudheitkundig Bodemonderzoek 27:* 191–215.

Hopkins, K., 1978. *Conquerors and Slaves,* Sociological Studies in Roman History, I.

* This paper was submitted in November 1981.

Hopkins, K., 1980. 'Taxes and trade in the Roman Empire (200 BC–AD 400)', *J. Roman Studies 70:* 101–25.
Jones, M., 1981. 'The developments of crop husbandry'. In M. Jones and G. Dimbleby (eds.), *The Environment of Man: The Iron Age to the Anglo-Saxon Period:* 95–127.
Kilbride-Jones, H. E., 1980. *Zoomorphic Penannular Brooches.*
Macgregor, M., 1976. *Early Celtic Art in North Britain: A Study of Decorative Metalwork from the Third Century B.C. to the Third Century A.D.*
Mackensen, M., 1975. 'The state of research on Norican silver coinage', *World Archaeol. 6:* 249–75.
Majewski, K., 1960. *Importy Rzymskie W Polsce* (Warsaw).
Möcsy, A., 1974. *Pannonia and Upper Moesia.*
Mytum, H., 1981. 'Ireland and Rome: the Maritime Frontier'. In A. King and M. Henig (eds.), *The Roman West in the Third Century:* 445–50.
Nash, D., 1976. 'The growth of urban society in France'. In B. Cunliffe and T. Rowley (eds.), *Oppida in Barbarian Europe:* 95–133.
Nash, D., 1978a. 'Territory and state formation in Central Gaul'. In D. Green, C. Haselgrove and M. Spriggs (eds.), *Social Organisation and Settlement:* 445–82.
Nash, D., 1978b. *Settlement and Coinage in Central Gaul c.200–50 BC.*
Partridge, C., 1981. *Skeleton Green: A Late Iron Age and Romano-British Site,* Britannia Monographs, 2.
Peacock, D. P. S., 1971. 'Roman amphorae in pre-Roman Britain'. In D. Hill and M. Jesson (eds.), *The Iron Age and its Hillforts:* 161–88.
Robertson, A., 1970. 'Roman finds from non-Roman sites in Scotland', *Britannia 1:* 198–213.
Royal Commission on Ancient and Historical Monuments in Wales & Monmouthshire, 1937. *An Inventory of the Ancient Monuments in Anglesey.*
Royal Commission on Ancient and Historical Monuments, 1956–64. *An Inventory of the Ancient Monuments in Caernarvonshire,* I: East (1956); II: Central (1960); III: West (1964).
Sakař, V., 1970. 'Roman imports in Bohemia', *Fontes Archaeologici Pragenses, 14.*
Schmid, P., 1978. 'New archaeological results of settlement structures (Roman Iron Age) in the north-west German coastal area'. In B. Cunliffe and T. Rowley (eds.), *Lowland Iron Age Communities in Europe:* 123–46.
Stevenson, R. B. K., 1966. 'Metal-work and some other objects in Scotland and their cultural affinities'. In A. L. F. Rivet (ed.), *The Iron Age in Northern Britain:* 17–44.
Stöckli, W. E., 1979. *Die Grob und Importkeramik von Manching,* Die Ausgrabungen in Manching, 8 (Wiesbaden).
Terray, E., 1974. 'Long-distance exchange and the formation of the state: the case of the Abron kingdom of Gyaman', *Economy and Society 3:* 315–45.
Thompson, E. A., 1965. *The Early Germans.*
Thompson, E. A., 1966. *The Visigoths in the Time of Ulfila.*
Todd, M., 1975. *The Northern Barbarians, 100 BC–AD 300.*
Todd, M., 1977. 'Germanic burials in the Roman Iron Age'. In R. Reece (ed.), *Burial in the Roman World:* 39–43.
Todd, M., 1981. *Roman Britain 55 BC–AD 400.*
Warner, R. B., 1976. 'Some observations on the context and importation of exotic material in Ireland', *Procs. Royal Irish Acad. 76C:* 267–92.
Webster, G., 1980. *The Roman Invasion of Britain.*
Wells, P. S., 1980. *Culture Contact and Culture Change: Early Iron Age Central Europe and the Mediterranean World.*
Wheeler, M., 1954. *Rome Beyond the Imperial Frontiers.*
Wild, J. P., 1976. 'Loanwords and Roman expansion in north-west Europe', *World Archaeol. 8:* 57–64.
Willers, H., 1907. *Neue Untersuchungen über die römische Bronzeindustrie von Capua und von Niedergermanien* (Hanover and Leipzig).

6

Regional organization in the western Early La Tène province: the Marne–Mosel and Rhine–Danube groups

H. Lorenz*

Attempts to establish large-scale regional groups frequently start from the investigation of individual attributes, whether the area of concern is that of material culture or socio-religious organization. The distribution of, for example, individual artefacts or artefact-types, elements of style or burial custom may be distinguished and only rarely is one closed attribute-complex studied in relation to another.[1] One such complex is the rites observed by a group on the death of one of their number. Archaeologically, these rites may be expressed by the external form and marking of the place of burial, the form of the grave itself, the method of interment or the articulation of the body within the grave, as well as the number and combination of the associated grave goods. Another approach might be the study of the costume worn by the dead at burial. 'Costume' should not here be understood in the narrow sense of clothing alone, but rather as a wider concept, incorporating all the visible attributes which combine to express the group identity and social status of an individual.[2] Thus in the La Tène period costume includes not only dress accessories such as brooches, but also – and these are the most important categories – weapons and ring ornaments (bracelets, anklets, finger-rings etc.). This paper aims to show that it is possible on this basis to isolate for the Early La Tène period two distinct, large-scale regional groups (fig. 6.1). The first is that of the Marne–Mosel area which extends from the Champagne (Sankot 1976–77) through the Ardennes into the Middle Rhine region, with offshoots to the north of the Main; the second is that of the Rhine–Danube area[3] which encompasses Switzerland (Sankot 1980), southern Bavaria, Baden-Württemberg and Alsace, with offshoots reaching the Main, and with an area of overlap with the Marne–Mosel group in the northern Upper Rhine valley.[4] Both groups are defined archaeologically by the Early La Tène character of the finds, although they are not in fact exactly contemporary, particularly in their early stages. The Marne–Mosel group originates as early as the beginning of the fifth century B.C., whereas the Rhine–Danube group

* trans. Susan Semmens

6 Regional organization in the western Early La Tène province

H. Lorenz

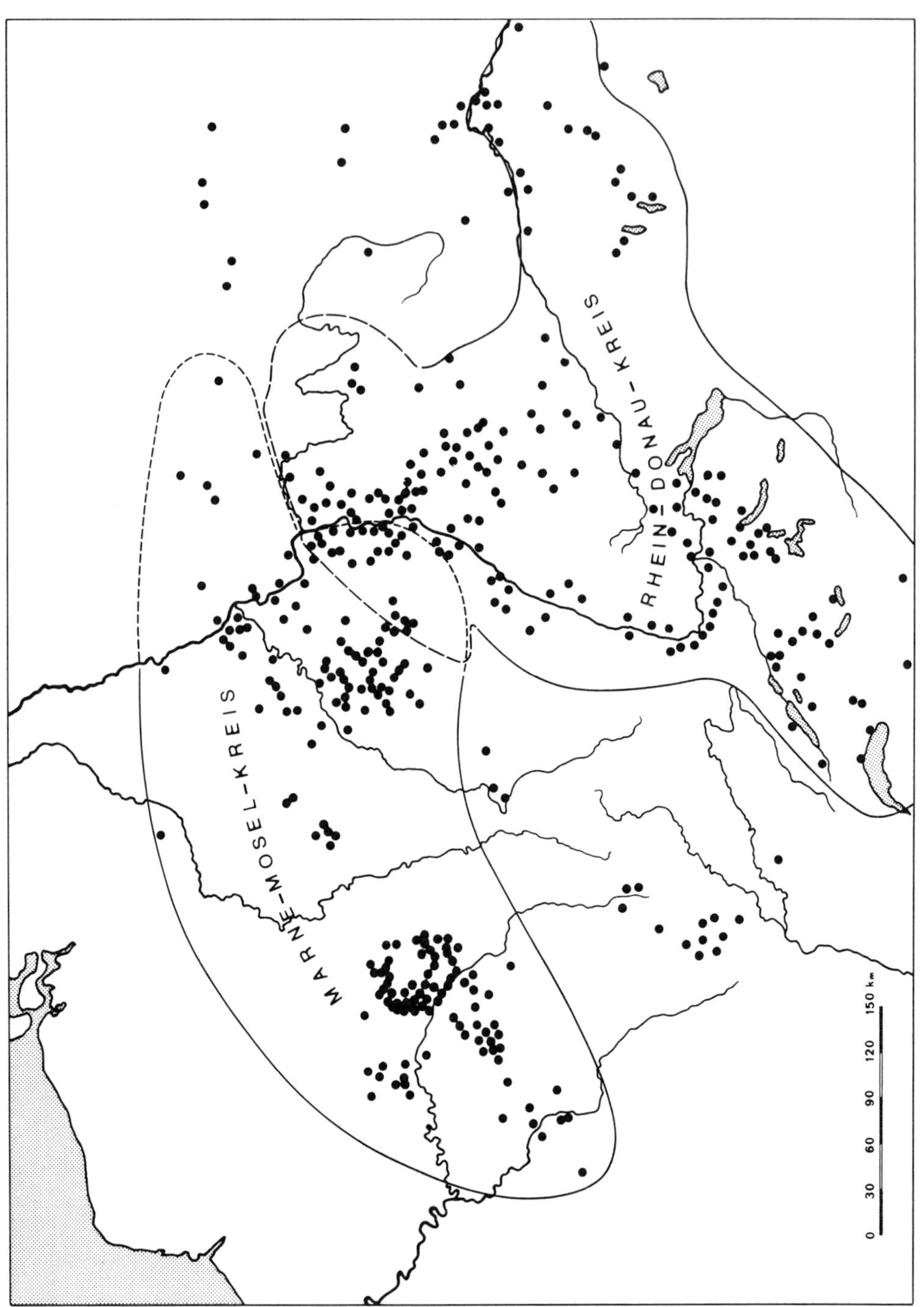

Figure 6.1 Distribution of the Marne–Mosel and the Rhine–Danube groups in the western Early La Tène province.

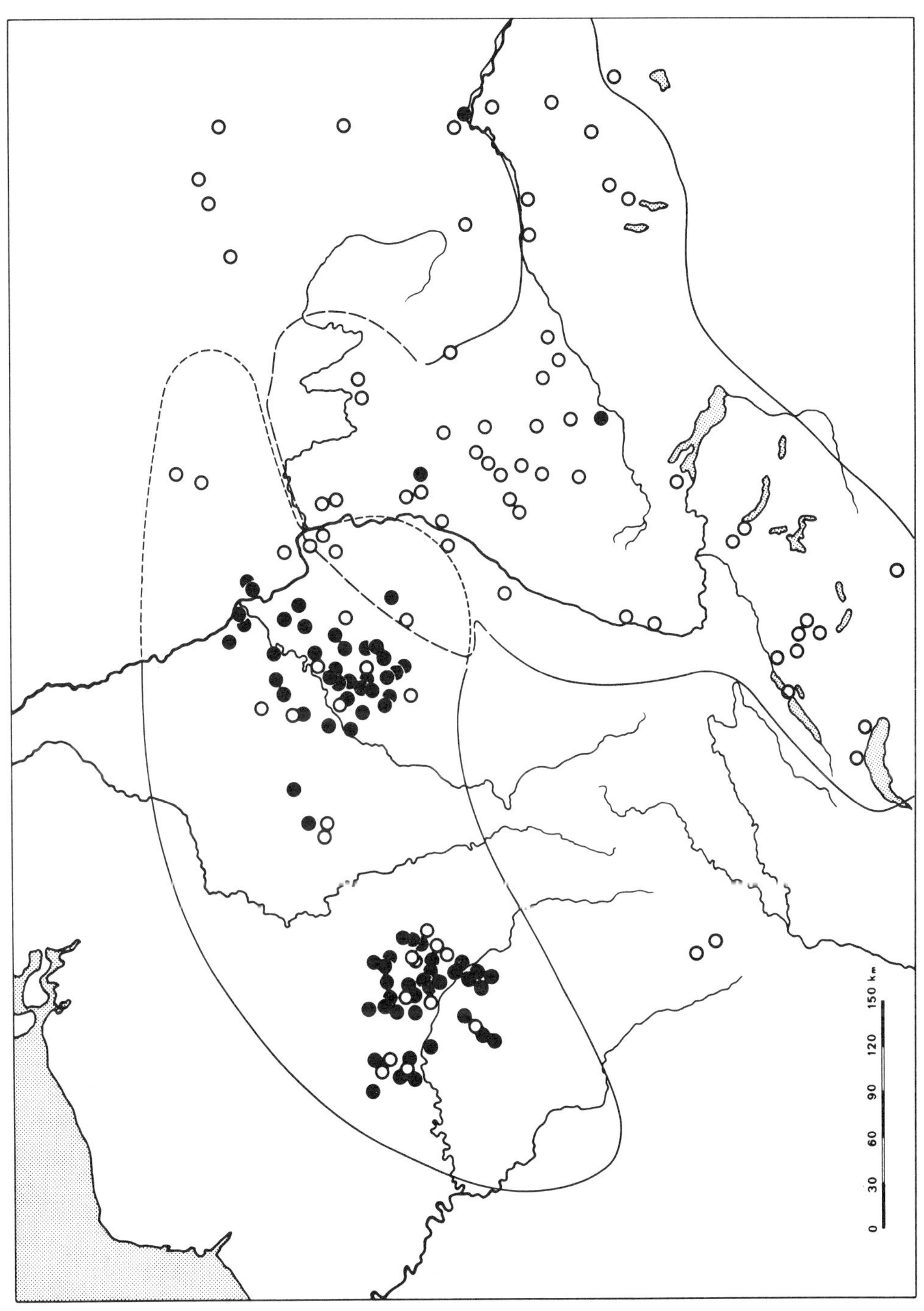

Figure 6.2 Early La Tène burials with weapons. (● Graves with more than one spear.)

develops at the end of the century and reaches its full extent only in the fourth century B.C.[5]

Graves containing weapons (figs. 6.2 and 6.3)[6]

Weapon graves of the Marne–Mosel group are dominated by the presence of the spear, with approximately half containing one example and the rest more than one. Analysis of the length and breadth of individual spear-heads suggests that they may represent either the thrusting or the throwing variety and that, when several are found together, they will tend to be a combination of the two types. A sword is often present in addition to the spears, although this combination is not very common in the Ardennes and the Eifel (Thénot 1971). It is, however, particularly strong in the Champagne and the Hochwald–Nahe area of the Middle Rhine where approximately every third weapon grave falls into this category. The possibility that swords were reserved for those of higher social rank is supported by their frequent appearance in the 'princely' graves of the Champagne and the Hochwald–Nahe region and by the small number of sword burials within individual cemeteries, in comparison to the very much larger

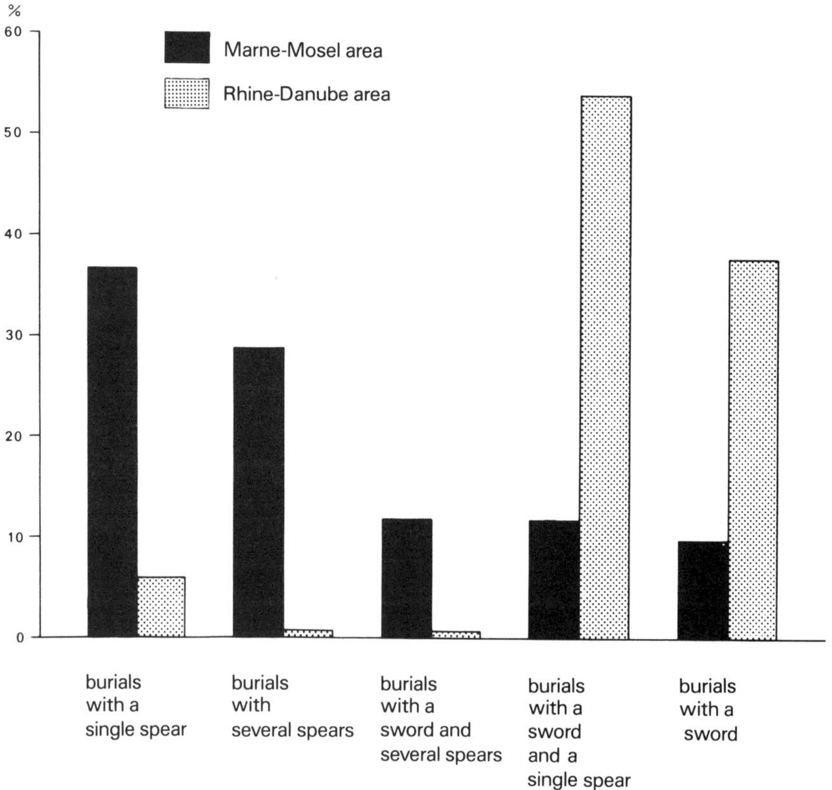

Figure 6.3 Comparison between weapon graves in the Marne–Mosel and Rhine–Danube areas.

number of burials with spears alone. Similarly, indications of the superior treatment afforded to the sword-wearer appears in the burial rite employed: in the Hochwald–Nahe area interment was generally in a much more spacious grave and covered with a mound both higher and more imposing than the others in the cemetery. Only very seldom are traces of protective armour found with weapons in graves, but it is not possible to say whether helmets, cuirasses and shields were in fact infrequent grave goods or whether this part of the equipment was made of organic material of some kind and thus difficult to establish archaeologically. Evidence can be brought in support of both interpretations. It is safe to assume, however, that armour was also undoubtedly an indication of the social position of the wearer – a suggestion again reflected in the 'princely' burials with metal helmets and body-armour in the Champagne (Schaaff 1973).

The variety of military equipment in the Marne–Mosel graves contrasts with the striking homogeneity of the Rhine–Danube group, in which a different weapon predominated. Central to this group was the sword, which was placed in the grave either alone or in association with a single spear which, judging from the dimensions of the head, is more likely to have been of the throwing than of the thrusting variety. The question of the provision of a sword alone and the combination of a sword and a spear seems, not least on the evidence from the cemetery of Münsingen-Rain, to be one of chronology rather than social status. In the earliest La Tène period at Münsingen the sword was generally placed on its own in the grave, whereas in the later period the combination of sword and spear was usual (Martin-Kilcher 1976). The provision of body-armour seems to have been no more frequent in the Rhine–Danube than in the Marne–Mosel area, although this is again subject to the qualification made above.

It comes as no surprise that the section of the population buried with weapons is suggested by anthropological analysis to be the adult males, although only a certain proportion of male burials contained weapons. At least half of the adult male burials in the Marne–Mosel group are represented here, whereas in the Rhine–Danube group the number is nearer a third. Thus it seems that the number of individuals entitled to be buried with weapons was different in the two areas.

Ring ornaments (figs. 6.4–6.7)

Ring ornaments are sometimes found in weapon graves; finger-rings infrequently, neckrings even more rarely,[7] and anklets not at all. Armrings or bracelets, usually worn by men on the lower left arm, are by far the most common type. The percentage of weapon graves involved is about 10 per cent in the Marne–Mosel and 20 per cent in the Rhine–Danube group. It is probably impossible to explain the restriction of this custom to so small a group of men, but it is reasonable to assume that social status was a factor. Thus in the Champagne and the Hochwald–Nahe area armrings are found in two out of three weapon graves which contained a sword and their occurrence in 'princely' burials is above the average (Harhoiu 1976). Among the adult graves without weapons are found a group in which the only grave good is a single ring on the

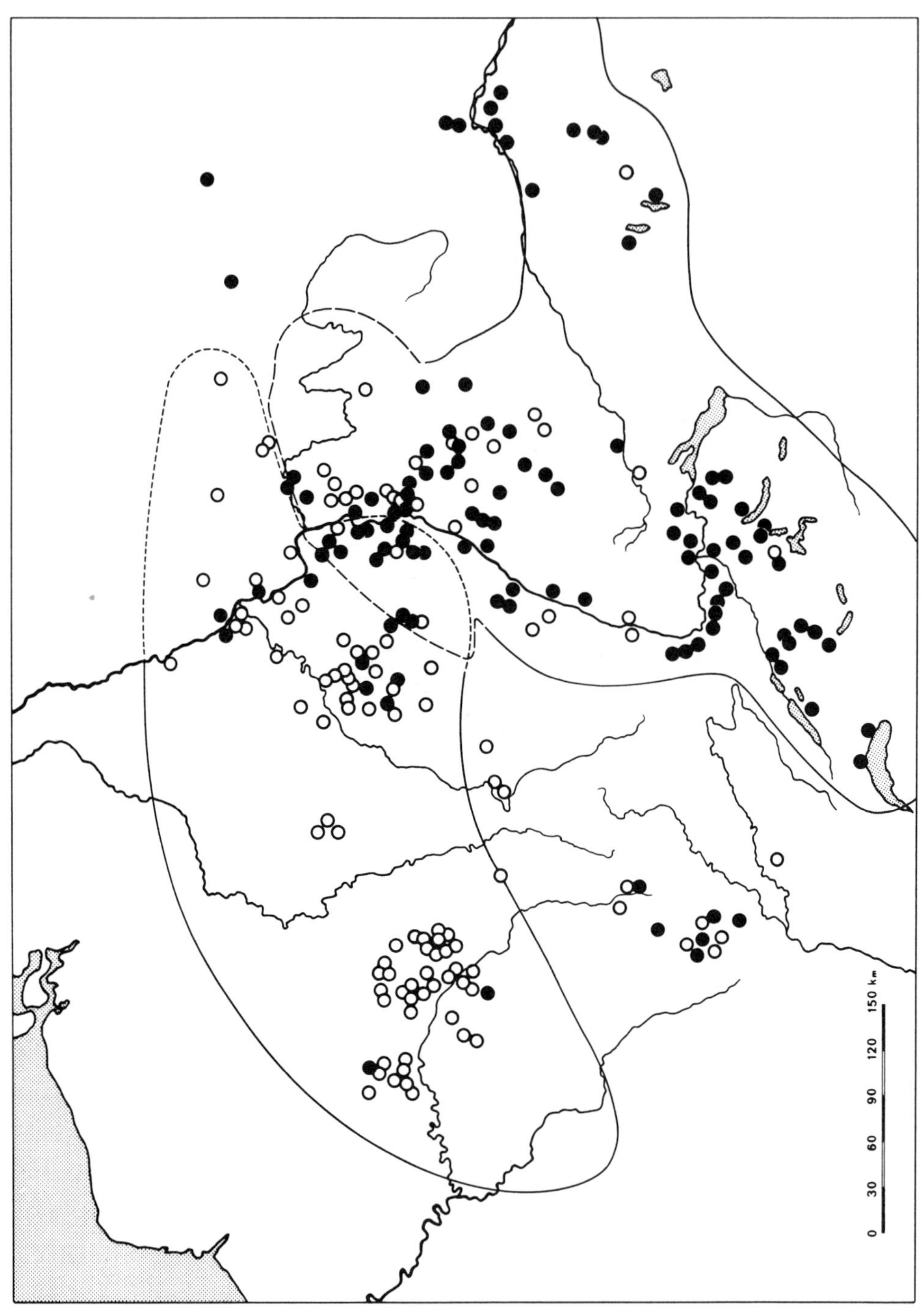

Figure 6.4 Early La Tène burials with ring ornaments. (● Graves containing anklets.)

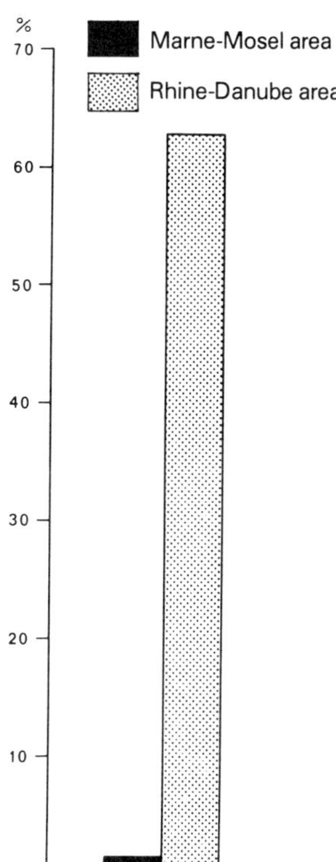

Figure 6.5 Percentages of those burials with ring ornaments which contain anklets. The area of western Switzerland is omitted.

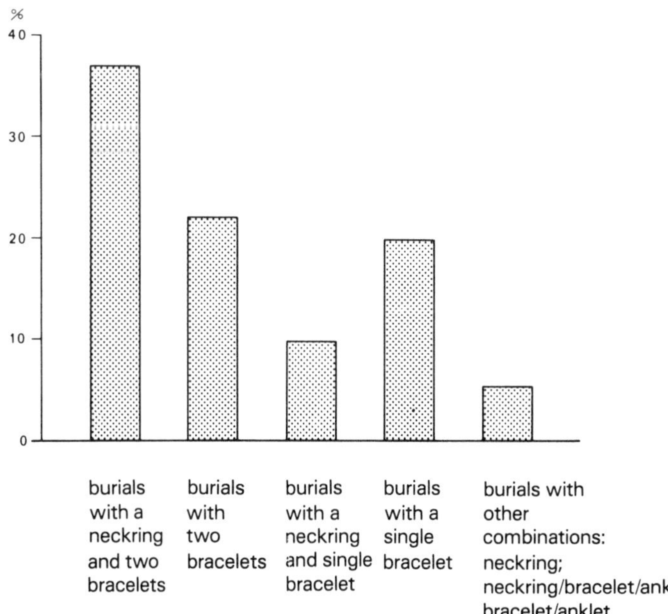

Figure 6.6 Ornament combinations in the Marne–Mosel area.

left wrist. The paucity of anthropological analyses and the lack of any sex-specific grave goods means that the sex of these burials can only infrequently be established and it must at present, therefore, remain unexplained whether the bracelet worn on the left arm was a general mark of a particular group of men or was only worn by those men who were provided with military equipment in the grave.

The association in a single grave of weapons and ring ornaments is the exception; as a rule graves contain only the ring ornaments. The types concerned here are principally bracelets, finger-rings, anklets and torcs, earrings and diadems being confined to certain geographical areas. The types and combinations of these rings allow clear distinctions to be drawn between the Marne–Mosel and the Rhine–Danube areas. Central to the combinations recognized for the Marne–Mosel group is the bracelet worn either as a pair, one on each wrist, or as a single example, usually found on the right wrist. In the majority of cases bracelets are worn in conjunction with a neckring or torc but regional variations occur, as in the Eifel where bracelets are generally found on their own. Finger-rings are rare in the Marne–Mosel group and the use of anklets is so unusual that they might even be an indication that the woman came from another area. The reasons for the variation in these combinations are again not known. Chronology does not appear to be the central factor, although ornament

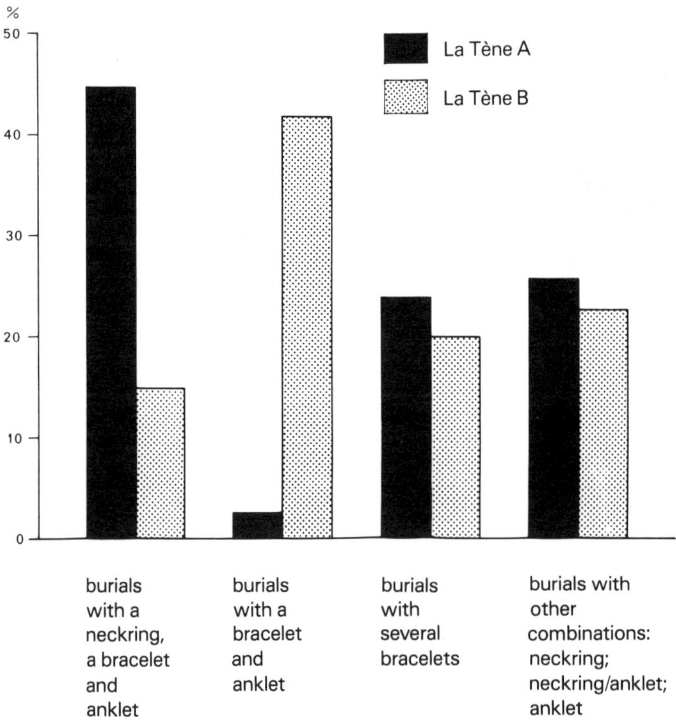

Figure 6.7 Ornament combinations in the Rhine–Danube area during the La Tène A and the La Tène B periods.

combinations certainly seem to have been dependent on the age of the individual. Graves which can be established as those of children were in the main furnished with a single bracelet.

The position in the Rhine–Danube group is more complex; besides neckrings and bracelets, finger-rings are found, as well as anklets, which are the characteristic type of this group. Both chronological and geographical distinctions can be identified in the ornament combinations. In the La Tène A period a single neckring, or very occasionally two, was generally worn, the lower arms being ornamented by a pair of bracelets and the lower legs by a pair of anklets. In west Switzerland an extra ring was common on the left leg, while in the central and northern areas of the country two pairs were frequently worn together. Finger-rings occur over the entire area but are especially frequent in the centre and north of Switzerland, where they are primarily found in graves with two sets of anklets. The change in the ornament combination which becomes clear in the La Tène B is based on the same principle throughout the Rhine–Danube area. A pair of anklets continued to be worn and bracelets nearly always appear, although they are no longer generally found in matching pairs but are of two different types. The decorated, perhaps more 'valuable', ring was worn on the right wrist whereas that on the left was a simple, undecorated example. It is also common to find the ring ornaments restricted to a single bracelet, generally found on the lower right arm. The neckring no longer forms an integral part of the ring set and now appears only infrequently. Finger-rings sustain their popularity over the whole Rhine–Danube area but again they appear most commonly in those graves in central and northern Switzerland which are furnished with two pairs of anklets rather than the more commonly recognized single pair. Developments in western Switzerland now take an individual course with the condensing of the extensive ornament group of the previous La Tène A into a single bracelet, worn on the right wrist. Similarly a different situation is found in the north of Baden-Württemberg where throughout the whole of the Early La Tène period, alongside the position already described, a combination appears which consists entirely of bracelets, worn either singly or as two together. This continues a phenomenon already observed in this area for the Late Hallstatt period. As well as the chronological and geographical distinctions described for the Rhine–Danube group, it seems likely that the age of the individual played a decisive role in determining the ornament combination. Children occasionally wore the same set of ornaments as adults, but were usually distinguished by the presence of a string of beads worn around the neck, although the majority – especially in the La Tène B period – wore an individual combination characterized by the complete absence of anklets.

Thanks to a series of anthropological investigations, the people buried with ring ornaments can now be identified more closely. The number of men in this category is small, children are more frequently represented, but the overwhelming majority are adult females. These analyses, however, make it quite clear that not all women possessed these ornaments, even if the proportion, around 80–90 per cent, far outweighed the proportion of men buried with weapons.

Dress accessories (figs. 6.8 and 6.9)

The brooches found in many burials in the westerly La Tène area can be assumed to have fastened the clothing worn by the dead. The number and size of these brooches are the main indicators of regional and social divisions. In the male weapon burials of the Marne–Mosel area the wearing of brooches seems to have been confined to a restricted group, being found in only about 20 per cent of the graves and generally represented by a single example. The regional differences already observed in the different combinations of weapons are also reflected here, as in the Ardennes and the Eifel the appearance of brooches seems to be the exception. As to those who wore fibulae in the graves of the Champagne and the Hochwald–Nahe, it is striking that the number of brooches is very much higher in sword-graves than in those furnished with spears alone. They are, indeed, most common in the 'princely' graves of the Champagne, as defined by the presence of a two-wheeled chariot, where they are represented in more than half

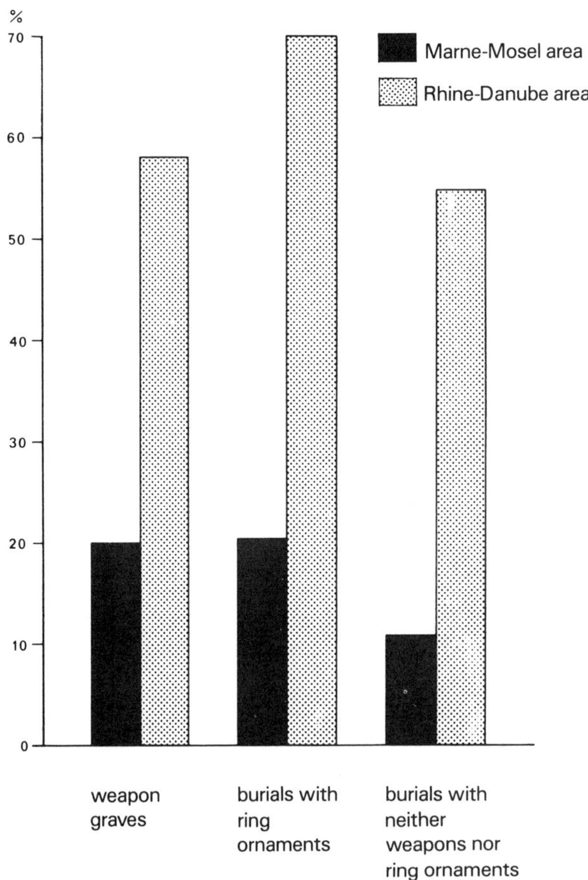

Figure 6.8 Percentage of burials with brooches.

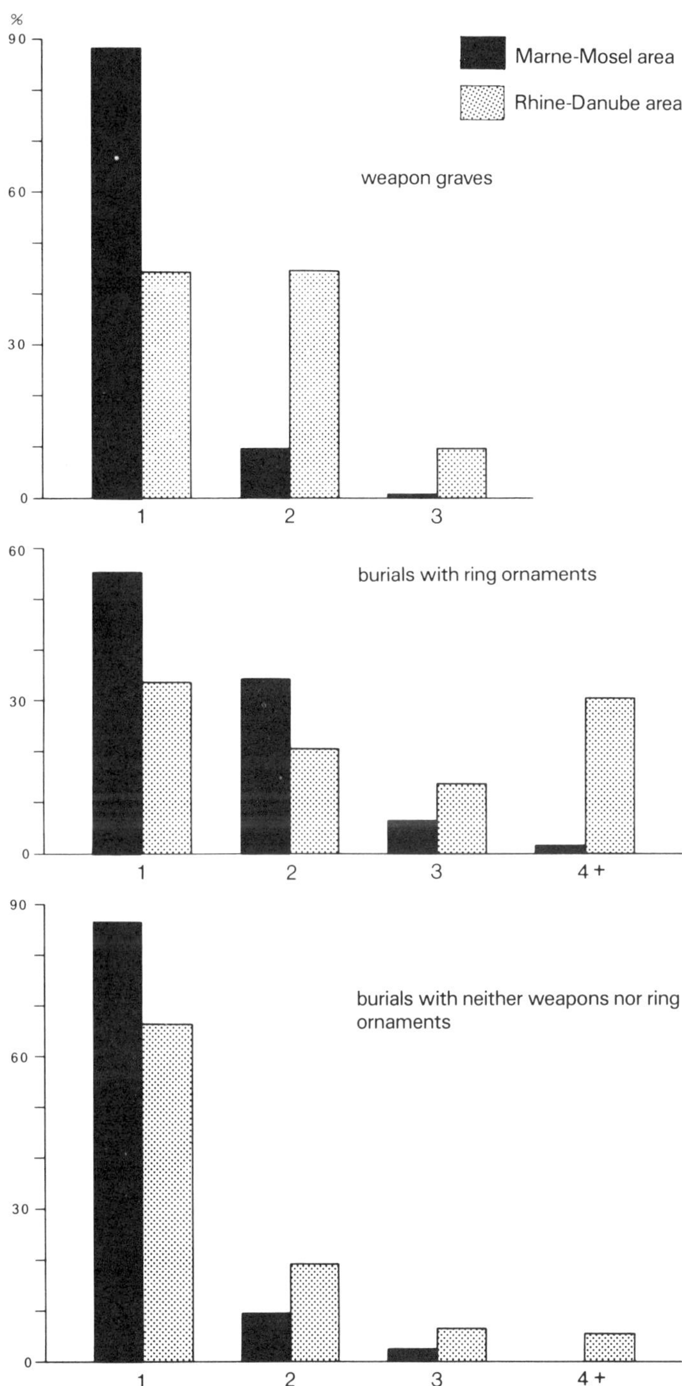

Figure 6.9 Numbers of brooches in burials.

the graves. This allows for the possibility that the wearing of brooches was reserved for a group of high-status individuals,[8] a suggestion strengthened by finds in the Rhine–Danube group, where a much larger circle were buried with brooches – indeed brooches were present in two-thirds of weapon graves. Except in Baden-Württemberg, where brooches generally occur singly, combinations of two and sometimes even three are found, frequently of different sizes.

A similar position in terms of provision of brooches is reflected in those graves which contain ring ornaments but are not furnished with weapons. In the Marne–Mosel group all indications again point to the restriction of brooches to a small circle of women, since they are found in only 20–25 per cent of the burials and, furthermore, in the Ardennes and in the Eifel brooches are very infrequent. The number of brooches varies but is in general higher in association with women than with men. Something like half the burials concerned contain one and the rest two or three examples, a higher tally occurring very seldom. In the Rhine–Danube group the situation is quite different, with brooches present in about 70 per cent of graves. However, this is not the only difference, the contrast also being reflected in the numbers of brooches themselves. As a rule two or three examples are found together but groups of four or more (up to a total of 23) are not uncommon. Even if these large numbers could not have contributed directly to the fastening of items of clothing, the situation revealed here seems to have been one unknown in the Marne–Mosel group. The reasons for wearing brooches with no practical function can no longer be ascertained, although it seems possible that social distinctions might have been expressed in this way. In central and northern Switzerland, after all, brooches were concentrated in burials with two pairs of anklets and with finger-rings which, it should be noted, were frequently of precious metals, such as gold, silver and electrum.

In addition to the burials in the western La Tène area with weapons and those with ring ornaments, there are also a large number of graves in which neither of these find-groups is represented. On the basis of anthropological analyses these comprise adult males with children being quite frequently represented but with very few adult females. The imbalance in numbers between males and females may also perhaps be expressed in the number of fibulae found in the respective graves. The general picture of regional groupings already established for the westerly La Tène province is confirmed here. In the Marne–Mosel area brooches are found in only about 10 per cent of graves and even more infrequently in the Ardennes and the Eifel. As in the male graves with weapons, these occur, almost without exception, as single examples.[9] In the Rhine–Danube area, however, the number of burials containing brooches is, as expected, higher and indeed reaches a figure of 50–60 per cent. In the majority of cases a single brooch is found although they are not infrequently found in twos and threes, and occasionally in even greater numbers.

Postscript

With the transition to the Middle La Tène changes occur over the entire La Tène province, changes which find their expression not only in the material culture but also in social and religious organization. The latter is expressed most clearly in a change of burial rite, which is identified archaeologically in a negative sense by the widespread absence of grave goods. This alteration, however, proceeds at different speeds in different areas so that, albeit on a more restricted basis, the general developments in costume can be appreciated both for the Marne–Mosel and for the Rhine–Danube area.

By this time the sword had become the dominant element in male weapon graves over the whole of the western La Tène region. These rarely appear alone in graves and are most commonly found in association with a single spear which, to judge by the dimensions, seems to have been a throwing spear. Only in the Middle Rhine area are a few burials found which, in place of the sword, contain a single spear.

A similarly united picture is provided by the female ring ornament sets, characterized at this time by the almost complete absence of anklets and by a concentration on bracelets, especially on the left arm: they were worn either on the left arm alone, or the number on the left arm exceeded that on the right. It is also worth remarking that bracelets were no longer worn simply on the lower arms but are also found, as armlets, on the upper arms. Finger-rings are a more common artefact type in the distribution area of the Early La Tène Rhine–Danube group, whereas the combination of bracelets and neckring or torc is generally centred in the Marne–Mosel area, with the greatest concentration in the Champagne.

In the wearing of brooches the western La Tène province shows a similarly unified aspect which is most clearly seen in the increase, in the area of the previous Marne–Mosel group, of the number of men and women who wore, or were in a position to wear, brooches; even if the total never attains that for the distribution area of the previous Rhine–Danube group.

At the transition to the Middle La Tène period changes can then be seen in the costume of the dead. In the area of the Rhine–Danube group these are not particularly significant and should probably be seen in terms of a further development. In the area of the Marne–Mosel group, on the other hand, the change is so fundamental that continuity is extremely difficult to envisage. The Early La Tène pattern is abandoned, to be replaced by another, orientated towards the principles of the Rhine–Danube area. However, the probability that behind this statement lies significant reorganization, not least of a social and political nature, is beyond the scope of this paper.[10]

Notes

1. For recent research into regional groups in the Early La Tène, see Dehn 1976.
2. For a definition of the concept of costume (*Tracht*), see Lorenz 1978:8 and 1980:133.
3. The appellation 'Rhine–Danube' is used here to mean only the western part of the

total Rhine–Danube area. For the full distribution see Lorenz 1978:219ff. and Appendix 10.

4. For the regional association of burials in Lorraine, Burgundy, north Bavaria and Thuringia, see Lorenz 1978:219f. and n. 916, and 230f.
5. For the Hallstatt D3/La Tène A problem, see *Hamburger Beiträge zur Archaeologie 2* (1972): 166f., with contributions by various authors, and most recently, Pauli 1978: 418ff.
6. In the following exposition only the most significant aspects will be discussed. More detailed analysis and examples can be found in Lorenz 1978:112 passim.
7. The absence of neckrings or torcs in weapon graves is in striking contradiction to the picture gained from literary and pictorial evidence of the Celtic warrior.
8. The complexity of this question is illuminated by the fact that brooches were also worn by men who were buried without weapons. Brooches seem, therefore, to characterize a particular group of men, a group defined without reliance on weapons in the grave.
9. See n.8.
10. For the historical situation and its interpretation, see Pauli 1978:443ff. and Lorenz 1978:245ff.

Bibliography

Dehn, W., 1976. 'Chronologische und geographische Gruppierungsmöglichkeiten in der älteren Latènekultur', *9. Congrès UISPP Nice 1976. Colloque XXIX, Le passage du 1er au 2e âge du fer en Europe:* 7–22.

Harhoiu, R., 1976. 'Tipuri de obiceiuri din mormintele princiare Hallstatt finale şi Latène timpurii din vestul R.F. Germania şi răsăritul Frantei', *Stud. Cerc. Ist. Veche 27:* 181–202.

Lorenz, H., 1978. 'Totenbrauchtum und Tracht. Untersuchungen zur regionalen Gliederung der frühen Latenezeit', *Bericht der Römisch-Germanischen Kommission 59:* 1–380.

Lorenz, H., 1980. 'Bemerkungen zur keltischen Tracht'. In *Die Kelten in Mitteleuropa* (Salzburger Landesausstellung Hallein): 133–7.

Martin-Kilcher, S., 1976. 'Zur Tracht und Beigabensitte im keltischen Gräberfeld von Münsingen-Rain (Kt. Bern)', *Zeitschrift Schweiz. Arch. und Kunstgeschichte 30:* 26–39.

Pauli, L., 1978. *Der Dürrnberg bei Hallein III. Auswertung der Grabfunde*, Münchner Beiträge zur Vor- und Frühgeschichte 18.

Sankot, P., 1976–77. 'Le rite funéraire des nécropoles latèniennes en Champagne', *Études Celtiques 15:* 49–94.

Sankot, P., 1980. 'Studie zur Sozialstruktur der nordalpinen Flachgräberfelder der La-Tène-Zeit im Gebiet der Schweiz', *Zeitschrift Schweiz. Arch. und Kunstgeschichte 37:* 19–71.

Schaaff, U., 1973. 'Frühlatènezeitliche Grabfunde mit Helmen von Typ Berru', *Jahrbuch RGZM 20* [1975]: 81–106.

Thénot, A., 1971. 'Les objets de fer dans les tombes d'enfant à La Tène I', *Antiquités Nationales 3:* 47–52.

7

Craft specialization and complex societies: a critique

D. A. Welbourn

This paper attempts to discuss some problems which face all archaeologists who are studying production and craft specialization. It is divided into two parts. First, I will discuss a sequence of assumptions concerning craft specialization which will be familiar to many; I will try to outline the difficulties involved in making these assumptions. Second, I want to discuss, in more general terms, the difficulties which archaeologists face in attempting to develop a theory for archaeological process and explanation for change. I do not pretend – or presume – to provide an answer to these problems, but hope that their discussion may help others to resolve them.

A 'familiar line of argument'

There is a chain of hypothetical argument in much archaeological literature concerning complex societies, which needs to be discussed and criticized. It concerns the analysis of these societies in terms of the scale of production within them. The argument might run like this:

> During a certain period there appears to be standardization of a certain group of artefacts over a large area. This suggests, therefore, [*Assumption 1*] that these artefacts were the result of large-scale production. This implies [*Assumption 2*] that specialist producers operated within the society. Since specialists have sufficient time to operate, there must [*Assumption 3*] have been sufficient division of labour within the society, or production of surplus within the society, to call it a stratified society or, in other words, to support an elite.

This line of argument has been employed very frequently in archaeological literature in order to support discussions about the evidence for the development of hierarchical societies. Rice (1981), for example, bases her paper on the evolution of specialized pottery production on this premise and writes (1981:227): 'In stratified societies behaviour, methods, pastes and forms are highly standardised, particularly in low-value/high-consumption utilitarian goods, with pottery production increasingly an exercise in mass production and cost-control.' (Rice even takes the progression further and maintains that variability in pottery will emerge again in elite wares. This further development of the argument will not, however, concern us here, since the same critique applies.) I do not intend to contradict Rice's or anyone else's conclusions concerning the complexity of past societies, but I do want to question the validity of the steps involved in their line of argument.

Standardization (Assumption 1)

That standardization of a certain group of artefacts over a large area suggests that the artefacts were the results of large-scale production.

Rice (1981) has developed this assumption, with reference to Rathje (1975) and others:

> If specialisation reflects in part restricted or regulated access to resources, then the products of such specialisation should have a narrow range of variation in properties, reflecting the range inherent in the raw materials. Unimodality may indicate the degree of consistency in achieving a desired result: multimodality may reflect the existence of multiple producers, each with his own slightly distinctive product or a predetermined set of variants consistently being produced.

This statement poses a number of problems, most of which will be discussed below. The most immediate objection to be raised, however, is about the assumed lack of standardization of objects used by 'non-stratified' or 'acephalous' societies. Rice (1981) even proposes that 'In an egalitarian or acephalous society . . . pottery production at the household level will likely be unstandardised and more or less random variations are likely to occur.' This generalization is clearly erroneous. One can cite several ethnographic examples (Turkana, Pokot, Njemps, Tugen) where standardization amongst domestically produced articles is at a very high level (e.g. Fedders and Salvadori 1977; Hodder 1977; Welbourn 1981). The idea that standardization of artefacts results only from specialization quite clearly needs to be re-assessed. If the material culture of 'acephalous' societies were more or less random, it would be a hard task indeed for the archaeologists to recognize such societies. As Binford wrote in 1972, 'The degree that differences in . . . degrees of variability can be demonstrated to be associated with or to covary with different forms of organisation . . . in the society stems represented is an area of research thus far not initiated.' What, then, is the role of standardized objects? It is certainly clear that some objects are used by some societies as more visual markers of social identity and differentiation than others. In the examples cited above, for example, female decoration and hut types clearly distinguish one social group from the next. In this case, however, pottery would not necessarily reflect the same social boundaries: one group, for example, trades pottery to another group and a third group has abandoned pottery for aluminium cooking pans which may be found in many other areas. Archaeologists have unfortunately placed too much emphasis on the importance of pottery as a prime visual marker of social identity. This mistake is understandable. As Nicklin explains (1971:47) 'Remains of pottery have always tended to be prominent in the archaeological record on account of its great abundance and variety in many cultures . . . it is thus not surprising that archaeologists have attempted to extract the maximum amount of information from pottery.' It is time now for the balance to be redressed.

To return again to the ethnographic examples cited above, the standardization of the domestically produced items is, at one level, a function of conformity to the group. Whilst a member of each group may be able to identify the maker of a particular object if that maker lives in the same village or herding area, this recognition is no longer possible beyond that area. In the case of the pottery 'specialists' in some of these groups (part-time seasonal workers), I would very much doubt the possibility of their maintaining a higher degree of standardization of products from one season to the next than the degree of standardization achieved by individual domestic producers of other items.

Finally, it is necessary to discuss what an archaeologist means by 'standardization'. Without my having undertaken a statistical analysis of my own Marakwet material, I could already quite safely state that the degree of similarity of these objects was quite high enough for everyone to recognize them as the products of a certain social group. Specialization of production of these objects, therefore, is by no means necessary for them to be recognized as a standardized form. This fact reflects the necessity of understanding the purpose involved in the standardization of an object – a problem which is, of course, most difficult for the archaeologist to solve. Until this problem begins to be addressed, however, one's assessment of degrees of standardization is inevitably going to be somewhat vague.

Specialization (Assumption 2)

This implies that specialist producers operate within the society and were involved in large-scale production.

Here I want to mention two areas of haziness. First, when 'specialization' is discussed, it is rarely clear whether people are thinking of part-time or full-time production, itinerance or permanent location of craft producers. Thus Bradley (1971) cites Peacock's seminal work (1969): 'several specialist potteries and their products have been isolated upon petrological considerations.' It must be added that even here it has yet to be proved that every manufacturing centre was in operation at the same time. Similarly, Clarke (1972) writes: 'the settlements would inexorably tend to become reciprocally specialised and mutually supporting within an area network embracing segments of fen and the Mendip slopes'. Neither of these statements really defines the precise social and economic relationships of the population of the area very clearly. While it may not be possible to be more precise with the limited data available, it may perhaps be the case that the general label 'specialization' masks the variety of options available and thus restricts our potential understanding of the situation.

Second, assumptions have frequently been made about increased specialization needing to have a market system to support its production level (e.g. Hodder 1972:888 – 'Service centres are necessary for the circulation and exchange of . . . specialised goods.'). There is a strong notion here of the economy at some stage getting up and away from its bedfellow (called social relations) and setting up shop on its own two market-oriented feet. Hodder, moreover, emphasizes the importance of effort minimization and trade maximization (*ibid.*:888–9) in market development. Yet as Nicklin clearly states, 'It should not necessarily be presumed that archaeological evidence of the exchange of pottery represents the occurrence of so-called "trade".' It is neither wise for us to assume that specialist production is connected with purely economic activity nor to suppose that our own expectations of a market-economy prevailed in other periods. It is quite unnecessary to assume that markets were an inevitable concomitant of specialization in the Iron Age or at any other time, or to suppose that, if markets did exist, economic factors overrode social or other issues. We understand, for example, that coinage used to be treated in a different way from its present western use (when it was first introduced in Poland, for example, it was treated *not* as a new exchange medium, but rather as another form of property – McFarlane 1978). It should be understood, therefore, that attitudes towards trade and exchange in general can also vary.

Stratification (Assumption 3)

There must have been sufficient division of labour within the society or production of surplus within the society to call it a stratified society or, in other words, to support an elite.

Renfrew (1973) for example makes use of the specialization-stratification connection in discussion of the development of Neolithic Wessex: 'craft specialisation is implied here, sustained perhaps by the central organisation, for the large scale of the operation makes freelance activity unlikely.' Rice (1981) adopts a similar argument: 'The production of elite or special-function or high-value ceramic goods is the first in which specialisation will take place.' There are many problems, however, with these assumptions. Adams (1981:228), for example, in his comments on Rice's paper, states: 'the emergence of social and political elites does not invariably result in the production of "elite" pottery wares. During most of Egyptian history and down at least to Roman and Byzantine times, pottery was not developed as an artistic medium or as a status symbol.' Indeed Renfrew too admits the high level of inference involved in his exercise and adds: 'there is no need to insist on full-time professionals for any of these enterprises, despite the skill displayed'. The problem here again is that too much is being inferred from insufficient data: it has been assumed that there is an evolutionary progression of developing specialization and concomitant control of resources. Formerly it used to be thought that wheel-made pottery, for instance, provided a greater opportunity for development, but as Nicklin explains, it can no longer be heralded as a great socio-economic advance (1971:48).

Technological specialization is often considered as the litmus test of elite societies. It is time now perhaps to realize that this is not a sufficiently general supposition to be safely used. On the one hand we have seen how some archaeological types may not have been specialized anyway, and on the other it is clear that the term 'specialization' needs to be more carefully employed.

While this redefinition is under way, it would also be helpful to assess the meaning of the word 'surplus'. This too has often been used in an imprecise way. Davis (1981:228), in commenting on Rice's paper, remarks: 'Within the narrow framework she adopts it seems a contradiction to speak of "specialisation" in a simple society.' This would often seem to be the case for 'surplus' too. Many 'unstratified' societies produce more of certain goods than they themselves need, in order to exchange them for other items. Is this over-production specifically *not* to be called surplus? If not, how should it be named?

Alternative strategies . . .?

There are certain issues which have become apparent from my argument so far, mainly concerning my discontent with the evolutionary nature of the specialization hypothesis. Archaeologists have spent a great deal of time in analysing stratified societies. The words 'standardization', 'specialization', 'surplus', and even 'stratification' have often been very loosely used and archaeologists on the whole have not attempted to appreciate the extent to which labour is divided in 'non-stratified' societies. If more attention were paid to the workings of production and exchange in such societies, archaeologists might begin to understand better the problems involved in their construction of models for development and collapse of hierarchical societies. It would certainly be interesting to see how control of production, access to resources, levels of production, output and uses of different styles could frequently be discussed with reference to 'unstratified' societies, where they can be and are determined by communal social factors, rather than by an hierarchical administration.

These last comments, however, are just remarks in passing and fall far short of solving the fundamental difficulties which I see for the archaeologists studying past material culture. Since so much of archaeological interpretation of past societies is based on the recognition and definition of *patterns* amongst archaeological remains, which are then used to support arguments concerning process and social formation, the archaeologists' theories concerning use of material culture are of crucial importance in any discussion. I contend that archaeologists assume that material culture is a passive reflection of society rather than being something which plays an active role in the creation and constant reformation of that society. People use objects to say things about themselves, and objects therefore acquire values or meanings through their use in specific contexts. As Turner (1969) and Lewis (1980) write about ritual, so I believe can material culture be viewed – as a reflection of and a reflection on the acted social world, both passive and active at once; and the material culture of a society is not something just tacked on the end for show but is rather manipulated by that society in such a way that it actually distinguishes its culture and embodies many of its beliefs and actions. Our own society, just like any other, recognizes the importance of different objects as means of conveying information. Thus Morris Minor cars and ethnic rugs mean one thing whilst Mercedes and Persian carpets mean another. It is also important to realize that objects only convey meaning to those who are in the know. So I can laugh when I see an American lady in a shop trying a tea-cosy on her elbow; and a traveller to a foreign land can take home a basketry fish trap for use as an exotic lampshade. The American lady was mystified, but the traveller managed to convert the object into something with meaning in her own field of reference.

When we begin to appreciate the power and the complexity of our own use of material culture, we can begin to appreciate the pitfalls involved in trying to discuss other people's. How, for example, are we to cope with trying to define past societies' categories of 'prestige' goods as opposed to 'ordinary' items? Hammond, in his discussion of Lubaantun (1972:795), writes:

> The list of goods exchanged includes items that are 'useful' and those that are 'functional'. . . . the former including obsidian, axes, pitch, pine, dyes and foodstuffs, and the latter including jade, incense, fine flint and obsidian work and fine pottery. Cacao falls into both categories, being functional as a currency and useful as a food, but the emphasis on its use is largely functional . . . [functional] products were sumptuary goods whose use was concentrated at the upper end of the social scale, and the exchange of lowland and sumptuary products for those of the highlands presumably took place between the top ranks of society.

Hammond has decided to divide these items into a 'functional' group and a 'useful' group and appears to be assured of a dichotomy between them. Yet he is having to rely on his own categories of prestige: it is still being assumed that the twentieth-century western mind is the ultimate in rational thinking and our ethno-centricity and subjectivity of interpretation, which are quite inevitable characteristics, are not being critically assessed. According to my understanding of the use of material culture, this dichotomy is a false one and only reflects the approach which has developed in archaeology of 'compartmentalization' or systems thinking. This extract from an article about Malinowski's work (Paluch 1981:282) reflects a similar problem:

> In his so-called general theory of culture, 'biological needs' form the crucial notion, while in the empirical work the same role is played by 'the native point of view'. When he develops the general theory of culture on the basis of biological imperatives, characteristic of human species, this vision appears very naturalistic and utilitarian, ruled by a very narrow biological determin-

ism. Contrary to that, when Malinowski analyses concrete social reality, such attributes of human kind as thought, emotion, tradition, all of them expressed in the context of changing social situations, play a decisive role.

Barrett and Bradley (1980) write: 'The truth is that the Bronze Age has been divided up into categories of specialist study, until the relationships between these essentially arbitrary parts seem to form the really important problems.' But rather than finding solace in subsistence data, which they advocate, I consider it to be far more fundamentally necessary to reintegrate the study of all spheres of activity, to realize that the ideas of a society are employed in all realms of social action, be they political, economic or symbolic. While we continue to ignore the influence which our own conditioning has upon our classifications of archaeological material, we will continue to rationalize past activity only in terms of our own limited experience.

Yet the solution does not lie with cross-cultural analogy as it has generally been used in archaeology. As I have already stated, material culture can only have value or meaning with relation to the society within which it is used. Throughout the first part of this paper I used several ethnographic examples to 'spoil' other writer's arguments. There are, no doubt, other societies who do things quite differently. This type of argument is, therefore, most unsatisfactory. Nonetheless, I do find that ethnographic examples stimulate one's capacity for understanding the possibility of means of social organization other than one's own and in that sense, therefore, these examples are helpful and enormously educative. Moreover, one can begin to understand the importance and indeed the vital role of a society's belief system in the formation of its past; its existing and its future archaeological record. In the end, however, the notion of lifting one example of use of a certain object or activity out of one social context and transplanting it somewhere else is not at all helpful, and is one which may only serve to confuse the issue. Rather, we need structural models and analogies which consider artefacts in the context of the structure of society as a whole.

So, if we are to recognize that material culture is more than a passive reflection of a society and that one-to-one cross-cultural comparisons are clumsy and ugly, where are we to turn? There is beginning to be a very good body of work studying the role of material culture in ethnographic contexts. Miller (1982), for example, has produced some very interesting work on pottery production amongst the caste system in India; and Donley (1982) has studied the role of the spatial organization of houses and of material culture in general in an Arab community. One fierce criticism that has come from other archaeologists is that in such a context these researchers are unable to look at any long-term diachronic development and are therefore unable to identify any dynamism in social process. I sympathize with this criticism, but I maintain that other archaeologists find this difficult too. Pattern recognition is one thing: archaeologists can see quite clearly that patterns change, and therefore they introduce 'centralizations' and 'intensifications' into their vocabulary to explain process. But I contend that archaeologists are no nearer to understanding *how* these changes come about. Snapshots can be very interesting, but we rely on the ingenuity of the commentator to make the sequence of events plausible. It used to be invasionist theories which held our attention, until we came to think them too simplistic and misleading. In the past ten years or so it has been the turn of the economists and marketeers. Surely now it is time for something else? The connections which archaeologists make at present between one snapshot and the next are as much mythological constructions of our own time as were the movements of the spheres for the Elizabethans. The conclusions may not be incorrect – we cannot say – and the myth is inevitable, but we ought at least to be able to give our own myth-making its due and acknowledge our own creation of social order.

Childe (1958:14) wrote: 'simply to avoid tedium I omit the question mark, the "probably" or "perhaps" that should qualify most statements.' I suggest that in future we make ourselves re-admit them.

Acknowledgments

I am most grateful to Sheena Crawford, Ian Hodder and Michael Mallinson for initial discussion and criticism, to Colin Haselgrove for inviting me to present a paper and to Micky Dietler and Ingrid Herbich for further advice.

Bibliography

Adams, W. Y., 1981. Comment on Rice 1981, *Current Anthropology 22:* 219–40.
Barrett, J. and Bradley, R., 1980. *Settlement and Society in the British Later Bronze Age* (BAR 83).
Binford, L., 1972. *An Archaeological Perspective* (New York).
Bradley, R., 1971. 'Trade competition and artefact distribution', *World Archaeol. 2:* 347–52.
Childe, V. G., 1958. *The Prehistory of European Society.*
Clarke, D. L., 1972. 'A provisional model of an Iron Age society and its settlement system'. In D. L. Clarke (ed.), *Models in Archaeology:* 801–70.
Davis, W. M., 1981. Comment on Rice 1981, *Current Anthropology 22:* 219–40.
Donley, L., 1982. 'House power: Swahili space and symbolic markers'. In I. Hodder (ed.), *Symbolic and Structural Archaeology:* 63–73.
Fedders, A. and Salvadori, C., 1977. *Turkana Pastoral Craftsmen* (Nairobi).
Hammond, N. D. C., 1972. 'Locational models and the site of Lubaantun: a classic Maya centre'. In D. L. Clarke (ed.), *Models in Archaeology:* 757–800.
Hodder, I. R., 1972. 'Locational models and the study of Romano-British settlement'. In D. L. Clarke (ed.), *Models in Archaeology:* 887–910.
Hodder, I. R., 1977. 'The distribution of material culture items in the Baringo District, Western Kenya', *Man 12:* 239–69.
Lewis, G., 1980. *Day of Shining Red.*
Macfarlane, A., 1978. *The Origins of English Individualism.*
Miller, D., 1982. 'Structures and strategies: an aspect of the relationship between social hierarchy and cultural change'. In I. Hodder (ed.), *Symbolic and Structural Archaeology:* 89–98.
Nicklin, K., 1971. 'Stability and innovation in pottery manufacture', *World Archaeol. 3:* 13–48.
Paluch, A. K., 1981. 'The Polish background to Malinowski's work', *Man 16:* 276–85.
Peacock, D. P. S., 1968. 'A contribution to the study of Glastonbury Ware from south-western Britain', *Ant. J. 49:* 41–61.

Peacock, D. P. S., 1969. 'The scientific analysis of ancient ceramics: a review', *World Archaeol. 1:* 375–89.

Rathje, W. L., 1975. 'The last tango in Mayapan: a tentative trajectory of production–distribution systems'. In J. Sabloff and K. Lamberg-Karlovsky (eds.), *Ancient Civilisation and Trade* (Albuquerque): 409–48.

Renfrew, A. C., 1973. 'Monuments, mobilisation and social organisation in Neolithic Wessex'. In A. C. Renfrew (ed.), *The Explanation of Culture Change:* 539–58.

Rice, P. M., 1981. 'Evolution of specialised pottery production: a trial model', *Current Anthropology 22:* 219–40.

Turner, V. W., 1969. *The Ritual Process.*

Welbourn, D. A., 1981. 'The role of blacksmiths in a tribal society'. *Archaeological Reviews from Cambridge 1:* 30–40.

8

Production and exchange in Early Iron Age central Europe

Sara Champion

We know almost nothing about artefact production and the dispersal of finished goods in Early Iron Age Europe. There is very little physical evidence, for reasons that will become clear, of industrial procedures, and such as there is tells us nothing of the organization which lies behind them. We have no records of exchange mechanisms from within central Europe, and almost none from the pens of literate Mediterranean historians and geographers. Nevertheless, it is just becoming possible to apply a variety of techniques of archaeological analysis to such material as is at present available and, I believe, to get nearer to an understanding of some of the processes of production and exchange that lie behind the bland terms like 'craftsman' and 'trade' that are currently scattered over the literature pertaining to the period. I hope to be able to show, by means of an examination of some of the mortuary data and of some classes of artefactual material, that over the period of around 300 years with which I am dealing (between 600 and 300 B.C.) there is a marked change in the milieu and the organization of production, and in the dispersal of finished goods, which reflects the changes in settlement and burial patterns frequently observed but rarely explained except by recourse to yet another invasion (though see Pauli, ch. 2 above).

Peter Wells has outlined elsewhere (Wells 1980a) the nature of society as it is at present perceived at the beginning of the period with which I am here concerned. By the middle of the sixth century B.C. we can see in west and central Europe a series of rich centres of population developing (Härke 1979:67–148), at Mont Lassois (Joffrey 1960) and the Camp-de-Château at Salins (Piroutet 1930), at the Heuneburg (Kimmig 1983) and Hohenasperg (Bittel, Kimmig and Schiek 1981:390–400), at the Britzgyberg in Alsace (Schweitzer 1973) and at Châtillon-sur-Glâne in Switzerland (Schwab 1975), possibly at Ipf (Schultze-Naumburg 1969), the Marienberg at Würzburg (Mildenberger 1963) and the Münsterberg (Bittel, Kimmig and Schiek 1981:314–17). These centres generally comprise a well-defended hill-top settlement and a series of rich burials containing a wealth of locally made fancy goods, from four-wheeled vehicles to fibulae, as well as pottery, metalwork and other materials imported from the Mediterranean. The emergence of these sites, and of the elite class they are always seen to represent, does not spring upon Early Iron Age Europe without warning, as some would suggest, for there are defended hill-top sites of size and importance dating back to the Bronze Age, and rich burials with vehicles and other fancy goods are also known before Hallstatt D. There is, however, a clearly recognizable intensification of these developments in the sixth century B.C., and Peter Wells has elsewhere suggested some of the possible reasons for it, emphasizing in particular the importance of trade with the expanding Mediterranean world. I would here take issue with one of his points, since it has relevance for my own theme, and that is his emphasis on Massalia and the Rhône route for imports reaching central Europe from the south. I am sure that this oversimplifies the complexity of the contacts with the Mediterranean world, and many scholars would strongly defend the equal importance of the Transalpine route, seeing both as participating in the process of interaction which takes place in the sixth and fifth centuries B.C. Objects of Italian manufacture, such as the pyxis from Kastenwald (Jehl and Bonnet 1968) and others, were clearly coming over the Alps to Switzerland, southern Germany and eastern France, and the same route can be shown too for coral, one of the classes of material I shall be concerned with here. The reduction in the significance of Massalia, which declines in commercial fortune by about 500 B.C., does not disrupt all the trade in luxury items, which it surely would were it the major or sole means of transmission of those items, and the essentially complex nature of these trans-cultural relationships is perhaps obscured by reducing them to a Massalia–central Europe relationship.

I have mentioned coral as one of the classes of material with which I shall be dealing. Coral is of particular importance in examining both the external and internal trade relations of central Europe, since on the one hand it is a certainly imported substance that forms part of the exchange in luxury items already mentioned, and on the other it is disseminated rather more widely in the Hallstatt period than other luxuries, and its transformation from raw material to finished ornament may permit the identification of craft centres. Its other, and in many ways greater, significance is that it continues to be an imported commodity after the trade in other luxuries has ceased, so that it is possible to trace, through analysis of its appearance in graves, changes in its use (and therefore manufacture) and destination (and therefore exchange) which cannot be demonstrated for any other imported substance or artefact. I shall also be looking at material inlaid with red enamel, very restricted in its temporal and spatial distribution but of exceptional importance in attempts to identify mechanisms of both production and exchange; and briefly at lignite and its variations, which serve to underline some of the exchange patterns established for the other material.

Since I shall use the term 'workshop products', and will be using material grouped by 'workshops' to illustrate certain points in my argument, I should perhaps begin by examining what I and others mean by a workshop, the physical and conceptual evidence for which is extremely flimsy. A fundamental idea underlying this and previous analyses of the production of specific groups of material is that objects may be ascribed to one craftsman, group of craftsmen, or workshop (e.g. Mansfeld 1973; Jope 1971). While technical similarity and geographical proximity of the findspots might suggest that a particular industrial centre produced particular goods, it cannot be necessarily inferred that all the products of one centre should exhibit such similarity or such geographical proximity. There are problems here which have frequently been glossed over by past researchers. At one extreme, stylistic and technical classification can be carried to the point where all objects which are not in every respect identical are attributed to separate producers; since there are few objects at this period and in this technological milieu which exhibit such extreme similarity, there results an implausible proliferation of manufacturers. At the other extreme, classification can be too general, so that all brooches with a high-arched bow and large-coiled spring may be labelled 'Marzabotto' brooches, implying at least for some that they are from a single source. For the investigation to continue, however, it is necessary to accept a degree of similarity that is appropriate to the problem and which lies somewhere between these two extremes. This 'appropriate' degree of similarity is likely to be largely subjective without the physical evidence of workshops, but the criteria used to differentiate between production centres must be characteristics of a type inherently likely to vary from one workshop to another. Furthermore, it is important to remember that a workshop might produce a variety of types in a variety of styles, and it may therefore be more relevant to look at characteristics other than those of pure typology. These might be chemically or physically discernible differences in the raw materials due to different sources of supply, or personal or workshop tricks of manufacture, either technical or ornamental. These variations should certainly be given more emphasis than minor variations in size or form. Unfortunately, analysis of the raw materials in question, bronze and gold, has for this period been extremely limited, and there are clear problems in this approach if, as may be suspected, there was considerable and continual recycling of old material. The isolation of certain technical tricks may be easier, but with regard to ornament there arises the question of an Iron Age version of a pattern book, which could well blur the distinctions between the workshops when details of beaded designs or engraved patterns are examined.

Some of these conceptual problems might be solved if there were anywhere satisfactory archaeological evidence for workshops – that is, the physical remains on site of a structure or area where high-class metalworking was going on. Such evidence is not in general forthcoming. Settlement sites on the Continent have received very little attention, apart from the exceptional sites like the centres already mentioned, and even for these only the Heuneburg has had sizeable excavations within the interior. Here there is ample evidence for metalworking, and the area in which it was happening can be identified to the excavators' satisfaction, but though moulds and waste metal material have been located, the organization and output of a particular workshop cannot be deduced. Evidence of metalworking has come from limited, mostly rescue, excavations on presumed settlement sites in central Europe, but in no case have structures been identified, and such a small area of the sites has been investigated that only fragments of the potential body of evidence are available. In Britain, where rich Iron Age burials do not detain us, excavations of settlement sites have long been our source of information on this period, but few have provided more than a scatter of evidence for metalworking. An exception, of course, is Gussage All Saints, Dorset (Wainwright 1979), where remarkable evidence of foundry debris was extracted, including a large series of moulds showing the range of goods made in that particular metalworking event: yet Spratling (Wainwright and Spratling 1973:124–6) was still pessimistic about being able to form any conclusions about the organization of smiths and workshops from that evidence.

If these lines of enquiry do not by themselves produce any useful answers, can ethnographic evidence be of assistance? Rowlands (1972) has shown the many different ways in which the production of metalwork can be organized, and the researcher may choose whichever of the examples appears to fit best the evidence he has. This at best is a precarious approach, and at worst will be misleading and worthless. It is of interest, however, that the often-quoted, Childean concept of an itinerant smith is the least common form of metal craftsman cited by Rowlands, although his data are not claimed to be exhaustive, and anyway lack of ethnographic parallel cannot be used to negate the possibility of itinerant craftsmen in prehistoric Europe. Despite the problems of using ethnographic data, there are persuasive parallels between the admittedly rather sparse evidence for the organization of metalworking in the wealthy milieu of the central European Hallstatt period, and the organizational structures hinted at by Rowlands in some of the societies with an elite; until there is more substantial evidence pointing to a different interpretation, these ideas lie behind my tentative suggestions as to the organization of metalworking in this period. As for the later, Early La Tène period, the evidence is less easy to manipulate, and the possible parallels in the ethnographic literature are correspondingly more numerous; I have therefore avoided any attempt to identify specific organizational structures for this phase.

Although I have stressed above the limitations both in the evidence and in the possible approaches to it, there are still grounds for optimism that a careful use of available data may lead to a greater understanding of the processes in which we are interested, and below I present just a selection of the material on which I have been working to illustrate this point.

Let us first examine artefacts made of or decorated with coral in the Hallstatt D period (sixth century B.C.) in central Europe (Champion 1976). These comprise fibulae, pins, beads, pendants and the occasional weapon. With a few exceptions these articles are geographically distributed near to, or actually on, those rich settlement and burial sites mentioned above. Few of the finds demonstrate the extreme degree of similarity which would allow an unhesitating ascription to the hand of one craftsman, but several tricks of construction or of decoration can be isolated which allow such an ascription to be suggested. An example is provided by a group of Hallstatt D2 kettledrum fibulae from Switzerland (Appendix 1). Their plain hemispherical bow, stop disc and foot

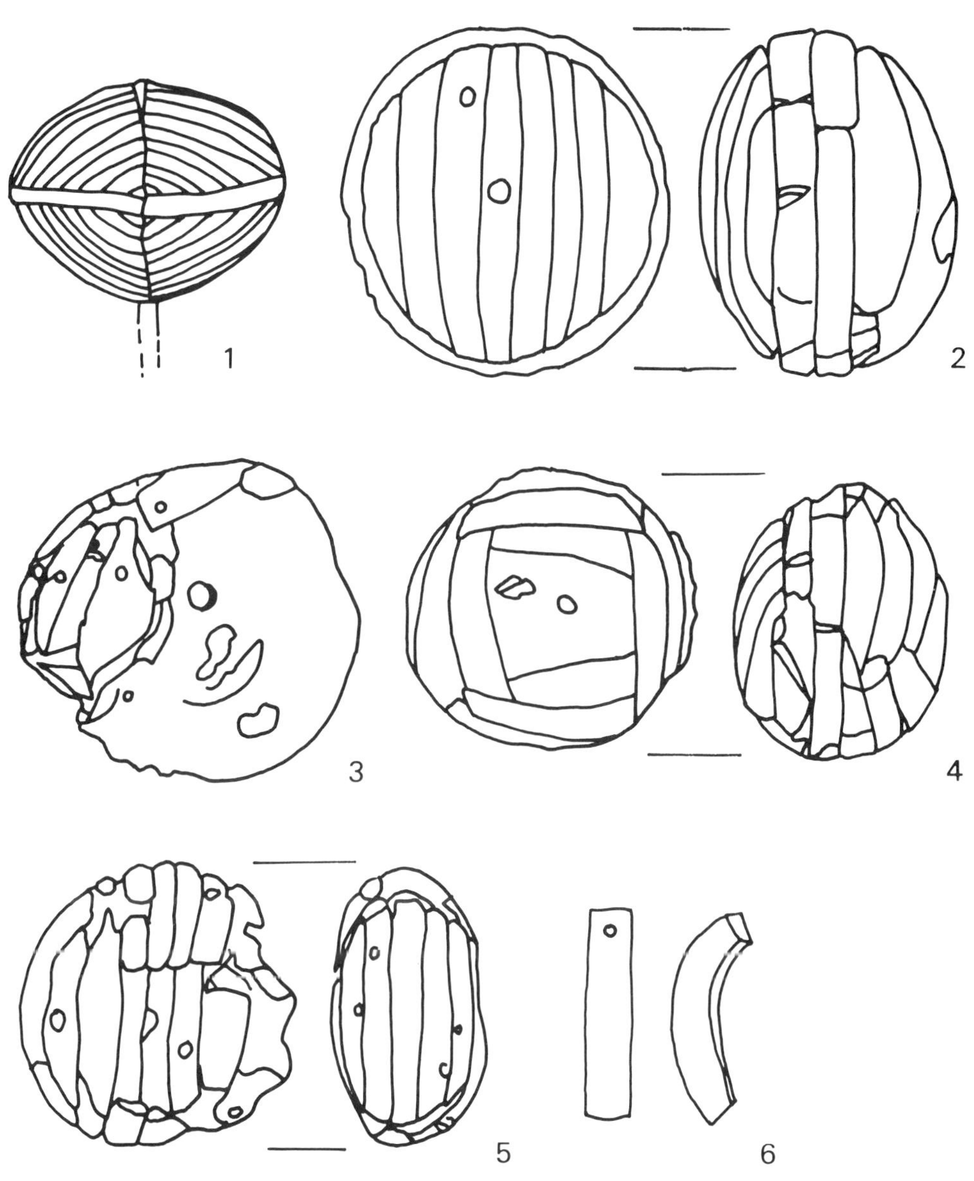

Figure 8.1 Composite coral beads and pinheads. 1 not to scale; 2–6 at 1:1.
1 Nordhouse; 2–5 Sirnau; 6 Mont Lassois.

decorated with a small bead of coral demonstrate a degree of similarity beyond that which simply groups them as kettledrum fibulae. Another group of Hallstatt D2 fibulae comprises those with a conical bow topped with a bead of coral (Appendix 2), found in eastern France and particularly associated with the rich centres at Mont Lassois and Camp de Château at Salins. A particularly persuasive group of objects is the small one comprising spherical beads and pinheads constructed of segments of coral fastened together with pins and resin (Appendix 3; fig. 8.1), which come from sites either side of the Rhine and possibly associated with Hohenasperg. A geographical outlier to the main group, comprising a single segment of coral probably from one of these spheres, was found at Mont Lassois, raising immediately interesting questions about the relationship between the rich centres themselves, to which we shall return. Other coherent groups of coral-decorated material seem to be concentrated in the Heuneburg area and again at Mont Lassois. In many cases, then, the groups of objects which could be claimed on technical and decorative grounds to be the product of one craftsman or workshop are distributed at or near the rich centres.

Excavations at these centres have in most cases been limited and not of a standard acceptable today. Nevertheless, some of the sites have produced evidence of manufacturing procedures on site: for example, there are half-finished fibulae at Mont Lassois (Joffroy 1960:fig.27.3). At the most recently, and more fully, excavated site of the Heuneburg, there is much more consistent evidence of metalworking and other manufacturing procedures taking place, as has been mentioned above. Of particular interest in this context is the find of a piece of partly-carved raw coral, which suggests that this material was being worked on the site (Kimmig and Gersbach 1971:57–8).

As well as looking at the objects themselves, and at the evidence from excavation of the settlements, I have examined the contexts of the majority of the finds, the burials. The mortuary data for the period and area in question are overwhelming in their quantity but are in many cases, sadly, of variable quality. The majority of the larger groups of tumuli were poorly excavated and/or recorded in the nineteenth and twentieth centuries A.D., and in many cases the exceptional, usually central, graves had already been pillaged in antiquity, often soon after deposition (for example, the central grave at Magdalenenberg, Spindler 1971; and the Grafenbühl, Zürn 1970). Despite the serious shortcomings of the data, which in general allow no really detailed analysis of the graves such as was accomplished for the Bronze Age cemetery of Branč (Shennan 1975), it has been possible to produce some very interesting results (summarized in Champion 1982). Analysis on a very basic level of a series of Late Hallstatt cemeteries, such as Grafenbühl and Mühlacker, showed that in each tumulus or group of tumuli there were several rather poorly endowed graves and proportionately few very wealthy, whether the wealth scoring was achieved simply by number of artefact types in the grave, by the total number of objects of each type, or by the value of the objects in terms of availability of raw material and the time and skill taken to produce them. Imported goods were exclusively associated with graves already designated as wealthy because of the number of artefact types, many local, that they contained, with the exception of the robbed central graves which for these analyses I assumed to have been very wealthy. The only Mediterranean import to reach graves below this top level was coral, which was found in graves richer in local goods than the average but containing no other imports. Coral would here seem to define a level of society below the richest and above the remainder of the population deemed worthy of interment in the tumulus, which itself may have been privileged. All the analyses carried out on Late Hallstatt cemeteries containing coral finds show clearly that coral was not available to the lower ranks of those buried, a factor which is important in the context of the organization of production in this period, and which will also be significant when we come to consider the cemeteries of the early La Tène period.

What do these different strands of evidence tell us of late Hallstatt society and the place of the craftsman within it? In the first place, there is enough evidence in the form of raw materials, waste materials and foundry debris to suggest that manufacturing of a variety of objects was carried out at the rich centres, and indeed, at the Heuneburg at least, the industrial area of the site has been identified. However, it is clear that metalworking, at least, was not confined exclusively to the major sites, as excavations at Hascherkeller (Wells 1980b), Hillesheim (Haffner 1971), Kornwestheim (Joachim 1977), Fellbach-Schmiden (Biel and Joachim 1979), and various sites in Switzerland (Wyss 1974) have shown. The limited amount of evidence from the major sites suggests the manufacture of fibulae, of local copies of Italian imports like flagons, and of objects of coral and shale or lignite. At least some of these items can be considered as luxury goods which were unlikely to have been available to the whole population, or so their distribution in graves would suggest. If we can believe the presence of craftsmen making luxury goods on the major sites, then we must envisage some kind of close relationship with the presumed elite who inhabited those sites. The picture presented by the goods examined is one of small batches of similar items or, more particularly, individual items with no exact parallels, giving the impression of goods made to special order rather than manufacture in bulk. There are examples in the anthropological literature of specialist craftsmen attached to high-status groups (Rowlands 1972:216). Such craftsmen might produce for those groups, and for redistribution by them to followers and subordinates, goods of a luxury and personalized nature. The raw materials, which in the case of these Iron Age sites include imported materials like coral as well as the ingredients for bronze which must have required imported tin, might be acquired by the patron through the wide-ranging contacts discussed elsewhere, and would be transformed into specially commissioned pieces. These would then be worn or used by the elite themselves, their wives and offspring, and may also have been redistributed to more distant family such as relations by marriage, and to followers whose relationship with the leader required strengthening and advertising in the form of fancy goods unavailable to the rest of the populace. This type of exchange mirrors on a more local scale the kind of relationship established between the elite north of the Alps and the Mediterranean world by the giving of ostentatious presents, referred to in the classical literature (Fischer 1973), and which can be interpreted as a means by which the elite legitimated their power over subordinates, while being a small price for the Mediterranean donors to pay for access to consumables and probably slave labour from the north.

The evidence which might be used to substantiate this interpretation is partly negative and partly positive. From the negative point of view, there is no evidence for the manufacture of fancy goods, nor the working of exotic materials, on ordinary settlement sites – which, if the excavation of such settlement sites were more commonplace, would be a powerful argument in favour of manufacture at the rich centres. In fact, as we have seen, few settlements have been excavated under other than rescue conditions. The only place where we have evidence of fine metalworking away from the major settlements is the recently excavated rich burial at Eberdingen-Hochdorf (Biel 1982). Here it is possible that some of the objects which accompanied the chieftain to his grave were actually made at the site of his tumulus, since remains of such processes have been found, and there is little wear on, for example, the goldwork. The presence of metalworking in close association with one of the rich graves only serves to accentuate the relationship between the elite and the processes of manufacture.

The absence of exotic goods, including coral, from all but the richest graves emphasizes the restricted distribution of this material, which would allow the interpretation suggested above of redistribution by the patron. Another possible explanation of such restriction might be that, given the assumption of manufacture at the centre, only the almost equally rich could afford to purchase goods of this quality, and that, though physically attached to the centre, the craftsman was able to manufacture for sale to outsiders. This would raise the question of the sources of bronze, gold and coral which under the previous interpretation we imagined to be acquired through the wide-ranging contacts of the patron. Rowlands (1972) has shown that one possible procedure would be for the person needing the object made to take the raw materials to the craftsman, and for the craftsman to take a small percentage of that material as payment for the manufacture of the object. This assumes a much more independent craftsman than can perhaps be envisaged for a man closely associated with what appears to be a centre of personal power. Also in favour of a patronized craftsman is the very slight evidence mentioned above for contact between the rich centres themselves. This is much easier to understand in terms of exchange between equals, if not rivals, than as one rich patron 'buying' goods from another centre. However, it could also be seen as evidence for a peripatetic craftsman, though this would be easier to assert were there more objects of similar kind from a number of the centres. The information available at present, though inadequate, does suggest that the interpretation as originally set out fits the evidence best, and new information from rescue excavation on rich burials, rich settlements and ordinary settlements seems to do nothing more than strengthen the likelihood of its becoming acceptable.

There are a number of object types which either require import of the raw material from a lesser distance, or which involve extremely highly skilled metal craftsmen: lignite and jet, for example, and the highly ornate bronze beltplates and barrel armbands. It would be of considerable interest to carry out the same type of cemetery analysis and a thorough search for manufacturing evidence in the form of raw and half-worked lignite as has been done for coral. A comparison of the patterns with those outlined above would, I suspect, show great similarities.

The end of the Hallstatt period has always been seen as signalling the demise of both the rich settlement sites and the associated rich graves. In fact there is evidence that for the Camp de Château at Salins, the Hohenasperg and for Dürrnberg in Austria, this was not the case, but this argument rests partly on what is meant by the Hallstatt period. In terms of the style of some of the objects found both in grave and on site, there is no doubt that the above-mentioned sites continue into at least the Early La Tène period; but in terms of real chronology, we are dealing with the problem of the possible contemporaneity of Hallstatt D and La Tène A, and it is impossible not to enter here into the thorny discussion surrounding this problem that has exercised the minds of, particularly, our German colleagues for many years (for example, *Hamburger Beiträge* 2.2, 1972; and Pauli, ch. 2 above). The problem is particularly bound up with the question of the La Tène A period in the area of the Middle Rhine, where an apparently similar type of elite society is in contact with the Mediterranean, just as was occurring further south in the Hallstatt period (Haffner 1976). There appear here rich burials with goldwork, daggers, imports and vehicles at a time which, according to one group of German archaeologists, coincides with that of the rich burials in southern Germany, and according to another, succeeds it. It is not relevant here to go into the protracted and sometimes acrid arguments that surround this particular chronological problem, though there are two points worth making. One is that much of the problem concerns terminology and the concepts which lie behind the use of such terms as 'Hallstatt' and 'La Tène'. The other is that discussion centres almost exclusively around the rich and well-known settlements and burials, taking little acount of the admittedly sparse but certainly available evidence for continuity (and succession) in the smaller, more ordinary settlements. It should be emphasized that if 'Late Hallstatt' in southern Germany and 'Early La Tène' in the Middle Rhine are in fact synchronic, then as much explanation is needed of the different nature of the imported material and the fact that the artefact types do not overlap as is needed to clarify the problems of why the imports and the associated elite cease further south if they are in fact successive. At this point I will do no more than to state my stance in this argument, which is to favour the successive rather than the synchronic view in general, and leave to a future occasion the reasoning behind my belief.

Many features of the Early La Tène period in the Middle Rhine are closely comparable with the Late Hallstatt period in southern Germany and eastern France. Rather suddenly there appear rich graves containing vehicles, high-class local goods and objects imported from the Mediterranean, and though the particular form, and perhaps the area of origin, of some of these imported goods may be different, it has generally been assumed that such graves appear as a result of the same processes and developments which produced the Hallstatt ones. There are differences, however. In the first place, the evidence comes entirely from graves; apart from those princely residences which have not yet ceased to function and which are at some distance from the area (for example, the Camp de Château), no rich centres, definable in terms of the imported materials they might contain on analogy with the earlier sites, have yet been located. This does not necessarily mean that they are not there: sites producing Attic black-figure and red-figure ware have only been located in the last few years in Alsace and in Switzerland, and with the current state of financial provision for large-scale settlement excavations the likelihood of a suitable programme of investigation being mounted recedes annually. It should also be noted that in the Middle Rhine the rich burials of the Early La Tène period are much more evenly spaced, much less clustered than those of regions further south during Hallstatt D, and that if this reflects a different kind of basis for the acquisition of wealth/power, then we might not be surprised to see differences in settlement organization among other things. Whether wealthy 'centres' eventually emerge or not, the archaeological data, in this case exclusively from cemeteries, suggest that there are similarities in the way that metalwork production was carried out. Though there are no physical remains of workshops, there is also no evidence for bulk manufacture of items in the form of rows of identical objects, and consumption of fancy goods is still restricted. Analyses of the mortuary data carried out in the same way as they were for the Hallstatt period show restricted access to imported materials and an identical pattern of access to coral (Champion 1982).

Further south, in the north-west Alpine region, the rich centres had disappeared by this time, and with them the tumuli and the imports. In Switzerland and southern Germany burial was now in flat graves, sometimes in small cemeteries, sometimes in sizeable ones, reflecting either a considerable variation in the sizes of communities served by the cemeteries or variations in the rules of access to cemeteries. Of their settlements we know almost nothing. Into this milieu, however, coral was still being imported, if anything in larger amounts than before if the profligate use of it in the decoration of fibulae is anything to go by (e.g. Münsingen Gr.156; Hodson 1968:142). There is no reason to suppose that it is coming in by any route other than a Transalpine one: cemeteries in northern Italy and the Italian part of Switzerland at this time also contain fibulae decorated with coral (e.g. Giubiasco; Ulrich 1914), and indeed there is no evidence of a break in the importing of coral which had probably always been carried out by this route, if not exclusively then at least to a considerable extent. Possibly for several reasons, one of which may have been the decline in ostentatious burial rites and monuments, many of the cemeteries remained unpillaged until the nineteenth century, and the mortuary data, while frequently still inadequate because of poor excavation, are at least in some instances more complete and therefore more suitable for analysis. Similar analyses to those outlined above were carried out for cemeteries in Switzerland (and also in the Marne region, to which we shall return later), and the results were striking (Champion 1982). There emerged a complete change in the availability of coral, imported substance though it was. Graves which on any scale would be rated poor (excluding, naturally, those which contain nothing in the way of grave goods), for example those containing only one object, may now have coral on that object, and coral need not appear in any greater volume in graves at the top of the wealth scale. The social restrictions on access to a luxury material seem to have gone, implying a fundamental transformation in the exchange mechanisms and perhaps also the production mechanisms at this time.

We return briefly to the question of the routes by which imports in general and coral in particular were reaching these areas north of the Alps. I have already indicated that in the Hallstatt period there was a considerable amount of Transalpine traffic, and this can be suggested not only for the fancy southern metalwork but also for coral, which was being used in a similar manner in Italy and southern Switzerland as it was north of the Alps. The continuing, indeed increasing, flow of coral to the north in the Early La Tène period must also have followed this route: again, it was in use in Cisalpine cemeteries, and north of the Alps it was used mainly in the north-west Alpine region, though it was more widespread than in previous periods, reaching further east, north and west. The decline in the fortunes of Massalia, which may well have continued to supply northern France on a more limited basis, is not matched by an interruption in the supply of coral to Switzerland and Germany, and indeed the picture suggested by the material is one of an unbroken supply of smaller, perhaps less obvious imports, from the Hallstatt to the La Tène period.

A new area and a new substance must be brought into the discussion here. Already in the latter part of Hallstatt D the Champagne region of France was acquiring coral to be used as pendants and in the decoration of fibulae, and analysis of one cemetery at Chouilly 'Les Jogasses' (Favret 1936) shows that access to coral is probably socially restricted in a manner similar to that discussed above for other regions, although the nature and contents of the graves themselves are different from the graves in southern Germany, Switzerland and eastern France. In the Early La Tène period there is a considerable increase in the number of cemeteries excavated, however badly, and a corresponding increase in the number of coral finds. In the well-known rich chariot burials such as Somme-Bionne (Morel 1875) and Condé-sur-Marne (unpublished, Châlons Museum; some finds in Jacobsthal 1944:no. 202) there are

Figure 8.2 Near Camp-de-Châlons, Marne. Iron boss, probably from shield, heavily decorated with coral. (Diameter 57mm.) (Musée des Antiquités Nat., St-Germain-en-Laye.)

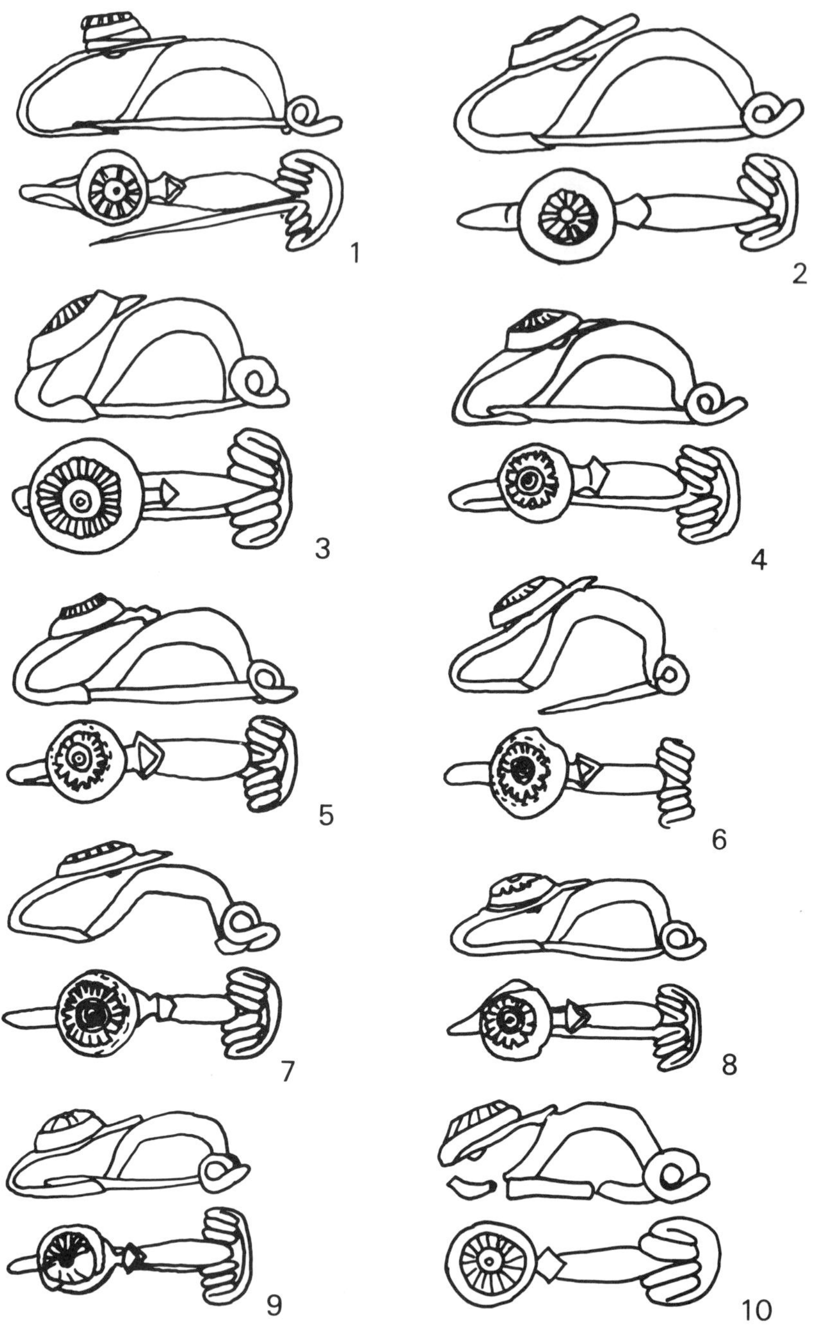

Figure 8.3 Münsingen-Andelfingen fibulae. Scale 1:1. 1 Dürrnberg Gr.28/1; 2 Nebringen Gr.4; 3 Andelfingen Gr.29; 4–9 Münsingen-Rain Grs.61, 93, 102, 121; 10 Boswil Gr.4.

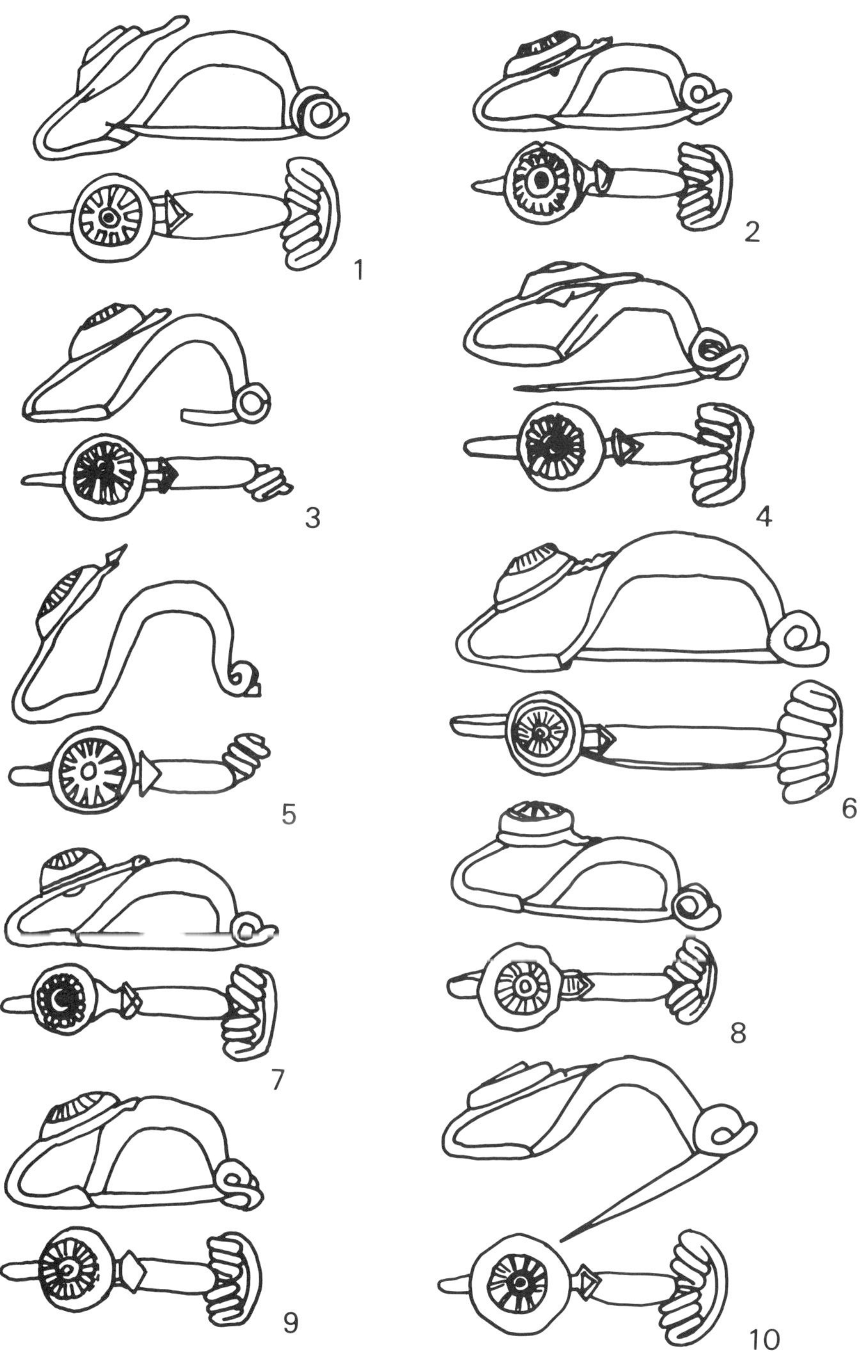

Figure 8.4 Münsingen-Andelfingen fibulae. Scale 1:1. 1,3 Winkel Gr.3; 2,4,7,9 Münsingen-Rain Grs.102, 152, 61, 84; 5 Rheinau; 6,8 Boswil Grs.6, 7; 10 Andelfingen Gr.6.

large amounts of coral used both on personal equipment and on horse-gear (fig. 8.2). There is, however, also a wider distribution of the substance socially, comparable to that seen in Switzerland and southern Germany; although the components of Hallstatt and La Tène in Champagne may differ to a certain extent from the areas to the east, nevertheless the same phenomenon of a wider availability of an imported material is in evidence.

The new substance relevant to this discussion is red 'enamel', or more accurately opaque red glass. Contrary to earlier assertions (e.g. Déchelette 1914:837), this material was not used as a later substitute for coral, but was developed and used during La Tène A and B, often with coral on the same object, and in nearly all areas went out of use in its early form before coral itself did. It is of significance here because in any discussion of workshops and production for the Early La Tène period the material which it adorns is of considerable value in defining workshop groups, and its intimate association with coral allows some startling comparisons to be made, with even more surprising conclusions to be drawn.

In contrast to the preceding period there now appear groups of artefacts that are to all intents and purposes identical, with many more which are very similar. These groups comprise fibulae and other types inlaid with coral and enamel, though some of the most impressive groups are enamelled fibulae. One of the more coherent coral-inlaid groups is that of fibulae found mainly in the Marne which I call the 'Berru' type (Appendix 4). Although some details of individual fibulae differ, all the items have a characteristic high, almost roof-shaped bow, a foot returning at 45° to the bow, inlaid disc(s) on the foot, and a long projecting finial beyond the disc. The bow is also frequently inlaid with coral in a long pointed oval furrow. All but one of the examples come from the Marne region (only one is from Doubs), and they must surely be the product of one or more closely associated workshops.

A remarkably homogeneous group of 'identical' objects is a group of small enamelled fibulae which I call the Münsingen-Andelfingen type, found mainly in Switzerland but also in southern Germany and with outliers as far away as Austria. Their characteristics include small size, an asymmetrical bow which leans back towards the 4-coil spring, an enamel disc fastened by a rivet with a sunburst-decorated head, and a triangular projection beyond the foot-disc (Appendix 5; figs. 8.3 and 8.4). There are at least 34 of these known, with others found since I compiled my list, and they are generally so easy to recognize that even without the inlay present examples can be confidently assigned to the group. Another homogeneous group of fibulae which I call the Münsingen-Deisswil type comprises those with a 4-coil spring and a bow inlaid with red enamel round an S-scroll. The foot has a disc of the same material, and where the head of the fastening pin is present it is in the form of a four-petalled flower (Appendix 6; fig. 8.5). There are at least eight of these known, with early reference to others which cannot be ascertained; six are from Swiss cemeteries, one is from southern Germany and another from Bas-Rhin. There can be little doubt that this group was manufactured in the same workshop, perhaps only in a limited number of production events. These are some of the most persuasive

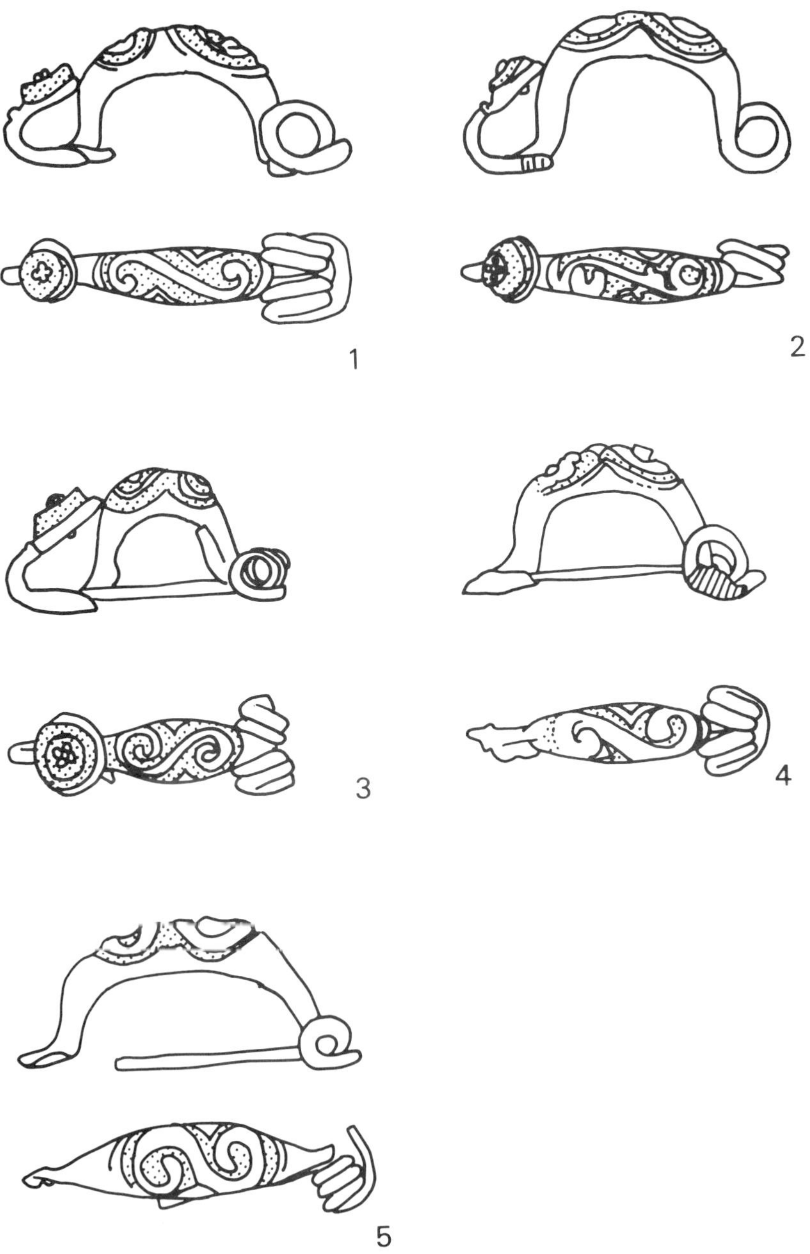

Figure 8.5 Münsingen-Deisswil fibulae. Scale 1:1. 1–2 Münsingen-Rain Grs.49, 80; 3 Schirrheinerweg Tum.8; 4 Deisswil Grs.2–4; 5 Birsfelden.

groups of identical or similar objects, but there are many others (including disc bracelets and torcs). In my view the fibulae at least can best be interpreted as batches of stock items, the kind of 'off-the-shelf' articles that a craftsman might have available for sale, forming part of his capital. While there is certainly the likelihood of special commissions still coming in, the appearance of numbers of identical items could be interpreted as a sign that the basis of production has changed. At the same time the dispersal of the objects shows evidence of a different set of exchange mechanisms from what has gone before (see below).

While it is in some ways easier with this material to spot the likely output of a single workshop, there are in truth as many, if not more, problems in understanding the organization of production. Firstly, there are no physical remains of any craft production centres of any type for the areas likely to have been at the heart of much of the manufacturing, for example the Swiss plateau. We have not a single fully excavated Early La Tène settlement site, so we have little idea of the size and complexity of such a site, let alone how small industries functioned. This is particularly unfortunate since detailed analysis of the metalwork has thrown up some important questions related to the organization of production which might well be answered by a few satisfactory excavations. These relate to the different types of material which may be worked in any one establishment, and could be answered were such a workshop, or even workshop debris, to be located.

I have already mentioned that the decorated rivet-heads on two of the groups of 'stock' items were consistent within each group. Having defined the three major classes of decorated rivet-heads (fig. 8.6), it becomes clear that they were not simply confined to enamelled fibulae but were used on disc torcs and bracelets as well. If these rivet-heads were a reliable guide to individual workshops, then it would greatly enlarge the range of goods attributable to one source. Unfortunately, it soon becomes apparent that while some groups comprising artefacts classed together on other grounds used exclusively one type of rivet-head, other groups which on all other evidence should belong together could be associated with all three main types of rivet-head. A particular case in point is a group of fibulae with coral-inlaid bows and enamelled disc foot (Appendix 7; figs. 8.7 and 8.8). There are at least 18 of these, nine of which have a Type I pinhead, five a Type II, and the rest Type IIIb or undecorated. On other grounds the majority of these examples, perhaps omitting the two very large ones, might have been considered the product of a single workshop.

The disc torcs, which can be grouped on the basis of several criteria, had all three main types of pinhead appearing in most of the groups. Only by grouping the torcs according to the pinheads could there be groups with identical pinheads, and then all the other, equally important characteristics were to be found spread among several groups, causing the separation of otherwise identical torcs. There are a number of possible explanations, some of which might be answered in a relevant excavation. In the first place there might be a slight chronological difference in the use of the pinheads, and I have argued elsewhere that there is some evidence for this (Champion 1977). A more interesting possibility, one that suggests more complex production procedures, is that the inlaying of metal ornaments might take place in a separate establishment where a choice of rivet-heads was available. Customers requiring a matching set of fibulae, torc and bracelet could choose one type for all three, even if the objects were manufactured in different workshops and/or at different times. Other customers wanting only one ornament might take the standard issue with the pinhead that the craftsman thought was suitable. Some might find this proliferation of craftsmen unlikely, but Rowlands (1972) has shown that in Nubia, for example, a customer might go to a smith with iron to be made into a dagger; take the blade on to another craftsman to be hafted; and go on to a third for a sheath to be fitted.

Against this, the inlaying of cut-out areas such as scrolls in fibula bows and on torcs would seem to be more sensibly carried out in the same production centre as the metalwork; again, the excavation of one suitable workshop should be able to show whether enamelling and bronzeworking were carried out in the same establishment. Another curiosity which points to complexities in production, and was brought up during the same analyses, is that although coral and enamel inlaid artefacts, particularly fibulae, are apparently made in the same geographical region (and from the decoration on the bows, even in the same workshop), there is not a single coral-inlaid fibula with its coral fixed by one of the three main types of rivet-head. Does this mean that coral-working was carried out in different establishments, and if so, how do we explain the group of fibulae inlaid with both substances? These are associated with all the main pinhead types – fastening the enamel discs – and yet the pinheads never cross the division between the two materials. Should we see in this evidence of the separation of production involving coral and enamel, and the carrying, by the client, of the completed bronze and enamelled fibula to a coral workshop or *vice-versa*? This is just a very small piece of evidence to suggest that different

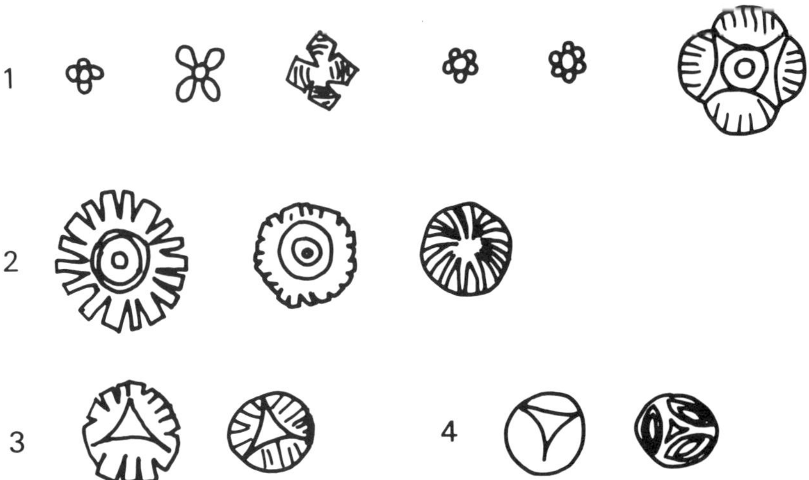

Figure 8.6 Decorated rivet-heads. Scale 2:1. 1 Type I; 2 Type II; 3 Type IIIa; 4 Type IIIb.

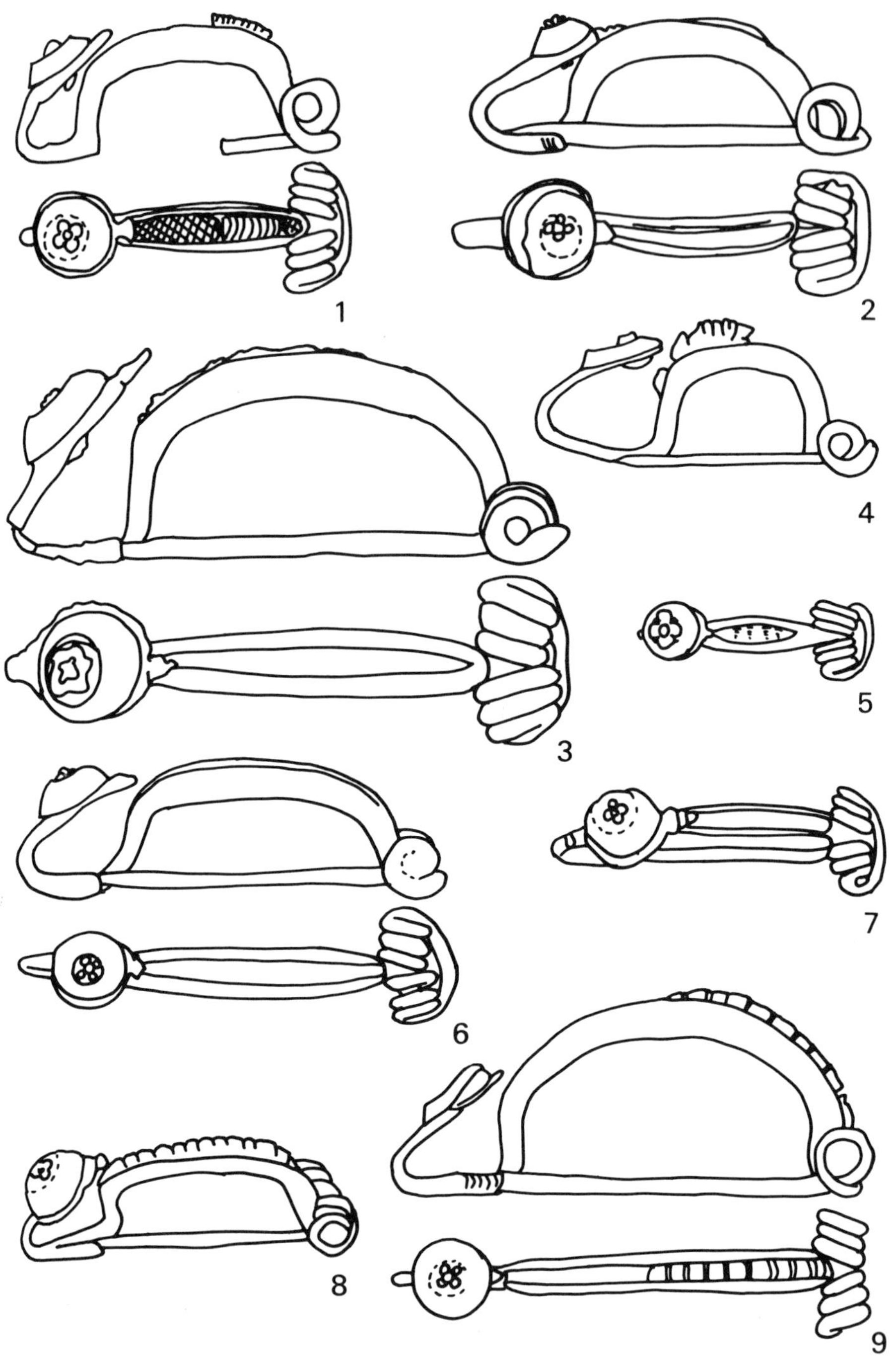

Figure 8.7 Fibulae with coral in bow and enamel on foot. Scale 1:1. 1,4 Nebringen Gr.17; 2 Deisswil Grs.8–15; 3 Worb Gr.11; 5 Andelfingen Gr.29; 6,9 Muttenz Gr.1; 7–8 Vevey Gr.29.

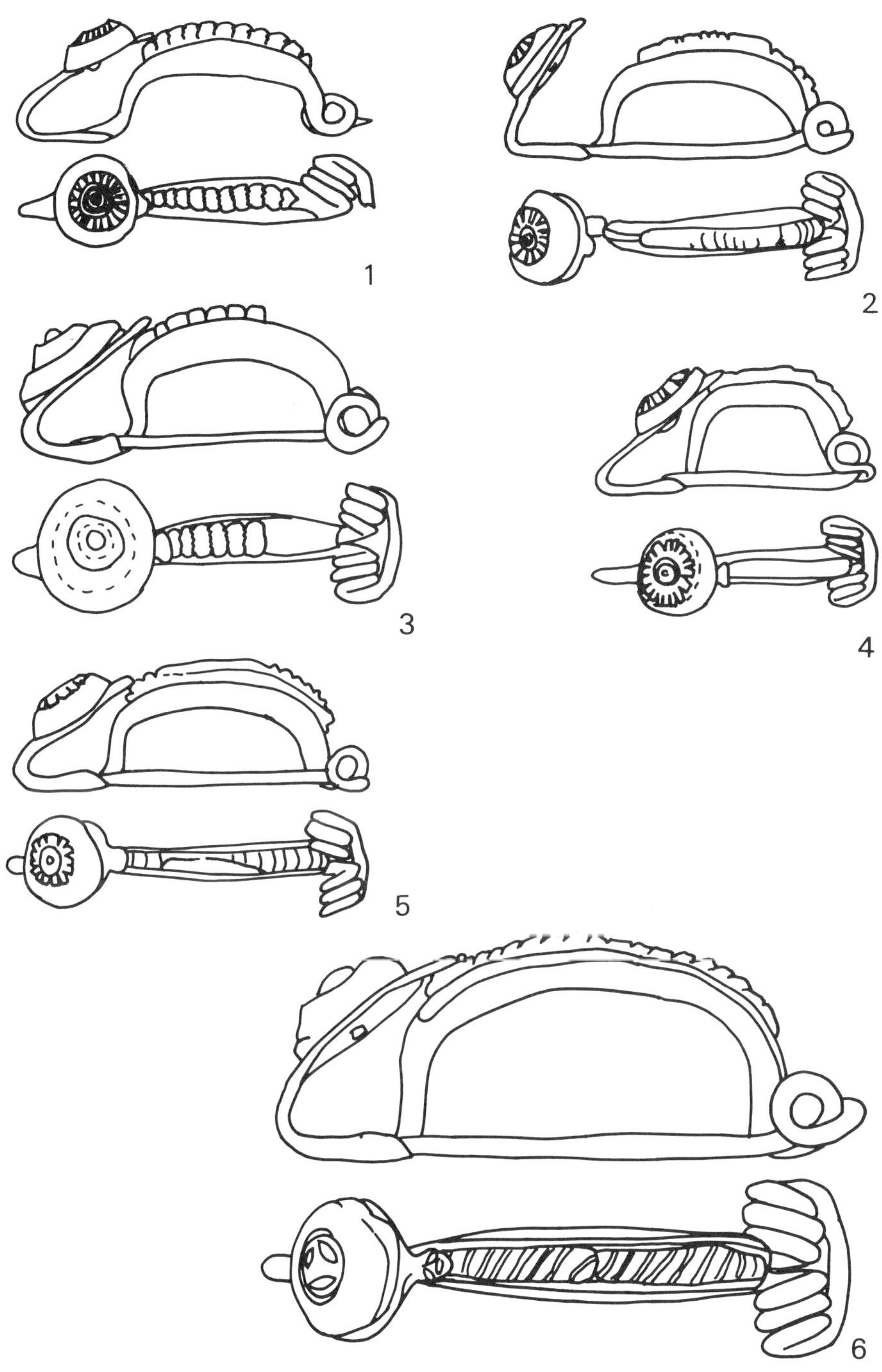

Figure 8.8 Fibulae with coral in bow and enamel on foot. Scale 1:1. 1,3 Altstetten Gr.1; 2,4–6 Münsingen-Rain Grs.84, 102, 86.

functions might have been carried out in different workshops, or that perhaps the rules governing the combination of features on an object were so strict that pinheads for enamel were never used for coral.

While problems of this nature remain intractable, we cannot say that we fully understand the organization of production in this period; however, a possible interpretation of the groups of standardized items is that specialized craftsmen acquired raw materials from their customers, taking a percentage so that stock items could be made, and manufacturing certain standard designs as well as the special orders that were still bound to be coming in. Such craftsmen appear not to have been associated with identifiable elite groups, as none such can be shown to have been in existence in this period, and both the positioning and the size of many of the cemeteries suggest small- or large-scale village life, where presumably a variety of items was made and exchanged. Doubtless some craftsmen became well-known for their excellent work, and we might see a workshop serving quite a large area with richly-decorated personal ornaments, some available for acquisition with no advance warning.

To sum up the evidence for production and local dispersal, there appear to be no more rich centres, and coral finds are dispersed widely in the regions round the putative manufacturing centres. There are no apparent social restrictions on what in the past seems to have been a socially restricted item, and one which must still be imported from the Mediterranean. There appears to have been a change in production procedures from patronized craftsmen attached to an elite group, manufacturing items to order for dispersal by the patron, to independent craftsmen probably based in large villages and possibly selling items from a pre-prepared stock as well as carrying out special orders. There is at least the possibility that some closely associated crafts are in fact carried out in different establishments, though evidence from other material suggests that enamelling and bronzeworking may take place in the same workshop.

Let us return to exchange. In the Hallstatt period we saw items from one putative source generally getting not much further than the hinterland of that source. The possibilities of inter-centre communications were raised by the occasional appearance, such as at Mont Lassois and the Camp de Château, of markedly similar types, though it would not be impossible to explain these by suggesting the existence of some sort of pattern book for fibulae and composite beads. When the rich defended sites came to an end, so did the finds of coral in those immediate areas, another indication of the role such sites played in its distribution. In the Early La Tène period interaction between different areas of Europe and over quite long distances becomes apparent, and emphasizes the ever-increasing complexity of society. For example, a small group of very decorative metal objects, some plaques and some disc brooches, which might well have been made in one workshop, appear not only in the rich graves of the Middle Rhine and the Marne, but also in one of the earliest La Tène flat graves in Switzerland, at St Sulpice (Appendix 8; figs.8.9–11). Here is an apparent link between two very different types of social organization which cannot yet be understood, though there are possibilities of pursuing such links further. When we look at the wider exchange patterns of the material manufactured in the north-west Alpine region we can see that the identification of workshop groups allows a more complex network to be uncovered. One of the most interesting features is the link between the Dürrnberg in Austria and the north-west Alpine region. A number of fibula types, decorated with coral or enamel and almost certainly manufactured on the Swiss plateau, are found in ones and twos in Dürrnberg graves (e.g. a pair of Münsingen-Andelfingen fibulae, Gr.28/1: Penninger 1972:Taf. 26, 1 and 2; fibulae with Type I pinheads, Gr.10/2: Penninger 1972:Taf.9, A1 and A3; a coral-decorated fibula, Gr.28/2: Penninger 1972:Taf.25, A1); and the evidence for this long-distance link – for there are no findspots in between – is augmented by the identification of much of the lignite used in Dürrnberg bracelets as being of south German origin, one example indeed having its only parallel on the Swiss plateau. There is even a possible piece of English shale from the Ramsaukopf (Moosleitner, Pauli and Penninger 1974:153–67).

The Swiss plateau appears to have been the hub of much activity in the Early La Tène period: coral-decorated brooches of almost certain Swiss manufacture are found in the Marne and in the south of France (Nages, Gard: *Gallia*, XXVII, 1969:406, fig.29; Uzès and Sommières, Gard: de Saint-Venant 1897:487–8 and fig.1; 508), while enamelled Swiss fibulae reach southern Germany in one direction and the far side of the Alps in the other. There can be no doubt that the silver bent ring from Park Brow in Sussex (Wolseley, Smith and Hawley 1927:fig.J) is of Swiss manufacture, and it is possible that at least one of the fibulae from Hunsbury, Northants. (Fell 1936:fig.2a), is also Swiss-made. The exact nature of these exchanges is not totally clear as yet, but at least we may now begin to identify what is going where from where, and can begin to look at how and why these objects went where they did. It is not difficult to understand the importance of the Dürrnberg in these exchanges, for it must have been

	SITE	METAL	METAL DECORATION		CORAL INLAY		OTHER INLAY	
			Long beading	Circles	Beads	Lengths	Type	Decoration
Brooches	Reinheim	Fe,Au	+	+	+		?amber	
	Reinheim	Fe,Au	+		+		?amber	
	Hoppstädten	Fe,Au	+	+	+			
	St Sulpice	Br,Au	+	+	+		amber	
	Wargemoulin	Br,Au	+		+	+	amber	circles
	Mauvilly	Br,Au		crosses	+		amber	
	Wargemoulin	Br,Au		small	+		?amber	
	St Sulpice	Br				+	enamel	
	Thayngen	Br	+		+			
Plaques	Schwabsburg	Fe,Au	+	+	+		amber	circles
	Weiskirchen	Fe,Au	+		+	+	amber	
	Kleinaspergle	Fe,Au	+		+		?amber	

Figure 8.9 Comparison of traits on coral-decorated brooches (fig.8.10) and plaques (fig.8.11), most with gold on iron or bronze.

intimately associated with the mining of salt, and it may have continued to play a central role, even as a sort of market; for goods from many different sources such as Greece and Hungary found their way there and may have been exchanged for items from other parts of Europe. Links with France and England are not yet so easy to understand, but however one envisages them they are nothing if not wide-ranging and are emphatically different from previous patterns.

Even without the physical remains of structures, and the records of exchange, it seems possible now to reconstruct in part the organization of production and the mechanisms of distribution and exchange for central Europe in the Early Iron Age. The socially restricted availability of imported goods in the earlier period is associated with the presence of elite groups who doubtless controlled the means of production; later on, imported material becomes available to all, and the tentatively suggested appearance of independent craftsmen emphasizes the social change already visible in the long-observed change in burial rite. The collapse of the rich Hallstatt fortified residences seems to have been the signal for the development of a much more complex society, probably with levels of status that could be achieved rather than inherited. Craftsmen began to be buried with the tools of their trade, surgeons with their instruments, and central Europe seemed set on the road to those transformations in social organization which would culminate, little over a century later, in the appearance of a recognizable form of early state.

Appendices

Appendix 1

Ins, Kt. Bern (2 examples) Drack 1958:19 and Taf.22, 248 and 250.
Mürzelen, Kt. Bern Drack 1958:25 and Taf.13, 15.
Rüssikon, Kt. Zürich Ulrich 1890:183–4.
Trüllikon, Kt. Zürich (2 examples) Bergmann 1958:46, no.15.
Wangen, Kt. Zürich (2 examples) Ulrich 1902–3:Taf.2, 16.

Appendix 2

Camp de Château, Salins, Jura Piroutet 1930:Taf.3, 22.
Fay en Montagne, Jura *Gallia, 24* (1966): 362, fig.25.
Mont Lassois, Côte d'Or (2 examples) Joffroy 1960:81 and pl. 21, 12 and 13.
Préty, Seine et Loire Jeannet 1964:Abb.34.
Königsbrück, Bas-Rhin Schaeffer 1930:fig.21n.

Appendix 3

Nordhouse, Bas-Rhin (2 pins) Forrer 1912:288–99, figs. 1–27.
Mont Lassois, Côte d'Or (segment) Joffroy 1960:p1. 17, 15.

Schöckingen, Kr. Leonberg (bead) Paret 1951:37.
Sirnau, Kr. Esslingen (4 beads) Paret 1936:246.

Appendix 4

Berru, Marne Schaaff 1973:82 Abb.6, 1.
Caurel, Marne Musée des Antiquités Nationales (Mus. Ant. Nat.) 80.030c.
Prosnes, Marne Mus. Ant. Nat. 33.331.
Besançon, Doubs Schaaff 1973:Abb. 7, 3.
Marson, Marne British Museum ML2150.
Bétheniville, Marne Mus. Ant. Nat. 78.258B.
Suippes, Marne Mus. Ant. Nat. 33.317.
Mus. Ant. Nat. unprovenanced: 65.694.
British Museum unprovenanced: ML2113.
Marne (unprovenanced) Mus. Ant. Nat. 80.148.

Appendix 5

Dürrnberg, Austria (2 examples) Penninger 1972:63, Taf.26, 1 and 2.
Mahlberg, Kr. Lahr Giessler and Kraft 1942:60 Abb.11, 4.
Nebringen, Kr. Böblingen (2 examples) Krämer 1964:Taf.2, 4; Taf.5, A2.
Tiengen, Kr. Waldshut Giessler and Kraft 1942:65 Abb.12, 6.
Viernheim, Kr. Bergstrasse Meier-Arendt 1968:101, Taf.49, 19.
Altstetten, Kt. Zürich (3 examples) Tanner 1979:vol.4/8, pp. 41, 42, and Taf.110, 11; Taf.111, 17.
Andelfingen, Kt. Zürich (4 examples) Tanner 1979:vol. 4/5, pp.20, 36, 40, and Tafs.9,9; 35,8; 42,12 and 14.
Belmont, Kt. Vaud Viollier 1916:pl.3, 108.
Bern, Kt. Bern (2 examples) Viollier 1916:pl.3, 104, 108.
Boswil, Kt. Aargau (3 examples) Tanner 1979:vol.4/3, pp.17, 21, 26, and Tafs.3,3; 7,16; 18,21.
Münsingen-Rain, Kt. Bern (11 examples+2 variants) Hodson 1968:101, nos.821, 822, 827; 105, no.582; 113, no.440c; 115, no.433; 116, no.476; 119, nos.495, 497, 498; 123, nos.344, 345; 141, no.282.
Rheinau, Kt. Zürich Tanner 1979:vol.4/7, p.31, Taf.79, B1.
Winkel, Kt. Zürich (2 examples) Tanner 1979:vol.4/8, p.26, Taf.102, 6 and 7.

Appendix 6

Münsingen-Rain, Kt. Bern (2 examples) Hodson 1968:96, no.779; 110, no.527.
Münsingen-Tägermatten, Kt. Bern Osterwalder 1971–2:19 Abb.15, 14.
Schirrheinerweg, Bas-Rhin Schaeffer 1930:81, fig.70.
Singen, Kr. Konstanz Giessler and Kraft 1942:67 Abb.13, 8.
Stettlen-Deisswil, Kt. Bern Tanner 1979:vol.4/14, p.59, Taf.60, B1.
Birsfelden, Kt. Basel Tanner 1979:vol.4/10, p.25, Taf.2, A4.
Corsier, Kt. Genf Viollier 1916:pl.3, 98.

Figure 8.10 a. Mauvilly, Côte d'Or. Bronze and gold disc brooch with small coral studs surrounding amber central stud. (Diameter 35mm.) (Musée des Antiquités Nat., St-Germain-en-Laye.)

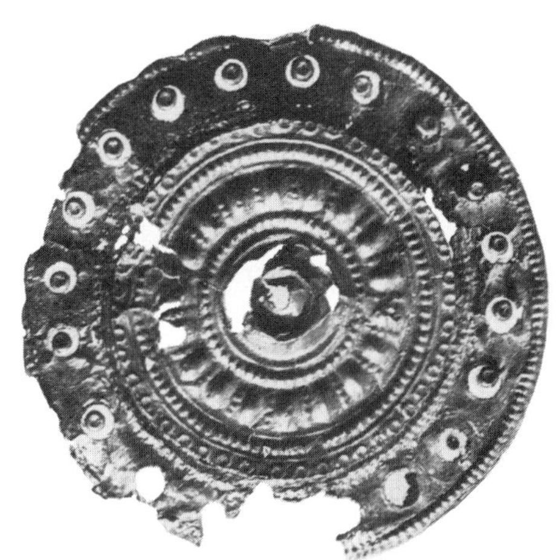

b. Reinheim, Kr. St Ingbert. Iron and gold disc brooch with small coral studs surrounding setting for ?amber central stud. (Diameter 41mm.) (Staatl. Konservatorant, Saarbrücken.)

c. Reinheim, Kr. St Ingbert. Iron and gold disc brooch with lyre-shaped extension settings for coral studs surrounding central amber stud. (Diameter 37.5mm.) (Staatl. Konservatorant, Saarbrücken.)

Figure 8.11 a. Weiskirchen, Kr. Merzig-Wadern. Gold and iron plaque with central setting for amber surrounded by 'lengths' of coral and settings for coral studs at left and right. (Width 80mm.) (Landesmuseum, Trier.)

b. Kleinaspergle, Kr. Ludwigsburg. Gold and iron plaque with central setting for amber and 12 settings for coral. (Width 68mm.) (Württ. Landesmuseum, Stuttgart.)

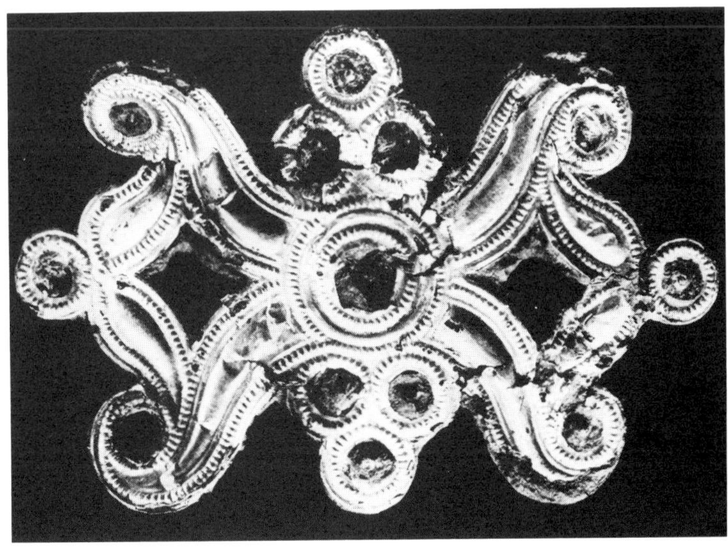

Appendix 7

With Type I pinheads:
Nebringen, Kr. Böblingen (2 examples) Krämer 1964:Taf.6, 1 and 2.
Andelfingen, Kt. Zürich Tanner 1979:vol.4/5, p.40, Taf.42, 10.
Stettlen-Deisswil, Kt. Bern Tanner 1979:vol.4/14, p.62, Taf.65, 5.
Muttenz, Kt. Basel (2 examples) Tanner 1979:vol.4/11, p.43, Taf.10, 10.
Vevey, Kt. Vaud (2 examples) Naef 1902:262, pl.XV, b and e.
Worb, Kt. Bern Tanner 1979:vol.4/16, p.26, Taf.105, 3.

With Type II pinheads:
Altstetten, Kt. Zürich (2 examples) Tanner 1979:vol.4/8, p.41, Taf.109, 9 and 10.
Münsingen-Rain, Kt. Bern (3 examples) Hodson 1968:113, nos.441, 442; 119, no.496.

With Type IIIb or plain pinheads:
Altstetten, Kt. Zürich Tanner 1979:vol.4/8, p.43, Taf.10, 9.
Münsingen-Rain, Kt. Bern Hodson 1968:114, no.452a.
Bern, Kt. Bern Viollier 1916:pl.3, 116.
St Sulpice, Kt. Vaud Gruaz 1914:264.

Appendix 8

Disc fibulae:
St Sulpice, Kt. Vaud (2 examples) Gruaz 1914:268.
Thayngen, Kt. Schaffhausen Zürich Museum 25494.
Hoppstädten, Kr. Birkenfeld Haffner 1976:187 and Taf.137, 2.
Reinheim, Kr. St Ingbert (2 examples) Keller 1965:36, Taf.16 and 17.
Mauvilly, Côte d'Or Henry 1933:83 and fig.33.
Wargemoulin, Marne (2 examples) Jacobsthal 1944:nos.348a and b.

Plaques:
Kleinaspergle, Kr. Ludwigsburg Jacobsthal 1944:no.22.
Schwabsburg, Kr. Mainz-Bingen Jacobsthal 1944:no.21.
Weiskirchen, Kr. Merzig-Wadern Jacobsthal 1944:no.20.

Bibliography

Bergmann, J., 1958. 'Entwicklung und Verbreitung der Paukenfibel', *Jahrbuch RGZM 5:* 18–94.

Biel, J., 1982. 'Ein Fürstengrabhügel der späten Hallstattzeit bei Eberdingen-Hochdorf, Kr. Ludwigsburg (Baden-Württemberg). Vorbericht', *Germania 60:* 61–104.

Biel, J. and Joachim, W., 1979. 'Vorgeschichtliche Siedlungsreste mit Gusstiegeln bei Fellbach-Schmiden, Rems-Murr-Kreis', *Fundberichte aus Baden-Württemberg 4:* 29–53.

Bittel, K., Kimmig, W. and Schiek, S. (eds.), 1981. *Die Kelten in Baden-Württemberg* (Stuttgart).

Bretz-Mahler, D., 1971. *La Civilisation de La Tène I en Champagne: Le Faciès Marnien* (Paris).

Champion, S. T., 1976. 'Coral in Europe: commerce and Celtic ornament'. In P-M. Duval and C. F. C. Hawkes (eds.), *Celtic Art in Ancient Europe. Five Protohistoric Centuries:* 29–40.

Champion, S. T., 1977. 'The use of coral and other substances to decorate metalwork in central and western Europe in the middle and later centuries of the first millennium B.C.' (D. Phil. thesis, University of Oxford).

Champion, S. T., 1982. 'Exchange and ranking: the case of coral'. In A. C. Renfrew and S. J. Shennan (eds.), *Ranking, Resource and Exchange:* 67–72.

Déchelette, J., 1914. *Manuel d'archéologie préhistorique, celtique et gallo-romaine,* II.3 (Paris).

Drack, W., 1958. *Ältere Eisenzeit der Schweiz: Kt. Bern,* I. Teil.

Favret, P. M., 1936. 'Les Nécropoles des Jogasses à Chouilly (Marne)', *Préhistoire 5:* 24–119.

Fell, C., 1936. 'The Hunsbury hill-fort, Northants: a new survey of the material', *Archaeol. J. 93:* 57–100.

Fischer, F., 1973. 'KEIMHΛIA: Bemerkungen zur kulturgeschichtlichen Interpretation des sogenannten Südimports in der späten Hallstatt- und frühen Latène-Kultur des westlichen Mitteleuropa', *Germania 51:* 436–59.

Forrer, R., 1912. 'Die Grabhügel bei Nordhausen', *Cahiers d'Archéologie et d'Histoire d'Alsace 1:* 288–99.

Giessler, R. and Kraft, G., 1942. 'Untersuchungen zur frühen und älteren Latènezeit am Oberrhein und in der Schwiez', *Bericht der Römisch-Germanischen Kommission 32:* 20–115.

Gruaz, J., 1914. 'Le Cimitière gaulois de St Sulpice (Vaud)', *Anzeiger für Schweiz. Altertumskunde* NF *16:* 257–75.

Haffner, A., 1971. 'Ein hallstattzeitlicher Eisenschmelzofen von Hillesheim, Kr. Daun', *Trierer Zeitschrift 34:* 21–29.

Haffner, A., 1976. *Die westliche Hunsrück-Eifel-Kultur,* RG Forsch. 36 (Berlin).

Härke, H., 1979. *Settlement Types and Settlement Patterns in the west Hallstatt Province* (BAR IS 57).

Henry, F., 1933. *Les Tumulus du département de la Côte d'Or* (Paris).

Hodson, F. R., 1968. *The La Tène Cemetery at Münsingen-Rain* (Bern).

Jacobsthal, P., 1944. *Early Celtic Art.*

Jeannet, M., 1964. 'Une fibule hallstattienne découverte à Préty (Saône-et-Loire)', *Rev. Arch. de l'Est et du Centre-Est 15.* 131–40.

Jehl, M. and Bonnet, C., 1968. 'La Pyxide d'Appenwihr (Haut-Rhin)', *Gallia 26.* 295–300.

Joachim, W., 1977. 'Untersuchung einer späthallstatt-frühlatènezeitlichen Siedlung in Kornwestheim, Kr. Ludwigsburg', *Fundberichte aus Baden-Württemberg 5:* 173–203.

Joffroy, R., 1960. *L'Oppidum de Vix et la civilisation hallstattienne finale dans l'est de la France* (Paris).

Jope, E. M., 1971. 'The Waldalgesheim master'. In J. Boardman, M. Brown and T. G. E. Powell (eds.), *The European Community in Later Prehistory:* 165–80.

Keller, F. J., 1965. *Das keltische Fürstengrab von Reinheim,* I (Mainz).

Kimmig, W., 1983. *Die Heuneburg an der oberen Donau=Führer zn arch. Denkmälern in Baden-Württemberg* (2nd edn, Stuttgart).

Kimmig, W. and Gersbach, E., 1971. 'Die Grabungen auf der Heuneburg 1966–1969', *Germania 49:* 21–91.

Krämer, W., 1964. *Das keltische Gräberfeld von Nebringen (Kr. Böblingen)* (Stuttgart).

Mansfeld, G., 1973. *Die Fibeln der Heuneburg 1950–1970,* RG Forsch. 33 (Berlin).

Meier-Arendt, W., 1968. *Inventar der ur- und frühgeschichtlichen Geländedenkmäler und Funde des Kreises Bergstrasse* (Frankfurt).

Mildenburger, G., 1963. 'Griechische Scherben vom Marienberg in Würzburg', *Germania 41:* 103–4.

Moosleitner, F., Pauli, L. and Penninger, E., 1974. *Der Dürrnberg bei Hallein,* II (Munich).
Morel, L., 1875. 'Découverte de Somme-Bionne (Marne)', *Cahiers archëologiques français 42:* 86–116.
Naef, A., 1902. 'Le Cimitière gallo-helvète de Vevey', *Anzeiger für Schweizen Altertumskunde* NF *3:* 104–14.
Osterwalder, C., 1971–2. 'Die Latènegräber von Münsingen-Tägermatten', *Jahrbuch des Bernischen Historischen Museum: 51–2:* 7–40.
Paret, O., 1936. 'Das Hallstattgrab von Sirnau bei Esslingen, Württemberg', *Germania 20:* 246–52.
Paret, O., 1951. 'Das reiche späthallstattzeitliche Grab von Schöckingen (Kr. Leonberg)', *Fundberichte aus Schwaben 12:* 37–40.
Penninger, E., 1972. *Der Dürrnberg bei Hallein,* I (Munich).
Piroutet, M., 1930. 'La Citadelle hallstattienne, à poteries hélléniques, de Château sur Salins (Jura)', *V. Congrès Internat. d'arch, Algiers:* 47ff.
Rowlands M., 1972. 'The archaeological interpretation of prehistoric metalworking', *World Archaeol. 3:* 210–24.
de Saint-Venant, J., 1897. 'Les Derniers Arécomiques. Traces de la civilisation celtique dans la région du Bas-Rhône, spécialement dans le Gard', *Bull. Arch. du Comité des travaux historiques et scientifiques* 1897: 481–531.
Schaaff, U., 1973. 'Frühlatènezeitliche Grabfunde mit Helmen von Typ Berru', *Jahrbuch RGZM 20* [1975]: 81–106.
Schaeffer, C., 1930. *Les Tertres funéraires préhistoriques dans la forêt de Haguenau II: Les Tumulus de l'Âge du Fer* (Hagenau).
Schultze-Naumburg, F., 1969. 'Eine griechische Scherbe von Ipf bei Böpfingen-Württemberg', in O.-H. Frey (ed.), *Marburger Studien zur Archäologie der Kelten, Festschrift W. Dehn,* Fundberichte aus Hessen, Beiheft 1: 210–12.
Schwab, H., 1975. 'Châtillon-sur-Glâne: ein Fürstensitz der Hallstattzeit bei Freiburg im Üechtland', *Germania 53: 79–84.*
Schweitzer, R., 1973. 'Le Britzgyberg – station du Hallstatt', *Bull. Mus. Hist. de Mulhouse 81:* 43–64.
Shennan, S., 1975. 'The social organisation at Branč', *Antiquity 49:* 279–88.
Spindler, K., 1971. *Magdalenenberg. Der hallstattzeitliche Fürstengrabhügel bei Villingen im Schwarzwald 1* (Villingen).
Tanner, A., 1979. *Die Latènegräber der nordalpinen Schweiz* (Bern).
Ulrich, R., 1890. *Catalog der Sammlungen der antiquarischen Gesellschaft in Zurich.*
Ulrich, R., 1902–3. 'Der Grabhügel im "Wieslistein" bei Wangen, Kt. Zürich', *Anzeiger für Schweizer. Altertumskunde* NF *4:* 8–17.
Ulrich, R., 1914. *Die Gräberfelder in der Umgebung von Bellinzona.*
Viollier, D., 1916. *Les Sépultures de second âge du fer sur le plateau Suisse* (Zürich and Geneva).
Wainwright, G., 1979. *Gussage All Saints – an Iron Age Settlement in Dorset.*
Wainwright, G. and Spratling, M., 1973. 'The Iron Age settlement of Gussage All Saints', *Antiquity 47:* 109–30.
Wells, P., 1980a. *Culture Contact and Culture Change. Early Iron Age Central Europe and the Mediterranean World.*
Wells, P., 1980b. 'The early Iron Age settlement of Hascherkeller in Bavaria: preliminary report on the 1979 excavations', *J. Field Archaeology 7:* 313–28.
Wolseley, G., Smith, R. A. and Hawley, W., 1927. 'Prehistoric and Roman settlements on Park Brow', *Archaeologia 76:* 1–40.
Wyss, R., 1974. 'Technik, Wirtschaft, Handel und Kriegswesen der Eisenzeit'. In W. Drack (ed.), *Ur- und frühgeschichtliche Archäologie der Schweiz 4; Die Eisenzeit* (Basel): 105–38.
Zürn, H., 1970. *Hallstattforschungen in Nordwürttemberg,* Veröffentlichungen des staatlichen Amtes für Denkmalpflege Stuttgart, Reihe A, 16 (Stuttgart).

9

Meditations on a Celtic hobby-horse: notes towards a social archaeology of Iron Age art

J. V. S. Megaw

The title for this essay is offered in tribute to one whose writings and kind counsel have influenced me much over the last 30 years. Sir Ernst Gombrich in the eponymous study of a trilogy examines the roots of artistic form; he is concerned to explore an apparent dichotomy in representation between so-called naturalistic art and 'conceptual images' (Gombrich 1978:1–11) based often on simple symbols or, in Robert Layton's useful phrase, 'visual metaphors' (Layton 1981), whose meaning changes with context. Gombrich also – and not for the first time – draws attention to what he sees as an innate automatic response towards certain 'readings' of forms in terms of physiognomic vision, 'the elusive mask' (Gombrich 1979:264ff.). The all-pervading role of the reversible face, for example, I have followed in my own attempts to find meaning in pre-Roman Celtic art (Megaw 1970b) and I wish to look again at some of the problems in studying the prehistory of art with particular reference to three perennial areas of enquiry in the examination of art – the role of the artist in contemporary society, the meaning of the art he or she produces and the manner in which themes or motifs may be transmitted.

The proper study of art

During an Adelaide seminar in which I was discussing with my students the problems of studying prehistoric and ethnographic art (Silver 1979), I was asked: 'if one cannot define use from form, what chance is there of deducing meaning from art?'. In this the questioner was echoing the pessimistic view of the anthropologist Anthony Forge who has written: 'there seems little chance of establishing for prehistoric or now destroyed primitive cultures any iconography that will enable the meanings of these long dead masters to be accurately translated into verbal terms' (Forge 1973:xiv). If anthropologists are not particularly helpful for the student of prehistoric art, what of critics or indeed artists themselves since, as André Malraux – not without reason – asserted in his *Le Musée imaginaire*, 'the most knowledgeable student of prehistory is not necessarily the most convincing interpreter of the art of the caves' (Malraux 1967:239)? Thinking of a suitably local reaction from the point of view of a continental European context one might consider the views of these like Gustav Klimt and his circle who regarded art as the object of disinterested contemplation divorced from the confines of the rest of life. But surely nothing can be further from the insights, however partial, into the nature of art rendered by the examination of those visual forms of expression which we call 'art' amongst so-called primitive or non-Western peoples. Art can be seen as a system of multiple reference, of communication, the employment of symbols or visual images to transfer sorts of meanings, the use of the same visual image – depending on context – to represent different meanings. Such observations, as Layton in his recent study *The Anthropology of Art* rightly points out, militate against those critics who too readily interpret visual imagery on the basis of assumptions that if objects ' "look like what they depict" then they can be "read" by members of alien cultures' (1981:23f.). Thus there is a double task demanded of the student of art, of whatever period or place: first, to identify the subject-matter depicted, and second, to obtain knowledge of its cultural significance. Layton continues: 'to understand the artist's aims we must understand the symbolism he utilized. The art object one observes is merely the tangible expression of a cultural, and therefore a mental construct expressed according to that culture's conventions of visual representation.' In the light of these observations is it surprising that such experiments as have been aimed at establishing cross-cultural aesthetic principles have by and large failed? In the same Adelaide seminar, I found myself offering the following definition of art; it is, I suggested 'that body of human creative activity which is least studied by archaeologists and anthropologists alike'.

But let us turn to a less pessimistic approach. James Ackerman once wrote: 'to be able to apprehend the importance of a work of art whether it be a painting or a poem, we must first learn its language' (Ackerman and Carpenter 1963:152). How then should we learn the language of an art which 'has no genesis', and what in fact is meant by this much-quoted statement (Jacobsthal 1944:158)? Before attempting to answer this question and to examine what currently may be said not only of the nature of Celtic La Tène art in the fifth to third centuries B.C. but also of its role in contemporary society as revealed by its geographical distribution and stylistic affinities, I wish first of all to examine a modern and possibly comparable phenomenon to that of La Tène art, with its clear and yet elusive allusions to the classical 'high arts' of the Mediterranean and orientalizing – if not oriental – world. I refer to what is occasionally termed the 'transitional' or more precisely 'assimilated fine arts' of the contemporary Third World, the adoption by its creators from North America to North Australia, from West Africa to West Irian, of at first totally foreign styles and techniques (Graburn 1976). Naturally, the degree to which successful assimilation can and does take place varies. In Indonesia one can perceive the contrast between the traditional styles of modern Balinese religious painting and the highly successful narrative or genre pictures, a result largely of the influence of expatriate European artists such as Walter Spies. In Australia in the 1930s Rex Battarbee introduced to the Aboriginal Albert Namatjira the conventions and techniques of European-trained landscape watercolourists, a style which today in the centre of Australia has become a sort of artistic *lingua franca*, largely unrecognized when compared with other attempts to revitalize so-called 'traditional' Aboriginal art, as for example in the acrylic paintings of the Western Desert (Megaw 1982b). To some degree La Tène art may also be regarded as 'assimilated' or 'integrated' art even as in its turn, and at a later period than that which this paper is largely concerned, such pieces as the Gundestrup, Aars, cauldron (Megaw 1970a:no.209) surely reflect the absorption in the Thraco-Getic culture of the eastern Danube basin of images – but, I must emphasize, by no means necessarily meanings – borrowed from Celtic iconography.

That the hobby-horse may actually exist in ancient Celtic society is not beyond the bounds of art-historical belief (Megaw 1983; Jope 1983), but then the art of the Celts has attracted almost as great a range of speculation as the art of the megalith builders. By and large, however, there is no doubt that the development and analysis of this art, an art which has no genesis – meaning of course that it has no readily discernible and gradual evolution – has repelled rather than attracted serious scholarship. Prehistoric art in general, with the possible exception of that of the palaeolithic period, has hardly produced a growth industry even in most recent years with the birth of such new 'newspeak' archaeologies as 'cognitive archaeology', 'contextual ethnoarchaeology' and of course the 'social archaeology' we now must practise. In seeking reason if not rationale, the unkind might comment, for studying these material manifestations of the past which are my own special concern, I have had recourse to some recent as well as some not so recent writings on the study of the art of the past. 'So many want to explain art and this is why professional archaeologists shy away from art prehistory, because they cannot find explanations . . . And they never will find explanations in a text-free archaeology', stated the 1969 Ferens Professor of Fine Art at the University of Hull, much concerned to support the study of art as leading ultimately to connoisseurship (Daniel 1970:esp.16–17). This is a view with which I am, I confess, not much in sympathy. I am not quite sure what constitutes 'art' as a separate, contemporarily meaningful entity within the context of the European Iron Age; far less what might have been considered 'good' or 'significant' within the society in which it was made. 'Artists are themselves the best judges of what is good and significantly new in art. They may show and define it by adapting their own art to deal with those options or insights that change perception' (Compton 1983:8, 11). Is not perhaps this statement – concerned not with prehistoric art but with the newest of new art and leaving aside the question of the existence in the Iron Age of the 'artist' – an indication of the kind of things that we must try to seek out if we are to begin to comprehend the art of the past?

But how? 'You can't make art outside your own period', says the artist David Hockney. How about those who would study art? If we look to the 'onlie begetters' of social archaeology itself we are not greatly helped even when they direct us towards an archaeology of the mind (Renfrew 1973; 1982). It is true that mensuration may have its place even in Celtic art (Spratling 1980) and certainly I prefer cognition to connoisseurship. The Doppler effect applies to fashions in archaeological theory as well as in the material objects to which such theories are supposed to be applied. The growth of cognitive anthropology has been welcomed by those who once more champion a view of archaeology as being concerned ultimately with data of a historical and cultural nature (Hodder 1982a). The use of ethnographic analogies in an attempt to flesh out the skinny relics of the past has been widely applied by those concerned to make some sense out of European Iron Age art (Megaw 1979; 1982a). All too often such attempts make unwarranted and untested inferential leaps in the process, ignoring 'the tedious basic-level testing of things like depositional processes in favour of investigating more interesting upper-level problems' (Tringham 1975:72). In a Celtic context those who sail into the treacherous waters of historical ethnography (Hawkes 1977; Pauli and T. C. Champion above) can no longer, it seems, safely look to such sources as the Old Irish hero tales (Jackson 1964; Megaw 1970a:16), since it is now generally agreed that like all folk tradition subsequently formalized, such sources represent a virtually indecipherable palimpsest of myth, actuality and interpetation; and Alice Welbourn's paper in this volume sounds a further timely cautionary note for those concerned with reconstructing craft specialization in particular.

There is in fact one thing that the study of ethnography and ethnographic art does make patently clear, and that is that – questions of changing taste within our own society apart – connoisseurship, the establishment of norms as to what-is-correct, may be very different in other societies from what some four centuries of Western European art-historical tradition has decided is that-which-is-good. There is, for example, nothing wrong in our regarding the Basse-Yutz flagons (Jacobsthal 1944:no.381; Megaw 1970a:no.60–1) (fig.9.1) or the Turoe Stone (Megaw 1970a:no.129; Duignan 1976) as masterpieces, as long as we do not delude ourselves into thinking that they were precisely so regarded by those who first made – or used – them; or, equally important, that a poorly cast *Maskenfibel* from, say, the Dürrnberg was not in its time regarded as more significant, 'better', art than either.

The nature and development of early Celtic art

Since this is an essay on archaeology, not aesthetics, perhaps I should return to what continues to be for me a real difficulty; not how *should* we study Celtic art, but how *can* we study Celtic art? In fact, most recently those concerned to study prehistoric or ethnographic art seem to be more or less agreed as to theory if not as to practice. Thus Duval (1982:7) sees the necessary steps as decipherment of form, reading of individual motifs and interpretation of meaning or symbolism. This view is not far from Hodder's (1982b:179) requirement for the study of art – or representation of the act of 'representing', to offer a further synonym (Brook 1980) – which is to study it within a social context. Renfrew (1982:236) approvingly notes Hodder's concern to identify objects as symbols; the prehistorian of art must seek symbols within the range of decoration of the object itself. Elsewhere in the same lecture, however, Renfrew – who like so many

Figure 9.1 Detail from the handle of one of the flagons from Basse-Yutz, Moselle, France, now in the British Museum. Width of face 36mm. (Photo: J. V. S. Megaw.)

archaeologists understandably does not seem to be altogether happy when writing on art – dismisses too lightly, I feel, the possibility of norms of perception as well as conception which may indeed allow the identification of significant symbols (and none so significant as the human head). Here of course I have most obviously followed Gombrich's lead in having recourse not to the uncertain field of trans-cultural aesthetics but rather to the principles established by perception psychology (Gombrich 1977; 1979: esp. 264ff.; Megaw 1970a,b); others have taken further my suggestion of the all-important symbolism of the head in Celtic art (Lenerz-de Wilde 1982) (frontispiece). Washburn, introducing a recent volume in the Cambridge *New Directions in Archaeology* series which has seemingly very little of directly archaeological material and certainly no Celtic art, quotes with approval the use of perception psychology in the study of art as exemplified by Arnheim (1974), and makes an important distinction: 'Physiology conditions how we see but culture conditions what we see and how we organise what we see into a given image' (Washburn 1983:1). The theory of the paramount importance in Celtic art of symbolic representation of the human head remains only a theory, but if one accepts the argument that in the Iron Age Celtic art had predominantly a religious or indeed a magical significance (Megaw 1970a:22; Pauli 1975; 1978: esp. 456ff.; p.170 below) then such a theory gains added credibility. The significance of the Early La Tène *Maskenfibeln*, whose individuality presents such a literal headache for the application of normal principles in establishing stylistic inter-relationships and groupings (Megaw 1982c:esp. 29), becomes, I think, clearer in the light of these approaches – a point I shall elaborate later. The curious concentration on compass-based ornamentation in both early continental La Tène and late insular ornamentation may also be interpreted in the context of a significant symbolism – and one which in the context of questions as to the status of Celtic craftsmen or the role they may have played in Iron Age society clearly points to individuals with the specialist knowledge as well as the skills for executing complex geometric formulae (Frey with Megaw 1976:esp. 60ff.; Lenerz-de Wilde 1977; Megaw 1979:esp. 51; Megaw 1983). That such knowledge must have been jealously guarded by a controlling class is a reasonable inference of Pauli's (1978:456ff.; p.177 below).

What can one say of the first stages of La Tène art, its role in society and its creators, an art which Ludwig Pauli sees as having its origin in the western Hunsrück–Eifel–Kultur/Champagne region (Pauli 1978:456ff.)? To begin with the broad cultural picture, recent writers have been frequently influenced by borrowed anthropological models and are not always free of the tendency to leapfrog. Frankenstein and Rowlands' (1978) generalized model for the southwest German Late Hallstatt/Early La Tène 'province' postulates a political system depending on the role of the Heuneburg, Kr. Biberach/Sigmaringen, as the centre of a paramount chief receiving in the first instance luxury imports (Kimmig 1983a:130ff. for summary), gift exchange as recognition of rank – the *keimelia* of Fischer's classical model (Fischer 1973; see also Freidin 1982). Equally to be regarded as tribute, raw materials would be received for on-site working and subsequent redistribution – at their more spectacular, Mediterranean coral as found in the unworked state on the Heuneburg or forming part of a necklace in a Late Hallstatt barrow at Kaltbrunn in Baden as it was to be used in Early La Tène Champagne (Champion S. 1976 and above), or the Chinese silk of the Hohmichele (Hundt 1969; 1970), and the possibly Italian embroidery in the tomb hangings of Eberdingen-Hochdorf, Kr. Ludwigsburg (Hundt, pers. comm.; see also Biel 1981; 1982a,b). Long-distance trade also brought Arabian incense where it was found in a *cista a cordoni* at Salvadonica in the area of Lake Como (De Marinis 1981:252); similar drug trafficking may also have reached the Heuneburg. How far, though, the clearly incomplete evidence of burial archaeology and the even more partial knowledge of contemporary settlements support Frankenstein and Rowlands' postulated descending order of hierarchies, any more than it does their views, following Driehaus (1965) in the limited concentration and exploitation of iron ore supplies, is a matter for continuing debate; there is need for a more thorough analysis of finds associations and their relative levels of reliability. Certainly Härke (1979), on the basis of his detailed examination of settlements and settlement patterns in the West Hallstatt province – itself the subject of some adverse criticism – and Wells (1980), in an admittedly geographically limited and somewhat over-selective view of culture contact and culture change in Early Iron Age Europe, support the now well-established distributional, and in material terms cultural, patterns of the beginning of the La Tène period. In a political shift of power to the north-west, Härke sees after an initial period of social differentiation – the evidence of the *Fürstengräber* – and continued redistribution, a rise in population and increased social fragmentation with less marked evidence of stratification and settlements both smaller and more numerous. Wells likewise writes of the western La Tène *Fürstengräber* zone as comprising a 'decentralised, dispersed, economic and social organisation with local chiefs of roughly equal status exercising their authority in small communities' (Wells 1980:116). Frankenstein and Rowlands relate the growth of the postulated Early Iron Age hierarchies to a dependent relationship with the Mediterranean cultures, a political structure built on external trade. They see a continuation of the system, at least in part, into the Early La Tène period, whose centre they maintain was on the Rhine east of the Hunsrück–Eifel, the Hochwald–Nahe group for example receiving its prestige goods by redistribution from the former area; with removal of the external links of trade, however, collapse of the political systems followed.[1]

The mobility of art styles and artists

Consideration of the contemporary role that Celtic craftsmen – or artists – may have played inevitably involves the old discussion as to whether they were mobile or sedentary, to which the simple answer seems to have been that they were both (Driehaus 1972a; Megaw 1979; Pauli 1978:esp. 443ff.). The significance of such key sites as the Dürrnberg as a link between the Alpine region, Italy and other parts of Europe cannot be over-emphasized (Pauli 1978:esp. pp.483–5; Moosleitner 1980), since as Jacobsthal (1944:esp. 160f.) was the first to point out, Italy provided, through such imports, many of the stimuli for Celtic art itself. There is no need to rehearse again the arguments I have presented elsewhere which suggest that it was largely through Italy and not direct from the East that the so-called 'orientalizing' elements in early Celtic art were transmitted despite the early fifth-century occupation of the Balkans by the Persians (Megaw 1975 *contra* Sandars 1976; Hawkes 1977:13ff.; Fischer 1983). This is not to deny the occasional import from, for example, the East Greek world – as recently shown by Frey-Asche (1980; see also Pauli 1980a:no.25) to be the case with the Weiskirchen ?drinking horn mount – or that there are Celtic objects with distinctly oriental features – for example the half-finished torc found on the Glauberg made not by *cire perdue* but in a two-piece mould, and with some telling oriental and indeed Persian antecedents (Frey 1981). Such isolated objects no more support a picture of Greeks bearing gifts than of a Celtic Marco Polo weighed down with Chinese silks (incidentally also probably obtained through ultimately Persian intermediaries). By similar down-the-line trading routes must have come perhaps the most significant aspect of indirect or direct trading, the transmission of ideas, as Colin Renfrew (1969) has frequently reminded us. This is of course not to deny the later evidence for Hellenistic influence, particularly in the eastern Celtic areas around the third century B.C. (e.g. Kruta and Szabó 1982). But personal links with Italy are more likely to have begun, if not as early as implied by Livy (*Histories*, bk v), then before the fourth century settlement of the Po valley. Following Wells (1980:137), one may envisage groups of Celtic *Gastarbeiter* gaining status in their own communities by returning home, not with second-hand Mercedes but with made-in-Italy *Schnabelkannen* and situlae.

The settlement of northern Italy by the Celts, a settlement which has recently been argued as corresponding to that established by our ancient Greek sources at c.388 B.C. (Sordi 1976–77) when the Celts may have moved into the Po valley, perhaps on acount of its renowned fertility, ended the central role played by the Golasecca culture (Pauli 1971; De Marinis 1977; 1981:esp.252ff.; Champion T. C. 1980:esp.34–6; p.171 below). It also followed the decline of imports through Massalia c.500 B.C., which in turn may have resulted from mainland Greece shifting its main market in food supplies from the West Mediterranean to the head of the Adriatic (Wells with Bonfante 1979). That Italic no less than Celtic craftsmen must have travelled seems to be the inevitable conclusion to be drawn from the fragmentary mould of a silen mask handle-mount from the Heuneburg (fig.9.2) (Kimmig and von Vacano 1973; Kimmig 1983a:130ff.; p.176 below). Even as in the Early La Tène period, when the Saarland and the Rhineland–Palatinate with their direct links through to Italy emerged as the new centre of power and Celtic craftsmen occasionally embellished or repaired precious imports (Jacobsthal 1944:no.32; Megaw 1970a:no.42; Pauli 1980a:no.27), so too in the Late Hallstatt *Fürstengräber* we occasionally come across suggestions that local smiths refurbished Mediterranean handiwork. This certainly seems the only reasonable explanation for the comically poor workmanship of one of the three lions on the rim of the fragmentary Greek cauldron from Eberdingen-Hochdorf, the great Hallstatt chieftain's grave in the neighbourhood of the Hohenasberg *Fürstensitz* (Biel 1981; 1982a; 1982b:esp.88–9 and Abb.21). The lure of gold (Pauli 1974), whether or not we are to regard the Erstfeld, Kt. Uri, gold-find as a religious offering rather than a personal cache or a travelling smith's hoard deposited *en route* for northern Italy (Megaw 1970a:no.84; Wyss 1975; Pauli 1980a: no.187), is another source of obvious north–south influences. But from the point of view of art the significance of Golasecca as a transmitter not only of objects but of artistic ideas must have been considerable. One obvious piece to cite here is the sword-sheath from Hallstatt grave 994. I would agree that this was most probably made by an itinerant craftsman, if not at Hallstatt itself then on the Dürrnberg (Jacobsthal 1944:no.96; Megaw 1970a:no.30; Megaw 1976:esp.20f.; Pauli 1980a:no.115). The decoration of the sheath clearly owes much to situla art and, in David Ridgway's happy phrase, 'the world of situla art is a world which stands still'[2] – not unlike some aspects of Celtic art itself and once more presenting obvious problems for the chronology of the art historian. If Hallstatt is clearly related to the art of the situla, the extraordinary scabbard from the warrior's grave in Hochscheid barrow 2, Kr. Bernkastel-Wittlich (Haffner 1977:esp. 165f. and Abb.2), with its Ferdinand the Bull or, more likely, cervid just sniffing the lotus flowers, is even closer to orientalizing Italo–Greek sources: another case of just how far travelling orientalizing elements reaching the Adriatic through Chiusi may have been. The problem remains, of course; where precisely did the Celtic swordsmith see his model? That occasional direct influence or contact with the Orient certainly also existed in the later La Tène period is, in the context of swords, nowhere made clearer than in the first-century A.D. Mihovo, Slovenia, grave 1846/5 (Frey 1980:91 and Abb.30; Pauli 1980a:no.136). The grave contains an iron sword with bronze appliqués in the form of a bird and ?bull with, below, two antithetical rams or goats in the iconography of the ram-in-the-thicket or the tree-of-life, well known from the 'Korisios' sword from the Late La Tène river deposit at Port, Kt. Bern (Megaw 1970a:no.190; see also Krämer 1982:489f.). Even if Windl's (1976) hypothesis of a Celtic warrior in Asia Minor having his sword locally embellished may be a bit far-fetched, if rejected then some other explanation involving direct rather than down-the-line influence seems inescapable.

Figure 9.2 Fragmentary silen mask mould for a handle-mount found on the Heuneburg, Kr. Biberach-Sigmaringen, Germany. Scale c.1:1. (Photo: courtesy of Professor Dr W. Kimmig.)

To return to an earlier period and more general matters, a more central question is how the beginnings of La Tène art can be fitted in with the scenario just sketched for the change-over in the West from Hallstatt to La Tène. A number of years ago (when I was even more disposed to sweeping generalities on the nature of prehistoric art than I am now I have anthropologically begun to come of age) I described La Tène art as 'predominantly a religious art . . . [employing] an iconography which imbues even the simplest objects with a degree of the mysterious or indeed the divine' (Megaw 1970a:38). Pauli, quoting this view with approval, expands the theory of La Tène art as religious art. He relates the growth of what he regards as the apotropaic element of faces and monsters to a time of stress and political uncertainty (Pauli 1975:205–7), although I would continue to maintain with Gombrich (1979:264ff.) that, for whatever initial reason, the ever-increasingly elusive mask becomes with time central to Celtic iconography and thus presumably to Celtic society itself. One may ponder indeed as to the line of development which transforms Italic 'naturalistic' faces – and the tricks played with them (witness the upside-down faces from Bad Dürkheim, Kr. Neustadt (Megaw 1970a:no.59;1970b; Lenerz-de Wilde 1982:esp. 182 and fig.1)) – into the well-nigh impenetrable foliage of the so-called 'Waldalgesheim' style. Pauli would consider the whole range of *Masken-*, *Tier-* and *Vogelkopffibeln* as part of this apotropaic symbolism, although it is interesting to note the distributional disconformities whereby such brooches seem by and large associated with male graves in the Rhineland while on the Dürrnberg – the site with by far and away the largest number (Pauli 1978:109ff.; Megaw 1982c) – the reverse is true.[3] What social circumstances can be suggested to explain this dichotomy? The seeming restriction of torcs to females in Early La Tène in contrast to later periods is another such case (Lorenz, above). The individuality of the decorated brooches, with more variation than would necessarily result from their *cire perdue* methods of casting, incidentally raises the salutary point made by Holmqvist in connection with the brooch moulds of the Helgö Migration Period workshop, surely the most extensive archaeological examination of the nature and organization of craftsmen in an early European context known to me.[4] Holmqvist writes: 'The variety of the form is in fact so great that if the original products had been found scattered throughout the country, one would have been impelled to think of them as having derived from a number of *different* workshops' (Holmqvist 1972: 256).

Reverting to the difficult area of meaning and Early La Tène iconography, it seems to me indisputable that in its motifs there must be something more than mere decorativeness or a descriptive 'naturalism' (compare East Greek 'export art' noted briefly in the following paragraph) when one looks in a different way at that small but related group of incised work which includes three very disparately distributed pieces: the Stupava, Okr. Teplice, plaque, the Hoppstädten, Ldkr. Birkenfeld, barrow sieve and, once more, the sword from the Hallstatt warrior grave no. 994 (Megaw 1975:20f. and figs. 1–3) to which one might now add the sword from Hochscheid. My inclination would be to regard all four pieces as products of the Hunsrück–Eifel or Rhineland; suffice it for the present to note not only the heraldic monsters, part-ancestors of later swordsmiths' 'dragon pairs' (see further p.183 below), but more particularly here the heroic battle on the Hallstatt sword which has its – again apotropaic? – counterparts in the struggling humans and beasts of what I maintain are also Rhenish products, the rings of Erstfeld, Kt. Uri, hoard. Birds, beasts and humans are all here. That the set was intended for an individual – woman, not man? – seems without dispute; this is 'made-to-order' finery, possibly personal goods transported by their owner, made by highly skilled (and at least one not so skilled) artisans who had access to no less than three sources of gold. Following Layton (1981:117ff. and fig.28), one might wonder if the iconography of Erstfeld, like the Predynastic Narmer palette, is a visual metaphor of conquest with chieftainly supporters? But these works follow the initial period of what might be termed the 'court school', or schools, of the *Fürstengräber* chiefs lying in state in their funerary chariots surrounded by made-to-measure finery to accompany them to the Otherworld.

It is instructive to contrast the art associated with the Western Celts and that of their near-contemporaries, the Eastern Scythians (Artamonov 1969; Charrière 1971; Metropolitan Museum n.d.; Rolle 1980). The latter too had a 'court school' but this was produced by foreigners, East Greeks albeit clearly within a formula of local or mythical images and indeed local forms; the fourth-century Chertomlyk golden bow-case is almost literally reflected in one of the Kul Oba cups, but this is not 'transitional art' in the sense that *Fürstengräber* gold-work may be so regarded. Both east and west of course received luxury imports; in the west some may have been actually made to order as for the Black Sea chiefs. But it was a native Celtic craftsman who embellished the Attic stemless cup by the Amphitrite painter and its plain companion found in the Early La Tène Kleinaspergle, Kr. Ludwigsburg, double-chambered grave (one of the later princely graves below the Hohenasberg), choosing as his starting-point a classical pattern-book (Jacobsthal 1944:no.32; Megaw 1970a:no.41; Pauli 1980a:no.27), even as the Celtic bronzesmiths responsible for the *Schnabelkanne* in the same tomb based the handle mount on the 'silen' masks of so-called 'Vulcian' Etruscan bronzes (Jacobsthal 1944:no.385; Megaw 1970a:50). The Amphitrite cup must have been traded through Italy where other examples occur and I need hardly refer again to the clear Italian connection between Etruria and the Early La Tène heartland through Switzerland and in particular the Ticino (Pauli 1971); there are both the *Schnabelkannen* themselves – and just how many of these in Celtic lands may after all not only be decorated by Celts but be of Celtic manufacture? – and the *Rhenisch-Tessinisch* situlae as again at Kleinaspergle which now can be demonstrated largely to be local products modelled on Alpine prototypes (Driehaus 1966; Pauli 1971:13ff.). As with regional variations in dress, so too one may detect patterns in the selection of imported goods – or their copies. Thus in the Middle Rhineland the so-called 'Hochwald–Nahe' and 'Rheinhessen–Palatinate' groups, burials are frequently accompanied by not only beaked flagons but a pair of Etruscan bronze basins as well as other imports. Further north where the situlae are common and where the flagons also occur, other imports are lacking in graves of the Rhine–Mosel group (fig.9.3). Patterns in local crafts products are also likely to have differed from region to region.

Celtic craftsmen and their tools

In the nature of prestige imports rather than the products of travelling craftsmen, occasional eastern Celtic masterpieces found their way to the west (Megaw 1970a:nos.182–3; 1973). In Middle La Tène, Swiss swords may have reached Slovenia and Croatia (Guštin 1977:esp. Tab.5:2, 8:2; 1982[5]) and into cre-

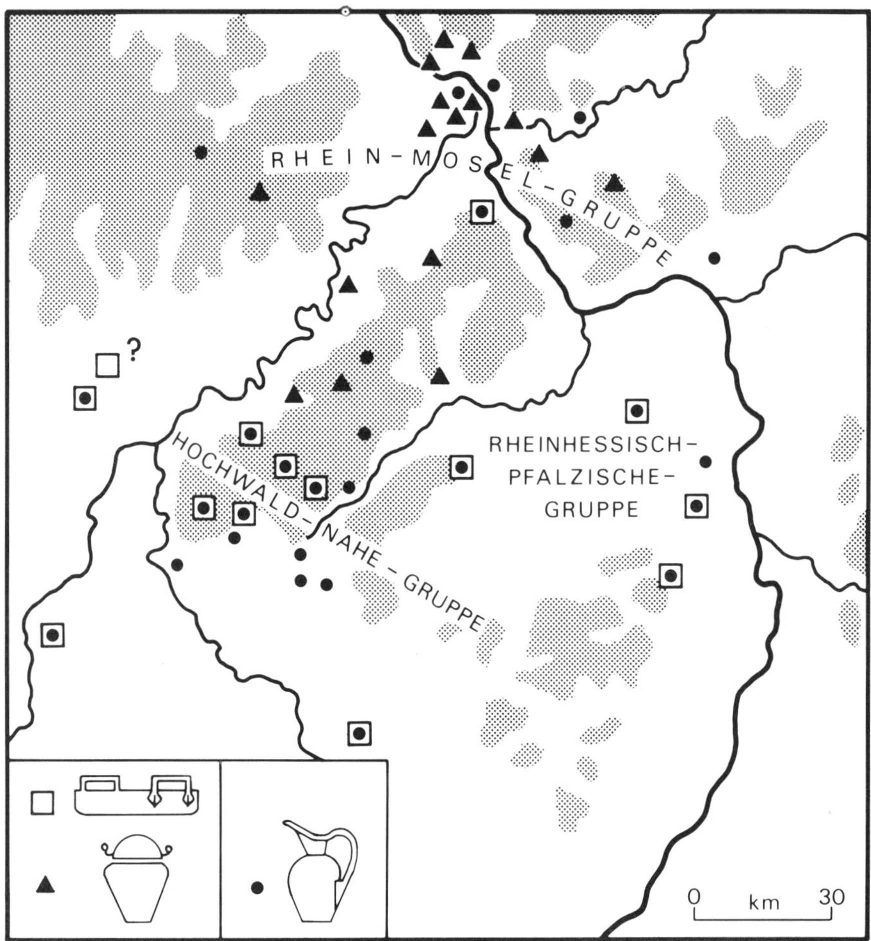

□ handled basins

▲ 'Rheinisch-Tessinische' situlae

● beaked flagons

Figure 9.3 Map showing the distribution of three imported types in the Middle Rhine. (Drawing: Ruth Rowell, after Driehaus, Frey, Haffner and Kimmig.)

mation cemeteries in Baden-Württemberg (Biel 1974) and Bavaria, where the Manching-Steinbüchel cemetery includes amongst earlier decorated sword scabbards one with all-over-stamp decoration, once more with general Hungarian parallels (Jacobi 1982:esp. Abb.2; Megaw 1978:esp. Fototaf.21:3; see also Frey 1978–79). The particular significance of the 'North Swiss Group B' sword with ring-punched chagrinage from the 'doctor's' burial in grave 7 at Obermenzing, Ldkr. München (De Navarro 1955; 1972:esp. pp.257ff.), is that here is certainly clear evidence of high status associated with material manifestations of smithing skill, skill to which magical properties are almost universally ascribed (Megaw 1979:51f.). However, how many of these so-called 'Hungarian' or 'Swiss' swords may again be of local manufacture – whatever the antecedents of their makers or the styles in which they worked – is a question which must also be kept in mind.

With regard to craftsmen-artists,[6] Hodson (1980) in a review of Pauli (1978:see here esp. 458–9) has recently briefly commented on such evidence as there is for craftsmen burials or at least the burial of tools in graves. In addition to high status burials with tools from graves 469 and 697 at Hallstatt one can not only cite the Early La Tène burial of the 'Kleine Hutweide' grave 13 at Au am Leithagebirge from the same general area of Lower Austria – a cremation with bent sword and scabbard (Nebehay 1973:esp. pp.14–16 and Taf.XI; Pauli 1980a:no.228) – but a slightly later burial from St Georgen am Steinfeld (Taus 1965; Pauli 1980a:no.229). Pauli's intriguing suggestion that the La Gorge-Meillet chariot grave might have been that of a master craftsman on the basis of the tools identified amongst the grave goods (Fourdignier 1878:esp.4 and pl.X; Bertrand 1879:esp.195) has recently been challenged on the grounds of uncertainty of association.[7] It is of course the helmet no less than the association in a chariot grave with an Attic black glaze stemless cup which links the Marnian chieftain of La Gorge-Meillet with his counterpart on the Dürrnberg where grave 44/2 may well be considered that of a western Celt. Does the helmet of Schaaff's 'Berru' type with its seeming eastern prototypes necessarily indicate direct or even indirect Persian links? I shall comment further on Marnian-Central European links; suffice it for the moment to observe that the 'Berru' helmet distribution as currently known is an east French phenomenon with central European outliers (Schaaff 1973). A more certain candidate for a chariot-owning craftsman, also noted by Pauli, is the discovery of a metalsmith's hammer with the bronze horse figurine in the Friesen, Kr. St Wendel, barrow (Jacobsthal 1944:no.390). A later burial from the same general area is cremation grave 39 (1980) in the extensive later Iron Age and Roman period cemetery at Wederath-Belginum, Kr. Wittlich/Bernkastel, with, in place of weapons as status markers, two chisels or gravers and a file (Haffner 1980:esp. 25f. and Abb.15). Despite the scanty evidence, the presence of smiths' graves in the metal-rich areas of western and central Europe is to be expected and with more and more attention being put into the excavation of relevant settlement sites it is not surprising if evidence for workshop groups and activities first summarized by Jacobsthal (1944:155) – including the occasional identification of tools from later Hallstatt and Early La Tène defended as well as open sites –

should be on the increase (Kimmig 1983a:118ff.; Pertlweiser 1969–1971; Joachim with Biel 1977; Wells 1981:esp.394 and Abb.4). From the increasing evidence for the settlement archaeology of the Dürrnberg comes an as yet unpublished field anvil associated with occupation material of La Tène B2–C1 date (fig.9.4), while for the Late La Tène phase the evidence naturally increases; however, it is not only from the well-known oppida sites such as Manching (Jacobi 1974a) but also from small-scale settlements and hoards that finds of tools are being recorded (e.g. Joachim 1980; Teodor 1980). As has been observed previously, detailed investigation of much later and culturally distinct north European centres not only offers interesting analogies for the possible organization of Celtic workshops but demonstrates the virtually unchanging typology of smiths' tools from later prehistory into the post-Roman period (Holmqvist 1972; Tomtlund 1978; Werner 1981). Again it must be observed in parenthesis that the commonly cited 'barrow' of Celles in the Puy-de-Dôme (fig.9.5) (Pages-Allary *et al.* 1903:esp.391ff.; Déchelette 1914:1353ff.), referred to for example by Lenerz-de Wilde (1977:esp.7 and Abb.5), is almost certainly the debris from a Late La Tène workshop specializing in bone working rather

Figure 9.4 Field anvil found on the Dürrnberg bei Hallein, Austria, in association with occupation material of the La Tène B2–C1 period. Width 45mm. (Photo: F. M. B. Cooke, University of Leicester.)

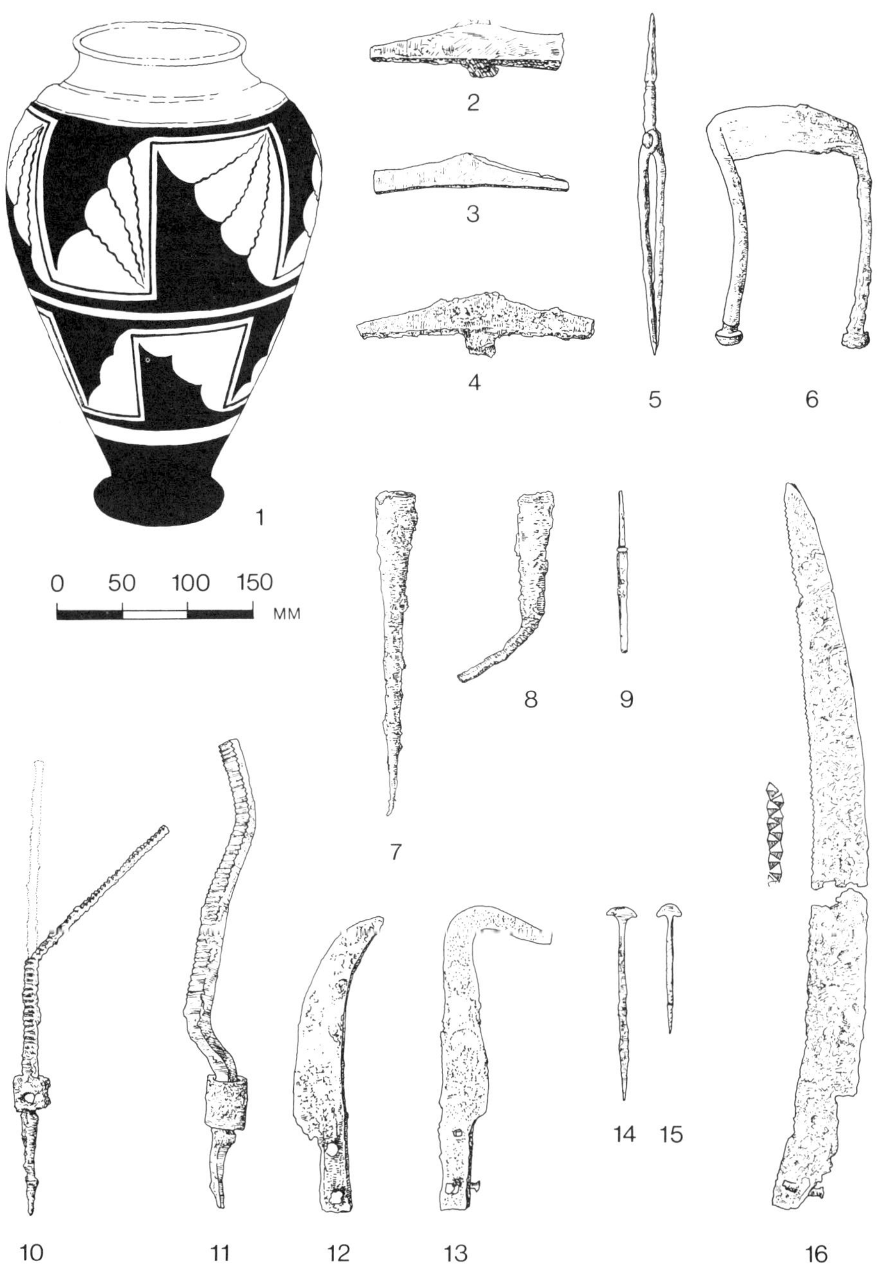

Figure 9.5 Celles, Puy-de-Dôme. Painted urn (1) and selection of iron tools (2–16) from 'barrow', comprising hammers (2–4), dividers (5), spoke-shave (6), awls or engraving tools (7–9), rasps (10–11), knives (12–13), chisels (14–15) and saw (16). (Drawing: Elizabeth Birkett, after Déchelette 1914.)

than evidence for high-status craftsmen.[8] Equally interesting is the evidence that that debris from the working of both gold and bronze was buried under the mound of the rich Hallstatt chieftain's barrow burial of Hochdorf, although Biel suggests that the actual workshops were probably on the princely settlement of the Hohenasperg itself (Biel 1982b:64 and 99f. and Abb.2, 30).

In the Greek world the legend of Daedalus and Achilles' kidnapping of craftsmen indicates their value in a stratified warrior society. The story of the Helvetic smith Helico's initiation of the Celtic incursions into Italy extends this tradition into the period under review (Pliny, *Nat. Hist.* xii.5; see p.177). As far as workshop activities and their relationship to trade and social hierarchies go, the Arbedo, Kt. Tessin, fifth-century B.C. workshop hoard (Primas 1972) with its Alpine and Etruscan types adds to the evidence for the key position held by the region at the beginning of the development of Early La Tène fine metalwork. As has already been mentioned, surely the Heuneburg mould fragment (Kimmig and von Vacano 1973), no less than the fragmentary mould for an Early La Tène *torques à tampons* from the settlement of Vayres in the Gironde (Mohen 1979:esp. fig.1:2), surely indicates the power to command the services of foreign specialist craftsmen (for a further possibility see Spindler 1980). In Britain as on the continent, there is evidence for metalsmiths in oppida, as has recently been recognized amongst material recovered earlier from the Brigantian centre at Stanwick (Spratling 1981). On the other hand it is not only the workshop debris from Gussage All Saints – like Stanwick, associated with the manufacture of harness sets (Spratling 1979; Foster 1980a,b) – and a mould from Worms Head (Savory 1974) which suggest that prestige goods were not always produced in the wealthiest centres. The unfinished Early La Tène *Maskenfibel* from a small fortified settlement, the Kleine Knetzberg in Bavaria (fig.9.6), is amongst the strongest evidence for itinerant skilled craftsmen producing on site particular prestige goods (Wamser 1982; Megaw 1982c:esp.26–7).

The most promising but as yet not fully exploited body of material for establishing not only stylistic development but workshop practice, trade and cultural association – in other words a seemingly perfect test bed for theories on Iron Age social archaeology – is of course the Early and Middle La Tène range of *Stempelkeramik* (Schwappach 1973; 1977; Linksfeller 1978).[9] Pottery stamps, usually of antler and for production of the ubiquitous concentric circle patterns (fig.9.7), are now known from a number of settlement sites, including pottery workshops – notably as yet not from graves, possibly indicating a differentiation in status between potters and metalsmiths – from the Late Hallstatt to the Late La Tène period (Pauli 1980b:esp.171–2, and no.117; Ludikovský 1964:esp. obr.3; Schwappach 1977:esp.142 and Abb.21; Linksfeller 1978: esp.83; Kappel 1969:esp.45 and Taf.59:1–4; Jacobi 1974a:esp.64 and Taf.81:1609–10; Dumitraşcu 1979; 1982:esp. fig.6:1, 3). From the Late Hallstatt and earlier La Tène cemetery of Polešovice in Moravia (Snášil and Ludikovský 1973), and hitherto unpublished following the untimely death of the excavator, is the only example of a more complex bone stamp so far known to me (fig.9.8);[10] this is in the form of a typical simplified lotus bud and reminds one of the technological relationship between such stamps and those producing the decoration of some

Early La Tène sword-sheaths (Jacobi 1982; Megaw 1978).[11]

Further on the question of the role and status of the early La Tène craftsman-metalsmith, there is one detail of the La Gorge-Meillet helmet to be recalled: the incised geometric decoration incorporating *tremolo* or rolled nosed scraper work. One possible source for such engraved metalwork can be found in a restricted group of western Swiss Late Hallstatt sheet metal belt plaques. As I have discussed in connection with the decorated sword scabbard from Méroux, terr. de Belfort (Megaw 1968), this piece, together with the Reinheim, Kr. St Ingbert, and the re-studied Waldalgesheim, Ldkr. Kreuznach, flagon (frontispiece), display a mastery of design and technique which must be studied now in the light of the detailed analyses by Majolie Lenerz-de Wilde (1977; 1979) of compass ornament in both early and insular Celtic art. Pauli's (1978) argument, already referred to, for such skills and their mathematical bases only being proper to an upper class, seems another point well taken. Even setting aside the claim that a quarter of all known *Fürstengräber* art is the product of compass-based ornament, the use of such ratios as the Golden Mean again offers a hint as to the transmission of ideas as well as objects and stylistic prototypes from the Mediterranean. From a later context we may recall Jacobi's (1974b) comments on trade as a means of the transferring of written skills to an aliterate society.[12] Certainly in such societies visual communication assumes a major role.

But if I am correct in expecting meaning behind the iconography of Early La Tène 'non-representational' art, recalling with Gombrich (1977) Karl Popper's belief in a universal need for regularity, then ornament may be seen as a system of multiple reference, and one may presuppose its use for the transference of 'sets' of meanings. Returning to ethnography, such sets may be found in the

Figure 9.6 Unfinished Early La Tène *Maskenfibel* from the Kleine Knetzberg, Ldkr. Hassberge, Germany. Length 70mm. (Photo: courtesy of Dr L. Wamser.)

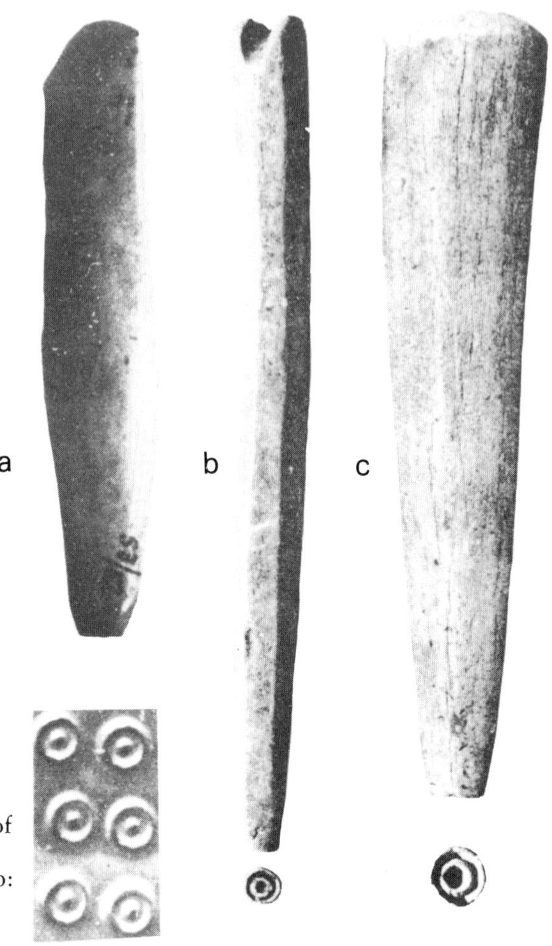

Figure 9.7 Antler pottery stamps with concentric circle design. Scale c.1:1. (a) Igersheim, Kr. Bad Mergentheim. (Photo: courtesy of Dr F. Schwappach.) (b) and (c) Manching, Kr. Ingolstadt. (Photo: courtesy Römisch-Germanisch Kommission.)

Figure 9.8 (*left*) Detail of end, and (*right*) impression of bone pottery stamp in the form of a simplified lotus bud from Polešovice, Okr. Uherské Hradiště, Czechoslovakia. Width 8mm. (Photos: AU CŠAV Brno; F. M. B. Cooke, University of Leicester.)

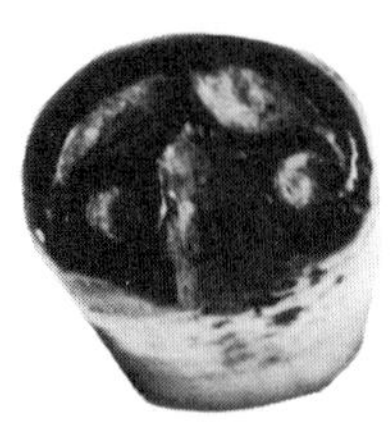

modern Australian Western Desert acrylics with their use of a limited range of symbols – indeed visual metaphors – whose meaning alters with context, a context which may not visually be discernible (Megaw 1982b). It follows then, in contrast with contemporary decorative art in fifth- and fourth-century Greece and Italy, that there may well be meaning to be found in compass designs. It is hardly surprising that, unlike high-status art, direct compass ornament is largely lacking on 'crafts' objects such as pottery; shared motifs on metalwork and *Stempelkeramik*, often cutting across Schwappach's (1973; 1976) east–west stylistic division of Early La Tène art, should not cause one to forget that not only the economics but the social anthropology of pottery-making is a very different thing from the production of metalwork.

Art styles, distribution, dispersion and migration

I must now return to a topic which I have discussed before: how to interpret the observed distributions of art objects, the surviving stylistic patterns of the influence of Greeks – and others – bearing gifts (Megaw 1982a). The problem begins with those who believe that rules born of the very structure of society largely determine each and every one of the major factors concerning the deposition and distribution of objects. Such views raise major issues in the valid reconstruction of past societies from archaeological evidence. Form follows function; 'art, it is said, is not a mirror but a hammer; it shapes', stated Leon Trotsky, darling of the Surrealists and thus perhaps not too wildly inappropriate a source to quote in the context of early Celtic art, particularly if one regards this art as a form of communication. A number of scholars concerned with problems of style and its interpretation have, again largely on the basis of ethnographic observation, been gradually building up a considerable literature on theories of stylistic variation. Thus Stephen Plog, favouring the 'information exchange theory of stylistic variation', where style is seen as a form of social behaviour encoding information as to social grouping and so forth (Plog 1980:5f.), quotes Ian Hodder's Kenya-based observations of a lack of correlation between degrees of interaction and cultural similarity (more recently Hodder 1982b:194). There is inherent in much contemporary work an attempt to present art styles as cultural cognitive maps, to employ J. L. Fischer's (1961) phrase. However, Jon Muller, who to my mind has written more sense on this difficult area than any other anthropologist or archaeologist, comments that 'styles are not necessarily contiguous with whole societies and examination of living societies suggests that they rarely are. Participation of an individual in a style, however, does imply membership of some kind of social group' (Muller 1977:35). A further element which seems largely to have been ignored in current discussion of the continental Iron Age is the question of competition and the manner in which the field of operation of an individual craftsman (or his products) will tend to repel the operation of others – an explanation for mutually exclusive distributions (Bradley and Hodder 1979; see also Bradley 1982). 'Competitiveness' must also have resulted when craftsmen worked within a certain area but nonetheless moved from chieftainly centre to centre. In a late and insular context Spratling, in his analysis of the I B.C./A.D. Gussage All Saints, Dorset, bronzesmithing debris, sees a growth of specialization running parallel with archaeological evidence for regional competition and the increase of multivallate fortification (Spratling 1979:esp.144f.).

Can one in fact then usefully map stylistic distributions of the early phases of the La Tène period? There is nothing new in trading objects across cultural boundaries, and the presence uniquely at the Dürrnberg of all the major styles of the period simply underlines its significance as the central place and redistribution centre *par excellence*. Kruta (in Duval and Hawkes 1976:161f.; cf. Schwappach 1973:96) has argued cogently that Schwappach's occasional conflation in his published distribution maps of motifs from fine metalwork and stamped pottery is comparing unlike with unlike. I have argued (Megaw 1982a:223f. and figs.3–4) that regional trends are difficult to discern in the broad distribution of both *Fürstengräber* plant and, particularly, palmette-based material and the compass-derived 'intersecting arc' motifs (Schwappach's (1976) 'western' and 'eastern' groups respectively); the same exists with the Waldalgesheim tendril, which it is now generally agreed considerably overlaps in time objects decorated with the other style elements (Frey 1976).

Certainly there is an expected western bias, extending noticeably to the south with the tendril designs, and with clusters in the Marne and Middle Rhine for the other two groups. Detailed examination of these distributions suggests, however, that there are important groupings of both palmette-based and arc design in the east – confirmation, for example, of the links between eastern France and east-central Europe as observable on the Dürrnberg and in the flat grave cemeteries of Transdanubia. If, while being mindful of Kruta's further stricture (in Duval and Hawkes 1976:161–2) that in art different factors are at work from in the selection of burial rites, one superimposes the stylistic distributions on Lorenz's cultural grouping based on detailed analysis of grave associations summarized in chapter 6 above, the basic point is, I think, immediately clear visually.

Frey (in Duval and Kruta 1982:2336) has argued that, despite my denial of a close fit of styles with Lorenz's regional groupings (chapter 6 above), in fact not only does the early palmette ornamentation cluster in the west, reflecting as it does prestige material produced for the chieftains of the Marne–Mosel zone (Lorenz group 1), but the arcs when observed on pottery concentrate in the eastern Rhine–Danube zone (Lorenz group 3 where decorated pottery is a particular feature in contrast to its virtual absence in graves further west); 'Waldalgesheim' or 'vegital' decoration is then shared between the western and eastern Rhine–Danube zone, as one would expect on the basis of the general archaeological evidence for the period of Celtic expansion in the fourth century. I continue to believe, however, that although such general correlations may exist there is no close fit between style elements and cultural sub-zones *as defined on the basis of grave goods* and that indeed on the basis of analysing the distributions as originally presented there is overall no statistically significant difference in the distribution of the varying styles within each zone.[13] The origin of what I certainly prefer with my French colleagues to term the 'vegital style'

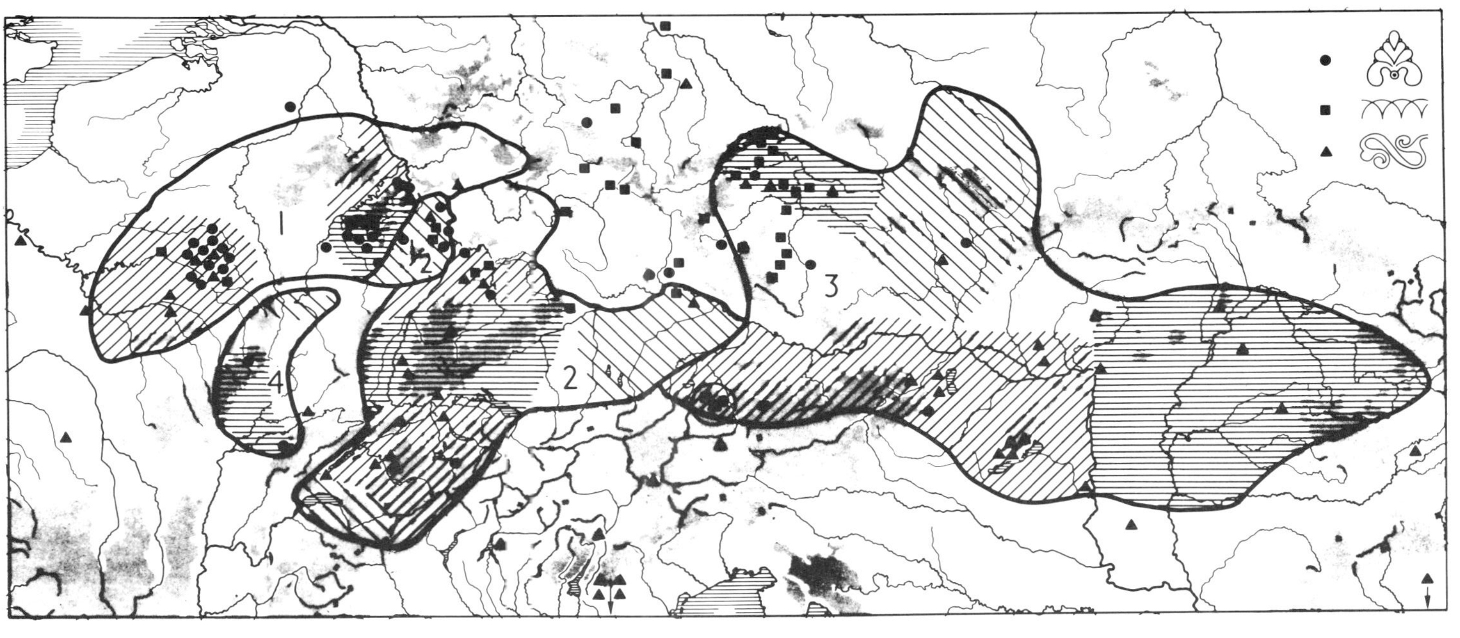

Figure 9.9 Distribution map showing regional divisions in burial customs of the Early La Tène period with (superimposed) palmette designs (circles), arcs (squares) and Waldalgesheim motifs (triangles).

The main groups are: 1. Marne–Mosel area; 2. Western Rhine–Danube area; 3. Eastern Rhine–Danube area; 4. Burgundy–Lorraine 'group'. Hatching represents subgroups; the large open circle is the Dürrnberg bei Hallein, Austria. (Drawing: Ruth Rowell, after Lorenz, Frey and Schwappach, with additions.)

(q.v. Kruta 1976–77), in view not least of the eponymous Waldalgesheim grave's comparative lateness and distributional outlying position, is Italy. This is as Jacobsthal originally conceived and as has been confirmed and elaborated by Frey (1976) and the work of the Krutas (Kruta 1978a,b; 1980; 1983; Kruta Poppi 1975) and other Italian writers (De Marinis 1977). Lacunae still of course exist; the later classical Italo–Greek – or more precisely Tarentine or Campanian – sources might lead one to expect a hybrid Italo–Celtic style, notably amongst the culturally mixed cemeteries of northern Italy. Graves such as Moscano di Fabriano with its chariot, Apulian pottery and Etruscan metal-work (Frey 1971) postdate the Celtic invasions and are rather to be regarded as contemporary with eastern movements into the Carpathian Basin which must have produced the opportunity for craftsmen to renew contact with classical products otherwise missing in the later fourth century north of the Alps. Even if the new settled territory of the Senones (Kruta 1981) – which Polybius notes as extending as far south as Syracuse by about 360 B.C. – has produced several sword scabbards in the newly evolving style, other scabbards, and of course the range of brooches mainly of Kruta's Duchcov-Münsingen horizon, suggest either Switzerland or the Marne as a possible centre for development; Kruta's examination of brooches of the period from the first half of the fourth to the beginning of the third century indicates another common disconformity in early Celtic art: stylistic ornamentation is never restricted to any single particular class or type of artefact. There is reason to support the theory of western Switzerland as the 'cross-roads of culture contact between the Celtic world and northern Italy' (Kruta 1976–77:44), and the key developmental area from which stylistic tendrils reached out both west to the Marne and even more particularly east to Bohemia and the Danube Basin. The helmet from Amfreville-sous-les-Monts, Eure (Kruta 1978b; Pauli 1980a:no.40), is a key piece in this discussion to which must now be added the south-westerly example from Agris, Charente (Gomez 1981; 1982) and the helmet from grave 14 of the Monte Bibele, Monterenzio, cemetery (Vitali 1982).

The context within which such obvious prestige objects as elaborately decorated sword scabbards are found, as noted in the following paragraph, is not only an indication of rank attained by their owner but also must indicate the high esteem in which certain craftsmen–artists were held. I do not wish here at the close to return to questions concerning models of hierarchy; despite the work of Lorenz and others on burial groupings (Lorenz, chapter 6 above; Sankot 1980; Bujna 1982), the material evidence for such analysis still seems to me to offer uncertain support for any particular theory unless on a restricted regional basis where comparison between both settlement patterns and burial customs can be made, and this of course is largely lacking although, as in Britain and the United States, there is in Europe no shortage of overviews on the subject of social structure (Steuer 1982). Hodson's (1977; 1979) cautionary remarks on inferring status from burials deserve continual re-reading and the wider issue of the cultural dispersal of archaeological material equally needs further discussion than I have recently offered (Megaw 1982a:esp.218ff. and fig.1; cf. Schiffer 1972 and

Bradley 1982), particularly when considering the influence on the selection of motifs and styles which must have occurred in the Iron Age as it does now (Becker 1982) as the result of market factors. But with regard to both art and social archaeological studies the development and distribution of the various sub-styles of Early and Middle La Tène decorated swords has a vital part to play in understanding both east–west and west–east movements of cultural symbols in the form of artistic motifs. Thus, recalling the previously mentioned dispute concerning the dissemination of 'orientalizing' motifs in Iron Age art, it seems quite clear now that the immediate origin and development of the 'dragon-' or 'bird-pair' was not in the east but the west (Bulard 1982; Petres 1982); similarly, it now seems certain that the so-called 'Hungarian' sword style, so often reinvoked in insular contexts (Megaw 1983:esp.138ff.),[14] developed first with Celtic expansion into Transdanubia coincidental with the evolution of Jacobsthal's 'Waldalgesheim style' (Szabó 1977; 1982). Frey has made clear that despite the lack of imports Mediterranean influences are strong in the period of the sword styles (Frey with Megaw 1976:50f.).

As has already been observed, Waldalgesheim itself must represent an outlier, a 'foreigner's grave' since the style is foreign to the Hunsrück–Eifel (see comments by Wolfgang Dehn in Duval and Kruta 1982:231–2). If Switzerland appears to lack the scabbards decorated in the 'vegetal' style, I no longer see any reason to doubt as I did in 1970 the local production of such material in north Italy, and the Waldalgesheim woman's grave could well be that of a locally marrying Celtic outsider with at the very least close connections to the south and west. That Bohemia, as Kruta (1975a; 1979) has repeatedly shown, is an important bridging region is again brought out by the brooch evidence, and Bohemian armlets and Duchcov-Münsingen brooches at the Dürrnberg yet again underline the site's claim as the cultural capital of the later phases of Early La Tène (Pauli 1978:esp.483–5). The Marnian contribution to eastern Celtic culture is clear in the evolution of the so-called 'Hungarian' sword style with its marked asymmetric layout on such pieces as the Litér, Kom. Veszprém scabbard with its Type II 'dragon-pair' (Szabó 1977:214 and fig.3; 1982:179). The local evolution in Hungary of the third-century sword style must have followed the pattern suggested by De Navarro (1972) for the western Swiss swords, with local specialist smiths – not necessarily those responsible for the swords as well as their scabbards – producing prestige goods, as has already been noted, occasionally for export as in the case of the Obermenzing surgeon. Both 'sword style' and the previous vegetal decorated material can be followed to the east as well, to Transylvania for example, with prestige swords present in the grave goods of such major Celtic Romanian cemeteries as Fîntînele, Pişcolt and Sanislău unfortunately as yet largely unpublished (but see Crişan 1975; Németi 1975).[15]

That eastern Celts also bore gifts can occasionally be seen as in the Cernon-sur-Coole, Marne, burial with the eastern sword and scabbard so closely related to that from Drňa in Slovakia (Megaw 1978), both demonstrating stylistic features which look back to the vegetal style and forward to the later eastern sword style. The relative date for such pieces is fixed by the pair of La Tène II decorated brooches from Conflans, Marne – one with the griffon-bird of the sword scabbards – recently discussed by Kruta (1975b), who persuasively argues that here too is evidence for the strength of a third-century Marne–Middle Danube cultural relationship. But how can one best explain the strange dispersal of the vegetal style? Certainly this was a time of population movements both small and great and many of the sword-bearers will have been mercenaries. It must be observed also that in the third century in the so-called Illyro-Pannonian region there are clear indications of how strong certain Hellenistic influences were on the eastern Celts (Kruta and Szabó 1982). Perhaps the occasional blurring of clear-cut and matching distributions between burial groupings and style elements may, in contrast to models cited earlier for the Late Hallstatt–Early La Tène change-over in the West, reflect the control exercised by local centres in a general time of mobility but comparative peace, a control which produced stability and thus removed the need for the ostentatious material display of identity which would result in such matching distributions.

But I have ridden my hobby-horses too hard and too long; adequate discussion of this last point would require another paper and, as has been said of insular Celtic art, 'theories concerning the social and economic implications of this group of material will no doubt reverberate in archaeological circles for some years to come' (Foster 1980a:187).

Notes

1. On the whole question of Mediterranean and particularly Greek influence on the early Celtic world see now the comprehensive overview by Kimmig (1983b:esp.47ff.).
2. I borrow this quotation from his lecture 'The first Western Greeks and the archaeology of Europe', given before the Society of Antiquaries of London, 18 December 1980.
3. A frequently quoted late source apparently citing a third-century B.C. account of a fifth-century Celtic attack on Massalia led by one Catumarandus includes a description of the strange staring features of the goddess seen in a dream, and the fear thus instilled in him recalls the apotropaic aspect of the *Maskenfibeln* which Pauli (1975:205ff.; 1978:111) remarks on; cf. Pompeius Trogus, *Historiarum Philippicarum Epitoma* xliii.5, 4–7, cited by Justin (see J.-J. Hatt in Pauli 1980a:52f.).
4. Mr Ronald Lightbown of the Victoria and Albert Museum, London, has also drawn my attention to the description of the workings of an early twelfth-century A.D. north-west German metalsmith's workshop contained in the late Latin text of Theophilus Monachus, *De diversis artibus* (q.v. Dodwell 1981; esp. Book III). See also here Driehaus (1972b).
5. The sword scabbard from Veliko Mraševo, gr. 1, with ring-dot punched chagrinage is surely 'Swiss' not 'Hungarian style' as suggested by Guštin.
6. The continued use of the male term 'craftsman' in this essay I believe to be defensibly non-sexist, at least as far as metalworkers go, in the absence of any evidence known to me – ethnography included – for women specialists in this area.
7. The tools, not currently available for study, were originally identified as a small hammer, punches, a borer, reamer and tweezers. Information from M. Alain Duval, Musée des Antiquités Nationales, St-Germain-en-Laye.

8. This interpretation I owe to M. Jean-Paul Guillaumet, Autun; see now Guillaumet (1983).
9. One eagerly awaits publication of Christopher Gosden's University of Sheffield doctoral thesis on central European fine pottery of this period, the more particularly since it will add considerably to the information currently available on fabric analysis.
10. I am grateful to my friends at the Archeologické Ústav ČSAV Brno for allowing me to study this piece found with another simpler stamp and to reproduce the illustration used here.
11. See in this context another sword scabbard perhaps of Hungarian origin – but *not* in the 'Hungarian sword style' – from Graz-Laubgasse (Megaw 1978:n.6; Frey 1978–79).
12. Add here the recent discovery on the Dürrnberg of an apparent script incised on a pottery slab considered to be from a La Tène B settlement deposit which would considerably pre-date the graffiti on sherds from Manching as 'die ältesten einheimisch Schriftdenkmäler aus dem prähistorischen Mitteleuropa nördlich der Alpen' (Krämer 1982:esp.499); it must be noted that the first published illustration (Moosleitner and Zeller 1982:esp. Abb.4) suggests the possibility of a much later date . . . I owe this information to Matt Murray, Department of Anthropology, Harvard University.
13. I am grateful to my former colleague Roger Martlew, now of the University of Loughborough, for making a first attempt to test my views statistically.
14. A fuller picture will emerge following the publication of Barry Raftery's (1984) and Ian Stead's continuing work on the Irish and British decorated sword scabbards respectively. Suffice it to note the recognition in the British Museum of two scabbards with dragon-pairs from the Thames, one from Hammersmith with well-defined Type I zoomorphic lyre (inv. no.1862.10.11). See now Stead 1984:50.
15. I am grateful to a number of Romanian colleagues for showing me much of this material in 1975 during a study tour under the auspices of the Anglo-Romanian Cultural Exchange Programme.

Bibliography

Ackerman, J. P. and Carpenter, R., 1963. *Art and Archaeology* (Englewood Cliffs, N.J.).

Arnheim, R., 1974. *Art and Visual Perception* (Berkeley, Los Angeles and London).

Artamonov, M. I., 1969. *Treasures from Scythian tombs.*

Becker, H. S., 1982. *Art Worlds* (Berkeley, Los Angeles and London).

Bertrand, A., 1879. In Travaux, *Bull. Soc. Nat. Antiq. de France*, 193–8.

Biel, J., 1974. 'Ein mittellatènezeitlicher Brandgräberfeld in Giengen an der Brenz, Kr. Heidenheim', *Arch. Korr. 4:* 225–7.

Biel, J., 1981. 'The late Hallstatt chieftain's grave at Hochdorf', *Antiquity 55:* 16–18.

Biel, J., 1982a. 'Das Fürstengrab von Eberdingen-Hochdorf, Kr. Ludwigsburg', *Antike Welt 13:* 22–37.

Biel, J., 1982b. 'Ein Fürstengrab der späten Hallstattzeit bei Eberdingen-Hochdorf, Kr. Ludwigsburg (Baden-Württemberg)', *Germania 60:* 61–104.

Bradley, R. J., 1982. 'The destruction of wealth in late prehistory', *Man 17:* 108–22.

Bradley, R. and Hodder, I., 1979. 'British prehistory: an integrated view', *Man 14:* 93–104.

Brook, D., 1980. 'A new theory of art', *British J. Aesthetics 20:* 305–21.

Bujna, J., 1982. 'Spiegelung der Sozialstruktur auf Latènezeitlichen Gräberfeldern im Karpatenbecken', *Památky Archeologické 73:* 312–431.

Bulard, A., 1982. 'À propos des origines de la paire d'animaux fantastiques sur les fourreaux d'épée latèniens'. In Duval and Kruta 1982:149–60.

Champion, S., 1976. 'Coral in Europe: commerce and Celtic ornament'. In Duval and Hawkes 1976: 29–37.
Champion, T. C., 1980. 'Mass migration in later prehistoric Europe'. In P. Sörbom (ed.), *Transport Technology and Social Change* (Stockholm): 33–42.
Charrière, G., 1971. *L'Art barbare scythe* (Paris).
Compton, M., 1983. *New Art at the Tate Gallery 1983.*
Crişan, I. H., 1975. 'La Nécropole de Fîntînele et son importance pour la problème des Celtes de l'Europe Centrale'. In J. Fitz (ed.), *The Celts in Central Europe=Alba Regia 14:* 185–6.
Daniel, G. E., 1970. *Archaeology and the History of Art: an inaugural lecture delivered in the University of Hull on 21 January 1969.*
Déchelette, J., 1914. *Manuel d'archéologie préhistorique Celtique et Gallo-Romain* II. 3 (Paris).
De Marinis, R., 1977. 'The La Tène culture of the Cisalpine Gauls'. In M. Guštin, (ed.), *Keltské Študije=Posavski Muzej Brežice 4:* 23–50.
De Marinis, R., 1981. 'Il periodo Golasocca IIIA in Lombardia', *Studi Archeologici, I* (Bergamo): 21–286.
De Navarro, J. M., 1955. 'A doctor's grave of the Middle La Tène period from Bavaria', *Procs. Prehist. Soc. 21:* 231–48.
De Navarro, J. M., 1972. *The Finds from the Site of La Tène I: Scabbards and the Swords Found in Them.*
Dodwell, C. R. (ed. and trans.), *Theophilus Monachus: De diversis artibus.*
Driehaus, J., 1965. ' "Fürstengräber" und Eisenerze zwischen Mittelrhein, Mosel und Saar', *Germania 43:* 32–49.
Driehaus, J., 1966. 'Zur Verbreitung der eisenzeitlicher Situlen in mittelrheinischen Gebirgsland', *Bonner Jahrb. 166:* 26–47.
Driehaus, J., 1972a. Review of Megaw 1970a, *Bonner Jahrb. 172:* 26–47.
Driehaus, J., 1972b. 'Zum Problem merowingerzeitl. Golschmiede', *Nachrichten der Akademie der Wissenschaften Göttingen, phil. -hist. Klasse 7:* 4–18.
Duignan, M., 1976. 'The Turoe stone: its place in insular La Tène art'. In Duval and Hawkes 1976: 201–17.
Dumitraşcu, S., 1979. 'Un atelier de olĕarie (La Tène) descoperit la Biharea', *Sargeţia 14:* 45–58.
Dumitraşcu, S., 1982. 'Les fours de poterie découverts à Biharea', *Dacia 26:* 157–66.
Duval, P-M., 1982. ' Comment analyser, reproduire et expliquer les formes d'art celtique'. In Duval and Kruta 1982: 3–23.
Duval, P-M. and Hawkes, C. F. C. (eds.), 1976. *Celtic Art in Europe: Five Protohistoric Centuries.*
Duval, P-M. and Kruta, V. (eds.), 1979. *Les Mouvements celtiques du V*[e] au 1er siècle avant notre ère (Paris).
Duval, P-M. and Kruta, V. (eds.), 1982. *L'Art celtique de la période d'expansion: IV*[e] *et III*[e] *siècles avant notre ère*, École Pratique des Hautes Études, IVe section III. 13.
Fischer, F., 1976. 'KEIMHΛIA: Bemerkungen zur kulturgeschichtlichen Interpretation des sogenannten Südimports in der späten Hallstatt- und frühen Latène-Kultur des westlichen Mitteleuropa', *Germania 51:* 436–59.
Fischer, F., 1983. 'Thrakien als Vermittler iranischer Metallkunst an die frühen Kelten'. In R. M. Boehmer and H. Hauptmann (eds.), *Beiträge zur Altertumskunde Kleinasiens: Festschrift für Kurt Bittel* (Mainz): 191–202.
Fischer, J. L., 1961. 'Art styles as cultural cognitive maps', *American Anthropologist 63.1:* 79–93.
Forge, A. (ed.), 1973. *Primitive Art and Society.*
Foster, J., 1980a. 'Metalworking at Gussage All Saints, Dorset: a review of recent work'. In W. A. Oddy (ed.), *Aspects of Early Metallurgy,* British Museum Occasional Paper 17: 185–7.

Foster, J., 1980b. *The Iron Age Moulds from Gussage All Saints*, British Museum Occasional Paper 12.

Fourdignier, E., 1878. *Double sépulture gauloise de la Gorge-Meillet: Étude sur les chars gaulois et les casques dans la Marne* (Paris and Châlons-sur-Marne).

Frankenstein, S. and Rowlands, M. J., 1978. 'The internal structure and regional context of early Iron Age society in south-western Germany', *Bull. Inst. Archaeol. Univ. London 15:* 73–112.

Freidin, N. P. G., 1982. 'Early Iron Age imports into the Paris Basin', *Expedition 24.3:* 21–9.

Frey, O-H., 1971. 'Das keltische Schwert von Moscano di Fabriano', *Hamburger Beiträge zur Archaeol. 1:* 173–9.

Frey, O-H., 1976. 'Du Premier Style au Style de Waldalgesheim'. In Duval and Hawkes 1976: 141–65.

Frey, O-H., 1978–79. 'Ein verziertes La-Tène-Schwert aus Graz', *Schild von Steier 15–16:* 67–73.

Frey, O-H., 1980. 'Die keltische Kunst'. In Pauli 1980a: 76–92.

Frey, O-H., 1981. 'Zu einem bedeutenden Zeugnis der frühen keltischen Kunst vom Glauberg', *Wetterauer Geschichtsblätter 30:* 13–21.

Frey, O-H. with Megaw, J. V. S., 1976. 'Palmette and circle: early Celtic art in Britain and its continental background', *Procs. Prehist. Soc. 42:* 47–65.

Frey-Asche, L., 1980. 'Zu einem goldenen Trinkhornbeschlag aus Weiskirchen'. In H. A. Cahn and Erika Simon (eds.), *Tainia. Festschrift R. Hampe* (Mainz): 121–32.

Gombrich, E. H. J., 1977. *Art and Illusion: a Study in the Psychology of Perception* (5th edn).

Gombrich, E. H. J., 1978. *Meditations on a Hobby-Horse and Other Essays on the Theory of Art* (3rd edn).

Gombrich, E. H. J., 1979. *The Sense of Order: a Study in the Psychology of Decorative Art.*

Gomez, J., 1981. 'A helmet from La Rochefoucauld', *Current Archaeol. 7:* 301.

Gomez, J., 1982. 'Un casque princier gaulois', *Archéologia 164:* 6–7.

Graburn, N. H. H. (ed.), 1976. *Ethnic and Tourist Arts: Cultural Expressions from the Fourth World* (Berkeley, Los Angeles and London).

Guillaumet, J-P., 1983. 'Le matériel du tumulus de Celles (Cantal)'. In J. Collis, A. Duval and R. Périchon (eds.), *Le Deuxième Âge du Fer en Auvergne et en Forez* (Sheffield and St Etienne): 189–211.

Guštin, M., 1977. 'Relativna Kronologija grobov "Mokronoške skupine" [Relative chronology of the graves of the "Mokronog group"]'. In M. Guštin (ed.), *Keltske Študije=Posavski Muzej Brežice 4:* 67–103.

Guštin, M., 1982. 'Zeitliche Einordnung der verzierten keltischen Schwerter aus Jugoslawien'. In Duval and Kruta 1982: 191–202.

Haffner, A., 1977. 'Die frühkeltischen Fürstengräben von Hochscheid – "Fuckerichscheide" ', *Westlicher Hunsrück=Führer zu vor- und frühgeschichte Denkmälern 34:* 163–71.

Haffner, A., 1980. 'Neue Ausgrabungen im keltisch–römischen Gräberfeld von Wederath–Belginum,' *Funde und Ausgrabungen im Bez. Trier 12:* 16–45.

Härke, H. G. H., 1979. *Settlement Types and Settlement Patterns in the West Hallstatt Province* (BAR IS57).

Hawkes, C. F. C., 1977. *Pytheas: Europe and the Greek explorers* (Eighth J. L. Myres Memorial Lecture, Oxford).

Hodder, I., 1982a. 'Theoretical archaeology: a reactionary view'. In I. Hodder (ed.), *Symbolic and Structural Archaeology:* 1–16.

Hodder, I., 1982b. *The Present Past: an Introduction to Anthropology for Archaeologists.*

Hodson, F. R., 1977. 'Quantifying Hallstatt: some initial results', *American Antiquity 42:* 394–412.

Hodson, F. R., 1979. 'Inferring status from burials in Iron Age Europe: some recent attempts'. In B. C. Burnham and J. Kingsbury (eds.), *Space, Hierarchy and Society* (BAR IS59): 23–30.
Hodson, F. R., 1980. Review of Pauli 1978, *Ant. J. 60:* 118–20.
Holmqvist, W., 1972. 'The Helgö workshop'. Summary in W. Holmqvist (ed.), *Excavations at Helgö*, IV.1: *Workshop* pt 1 (Stockholm): 256–62.
Hundt, H-J., 1969. 'Über vorgeschichtliche Seidenfunde', *Jahrbuch RGZM 16* (1971): 59–71.
Hundt, H-J., 1970. 'Gewebefunde aus Hallstatt: Webkunst und Tracht in der Hallstattzeit', *Krieger und Salzherren: Hallstattkultur im Ostalpenraum=RGZM Ausstellungskataloge* Bd 4: 53–71.
Jackson, K. H., 1964. *The Oldest Irish Tradition: a Window on the Iron Age.*
Jacobi, G., 1974a. *Werkzeug und Gerät aus dem Oppidum von Manching=Die Ausgrabungen in Manching 5* (Wiesbaden).
Jacobi, G., 1974b. 'Zum Schriftgebrauch in keltischen Oppida nördlich der Alpen', *Hamburger Beiträge zur Archäol. 4:* 171–81.
Jacobi, G., 1982. 'Verzierte Schwertscheiden vom Frühlatèneschema aus den Flachgräbern von Manching', *Germania 60:* 565–8.
Jacobsthal, P. F., 1944. *Early Celtic Art* (rev. edn 1969).
Joachim, H-E., 1980. 'Jüngerlatènezeitliche Siedlungen bei Eschweiler, Kr. Aachen', *Bonner Jahrb. 80:* 355–459.
Joachim, W. with Biel, J., 1977. 'Untersuchung einer Späthallstatt-frühlatenezeitlicher Siedlung in Kornwestheim, Kr. Ludwigsburg', *Fundberichte aus Baden-Würrtemberg 3:* 173–203.
Jope, E. M., 1983. 'Torrs, Aylesford and Padstow hobby-horse'. In A. O'Connor and D. V. Clarke (eds.), *From the Stone Age to the 'Forty-five: Studies presented to R. B. K. Stevenson:* 149–59.
Kappel, I., 1969. *Die Graphitonkeramik von Manching=Die Ausgrabungen in Manching*, II (Wiesbaden).
Kimmig, W., 1983a. *Die Heuneburg an der oberen Donau=Führer zu arch. Denkmälern in Baden-Württemberg*, I (2nd edn, Stuttgart).
Kimmig, W., 1983b. 'Die griechische Kolonisation im westlichen Mittelmeergebiet und ihre Wirkung auf die Landschaften des westlichen Mitteleuropa', *Jahrbuch RGZM 30:* 3–78.
Kimmig, W. and Von Vacano, O-W., 1973. 'Zu einem Gussform-Fragment einer Etruskischen Bronzekanne von der Heuneburg an der Oberen Donau', *Germania 51:* 72–85.
Krämer, W., 1982. 'Graffiti auf Spätlatènekeramik aus Manching', *Germania 60:* 489–99.
Kruta, V., 1975a. *L'Art celtique en Bohême*, École pratique des Hautes Études 324 (Paris).
Kruta, V., 1975b. 'Les Deux fibules laténiennes de Conflans (Marne)', *Études Celtiques 14:* 377–89.
Kruta, V., 1976–77. 'Les fibules laténiennes a décor d'inspiration végétale au IVe siècle a.n.e.', *Études Celtiques 15:* 19–47.
Kruta, V., 1978a. 'Celtes de Cispadane et Transalpins aux IVe et IIIe siècles a.n.e.', *Studi Etruschi 46:* 149–74.
Kruta, V., 1978b. 'Le casque d'Amfreville-sous-les-Monts et quelques problèmes de l'art du IV siècle a.n.e.', *Études Celtiques 15:* 405–24.
Kruta, V., 1979. 'Duchcov-Münsingen: nature et diffusion d'une phase laténienne'. In Duval and Kruta, 1979: 81–115.
Kruta, V., 1980. 'Les Boïens de Cispadane', *Études Celtiques 17:* 7–32.
Kruta, V., 1981. 'Les Sénons de l'Adriatique, *Études Celtiques 18:* 7–38.
Kruta, V., 1983. 'Facies celtiques de la Cisalpine aux IVe et IIIe siècles a.n.e.', *Popoli e facies culturali celtiche a nord e a sud delle Alpi dal V al I secolo a.c.=Atti del Colloquio Intern.* (Milan): 1–15.

Kruta, V. and Szabó, M., 1982. 'Canthares danubiens du IIIe siècle a.n.e. Un exemple d'influence hellénistique sur les Celtes orientaux', *Études Celtiques 19:* 51–67.
Kruta-Poppi, L., 1975. 'Les Celtes à Marzabotto (Province de Bologne)', *Études Celtiques 14:* 345–76.
Layton, R., 1981. *The Anthropology of Art.*
Lenerz-de Wilde, M, 1977. *Zirkelornamentik in der Kunst der Latènezeit,* Münchner Beiträge zur Vor- und Frühgeschichte 25.
Lenerz-de Wilde, M., 1979. 'Zur Verzierung der Röhrenkanne aus dem Fürstengrab von Waldalgesheim', *Arch. Korr. 9:* 313–16.
Lenerz-de Wilde, M., 1982. 'Le "style de Cheshire Cat", un phénomène caractéristique de l'art celtique'. In Duval and Kruta 1982: 101–14.
Linksfeller, D., 1978. 'Die stempelverzierte Keramik in Böhmen und Mähren', *Arch. Informationen 4:* 82–108.
Ludikovský, K., 1964. 'Dílny na Moravských nížinných keltských sídlištich', *Arch. Stud. Materiály 1:* 126–34.
Malraux, A., 1967. *Museum without Walls* (trans. S. Gilbert and F. Price).
Megaw, J. V. S., 1968. 'Une épée de la Tène I avec fourreau décoré, *Revue Arch. de l'Est et du Centre-Est 19:* 129–44.
Megaw, J. V. S., 1970a. *Art of the European Iron Age: a Study of the Elusive Image.*
Megaw, J. V. S., 1970b. 'Cheshire Cat and Mickey Mouse: analysis, interpretation and the art of La Tène Iron Age', *Procs. Prehist. Soc. 36:* 261–79.
Megaw, J. V. S., 1973. 'The decorated sword-scabbard from Cernon-sur-Coole (Marne) and Drňa, Rimavska Sobota (Slovakia)', *Hamburger Beiträge zur Archäol. 3.2:* 119–37.
Megaw, J. V. S., 1975. 'The orientalizing theme in Early Celtic art: East or West?' In J. Fitz (ed.), *The Celts in Central Europe. Papers of the II Pannonia Conference, Székésfehervar 1974=Alba Regia 14:* 15–33.
Megaw, J. V. S., 1978. 'The decoration on the sword-scabbard from Jenišův Újezd, gr. 115'. In J. Waldhauser (ed.), *Das Keltische Gräberfeld bei Jenišův Újezd* II (Teplice [1980]): 106–13.
Megaw, J. V. S., 1979. 'Celtic art – product of travelling craftsmen or chieftainly vassals?' In Duval and Kruta 1979: 49–54.
Megaw, J. V. S., 1982a. 'Finding purposeful patterns: further notes towards a methodology of Pre-Roman Celtic art'. In Duval and Kruta 1982: 213–29.
Megaw, J. V. S., 1982b. 'Western Desert acrylic painting – artefact or art?', *Art History 5:* 205–18.
Megaw, J. V. S., 1982c. 'An early La Tène *Maskenfibel* from Slovenské Pravno, okr. Martin, Slovakia', *Études Celtiques 19:* 7–34.
Megaw, J. V. S., 1983. 'From Transdanubia to Torrs: further notes on a Gabion of the late Jonathan Oldbuck'. In A. O'Connor and D. V. Clarke, (eds.), *From the Stone Age to the 'Forty-five: Studies presented to R. B. K. Stevenson:* 127–48.
Metropolitan Museum of Art [n.d.]. *From the Lands of the Scythians: Ancient Treasures from the Museums of the USSR* (n.d. [1975]).
Mohen, J-P., 1979. 'La présence celtique de la Tène dans le sud-ouest de l'Europe: indices archéologiques'. In Duval and Kruta 1979: 29–48.
Moosleitner, F., 1980. 'Handwerk und Handel'. In Pauli 1980a: 93–100.
Moosleitner, F. and Zeller, K., 1982. 'Beschriftete Tontafel aus keltischer Zeit am Dürrnberg', *Salzburger Museumsbl. 43:* 29–30.
Muller, J., 1977. 'Individual variation in art styles'. In J. N. Hill and J. Gunn (eds.), *Individual in Prehistory: Studies of Variability in Style in Prehistoric Technologies* (New York and London): 23–39.
Nebehay, S., 1973. *Das latènezeitliche Gräberfeld von der kleinen Hutweide bei Au am Leithagebirge,* Archaeologia Austriaca Beiheft 11.
Németi, J., 1975. 'Contributions concernant le facies latènien du Nord-Ouest de la Roumanie à la lumière des découvertes celtiques de Pişcolt'. In J. Fitz (ed.), *The Celts in Central Europe=Alba Regia 14:* 187–97.

Pages-Allary, J., Déchelette, J. and Lauby, A., 1903. 'Le tumulus arverne de Celles', *L'Anthropologie 14:* 385–416.

Pauli, L., 1971. 'Die Golasecca-Kultur und Mitteleuropa: Ein Beitrag zur Geschichte des Handels über die Alpen', *Hamburger Beiträge zur Archäol. 1.*

Pauli, L., 1974. 'Die Goldene Steig'. In *Studien zur Vor- und Frühgeschichte: Festschrift J. Werner*, Münchner Beiträge zur Vor- und Frühgeschichte Ergbd. 1: 115–39.

Pauli, L., 1975. *Keltische Volksglaube: Amulette- und Sonderbestattungen am Dürrnberg bei Hallein und im Eisenzeitlichen Mitteleuropa*, Münchner Beiträge zur Vor- und Frühgeschichte 28.

Pauli, L., 1978. *Der Dürrnberg bei Hallein* III, Münchner Beiträge zur Vor- und Frühgeschichte 18.

Pauli, L. (ed.), 1980a. *Die Kelten in Mitteleuropa: Kultur-Kunst-Wirtschaft: Salzburger Landesausstellung 1. Mai–30 Sept. 1980* (Salzburg).

Pauli, L., 1980b. 'Eine Siedlung mit hallstattzeitlichen Töpferei bei Mintraching, Ldkr. Regensburg'. In K. Spindler (ed.), *Vorzeit zwischen Main und Donau=Erlangen Forschungen A:26:* 159–72.

Pertlweiser, M., 1969; 1970; 1971. 'Die Hallstattzeitl. Hohensiedlung auf dem Waschenberg bei Bad Wimsbach-Neuharting, Poltischer Bez. Wels, Oberösterreich', *Jahrbuch des Oberösterreich. Musealvereines 114:* 29–48; *115:* 37–70; *116:* 51–80.

Petres, É. f. 1982. 'Notes on scabbards decorated with dragons and bird pairs'. In Duval and Kruta 1982: 161–74.

Peyre, C., 1982. 'Y a-t-il un contexte italique au style de Waldalgesheim?' In Duval and Kruta 1982: 51–82.

Plog, S., 1980. *Stylistic Variation in Prehistoric Ceramics.*

Primas, M., 1972. 'Zum eisenzeitlichen Depotfund von Arbedo (Kt. Tessin)', *Germania 50:* 76–93.

Raftery, B., 1984. *A Catalogue of Irish Iron Age Antiquities,* Veröffentlichungen des Vorgeschichtlichen Seminars Marburg, Sonderband 1.

Renfrew, A. C., 1969. 'Trade and culture processes in European prehistory', *Current Anthropology 10. 2–3:* 151–69.

Renfrew, A. C., 1973. *Social Archaeology: an inaugural lecture delivered at the University of Southampton, 20 March 1973.*

Renfrew, A. C., 1982. *Towards an Archaeology of mind: an inaugural lecture delivered before the University of Cambridge on 30 November 1982.*

Rolle, R., 1980. *Die Welt der Skythen: Stutenmelker und Pferdebogner: Ein antikes Reitervolk in neuer Sicht* (Lucerne and Frankfurt).

Sandars, N. K., 1976. 'Orient and orientalizing: recent thoughts reviewed'. In Duval and Hawkes 1976: 41–60.

Sankot, P., 1980. 'Studien zur Sozialstruktur des nordalpinen Flachgräberfelder der La-Tène-Zeit im Gebiet der Schweiz', *Zeitschrift Schweiz. Arch. und Kunstgeschichte 37:* 19–71.

Savory, H. N., 1974. 'An Early Iron Age metalworker's mould from Worms Head', *Archaeologia Cambrensis 123:* 170–4.

Schaaff, U., 1973. 'Frühlatènezeitliche Grabfunde mit Helmen von Typ Berru', *Jahrbuch RGZM 20* [1975]: 81–106.

Schiffer, M. B., 1972. 'Archaeological context and systemic context', *American Antiquity 37. 2:* 156–65.

Schwappach, F., 1973. 'Frühkeltischen Ornament zwischen Marne, Rhein und Moldau', *Bonner Jahrb. 173:* 53–111.

Schwappach, F., 1976. 'L'art ornamental du "Premier Style" celtique'. In Duval and Hawkes 1976: 61–110.

Schwappach, F., 1977. 'Die Stempelkeramik aus den Gräbern von Braubach', *Bonner Jahrb. 177:* 119–83.

Silver, H. R., 1979. 'Ethnoart', *American Rev. of Anthropology 8:* 267–307.

Snášil, R. and Ludikovský, K., 1973. 'Vorlaüfige Grabungsergebnisse auf der hallstatt- und Latènezeitliche Siedlung in Polešovice im Jahre 1972 (Bez. Uherscké Hradiště)', *Přchled Výzkumů 1972:* 35–7.
Sordi, M., 1976–77. 'La Leggenda di Arunte chiusino e la prima invasione gallica in Italia', *Scritti in memoria di Gianfranco Tibiletti=Rivista storiche dell' antichità 6–7:* 111–17.
Spindler, K., 1980. 'Zur Elfenbeinscheibe aus dem hallstattzeitlichen Fürstengrab vom Grafenbühl', *Arch. Korr. 10:* 239–48.
Spratling, M. G., 1979. 'The debris of metal working'. In G. J. Wainwright, *Gussage All Saints: an Iron Age Settlement in Dorset=DOE Archaeol. Reports 10:* 125–49.
Spratling, M. G., 1980. 'Weighing of gold in prehistoric Europe'. In W. A. Oddy (ed.), *Aspects of Early Metallurgy=British Museum Occasional Paper 17:* 179–83.
Spratling, M. G., 1981. 'Metalworking at the Stanwick oppidum: some new evidence', *Yorks. Archaeol. J. 53:* 13–16.
Stead, I. M., 1984. 'Some notes on imported metalwork in Iron Age Britain'. In S. Macready and F. H. Thompson (eds.), *Cross-Channel Trade between Gaul and Britain in the pre-Roman Iron Age*, Soc. Antiquaries of London Occ. Paper (n.s.) 4: 43–66.
Steuer, H., 1982. *Frühgesch. Sozialstruktur in Mitteleuropa,* Abhandlungen der Akademie der Wissenschaften in Gottingen, phil. -hist. Klasse 128.
Szabó, M., 1977. 'The origins of the Hungarian sword style', *Antiquity 51:* 211–20.
Szabó, M., 1982. 'Remarques sur la classification des fourreaux d'epée dits hongrois'. In Duval and Kruta 1982: 175–90.
Taus, M., 1965. 'Ein spätlatènezeitliches Schmied-Grab aus St Georgen am Steinfeld', *Archaeologia Austriaca 34:* 13–17.
Teodor, S., 1980. 'Das Werkzeugdepot von Lozna (Kr. Botaşani)', *Dacia 24:* 133–50.
Tomtlund, J-E., 1978. 'Tools'. In K. Lamm *et al.* (eds.), *Excavations at Helgö,* V.1: *Workshop* pt 11 (Stockholm): 15–29.
Tringham, R. 1975. 'Experimentation, ethnography, and the leapfrogs in archaeological methodology'. In R. A. Gould (ed.), *Explorations in Ethnoarchaeology* (Albuquerque): 169–99.
Vitali, D., 1982. 'L'elmo della tomba di Monte Bibele a Monterenzio (Prov. di Bologna)', *Études Celtiques 19:* 35–49.
Wamser, L., 1982. 'Frühkeltischer Fibelschmuck vom Kleinen Knetzberg', *Arch. Jahr in Bayern 1981:* 120–1.
Washburn, D. K., 1983. 'Towards a theory of structural style in art'. In D. K. Washburn (ed.), *Structure and Cognition in Art.*
Wells, P. S., 1980. *Culture Context and Culture Change: Early Iron Age Central Europe and the Mediterranean World.*
Wells, P. S., 1981. 'Siedlungsweise und Wirtschaft der Hallstattkultur'. In *Die Hallstattkultur: Bericht über das Symposium in Steyr 1980* (Linz): 389–97.
Wells, P. S. and Bonfante, L., 1979. 'West-central Europe and the Mediterranean: the decline in trade in the fifth century B.C.', *Expedition 21:* 18–24.
Werner, G., 1981. 'Goldsmiths, silversmiths and carpenters' tools'. In A. Lundström *et al.* (eds.), *Excavations at Helgö,* VII: *Glass–Iron–Clay* (Stockholm): 39–62.
Windl, H. J., 1976. 'Ein verzierter Schwertscheidenbeschlag aus dem Gräberfeld von Mihovo, Unterkrain (Dolejnsko)', *Mitteilungen der Anthropologischen Gesellschaft, Wien 106:* 42–7.
Wyss, R., 1975. *Die Goldfund von Erstfeld: Frühkeltische Goldschmuck zur den Zentralalpen=Arch. Forschungen* 1 (Zürich).

10

First-millennium settlement and society in northern France: a case study from the Aisne Valley

Jean-Paul Demoule and Michael Ilett

Introduction: the Aisne Valley Project

Until recently there has been no prehistoric research on a systematic regional basis in the Paris Basin. In the absence of adequate institutional and financial backing, it has generally been impossible for research programmes to be established, even in the river valleys where gravel extraction is most intensive. In a few exceptional cases local amateurs have managed to rescue a minimum of sites and draw up representative distribution maps, acting on their own initiative and often with meagre resources. Outstanding examples are Carré's largely unpublished excavations in the Middle Yonne valley, the Mordants' excavations in the Bassée region – the Seine valley just upstream of the Yonne confluence (Mordant 1975) – and the work of the 'Centre de Recherches Archéologiques de la Moyenne Vallée de l'Oise' near Compiègne. Yet it is precisely in the river valleys that the majority of prehistoric settlements are to be found, and a comparison of these relatively well-researched areas with others already completely destroyed without any archaeological intervention or even surveillance highlights the irreparable damage suffered by large sectors of the Paris Basin.

The rescue programme carried out over the last ten years by Paris I University and the Centre National de la Recherche Scientifique in an 80km stretch of the Middle and Lower Aisne valley is thus the only regional project of sufficient scope to permit the formulation of general hypotheses about prehistoric cultural developments in the Paris Basin.[1] Preceded by several years of aerial survey (fig. 10.1) and rescue excavation by Boureux (Boureux 1978; Boureux and Coudart 1978), the project began on a large scale in 1974. More than 30 sites have been investigated (fig. 10.2), ranging from the beginning of the Neolithic (c.4,000 b.c.) to the Migration Period. A total surface area of over 135,000m^2 has been excavated, employing for the first time in France extensive machine stripping techniques previously developed by Soudský on the Czech Neolithic site of Bylany.

Before examining first-millennium developments in the Aisne valley it is worth stressing some basic interpretational problems. A major question is clearly the representativeness of the distribution of known sites. As the most spectacular destruction (gravel extraction) concerns the valley floor, it is here that most archaeological activity takes place. At present the valley slopes and the plateau itself are threatened only by ploughing; destruction of sites is consequently slower and less obvious. In addition, the soils of these zones are less suitable for producing crop-marks. These factors could partly explain certain gaps in the distributions, such as the absence of Bronze Age settlements. Another outstanding problem is the representativeness of excavated sites in relation to the total population of known sites (fig. 10.3). Neolithic and Chalcolithic sites, the least productive of crop-marks, represent less than a third of the known sites but account for half of the excavated sites (and two-thirds in terms of surface area excavated and work input, neither of which are included in fig. 10.3). Neolithic research was particularly underdeveloped in the Paris Basin, and an important objective of the project was to catch up with neighbouring countries in this respect. The Aisne valley excavations have thus produced 80 per cent of the 'Danubian' Neolithic houseplans and 60 per cent of the Neolithic/Chalcolithic ditched enclosures currently known in the Paris Basin. In contrast, large numbers of Bronze Age sites have been discovered through aerial photography. These are all funerary ring-ditches, which are easy to identify from the air or even on the ground in an active gravel pit; over 200 are known. However, they provide very little information. In 80 per cent of the excavated examples the central burial has apparently been lost to erosion. The ditches themselves were not used as refuse dumps and are usually sterile. Excavation of ring-ditches is

Figure 10.1 Distribution of crop-mark sites in the Aisne valley. (After Boureux 1976.)

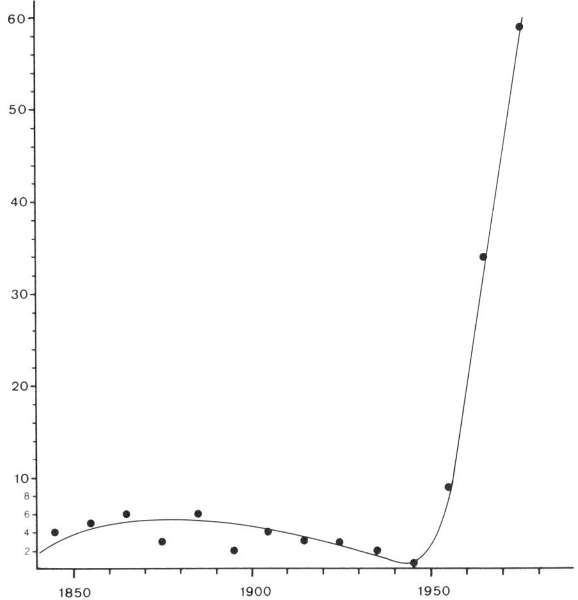

Figure 10.2 Number of excavations (by decade) in the Aisne valley, from the beginnings to the present day. The first peak corresponds to the rise of interest of local dignitaries and 'rentiers' in archaeology in the second half of the nineteenth century – an interest terminated by the twentieth-century economic crisis. The onset of the second peak reflects the development of gravel extraction. The final acceleration, a result of the current project, would be increased *tenfold* if the surface area excavated were taken into account.

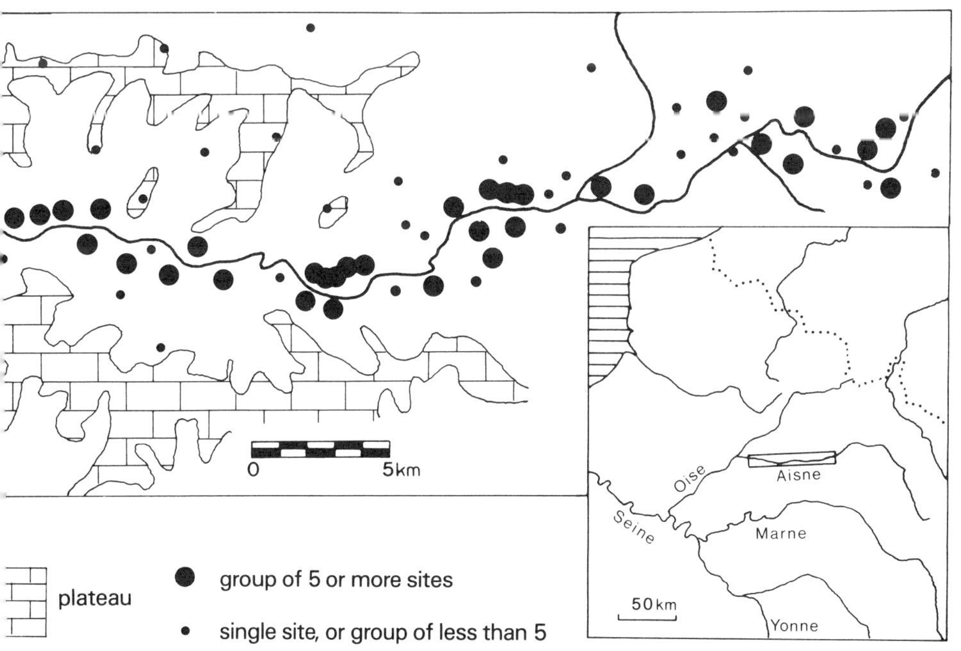

	Project's excavations %	Other excavations %	Sites discovered by Survey (excavated or not) %
Neolithic/Chalcolithic	50	35	30
Bronze Age	15	25	40
Iron Age	20	25	15
Gallo-Roman/Migration Period	15	15	15
	100	100	100

Figure 10.3 Survey and excavation in the Aisne valley listed by period. The dating of crop-mark sites is often difficult. Typologically undateable sites ('atypical' pits and ditches with no surface finds) represent about 20 per cent of the total of 200 sites, but are not included in this table. Ring-ditches are attributed to the Bronze Age since almost all those excavated (30 out of 200) proved to be of this date. Sites with rectilinear ditch systems of variable size are attributed to the Iron Age. More extensive field systems are equally divided between the Iron Age and later periods.

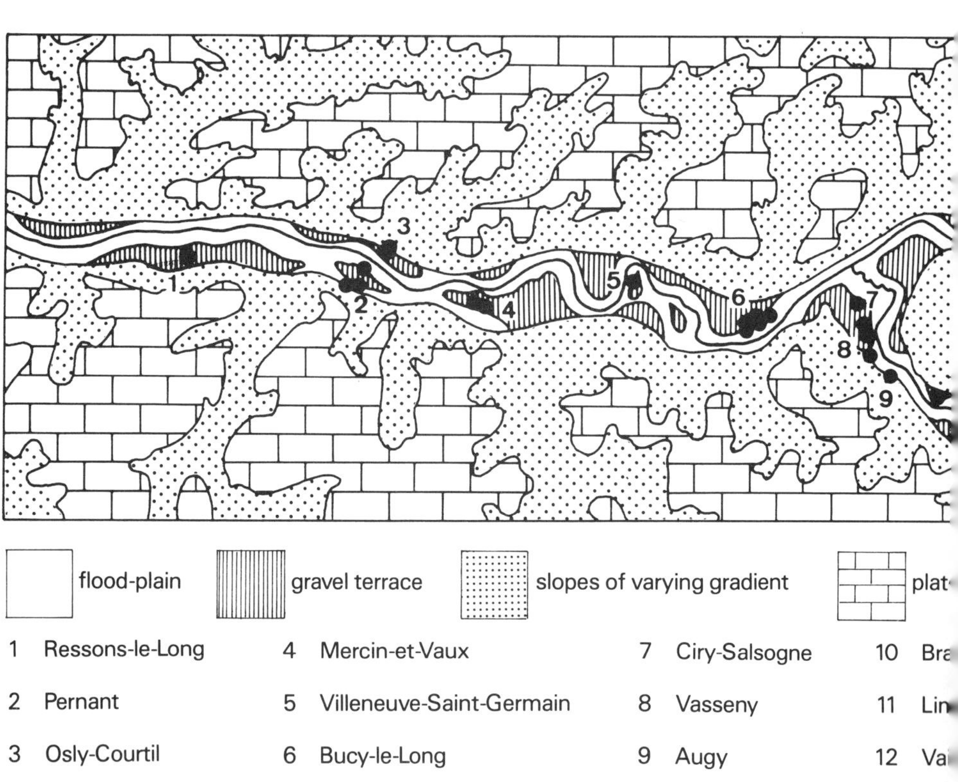

Figure 10.4 Distribution of Bronze Age ring-ditches in the Aisne valley. (After Boureux 1978.)

therefore limited to the small number that face immediate threats of destruction. Settlements of this date are virtually unknown and undetectable. Turning to the Iron Age, much previous excavation concentrated on Early La Tène cemeteries; present efforts concentrate on settlements. The Gallo-Roman period is very well researched in other regions, and the project's policy is merely to rescue sites when the need arises and to reconstruct the general pattern of settlement, rather than to concentrate on one particular site. Finally, research objectives have yet to be defined for the Merovingian period, for historical reasons one of the most notorious blanks in French archaeology; however, some settlement excavation has recently taken place in the valley.

The Bronze Age

The particular difficulties attached to this period have already been mentioned; an abundance of burial structures containing very few finds, and a near absence of settlements. The sheer quantity of tombs suggests that this absence is not a result of depopulation (fig. 10.4); neither is it a result of erosion, as post-hole structures survive from both the Neolithic and the Iron Age, and in certain cases

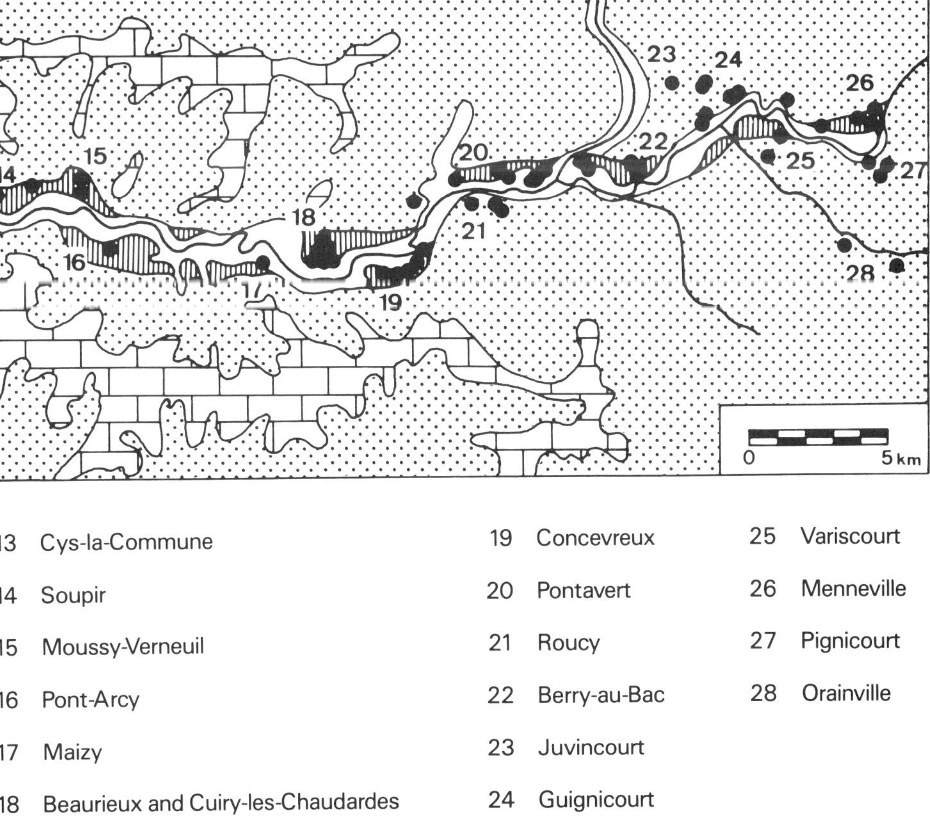

occupation layers seem to have been partially preserved by flood-silts (Bailloud 1975). Aerial survey has been intensive and excavations have taken place along most of the valley, so it is unlikely that the elusive settlements reflect insufficient fieldwork. The possibility therefore arises that the settlements either consisted of light structures without deep foundations and pits, or were located away from the valley floor on the slopes and plateaux, zones where only the more substantial features are susceptible to aerial survey. A further possibility, in the light of recent work elsewhere in north-west Europe (summarized in Bradley 1978), is that some of the many unexcavated field or boundary systems known from aerial survey of the valley floor may eventually prove to be of Bronze Age date. Not everyone can have been buried within ring-ditches as there are only two important concentrations, at Bucy-le-Long and at Beaurieux. Finally, the few rubbish pits that have been found are all close to ring-ditches. It is therefore unclear, in the absence of accompanying buildings, whether or not the pits represent permanent settlement.

The currently unsolved problem of the origin and early development of the Bronze Age in the Paris Basin (Gaucher 1981) lies outside the scope of this article. Early Bronze Age material has yet to be found in the Aisne valley, but Middle Bronze Age pottery (Letterle 1982) is related to the rare Early Bronze

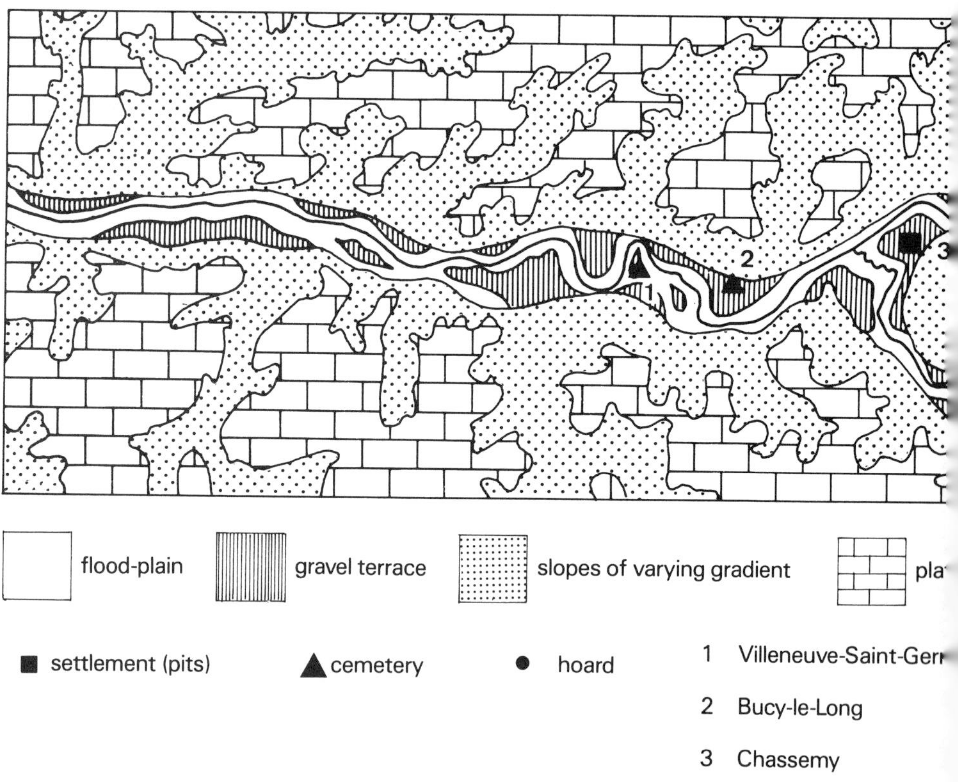

Figure 10.5 Distribution of excavated Late Bronze Age sites in the Aisne valley.

Age finds elsewhere in the Paris Basin, notably from Videlles (Bailloud 1958; Bailloud and Coiffard 1967), as well as to the Middle Bronze Age material from Videlles and Marion des Roches (Bailloud 1961; Blanchet 1976; 1979). The present evidence suggests that although the first tumuli appear in the Middle Bronze Age, the closest links are with the Atlantic façade and the British Isles rather than with Germany and central Europe.

It is only with the onset of the Late Bronze Age, with its clear 'Urnfield' affinities, that the distribution map begins to match the density of Neolithic and Celtic Iron Age sites (fig. 10.5). Nevertheless, the evidence is still very incomplete. Nothing is known about domestic structures; the few sites with rubbish pits do not indicate functional variation between settlements. The only hoard was discovered by German soldiers at Juvincourt during the First World War (Jockenhövel and Smolla 1974). Burial structures vary considerably. Clusters of cremations at Pont-Arcy and Vieil-Arcy (Chevallier 1960; Boureux 1974) produced typical Late Bronze Age cups; a group of several dozen ring-ditches or similar sub-circular features at Beaurieux contained cremations but little else (Beeching *et al.* 1976). Small clusters of ring-ditches, or isolated ring-ditches, have been noted elsewhere and in themselves are very variable. Apart from 'classic' types, some of which are double (Boureux 1975; Audouze 1981), some

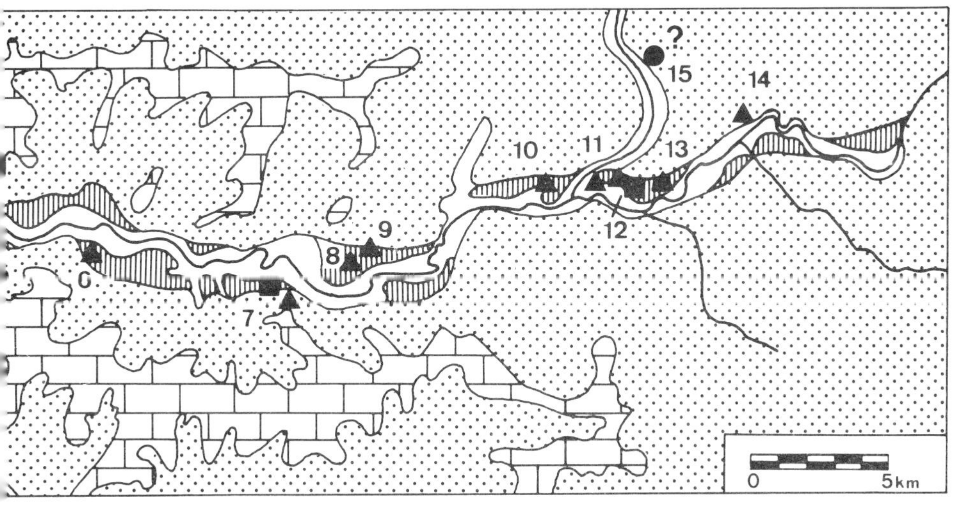

Cys-la-Commune *les Longues Raies*	10 Pontavert le Marteau
Cys-la-Commune *le Mont sans Pain*	11 Berry-au-Bac *le Vieux Tordoir*
Vieil-Arcy	12 Berry-au-Bac *le Chemin de la Pêcherie*
Maizy	13 Berry-au-Bac *la Croix Maigret*
Cuiry-lès-Chaudardes	14 Guignicourt
Beaurieux	15 Juvincourt

ring-ditches possess a single interruption, usually to the south-east. This is a feature that occurs in Late Bronze Age contexts both in neighbouring regions, as at Les Marais de Saint-Gond (e.g. Aulnay-les-Planches; Hatt and Brisson 1953), and further afield in the Netherlands. The ring-ditches vary between 5m and 20m in diameter, and are sometimes oval (Beaurieux) or irregularly shaped (Cuiry-lès-Chaudardes). Post-hole alignments occasionally replace the ditch, as at two Berry-au-Bac sites (*la Croix Maigret* and *le Chemin de la Pêcherie*). When the evidence has survived, the burial rite is also quite variable. Both cremations and inhumations occur; some cremations were placed in the ditch itself (Cys-la-Commune; Joullié 1962a). The former presence of a mound can sometimes be extrapolated from the ditch fill, but this does not always seem to have been the case (Joullié 1962b; Villes 1974). Although these monuments imply social differentiation their only contents are small quantities of pottery. The central grave at Berry-au-Bac *la Croix Maigret*, encircled by a double ring-ditch, contained a child's skeleton without grave goods (Demoule and Ilett 1978). At the present stage of research it is not possible to isolate the social, chronological, or regional factors underlying this variation in burial practices.

Finds from the various sites can be attributed to Hatt's 'Late Bronze Age II and III', and resemble material from the settlements of Les Marais de Saint-Gond, 40km to the south, on which the chronology of the Champagne Late Bronze Age is based (Hatt and Brisson 1966–67). Two radiocarbon dates are available; 1360±120 b.c. for a double ring-ditch with no finds at Cys-la-Commune *les Longues Raies* (Joullié 1962a), and 820±160 b.c. for a pit (55) at Berry-au-Bac *le Chemin de la Pêcherie* containing material dateable to Hatt's 'Late Bronze Age IIb' phase (fig. 10.6), which is normally placed in the thirteenth century B.C.

The Early Iron Age

Here again, information is scarce. Only one site, Cuiry-lès-Chaudardes (*les Fontinettes* and *le Champ Tortu*) has provided substantial evidence in the form of post-built structures, palisades with entrances, and rubbish pits (Demoule and Ilett 1982). Excavation is still in progress. The finds exhibit typological continuity with Late Bronze Age material. Limited excavations at Berry-au-Bac, Chassemy, Variscourt, Villeneuve-Saint-Germain, and Cuiry-lès-Chaudardes *la Croix Blanche* have all uncovered traces of Early Iron Age occupation. The pottery can broadly be integrated into the sequence from the Aisne-Oise confluence site at Choisy-au-Bac, outside the sector of the valley covered by the project. This settlement contains several stratified layers spanning the Late Bronze/Early Iron Age transition (Blanchet and Decormeille 1980). It therefore appears unlikely that the present scarcity of information results from cultural discontinuity. It is also possible that some ring-ditches may date from this period, as may a group of 30 small cremation pits at Villeneuve-Saint-Germain (F.P.V.A. 1977: 77 and fig. 44; Cadoux 1979) which produced two small gold-plated bronze rings with parallels in France and Britain (Toupet 1979).

In terms of artefact typology, the real break falls between the 'Urnfield

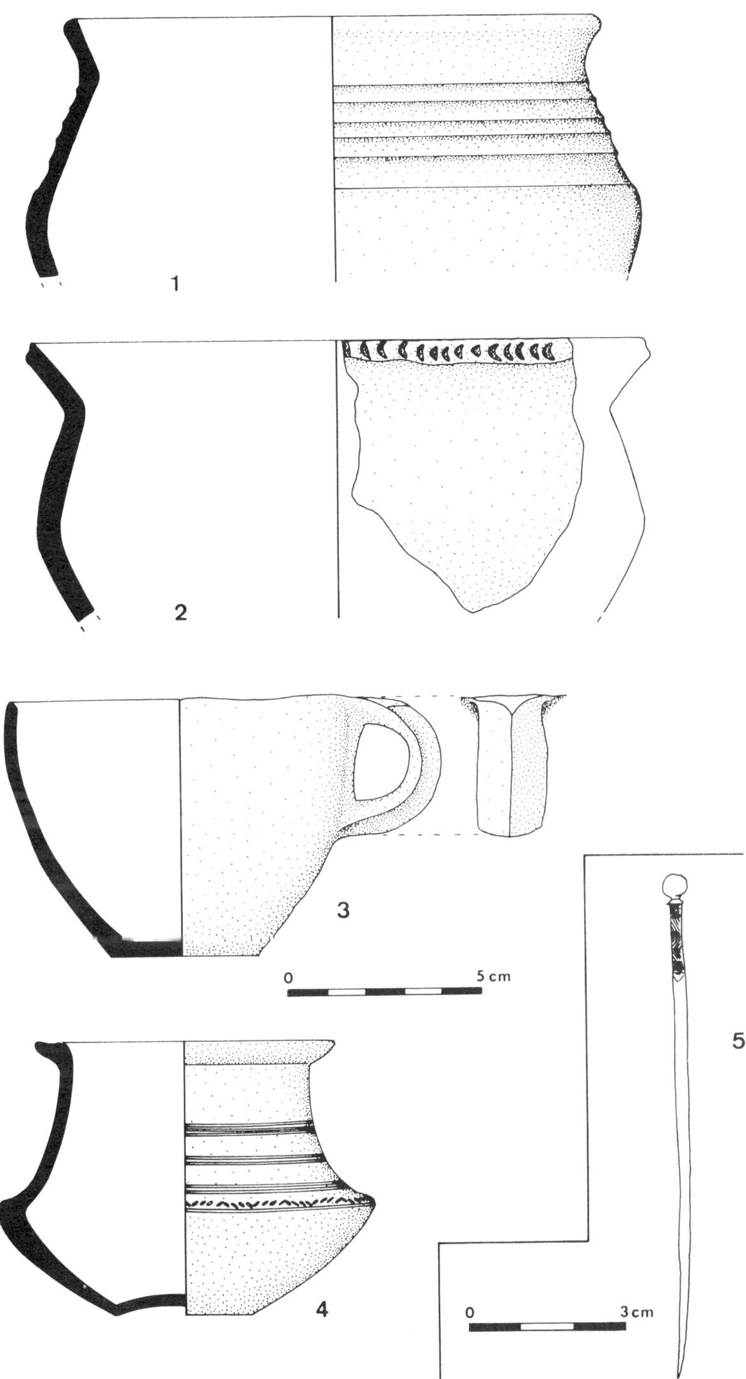

Figure 10.6 Late Bronze Age material from Berry-au-Bac *le Chemin de la Pêcherie*. 1–3, pit 65; 4–5, pit 55. (After F.P.V.A. 1978; 1981.)

tradition' Hallstatt and the Hallstatt immediately preceding Early La Tène. The reason for this is unclear.

Early La Tène and the origins of Celtic civilization

Settlement pattern and previous research

The Aisne valley lies at the north-western edge of Champagne, a region with an exceptional density of Early La Tène (La Tène I or A–B), 'Marnian' or 'Marnian Culture' sites. Unfortunately the majority are cemeteries that were pillaged in the second half of the nineteenth century; records are only available for a few hundred out of an estimated total of 50,000 robbed burials belonging to at least 400 cemeteries. Often this information has been exploited in a purely typological manner (Bretz-Mahler 1971). Research into the long-neglected settlements is only just beginning, and is largely unpublished (Villes 1980). Distribution maps of cemeteries and settlements, however impressive (Bretz-Mahler 1971), have never taken account of *all* the excavated evidence and reflect the work of the

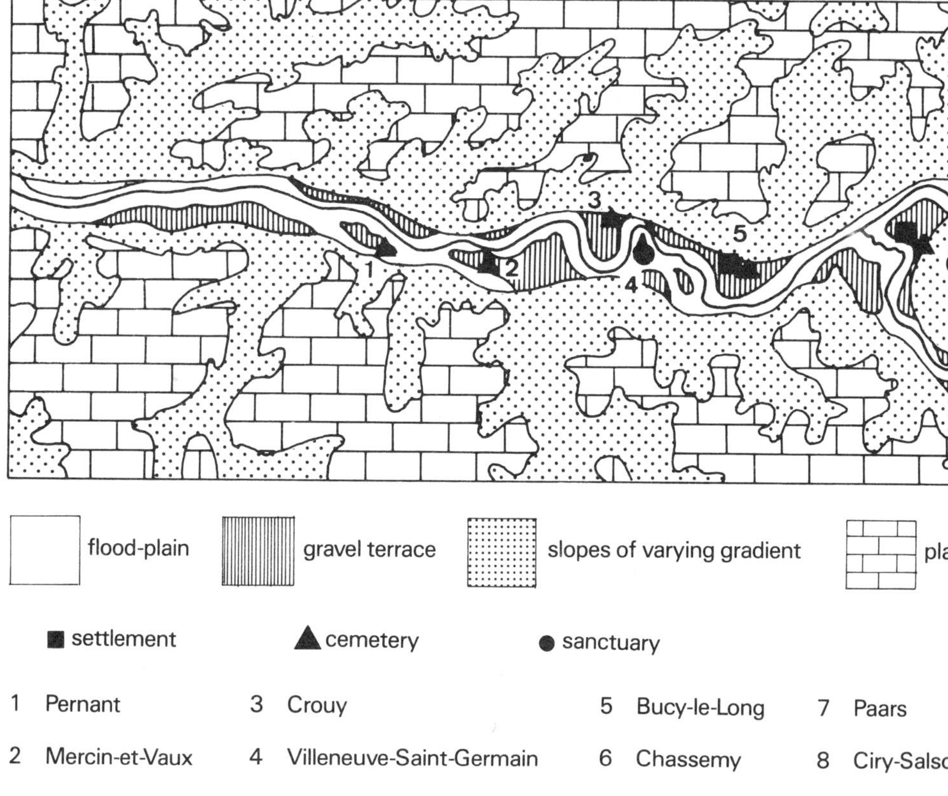

Figure 10.7 Distribution of La Tène I sites in the Aisne valley.

more active excavators rather than systematic micro-regional survey. The Aisne valley therefore offers a unique and valuable opportunity for the analysis of 'Marnian Culture' settlement patterns.

Sixteen cemeteries, four settlements, and one 'sanctuary' are currently known from the sector of the Aisne valley under investigation (fig. 10.7). In two cases cemetery and settlement seem associated; the cemeteries belonging to the other two settlements have yet to be located. The valley floor can be divided into a linear series of more or less discrete segments of gravel terrace ('micro-areas'), defined by the meandering course of the river and its flood-plain, the valley sides, and the secondary drainage network (Boureux and Coudart 1978:343–4). The distributional evidence, and typological dating of finds, suggest that about 20 'micro-areas' were in use at the same time. Site density in fact matches the Neolithic Bandkeramik and Michelsberg periods, and the misleading impression of abrupt 're-settlement' or invasion in the Early La Tène is largely created by the elusive nature of Bronze Age and Early Iron Age settlements.

To what extent is this distributional evidence complete? The rate of discovery of Early La Tène sites (fig. 10.8) resembles that of other sites (fig. 10.2); both are governed by similar factors. At the same time, there are blanks on the distribu-

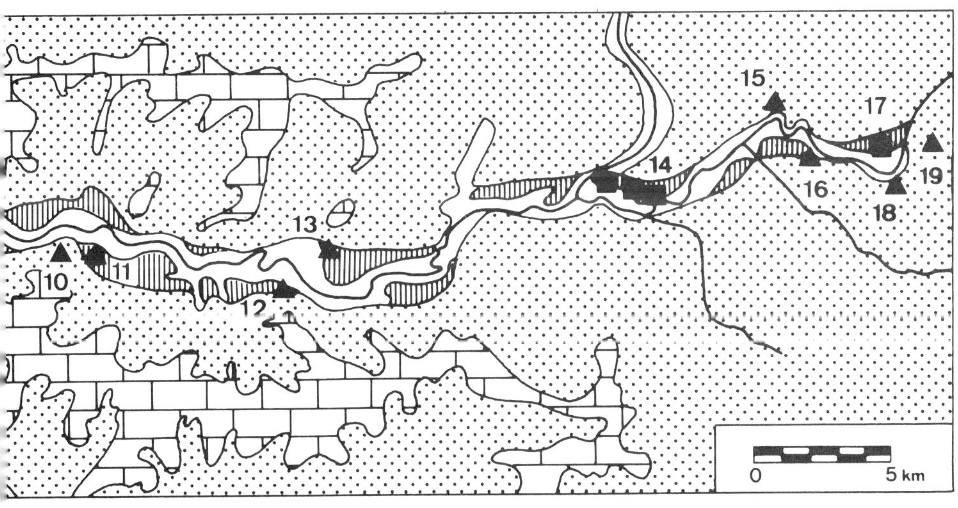

9 Cys-la-Commune

10 Villers-en-Prayères

11 Pont-Arcy

12 Maizy

13 Beaurieux

14 Berry-au-Bac *(le Vieux Tordoir, le Chemin de la Pêcherie, la Croix Maigret)*

15 Guignicourt

16 Variscourt

17 Menneville *(Derrière le Village* and *la Fourche)*

18 Pignicourt

19 Aguilcourt

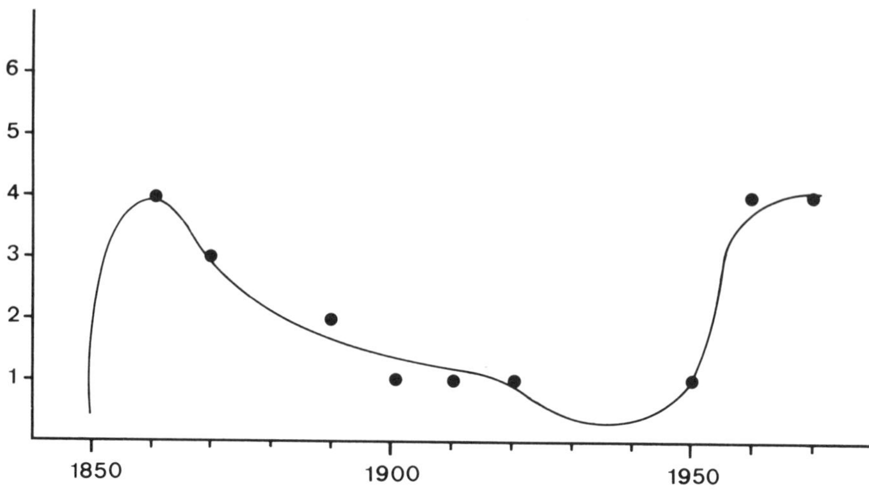

Figure 10.8 Rate of discovery of La Tène I cemeteries in the Aisne valley (cf. fig. 10.2).

tion map which cannot be put down to a lack of research. It is also worth noting the scarcity of reliable cemetery data in the Aisne valley. Of the hundreds of burials excavated by the collector Moreau in the nineteenth century, a few dozen alone have survived. Only two cemeteries have been excavated recently; Pernant (Lobjois 1969), part of which was destroyed before archaeological intervention, and Bucy-le-Long (Lobjois 1974a,b), which is incompletely published.

Settlements

Excavation has been limited and has often taken place under rescue conditions. There are thus no complete village plans although several sites are still intact; pits constitute the majority of features. A partial house-plan (fig. 10.9D) is available from Chassemy (Rowlett *et al.* 1969). The settlements nevertheless cover several hectares, and at Berry-au-Bac Early La Tène features have been discovered, for the most part fortuitously, along a 4km stretch of the valley floor. As in other periods, sites occupy terrace locations out of reach of flooding but as near as possible to the river. Storage pits are the most recognizable type of settlement feature. These are circular in plan, and have bell-shaped sections with occasional layers of carbonized cereal grains. Similar pits were cut into the Champagne chalk, and experiment has shown that even in gravel subsoil the walls of the pits remain relatively stable. The function of these pits has been confirmed by discoveries of storage vessels buried at the bottom (fig. 10.9A). Some of the pits contain layers of burnt clay and earth, as at Menneville (fig. 10.9B; Coudart *et al.* 1981). A further category of pit of more irregular shape, and containing less settlement debris, occurs on patches of Pleistocene flood-silt capping the gravel terrace; these are best interpreted as quarry pits to extract raw material for daub and pottery. There is some poorly preserved evidence of

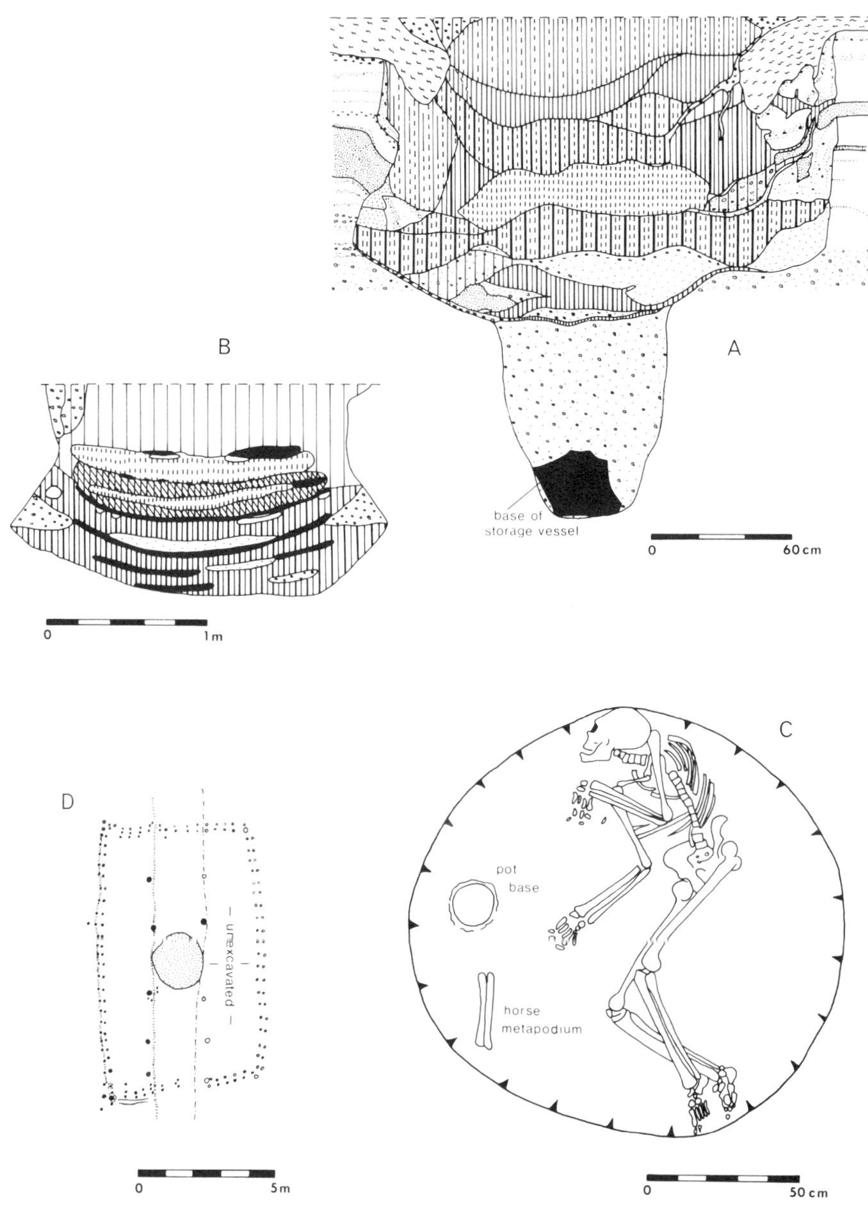

Figure 10.9 La Tène I settlement features: (A) pit with storage vessel partly preserved in cavity at base (Berry-au-Bac *le Vieux Tordoir*); (B) pit with burnt layers in black (Menneville); (C) burial at bottom of pit (Menneville); (D) partial house-plan (Chassemy). (After F.P.V.A. 1981; Coudart *et al.* 1981; Rowlett *et al.* 1969.)

iron-smelting from Menneville and Chassemy. Burials can occur within settlements; a storage pit at Menneville contained a skeleton without the usual grave goods (fig. 10.9c).

The considerable density of pits on these sites argues for a similar density of occupation. In the absence of complete plans, however, it is difficult to interpret settlement structure in social terms, and analyses of ceramics, animal bones, and flotation samples are still in progress. A possible 'sanctuary', in the form of a 130m² ditch enclosure, has been discovered at Villeneuve-Saint-Germain. This has yet to be extensively excavated (Debord 1981).

Cemeteries: chronology and society

In contrast, the cemeteries permit a more detailed investigation of social organization and chronology. Almost all the burials are inhumations, the body lying extended on its back, accompanied by functionally positioned objects and weapons. The sole cremation in the Aisne valley is at Pernant.

What are the origins of this 'Marnian Culture'? For a long time it was considered intrusive, but there are no close typological links with earlier material from either eastern France or Germany. Recent chronological studies, employing combinatorial (Babeş 1974; Demoule, in press) and typological (Hatt and Rouallet 1976–77) methods, of two Late Hallstatt (Hallstatt D 2–3 or IIb or Jogassian) cemeteries in Champagne (*Les Jogasses* at Chouilly, *Charvais* at Heiltz l'Evêque) have clearly demonstrated continuity with the initial phases of Early La Tène, defined by identical methods at other cemeteries (Hatt and

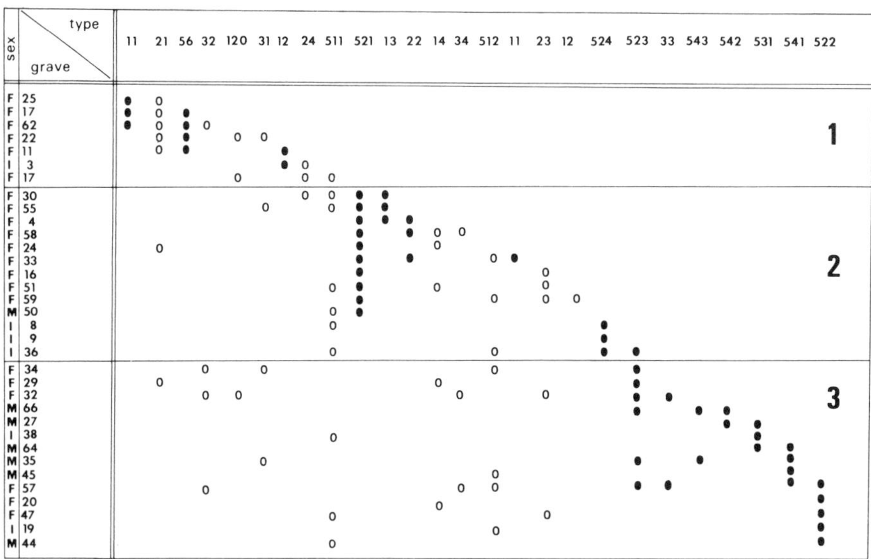

Figure 10.10 Ordered matrix of graves and grave goods from the La Tène I cemetery at Pernant. (After Demoule 1979.)

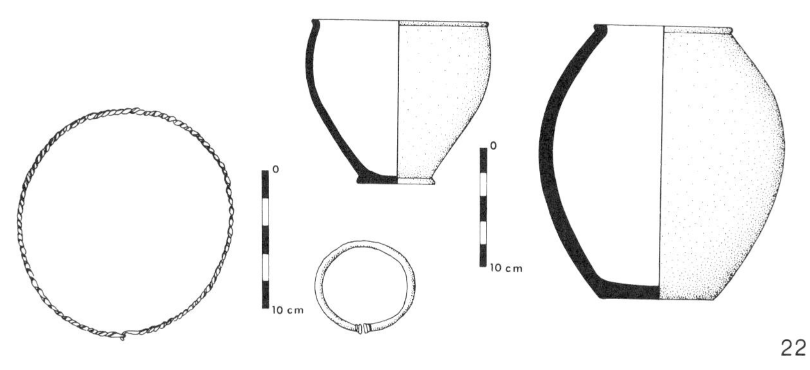

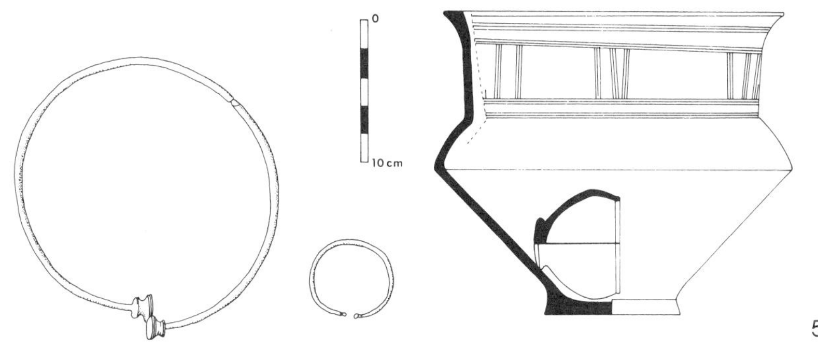

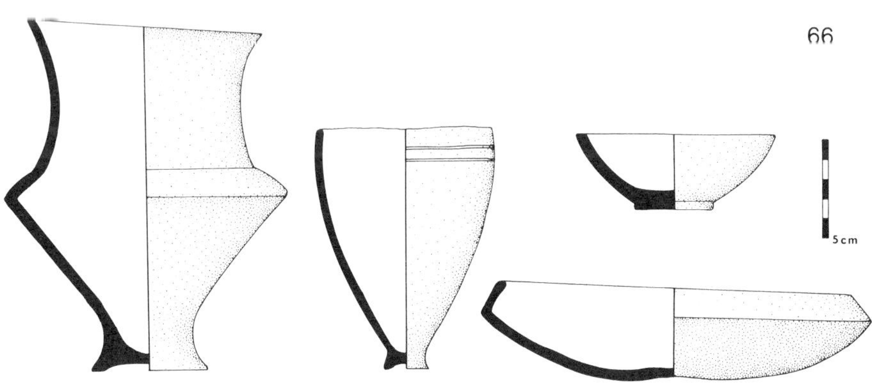

Figure 10.11 Examples of diagnostic graves, Pernant. 22 (Pernant 1); 51 (Pernant 2); 66 (Pernant 3). (After Lobjois 1969.)

Rouallet 1976–77; Demoule 1979). In fact most of the characteristic Early La Tène artefacts – hollow decorated torcs, square-sectioned solid torcs, incised open bronze bracelets, disc-element and straight-footed fibulae, boat-shaped earrings, pottery with low carinations, situla-shaped vessels – already occur in Late Hallstatt contexts. The burial rite – orientation and position of the body, types of grave good, shape of the grave – is also identical. The few new artefact types, such as twisted torcs and bracelets, do not point to a foreign origin. This uninterrupted sequence is paralleled, in the only neighbouring region where a similar study has been carried out, by the Hunsrück–Eifel Culture (Haffner 1976).

While continuity applies to the whole Marnian zone, the Aisne valley, on its north-western edge, has yet to produce material which can be closely related to the Jogassian. The precise borders of the true Marnian zone remain undefined, and there have been no comparable regional studies elsewhere in the Paris Basin.

It seemed paradoxical in Champagne, where pottery is abundant but fibulae rare (and this is especially so of the Aisne valley), to use the La Tène I a–b–c subdivisions defined in Switzerland, in the absence of pottery, with fibulae. A combinatorial analysis (Demoule, in press), essentially based on ceramic, bracelet, and torc typology, has led to the definition of an 'Aisne–Marne Culture' with three main periods. The first of these corresponds to the Jogassian. The second, broadly parallel to La Tène A or Ia, is characterized by carinated vessels and twisted metal ornaments. The cemetery at Pernant (Aisne) is the most representative of this period, and can be subdivided into three phases (figs. 10.10 and 10.11), the attributes of which are shared by the other Aisne valley cemeteries.

Pernant 1: thin or broad twisted torcs with hook fasteners; square-sectioned bracelets; vessels with low carinations or rounded profiles.
Pernant 2: the appearance of buffer terminals on the ornaments, and of 'classic' carinated vessels (carination at mid-height).
Pernant 3: vessels with very accentuated high carinations.

The third period, broadly equivalent to La Tène B or b–c, sees the replacement of carination by more rounded shapes, the introduction of 'lost-wax' ornaments, and an increase in chariot burials. While this period is attested in the Aisne valley at Bucy-le-Long, it is only at Beine (*l'Argentelle*), 20km to the south near Reims, that a three-phase subdivision is possible. In Champagne the start of Middle La Tène sees the abandonment of most of the larger cemeteries in favour of new cemeteries associated with quadrangular enclosures.

The principal interest of this chronological sequence is that it enables us to trace the development of the society to which the cemetery belonged. The plan of the Pernant cemetery shows that the burials are grouped in small clusters, within which orientations are identical, separated by empty spaces (fig. 10.12); and that the three successive phases of the cemetery occur in each of the clusters (fig. 10.13). It seems very likely that the clusters of graves represent social groups, and more specifically, since all ages and both sexes occur in each cluster, family

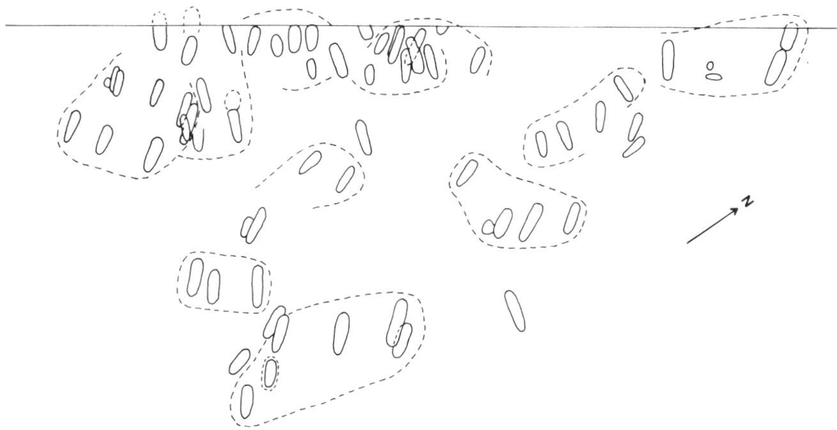

Figure 10.12 Pernant: orientation groups in the cemetery. (After Demoule 1979.)

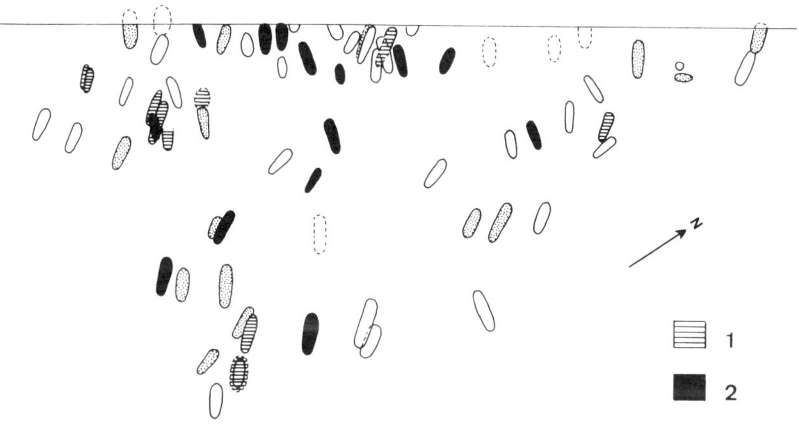

Figure 10.13 Pernant: cemetery phases. (After Demoule 1979.)

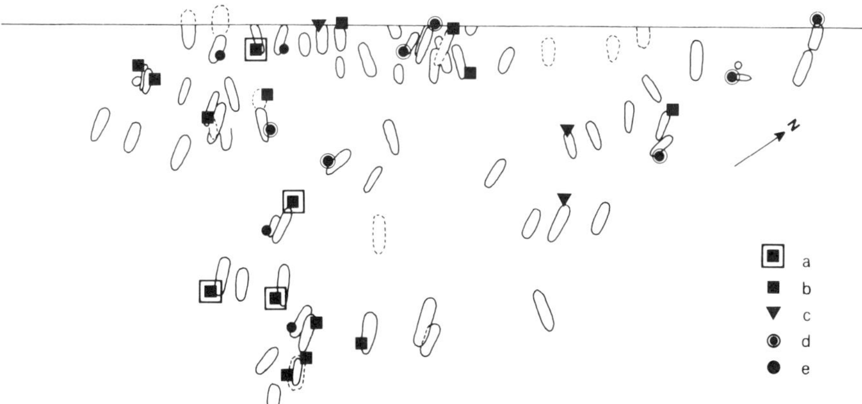

Figure 10.14 Distribution of 'wealth' in female graves at Pernant: (a) torc+2 bracelets+beads; (b) torc+1 bracelet+beads *or* torc+2 bracelets without beads; (c) torc; (d) bracelet with or without beads; (e) beads. (After Demoule 1979.)

groups. The cemetery at Beine has been interpreted in the same way (Morgen and Rouallet 1975–76). The clusters can be seen as a continuation of Late Hallstatt cemetery organization; in the early phases at *Les Jogasses* the graves are grouped by sex, but in the second the sexes are mixed (Babeş 1974). The grave goods at Pernant are not evenly distributed amongst the family groups. This is particularly true of ornaments of varying wealth in the female graves (fig. 10.14); however, all female graves seem to have contained ornaments of some kind. The same hierarchy can be seen in male burials; some have no grave goods, others contain only pottery, others pottery and spear-heads, while a small number contain pottery, spear-head, and sword. Chariot burials are even rarer and are always accompanied by large numbers of grave goods. In the Aisne valley they have been found at Ciry-Salsogne, Chassemy and Pernant. Most of the chariot burials appear to belong to the more recent phases, indicating that social ranking increased during Early La Tène. The existence of this social hierarchy is likely to be confirmed by settlement data.

Some tentative comments can finally be made about demography. The usual estimate of the duration of Early La Tène, based on Mediterranean chronology, is 250 years. It can reasonably be argued that each of the six phases outlined above roughly corresponds to a generation. A phase is generally represented by 20–30 burials in each cemetery. This suggests a figure of about 100 inhabitants per village and, assuming one village per 'micro-area', a total population of around 2,000 for the 20 'micro-areas' in the valley. It is striking that these

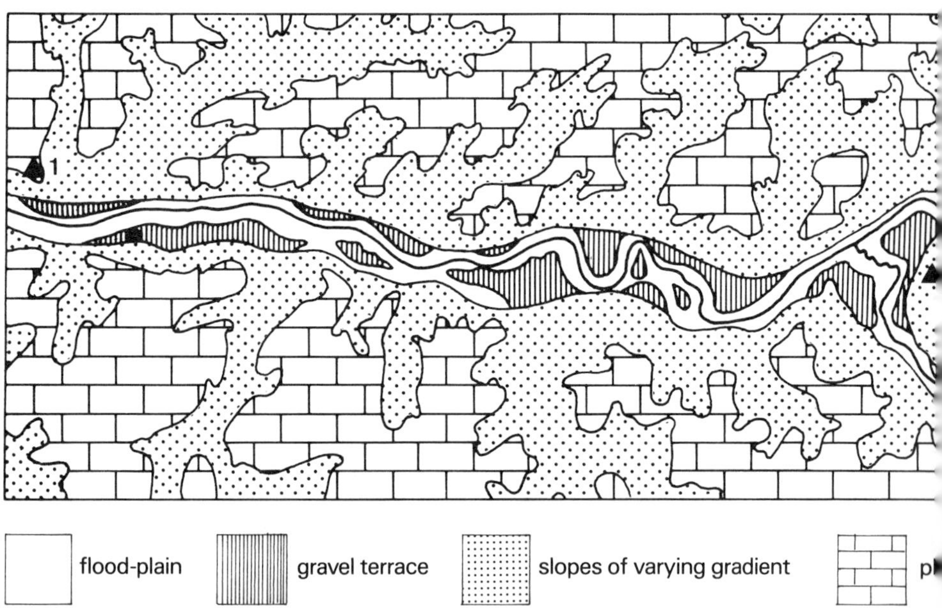

Figure 10.15 Distribution of La Tène II sites in the Aisne valley. The unnumbered circles represent crop-mark sites with small quadrangular enclosures (possible La Tène II cemeteries).

figures differ very little from population estimates for the Neolithic Bandkeramik (Soudský and Pavlu 1972), the first sedentary occupation of the valley over 3,000 years earlier.

Middle La Tène: a gap in the evidence

The map of Middle La Tène sites offers an obvious contrast (fig. 10.15). There are no settlements, and only seven 'cemeteries'. The latter term refers to isolated and poorly recorded discoveries; several of these are cremations. A number of small quadrangular enclosures known from aerial survey can probably be added to this information, as they resemble Middle La Tène cemeteries from Champagne. This dating has yet to be tested by excavation. In face of the inadequate evidence currently available, any discussion of possible depopulation in Champagne, as a result of Celtic migrations towards the Mediterranean, would clearly be unrealistic.

Late La Tène and the beginnings of urbanization

Although the quantity of sites is relatively small, the Late La Tène distribution map (fig. 10.16) indicates, for the first time, functional variation between settlements. A distinction can be made betwen valley floor sites and those on the edge of the plateau, which is on average about 100m above the valley floor. The

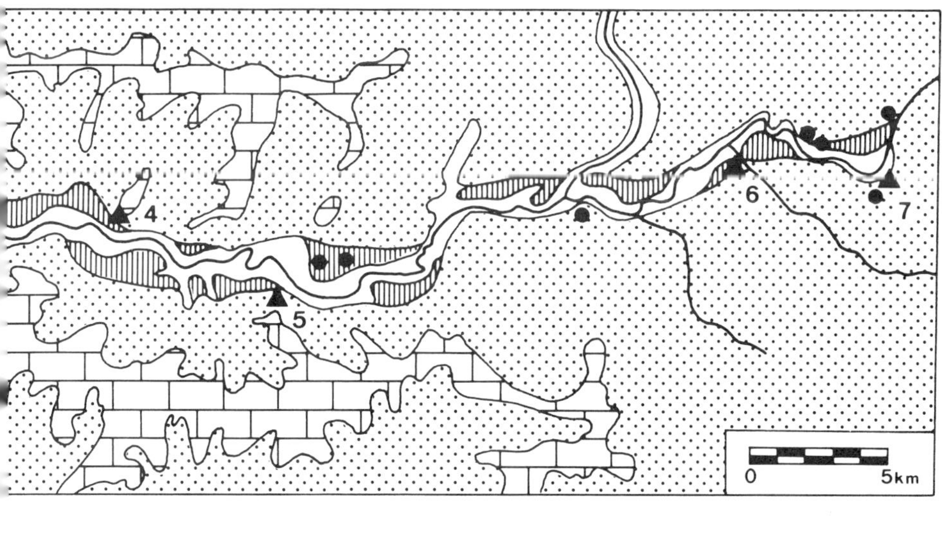

tichy	3 Soupir	5 Maizy	7 Pignicourt
assemy	4 Bourg-et-Comin	6 Condé-sur-Suippe	▲ cemetery

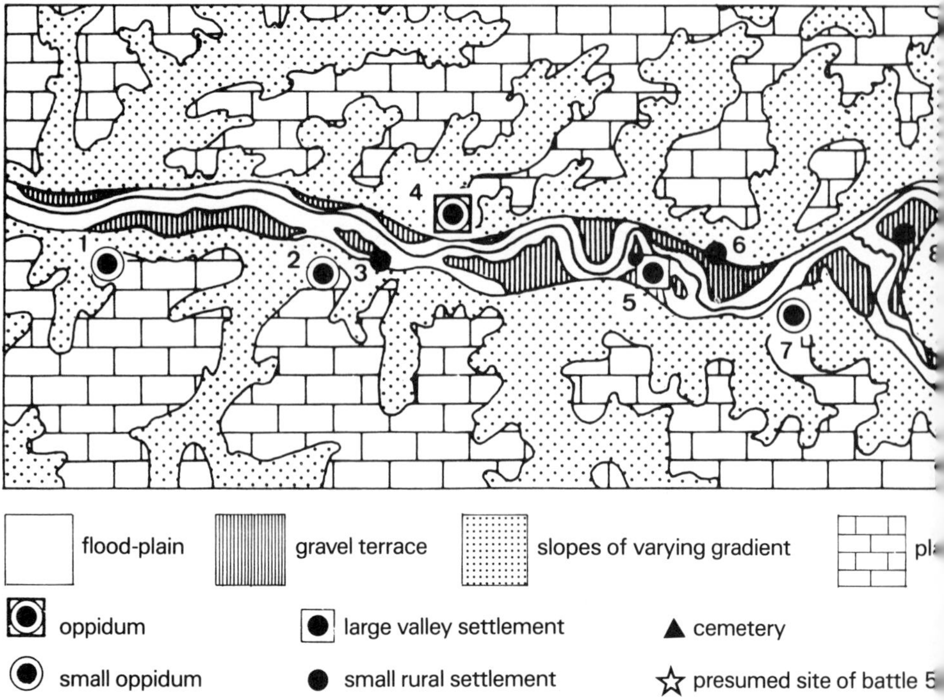

Figure 10.16 Distribution of La Tène III sites in the Aisne valley.

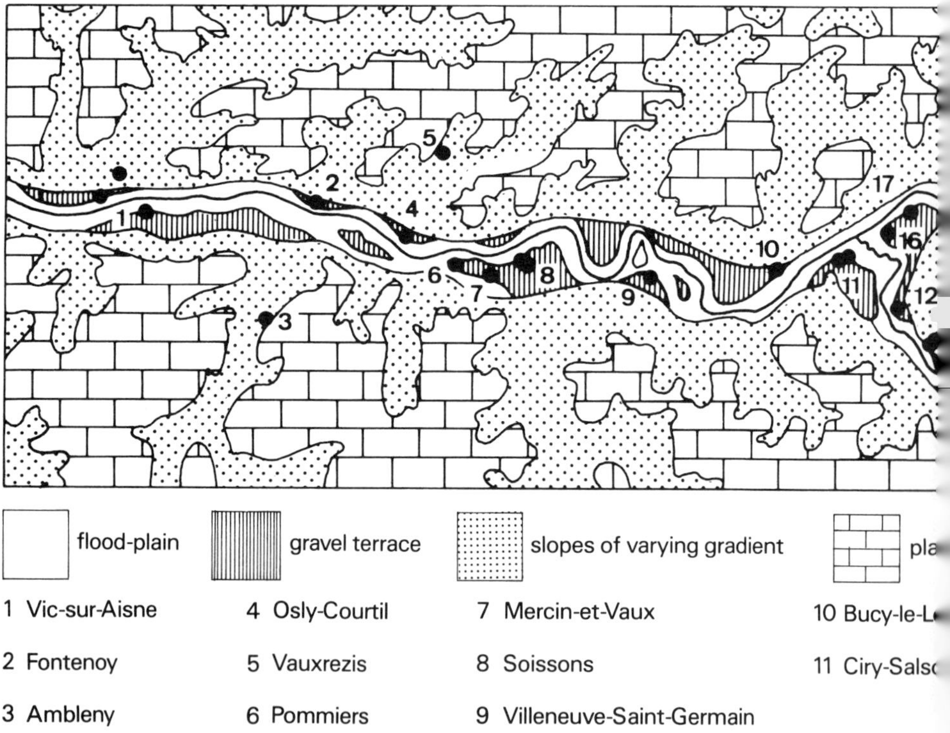

Figure 10.17 Distribution of 'fermes indigènes' in the Aisne valley. (After Boureux 1978.)

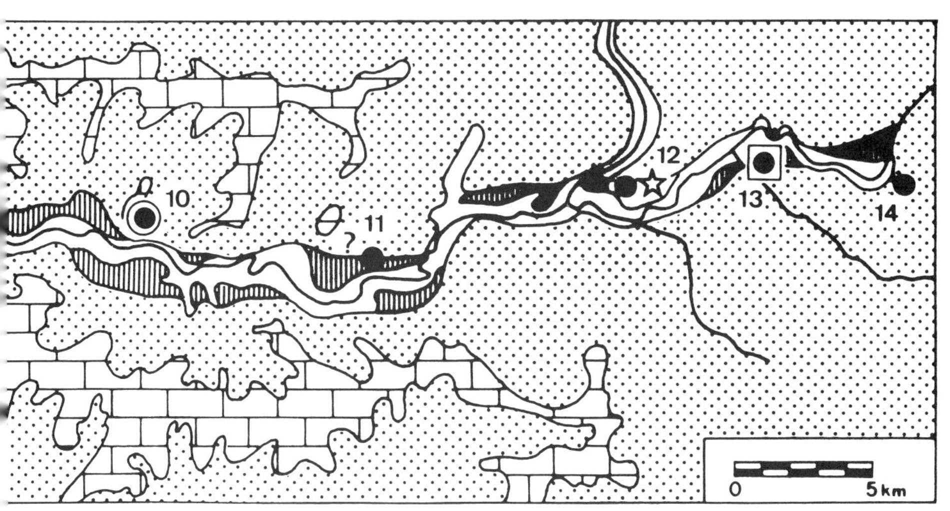

ontigny-Lengrain	6	Bucy-le-Long	11	Cuiry-lès-Chaudardes *la Croix Blanche*
mbleny	7	Sermoise	12	Berry-au-Bac *le Chemin de la Pêcherie*
rnant	8	Chassemy	13	Condé-sur-Suippe
mmiers	9	Presles-et-Boves	14	Pignicourt
lleneuve-Saint-Germain	10	Bourg-et-Comin		

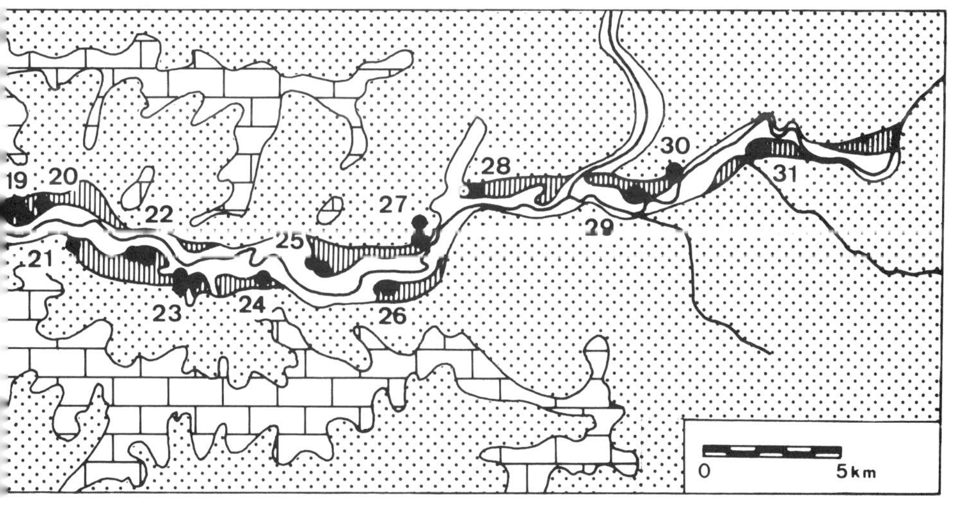

assemy	17	Vailly	22	Villers-en-Prayères	27	Chaudardes
ine	18	Cys-la-Commune	23	Pont-Arcy	28	Pontavert
urcelles-sur-Vesle	19	Soupir	24	Maizy	29	Berry-au-Bac
né	20	Moussy-Verneuil	25	Beaurieux	30	Juvincourt
ndé-sur-Aisne	21	Vieil-Arcy	26	Concevreux	31	Condé-sur-Suippe

plateau sites differ in size but are invariably defended. Within the category of valley sites a further distinction can be made between small rural settlements and proto-urban defended centres covering several dozen hectares in either confluence (Condé-sur-Suippe) or meander locations. This evidence points to an increasingly complex network of settlement, the hierarchical nature of which must be symptomatic of urbanization. Some of the 30 or so crop-mark sites with pits and ditch systems, loosely termed 'fermes indigènes' (fig. 10.17), can probably be attributed to Late La Tène, although only two so far have been positively dated (Pommiers and Bucy-le-Long). Others could be of rather later date.

Re-occupation of the plateau is an important aspect of this period. At present the only other evidence for major settlement of the plateau edges dates back to the late fourth and early third millennia b.c. (Michelsberg-Chasséen horizon). Sites range from the impressive *Villé* oppidum at Pommiers, reputed to be the Noviodunum of Caesar's campaign against the Belgae in 57 B.C. and first investigated at the end of the nineteenth century, to much smaller defended spurs. It must be stressed that none of the northern French oppida has been extensively excavated.

An equally important aspect has come to light with recent excavations of the largest valley settlements. The sites at Villeneuve-Saint-Germain (figs. 10.18 and 10.19) and Condé-sur-Suippe (fig. 10.20), with their strict orthogonal lay-out and functional division into living, workshop, and agricultural zones (Ilett *et al.* 1981), reflect a genuine urban organization. At Villeneuve-Saint-Germain each house is surrounded by a fenced enclosure; within these enclosures there is evidence for granaries, pits of varying function, wells and square cellars with wooden walls and plaster floors. This site alone has provided a great deal more architectural information for the period than was previously available for the whole of northern France. The houses vary both in construction and orientation. Two have already been reconstructed at a newly established experimental archaeology centre near Chassemy, a few kilometres along the Aisne to the east (fig. 10.21). Substantial traces of metal workshops have also been found; the metal tool-kit is largely renewed in this period. Analysis of part of an extremely large faunal assemblage has revealed very low percentages of wild animals; two-thirds of the domestic animal bones are pig. The faunal data thus imply a developed, waste-producing economy, and support textual information about the importance of the export of Gallic salted pork to Rome.

However, the precise dating of these settlements remains problematical. To judge from the homogeneity of ceramic assemblages and the rarity of intercutting features, Villeneuve-Saint-Germain was not occupied for very long. The site was probably abandoned with the founding by the Romans of the town of Soissons, Augusta Suessionum, just downstream. The chronology of the fibulae, Celtic coins, and Roman amphorae of Dressel I type, the only Roman imports on the site, is uncertain (Buchsenschutz 1981). There is disagreement about the dating both of the introduction of bronze coins in relation to the Roman conquest and of the disappearance of Dressel IA and IB amphorae. Precise dating will obviously be of vital importance to the final interpretation of these

Figure 10.18 Part of the Late La Tène settlement at Villeneuve-Saint-Germain (main sector excavated by the U.R.A. 12 between 1975 and 1981).

Figure 10.19 Aerial view of excavation at Villeneuve-Saint-Germain in 1977. The large central feature is a completely excavated cellar (see fig. 10.18). (Photo: Michel Boureux.)

Figure 10.20 Crop-marks revealing part of the Late La Tène settlement at Condé-sur-Suippe. (Photo: Michel Boureux.)

Figure 10.21 Reconstruction of Late La Tène building (based on house-plan from Villeneuve-Saint-Germain) at the experimental archaeology centre, Chassemy. (Photos: U.R.A. 12.)

sites, especially as the low-lying Villeneuve-Saint-Germain settlement is only 6km from the oppidum at Pommiers.

Only one cemetery, *Saint-Audebert*, Presles-et-Boves, has been discovered. This was excavated in the nineteenth century and records are insufficient for chronological or social analysis. Several cemeteries from the Hauviné area, further east in the Ardennes Département, have recently been published and a basic chronology established (Rouallet 1977–79). On this evidence, the currently available material from the Aisne valley belongs to the final phases of Late La Tène.

It was on the river Aisne, probably near Berry-au-Bac (fig. 10.16), that Caesar crushed the Belgic coalition in 57 B.C. but it is striking that there is so far no archaeological trace of the Gallic war in the valley. The Roman camp at Mauchamps, near Guignicourt, is traditionally dated to this campaign. Napoleon III's excavations produced only second-century A.D. finds, a date in agreement with the 'clavicula' gates. The exact nature of the Roman colonization is thus obscure, and its understanding is hindered by the absence of a chronology for Gallo-Roman domestic pottery. The villas themselves, easily detectable from the air, are difficult to date as none has been extensively excavated; the same applies to the 'fermes indigènes' mentioned above. As is the case with the earlier first millennium B.C., and indeed with the end of the Roman period, there is no marked cultural discontinuity.

Conclusion

The various gaps in the Aisne valley research programme cannot be overlooked. In the first millennium B.C. the Early Iron Age and Middle La Tène are the most poorly documented periods. Nevertheless, one of the most significant results of the project has been to emphasize cultural and structural continuity in the course of this millennium. The main breaks in the sequence do not appear, as has traditionally been supposed, at the Bronze Age–Hallstatt and Hallstatt-La Tène transitions, but rather at the onset of the Jogassian and Late La Tène. The latter break is more apparent in socio-economic factors such as the appearance of settlement hierarchy, the reoccupation of plateau locations, and the internal organization of proto-urban settlements, than in pottery and fibula typology. At a general level, structural continuity as far back as the Neolithic is reflected by the same type of settlement location (the valley floor 'micro-areas'), by similar building techniques (rectangular wooden wattle-and-daub houses), and even by comparable population levels for much of the millennium.

Such intensive regional studies are a vital preliminary step towards the explanation of cultural changes affecting large areas of Europe in the first millennium B.C.

Note

1. The Aisne Valley Project is run by the Centre de Recherches Protohistoriques, Paris I University (directed by B. Soudský, the project's founder, from 1973–76, then by M.

Lichardus) and by the Unité de Recherche Archéologique No. 12 of the Centre National de la Recherche Scientifique (directed by B. Soudský from 1973–76, then by G. Bailloud). The excavations and finds analysis are carried out principally by G. Bailloud, A. Beeching, M. Boureux, P. Brun, S. Cleuziou, C. Constantin, A. Coudart, J-P. Demoule, J. Dubouloz, J-P. Farruggia, G. Firmin, B. Fleury-Ilett, M. Ilett, M. Lasserre, M. Le Bolloch and M. Plateaux. Financial support is provided by Paris I and VII Universities, the C.N.R.S., the Aisne Département (Comité du Tourisme), the Sous-Direction d'Archéologie (Ministère de la Culture), and the Délégation Générale à la Recherche Scientifique et Technique (Ministère de la Recherche). Some excavations have been carried out by the Sous-Direction d'Antiquités. Annual reports, *Les Fouilles Protohistoriques dans la Vallée de l'Aisne,* have been published by Paris I University since 1972. A special volume of *Revue Archéologique de Picardie*, devoted to the Aisne valley, was published in 1982, and a preliminary survey of ten years of research entitled *Archéologie de la Vallée de l'Aisne I*, is in preparation.

Bibliography

Audouze, F., 1981. 'Le Double enclos circulaire du Grand-Marais à Bucy-le-Long (Aisne)', *Cahiers Arch. de Picardie 8:* 19–37.

Babeş, M., 1974. *Die relative Chronologie des späthallstattzeitliches Gräberfeld von Les Jogasses, Gem. Chouilly (Marne)*, Saarbrücker Beiträge zur Altertumskunde 13 (Saarbrück).

Bailloud, G., 1958. *L'Habitat néolithique et protohistorique des Roches à Videlles. Mémoires de la Soc. Préhistorique Française 5.*

Bailloud, G., 1961. 'Un habitat du Bronze Moyen en forêt de Fontainebleau: Marion des Roches', *Bull. de la Soc. Préhistorique Française 58:* 99–102.

Bailloud, G., 1975. 'Rapport sur les fouilles executées en 1975 à Cys-la-Commune (Aisne), lieu-dit Le Mont Sans Pain', *F.P.V.A. 3:* 32–7.

Bailloud, G. and Coiffard, P., 1967. 'Le Locus 5 des Roches à Videlles (Essonne). I. Etude archéologique', *Bull. de la Soc. Préhistorique Française 64:* 371–410.

Beeching, A., Constantin, C., Coudart, A., Demoule J-P., Fleury, B. and Ilett, M., 1976. 'La Nécropole de l'Age du Bronze à Beaurieux, La Justice', *F.P.V.A. 4:* 59–67.

Blanchet, J-C., 1976. 'Les tumulus des combles d'Eramecourt (Somme) dans leur contexte du bronze ancien et moyen en France du Nord-Ouest', *Cahiers Arch. de Picardie 3:* 39–56.

Blanchet, J-C. (in press). *Les Premiers métallurgistes du Nord de la France. Chalcolithique, Age du Bronze, Premier Age du Fer* (Mémoires de la Societé Prehistorique Française).

Blanchet, J-C. and Decormeille, A., 1980. 'Les Débuts du Premier Age du Fer à Choisy-au-Bac (Oise, France)', *Bull. Soc. Royale Belge d'Anthropologie et de Préhistoire 91:* 21–38.

Boureux, M., 1974. 'Le Site de l'Age du Bronze Final à Vieil-Arcy', *Cahiers Arch. de Picardie 1:* 51–66.

Boureux, M., 1975. 'Fouilles à Berry-au-Bac', *Rev. Arch. de l'Oise 8:* 3–7.

Boureux, M., 1976. 'Prospections aériennes de 1976', *F.P.V.A. 4:* 119–57.

Boureux, M., 1978. *Le Passé de l'Aisne vu du ciel* (Comité Départemental du Tourisme de l'Aisne, Laon).

Boureux, M. and Coudart, A., 1978. 'Implantations des premiers paysans sédentaires dans la vallée de l'Aisne', *Bull. de la Soc. Préhistorique Française 75:* 341–60.

Bradley, R., 1978. 'Prehistoric field systems in Britain and north-west Europe – a review of some recent work', *World Archaeol. 9:* 265–80.

Bretz-Mahler, D., 1971. *La Civilisation de La Tène I en Champagne.* 13e suppl. à Gallia Préhistoire (C.N.R.S. Paris).

Buchsenschutz, O., 1981. 'L'Apport des habitats à étude chronologique du premier siècle avant J-C.'. In *L'Age du Fer en France Septentrionale* (Mémoires de la Soc. Arch. Champenoise 2): 331–8.

Cadoux, J-L., 1979. 'Informations archéologiques Picardie: Villeneuve-Saint-Germain', *Gallia 37:* 305–9.

Chevallier, R., 1960. 'Notes préliminaires sur le champ d'urnes de Vieil-Arcy (Aisne)', *Bull. de la Soc. Arch. Champenoise 2:* 16–18.

Coudart, A., Dubouloz, J., and Le Bolloch, M., 1981. 'Un Habitat de La Tène ancienne dans la vallée de l'Aisne à Menneville (Aisne)'. In *L'Age du Fer en France Septentrionale* (Mémoires de la Soc. Arch. Champenoise 2): 121–30.

Coudart, A. and Ilett, M., 1978. 'Le Site néolithique, chalcolithique et de l'Age du Bronze de Berry-au-Bac, lieu-dit La Croix Maigret (Aisne)', *F.P.V.A. 6:* 51–77.

Debord, J., 1981. 'Un enclos quadrangulaire à remplissage de La Tène Ia, à Villeneuve-Saint-Germain (Aisne)'. In *L'Age du Fer en France Septentrionale,* Memoirs de la Soc. Arch. Champenoise 2): 107–20.

Demoule, J-P. (in press). *Les Nécropoles de l'Âge du Fer dans le Nord de la France* (Saarbrücker Beiträge zur Alterkumskunde).

Demoule, J-P. and Ilett, M., 1978. 'Le Site de Berry-au-Bac, La Croix Maigret', *F.P.V.A. 6:* 51–77.

Demoule, J-P. and Ilett, M., 1982. 'Les Installations du Premier Age du Fer à Cuiry-lès-Chaudardes', *Revue Arch. de Picardie*, numéro special 1982: 187–94.

F.P.V.A., 1972–80. *Les Fouilles Protohistoriques dans la Vallée de l'Aisne 1–7* (Université dé Paris I).

Gaucher, G., 1981. *Sites et cultures de l'âge du bronze dans le bassin parisien.* 15e suppl. à *Gallia Préhistoire* (C.N.R.S. Paris).

Haffner, A., 1976. *Die westliche Hunsrück–Eifel-kultur,* Römisch-Germanische Forschungen 36 (Berlin).

Hatt, J-J. and Brisson, A., 1953. 'Les Nécropoles hallstattiennes d'Aulnay-aux-Planches', *Rev. Arch. de l'Est et du Centre-Est 4:* 193–233.

Hatt, J-J. and Brisson, A., 1966–67. 'Fonds de cabanes de l'Age du Bronze Final et du Premier Age du Fer en Champagne', *Rev. Arch. de l'Est et du Centre-Est 17:* 165–97, and *18:* 7–51.

Hatt, J-J. and Rouallet, P., 1976–77. 'Le Cimitière des Jogasses et les origines de la civilisation de La Tène', *Rev. Arch. de l'Est et du Centre-Est 27:* 421–48, and *28:* 7–36.

Ilett, M., Demoule, J-P., Coudart, A. and Constantin, C., 1981. 'Structures d'habitat et urbanisme à Villeneuve-Saint-Germain (Aisne)'. In O. Buchsenschutz (ed.), *Les Structures d'habitat à l'Age du Fer en Europe tempérée* (Maison des Sciences de l'Homme, Paris): 201–6.

Jockenhövel, A., and Smolla, G., 1975. 'Le dépôt de Juvincourt-Damary (Aisne)'. *Gallia Préhistoire 18:* 289–309.

Joullié, H., 1962a. 'Découverte dans la vallée de l'Aisne, non loin de Vailly-sur-Aisne d'une tombe à incinérations multiples, entourée de deux fossés concentriques', *Bull. de la Soc. Préhistorique Française 59:* 324–32.

Joullié, H., 1962b. 'Brêve étude des tombes entourées d'un fossé circulaire, de leur région d'origine et de leur propagation', *Bull. de la Soc. Arch. Champenoise:* 6–28.

Letterle, F., 1982. 'Un site de l'Age du Bronze à Cuiry-lès-Chaudardes (Aisne)', *Revue Arch. de Picardie*, numéro special 1982: 175–86.

Lobjois, G., 1969. 'La Nécropole gauloise de Pernant', *Celticum 18:* 1–283.

Lobjois, G., 1974a. 'La Nécropole gauloise de La Tène I à Bucy-le-Long (Aisne)', *Cahiers Arch. de Picardie 1:* 67–96.

Lobjois, G., 1974b. 'La Nécropole gauloise de Bucy-le-Long (Aisne), première étude, les tombes de 001 à 051', *Cahiers Arch. du Nord-Est 17:* 1–74.

Lobjois, G., 1977. 'La Nécropole gauloise de Bucy-le-Long (Aisne), deuxième étude, les tombes 052 à 082', *Cahiers Arch. du Nord-Est 20:* 11–94.

Mordant, D., 1975. 'Quinze années d'activité archéologique en Bassée. Sauvetages et fouilles préventives', *Bull. du Groupement Arch. de Seine et Marne 16:* 15–40.
Morgen, M. L. and Rouallet, P., 1975–76. 'Le Cimitière gaulois de l'Argentelle à Beine (Marne)', *Mémoires de la Soc. d'Agriculture de la Marne 90:* pl. I–XXXI, and *91:* 7–44.
Rouallet, P., 1977–79. 'Cimitières à incinération d'Hauviné et de Saint-Clément-à-Arnes (Ardennes)', *Mémoires de la Soc. d'Agriculture de la Marne 92:* 35–53, *93:* 23–34, and *94:* 17–30.
Rowlett, R. M., Rowlett, E. S. J. and Boureux, M., 1969. 'A rectangular Early La Tène Marnian house at Chassemy (Aisne)', *World Archaeol. 1:* 106–35.
Soudský, B. and Pavlu, I., 1972. 'The Linear Pottery Culture settlement patterns of Central Europe'. In P. J. Ucko, R. Tringham and G. W. Dimbleby (eds.), *Man, Settlement and Urbanism:* 317–28.
Toupet, C., 1979. *Une nécropole à incinération à Longuesse (Val d'Oise)* (Service Départemental d'Archéologie du Val d'Oise, Cergy-Pontoise).
Villes, A., 1974. 'Les Enclos de Juvigny (Marne) et le remplissage des fossés des enclos funéraires protohistoriques en milieu alluvial', *Bull. de la Soc. Arch. Champenoise 5:* 25–58.
Villes, A., 1980. *La Maison protohistorique et ses annexes en Champagne et en France septentrionale dans le contexte de l'Europe moyenne tempérée* (thesis, Université de Besançon; forthcoming Mémoire de la Soc. Arch. Champenoise).

11

Approaches to the problem of settlement patterns in eastern Scania in the first millennium B.C.

Berta Stjernquist

First of all, it must be emphasized that the cultural development of Scandinavia has a different rhythm from that of central and western Europe. In southern Scandinavia, the Iron Age begins in the middle of the first millennium B.C. On the other hand, it dominates developments up to the eleventh century A.D. This means that the first millennium B.C. includes the Late Bronze Age as well as the beginning of the Iron Age, while the major part of the Iron Age comes after the birth of Christ. In order to understand our Iron Age, it is necessary to consider the period after the birth of Christ. I will therefore take the liberty of using the Gårdlösa Investigation, my own research project for analysing Iron Age settlement, to illustrate current approaches to the problem of settlement patterns in the first millennium B.C.

Problems

It is apparent that the term 'settlement patterns' in archaeological research is used in a rather wide sense. It is no doubt also the case that the papers presented here need not be too narrowly restricted. But it is important to clarify the problems involved and to discuss the theoretical background, for only if this is clarified is it possible to go on to choose material and to perform analyses.

One important task is to illuminate the distribution of settlements over the landscape and their relation to natural resources: soils, water, etc. On a macro-level, one can, through a study of these relationships, establish general characteristics and reasons for the localization. This type of analysis deals with general connections between the settlement and one or more external factors. In order to be able to develop hypotheses about more complex connections, it would seem to be necessary to study individual patterns and structures through intensive analysis of minor entities: case-studies. One can go further and make comparisons between different individual structures and in this way arrive at general features of the structures.

One could say that the analysis of general patterns of settlement structures can have two angles of approach; of these, one lies on the macro-level and involves the study of general connections between settlement and external factors, while the other lies on the micro-level and involves the analysis of individual settlement structures, as expressed in the model (fig. 11.1). It is necessary that an interaction between the different approaches occurs. If a survey analysis is performed, it is not possible to see if the relations are real. Individual tests, in which more complex causal relations can be explored, are necessary for this. One must investigate how man adapts to the environment and exploits natural resources in developing social systems of simpler or more complex nature. This is the driving force for the development of the cultural landscape.

What possibilities are there for analysing the settlement patterns of the first millennium B.C. in the area in question? In principle, the methods are the same regardless of the period with which one works. The starting point is our knowledge of the archaeological material. Hoards rich in bronzes, grave-fields with cremation graves, and some occupation sites are known from the first 500 years of the first millennium B.C., here as in other places in southern Scandinavia. The occupation sites are few (fig. 11.2), but their number is continuously increasing (Stjernquist 1969a; Strömberg 1975a:101) thanks to the new investigations which are being carried out in connection with expansion in modern settlement areas or in other areas subject to modern planning. At the same time we have begun to gain insight into the structure of these settlements, as house foundations – of which we had very little knowledge earlier – are beginning to show up as patterns of post-holes and other features when large excavation areas are opened up. By studying an extensive system of simple arrangements of pits, one of my doctoral students has been able to show that they could be material pits and could have a connection with house foundations which have subsequently disappeared due to farming activity (Widholm 1980:29). Such traces indicate that settlement has been frequent and that it can be studied even if the constructions are badly damaged.

In the graves, which consist of cremation burials spread over the landscape, hints of relatively extensive settlement have long been available. This idea was confirmed by the bronze-rich hoards which also occur (fig. 11.3). However, there are many uncertain factors connected with drawing conclusions about settlement patterns from such material. The known cremation graves consist mainly of smaller accumulations. Only three larger grave-fields are known in

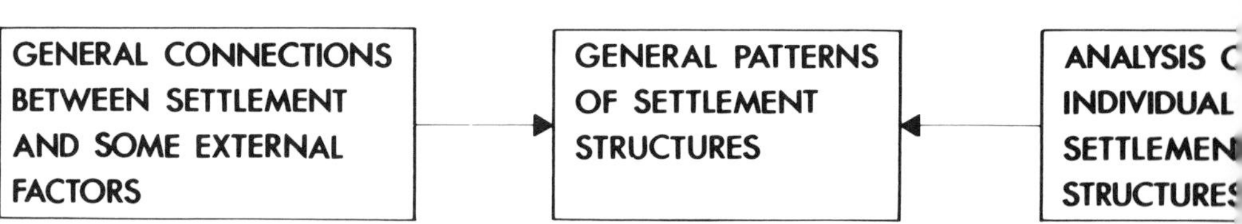

Figure. 11.1 Model showing two angles of approach in analysing general patterns of settlement structures.

south-eastern Scania (fig. 11.4), namely the Simris grave-field which I investigated from 1949 to 1951 (Stjernquist 1961)), the Löderup grave-field (Strömberg 1975b), and a complex of graves in the Svarte-Ruuthsbo area (Hansen 1923:119). However, it must be said that these large grave-fields have been investigated through large-scale archaeological efforts, and we know by experience that the simpler cremation graves to a large extent are destroyed and can disappear without a trace in connection with farming and exploiting of gravel-pits in the landscape. The material of which we are aware is thus only fragmentary.

There are researchers who have suggested, based on the few settlements which have been mapped, that there was a population increase during the Late Bronze Age (Welinder 1977). This is possible, but the uncertainty factors are numerous. If one assumes that subsistence was characterized by extensive agriculture and

Figure 11.2 Bronze Age settlements in Scania. (After Stjernquist 1969a with additions – the solid triangles.)

stock-raising, one cannot rule out the possibility of a mobility of settlement, with moves perhaps so frequent that we, limited by our coarse dating methods, have difficulty seeing the connection. In this case the graves can be of help, as one can gain more reliable information about settlement continuity through them. But considerably more investigations are needed.

One of the more interesting excavation sites in eastern Scania is in Stora Köpinge parish, where salvage work has been carried out. Phosphate mapping for reconnaissance of the area has been undertaken parallel with the excavation. The method of excavation has entailed uncovering large areas in which house foundations in the form of series of post-holes have been traced. Groups of house foundations from the period corresponding to the first part of the first millennium B.C. (that is, our Late Bronze Age) have been identified. Cooking

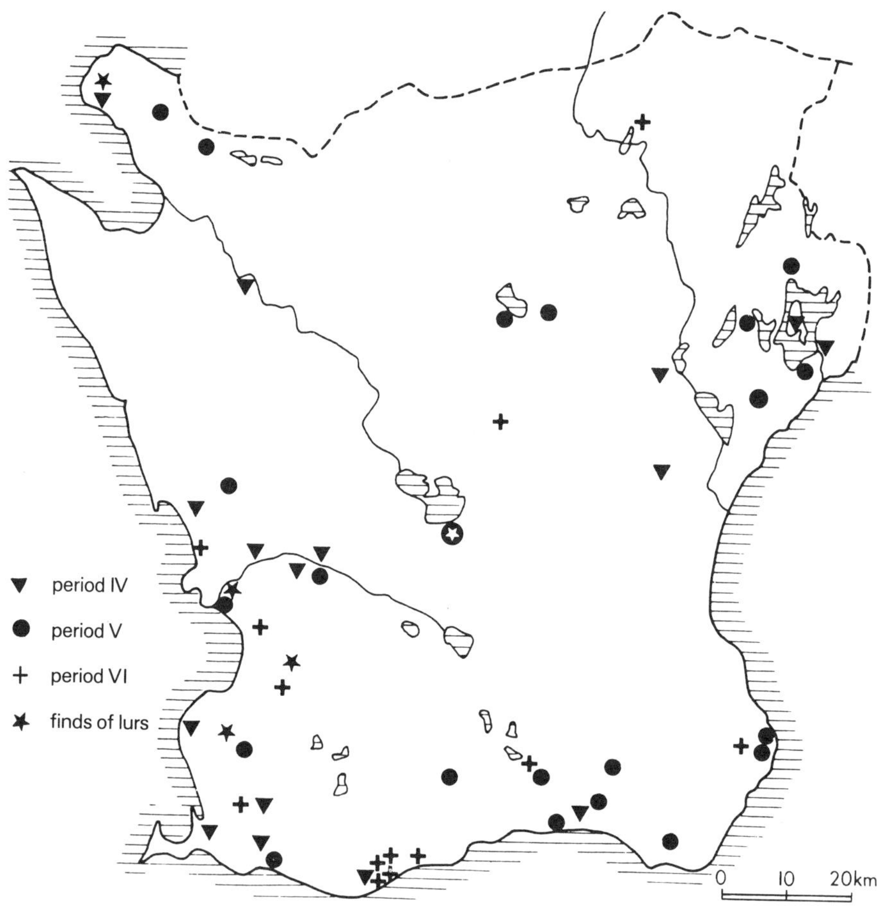

Figure 11.3 The distribution of the Late Bronze Age hoards of Scania. (After Larsson 1975.)

pits, refuse layers, and house foundations proved to lie within the 100m×150m area which had shown markedly higher amounts of phosphate (Widholm *et al.* 1975; Tesch 1980).

The house foundations correspond typologically to those from Denmark from the same period (Becker 1976:70; 1980:127). These are now also appearing in excavations in other parts of Scania, especially in the area around Malmö. In newer works on Bronze Age society, and under the influence of social anthropology, it has been common to view Bronze Age society as strongly integrated in the form of a chiefdom. In Denmark, large-scale investigations on south-western Fyn have produced a large amount of rich material from graves and occupation sites from the Late Bronze Age. Using this material, Henrik Thrane has discussed, in an especially interesting way, possible dynamic

Figure 11.4 Map of Scania, southern Sweden, with find-places mentioned in the text.

settlement changes in occupation sites which are hierarchically constructed and which function in connection with a central place (Thrane 1980:165; fig. 11.5). At Voldtofte on Fyn, in an area rich in finds, settlement remains with among other things remains of painted wall-coverings have been investigated (Thrane 1979:10). Such features have been considered to indicate a high-status dwelling. Comparable finds are not known in southern Sweden. From its appearance, with simple graves and settlements, the material here seems to derive from an egalitarian society. Better knowledge of the society would be of help in studying

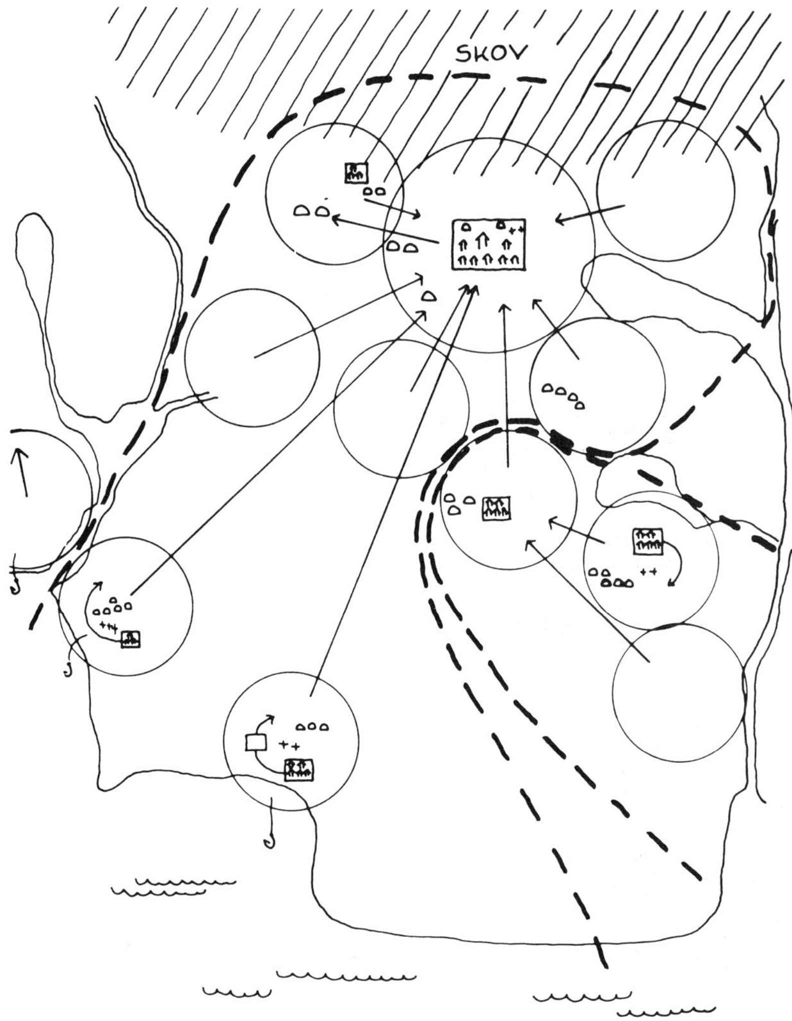

Figure 11.5 Model of the dynamic process in a hierarchic system of settlements. (After Thrane 1980.)

the settlement pattern as a whole, but the find material is still too meagre to support an analysis of social stratification (cf. Welinder 1977; Strömberg 1975b).

The question of the distribution system for goods is connected to that of social stratification. The hoard finds play an important part in this context. Thrane has discussed the successive spread of metal products from central Europe to Scandinavia, based on hoard finds. This is one possible way of approaching social structure, a question which is of importance for a more complex analysis of the settlement pattern (Thrane 1975).

An important question for the first millennium B.C. is that of continuity from the Late Bronze Age to the Early Iron Age in the middle of the millennium. Finds from the beginning of the Iron Age are few. However, it should be noted that the material from two of the Bronze Age grave-fields mentioned above, Simris and Löderup, indicate continuity. There are, among other things, graves without finds which can be dated to the beginning of the Iron Age by C14 analysis. But in order to gain a deeper understanding of settlement relations, it is necessary to combine the study of the archaeological remains with natural science methods of analysis.

Natural science methods, in particular pollen analysis, have shown changes in the landscape which indicate four different agricultural expansion phases during prehistoric times in southern Sweden. One of these occurs at the end of the first millennium B.C. and continues into the first millennium A.D. Archaeologically, the expansion periods should indicate population growth and technical development which brought about an expansion of the agricultural landscape. Technically, this period should correspond to a time when mobile agriculture successively became less mobile, leading to a permanent settlement of single farmsteads. It can be assumed that fertilization was practised and that a preliminary division into infields and outlying land was begun (Berglund 1969).

The pollen diagrams' evidence for increased human activity, with a more open landscape as a result, corresponds in Denmark to an expansion of settlement with colonization even to heavier soils. Settlements with house foundations have been sporadically identified even in Scania, and they continue without pause until after the birth of Christ. An example of such a settlement is Hötofta in the south-western part of the province (Stjernquist 1969a; Stjernquist 1969b:161). The period is represented at the above-mentioned settlement at Stora Köpinge in the south-east by long-house foundations dated to the period before as well as after the birth of Christ. The plan is the usual, with two rows of inner posts and a hearth in one part of the house. Such foundations lie in groups. This seems to be the same sort of settlement as the well-known concentrations of village-like settlements in Denmark, in spite of the fact that our material is poorer than what is known in Denmark. We now know it is necessary to uncover large areas in order to delineate structures. In connection with the find material from eastern Scania, I would like to mention here a very interesting settlement at Istaby. This lies just east of the boundary between Scania and Blekinge in an area which is the easternmost spur of the plains area of north-east Scania, the Kristianstad plain. Two students of mine have investigated here a settlement with a long-house which was later overlain by graves. The graves are from the period around and just after the birth of Christ. One house, which was 25m long and 6m wide and had rounded corners, differed from the normal house in that it had only one row of inner posts. The posts in the line of the wall showed that the house had been constructed in wattle and daub (Björkquist and Persson 1977:13) (cf. fig. 11.4).

The details of the house foundations which have been described yield some insights into housing conditions and settlement groupings. In order to get an idea of the relations between man and nature and about external relations, it is necessary to try to illuminate the activities as a whole. This lies behind the model which I constructed when I worked with the analysis of an Iron Age society, Gårdlösa, in south-eastern Scania (fig. 11.6). In a concrete manner this model takes up all the activities in a social system. Economic, social and religious activities, relationships between them and relations to the natural environment and to the social milieu are included here. Modern settlement archaeology aims at achieving a holistic picture of a society. A systematic analysis, starting from a model of this sort, not only gives positive results but is also of help in spotting gaps in the material. If the material is incomplete, it becomes clear in the analysis how far one can go under the conditions given. In the analysis, an interdisciplinary method becomes necessary to investigate the ecological connections around

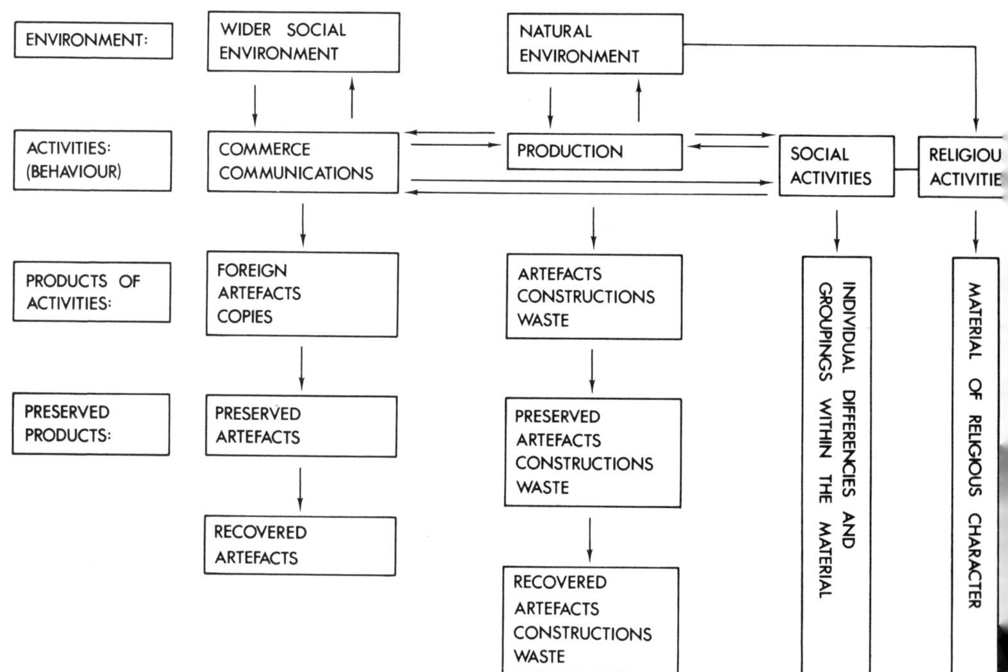

Figure 11.6 Model of components of a prehistoric community.

and in the settlement. The natural surroundings and their resources are preconditions for the activities which affect subsistence. The interdisciplinary analyses play a central part even in the discussion of the area outside the settlement which could have contributed to the subsistence activities. Important factors creating resources are climate, hydrological conditions, soil, flora, fauna, technology, communication, and organization. An integration of the information which the archaeological material yields with that from the interdisciplinary analyses is needed. This is illustrated by an idealized scheme of archaeological/paleoecological settlement studies compiled by Björn Berglund, Professor of Quaternary geology at the University of Lund and one of my co-workers in the

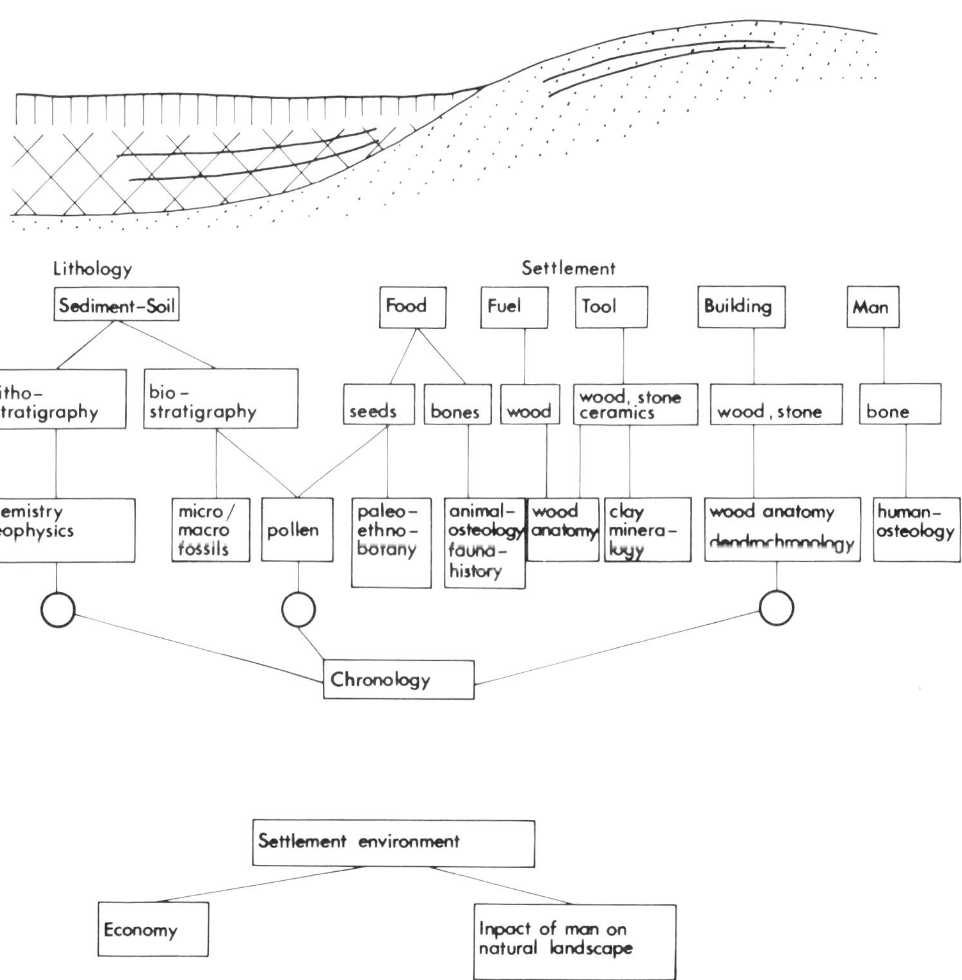

Figure 11.7 An idealized scheme of archaeological-paleoecological settlement studies compiled by Björn E. Berglund. (After Berglund 1981.)

project dealing with the cultural landscape which is being carried out at the university (fig. 11.7). The scheme illustrates a prehistoric settlement, with culture layers embedded in the sand of a beach ridge. There are traces of human activity in the sediments. With the help of the numerous biological and physical/chemical methods illustrated in fig. 11.7, one can study the details in the settlement and its changes and, through this, man's activity and the impact of man on the cultural landscape. Many of the factors which are studied are basic to the economy of the settlement and are therefore also basic to the settlement pattern as a whole.

In order to illustrate the methodology which I presently employ in the study of settlement patterns, I shall use the example of the previously mentioned Gårdlösa Research Project and more closely explore the material and the methods of analysis. The Gårdlösa Project deals with an Iron Age community in its natural and social setting (Stjernquist 1981). The area of investigation is part of the village of Gårdlösa, parish of Smedstorp, in south-eastern Scania (cf. fig. 11.4). Situated on the southern part of the Gårdlösa ridge which runs north-north-east–south-south-west, it is topographically fairly well delimited. The water system of the Tommarp river stresses the contours of the ridge.

The aim of the excavation was to make the investigation as complete as possible. Systematic fieldwork started in 1963 and was terminated in 1976. I cannot discuss the project in detail here but I want to present some aspects of the results and – as mentioned – the methods of analysis. The investigations have shown that the ridge was occupied during the greater part of the Iron Age. There are, in addition, some traces of occupation from the later part of the Bronze Age, but this occupation has been less extensive. The excavated material consists of different sorts of graves, remains of house foundations, occupation layers, pits, wells, ovens and some refilled springs. Variations in burial practices can be followed in this material, and remains of house constructions can be studied. In addition, the grouping of structures and their location in relation to each other can be studied.

The house foundations lay in three different groups. The oldest complex was discovered in the northern part of the excavated area. Here, remains of house foundations, which had lain on the surface and which therefore were seriously damaged, were investigated.

As a whole the period for the grave constructions agrees with that which the house remains represent. The question of the inner relationship will be more closely examined in connection with the intensive study of the finds. However, one can accept the hypothesis that the inner relationship is great. The investigations of the grave-field yield not only material for the interpretation of the inner connections in the settlement area, but also many new angles of approach for the interpretation of other grave-fields and for the question of the settlement's relation to the external social milieu (the contact net).

The three house foundation complexes are chronologically related to each other. Together, they cover the whole Iron Age from the first century B.C. to the eleventh century A.D. A variety of circumstances indicate that settlement relocation took place on two occasions. It is of particular interest that certain changes in settlement structure and in burial occur simultaneously with these relocations.

One of the conditions for completing the investigation is that the material should be set in a time perspective, i.e. that it should be possible to see a chronological relationship existing between the various entities. The methods used for this purpose are C14 analyses (Olsson 1981) and comparative analysis of the archaeological material with the help of typology. By employing both methods, increased certainty of the results will be assured. It was also possible to supplement the archaeological datings with C14 analysis, and through C14 analyses to obtain a chronological skeleton for the wood-anatomical identifications, so important for the milieu analyses. These are treated below.

If one chooses to investigate a prehistoric society as a social system; that is, chooses a problem-orientation about conditions of life and man's way of living and forming his existence in society, an interdisciplinary method of analysis becomes necessary to investigate the ecological connections around and in the settlement. The natural surroundings and their resources are preconditions for the activities which affect subsistence. The interdisciplinary analyses play a central part even in the discussion of the area outside the settlement which could have contributed to the subsistence activities, the site territory. In order to carry out the analysis according to this model, an integration of the information which the archaeological material yields with that from the interdisciplinary analyses is needed. A number of researchers from scientific and humanistic disciplines have taken part in and contributed to the analysis of Iron Age society. The basic information which has emerged from these analyses has been presented and will be published in a first part of the Gårdlösa Research Project.

The interdisciplinary analyses in the Gårdlösa Research Project have many angles of approach. First, a *geological* investigation has been carried out. This work has produced a map showing bedrock and soils as a basis for the analysis of vegetation through time. It also yields information about the occurrence of various materials, for example where limestone can be found. Limestone was used in the structures at the settlement, and it should have been quarried in one of the localities near the settlement, as shown (Mikaelsson and Sandgren 1981). Second, a *vegetation reconstruction* analysis has been completed through co-operation between specialists of Quaternary geology, dendrochronology and wood anatomy and plant ecology. It is not possible to obtain material for pollen analysis near the settlement. Instead, the standard profile which exists for Bjärsjöholm lake, c.25km from Gårdlösa, was used. However, this has been supplemented by material from the locality. In this work, two independent methods have been used (Bartholin *et al.* 1981). The first of these methods is wood anatomy – that is, the identification of charcoal from hearths on the site. Through this an idea could be gained as to which trees and bushes were used and therefore existed near the site. Thomas Bartholin has been responsible for this part of the analysis. The other method used here was developed by Nils Malmer and consists of drawing conclusions about the potential vegetation from present-day vegetation. This involved a theoretical construction to describe how the vegetational landscape today would have developed if it had been left alone without interference from man. In this way the area can be divided up into comprehensible ecological units and this can be used in the vegetation analysis. The cultural plants are also included in the vegetation analysis. The analysis of cultural plants also yields information for many questions which concern subsistence life.

The Iron Age landscape and its background in preceding periods has been reconstructed from these different angles. A picture of the vegetation commensurate with soils and other surface conditions, for instance humidity, has emerged. A mosaic landscape with small open areas existed on the lighter soils on the ridge during the Iron Age. The forest was dominated by oak, but birch, ash and Sorbus species existed as well. It can be seen that the vegetation became more open after c.500 A.D. – a grazing landscape. One can assume that conditions for agriculture grew worse during the Vendel Period due to the hydrological and nutritional conditions in effect.

It is assumed that the climate from 700 A.D. became warmer and drier, and this could have contributed to lower productivity and to the fact that the settlement moved from the ridge. Through the vegetation reconstruction analysis it has been possible to gain a fairly good impression of the environmental conditions for subsistence. The *osteological* material, burnt and unburnt human and animal bone, is a rich source of information about the settlement and of course also about the activities involved. Nils-Gustaf Gejvall has completed a thorough analysis of this material. The animal bones give information about the activities and subsistence conditions at the settlement. Cattle were the most common domestic animal, but sheep and pigs were of importance and horses occurred as well. There are also a few bones from some wild species of particular interest such as seal and beaver. The basic source for calculations about the size and composition of the population is found in the osteological material, even if there are many sources of error. It is, of course, necessary to combine different methods which can be of use for such calculations if one wishes to investigate population conditions (Gejvall 1981).

A *cultural geographical* analysis has been carried out by Staffan Helmfrid. He has examined and worked up the cartographic material. Since this material is relatively late and poor in information, and since fossil traces of cultivation are not and are not likely to be preserved in the sandy soil up on the ridge, the result of the analysis consists of possible hypotheses about culture geographical relationships. The preconditions for cultivation and forms for resource exploitation are discussed in this connection. This gives different interpretive possibilities (Helmfrid 1981).

The problems surrounding the removal and cessation of the settlement up on the ridge are central to the investigation. The cause of such changes can of course be wholly local, but on the other hand there may be causal connections and adaptive problems of more general nature in such a process. The interdisciplinary analyses play a central part in the microanalysis which is necessary to illuminate this. There is some support for the idea that the natural resources in the area very easily and relatively quickly could be over-exploited, especially if there was a period of desiccation during the later part of the Iron Age.

Other important problems of the Gårdlösa project concern the extent of the resource area of the settlement and wider social environment. The discussion of the resource area, inspired by ethnographic analogies, has been important among other things because it has quickened interest in the study of the varying activity patterns practised by man. But it is wholly theoretical to picture a resource area in a schematic fashion as a circle with the settlement as a centre, a common model in modern archaeological literature. Variations in the question of mobility, and therefore the size of the resource area, were undoubtedly dependent on a number of factors. The topography and other natural conditions play a large part. They are also dependent on other settlements and their resource areas. The subsistence structure is another factor of importance.

The topography of the settlement area suggests that the Tommarp river may have played some role in communication between the ridge settlement and the Baltic. In order to determine the wider social environment, other Iron Age communities in neighbouring regions must also be taken into account and form an independent part of the analysis.

The methodology used in the Gårdlösa Programme, including the study of

Figure 11.8 The project area in Scania, southern Sweden.

settlement and its relationship to nature and the social environment by means of intensive interdisciplinary studies, creates the possibility of gaining a holistic view of the settlement pattern. Through various case studies, one can develop the questions to be asked and can adapt the methods to these. Settlement is regarded as an integrated part of the cultural landscape, and the various settlement entities are seen as parts of a settlement pattern over larger areas. The methods are in principle applicable to any chronological period. In order to among other things further develop the method, researchers from humanistic and scientific disciplines at the University of Lund are collaborating in a project to study the cultural landscape over 6,000 years in an area in south-east Scania (fig. 11.8). The development of the settlement pattern during the Late Bronze Age and Early Iron Age, according to the Scandinavian chronology (that is, the first millennium B.C.), is included in the project. The name of the project is 'The cultural landscape during 6,000 years. An interdisciplinary study of man and landscape in a south Scanian district'. The aim is to describe the landscape and those changes which it has undergone in an area in southern Sweden. Through interdisciplinary collaboration, a deeper holistic understanding of the relationships between man, his external milieu such as land use, vegetation, animal life, production, etc., and his social milieu such as population development, social structure, economy, technology, etc., will be attained. The problems to be studied are attacked in two ways: first, through studies of changes in landscape in a long, continuous chronological perspective: time-vertical studies; and second, through interdisciplinary studies of a few time periods, chosen in consideration of their assumed importance in the development of the society and the landscape: phase studies. The major hypothesis is that a periodization can be seen in change in the cultural landscape, in that periods of expansion alternate with periods of regression. This involves some focus on the supposed periods of expansion, but does not mean that the supposed periods of regression are without interest.

The development of the agricultural landscape as seen from a long chronological perspective is studied, using Quaternary geological methods. Changes should be seen in relation to the natural preconditions for the different areas and to the social development. As in the Gårdlösa Programme, the natural preconditions are illustrated through plant ecological vegetational reconstruction based on the mapping of vegetation types, soils, and hydrological conditions in special areas. The paleoecological studies should lead to a holistic view of the natural resources and man's use of them in time and space.

The six time-vertical studies will deal with regional and local vegetation developments, paleohydrological changes, land erosion and vegetational reconstructions. Periods which against the research background can be assumed to have involved large changes in man's expansion over the landscape and in the use of natural resources have been chosen for the phase studies. Within each of these phases the analysis will be concentrated on the question of how the resources were used in man's activity in developing social systems of a simpler or more complex nature. One of these phases deals with the cultural landscape during the Bronze and Iron Ages. The central area for this study is that around St

Köpinge, where rich archaeological material from previous excavations is already available. I have mentioned house foundations and phosphate maps from this area. Questions of settlement concentrations in the prehistoric landscape and questions of structuring such as the relationship between settlement on the plain and in the hills, central district versus regional area, permanent versus temporary settlement, and infields versus outlying land, are central. Archaeology, Quaternary geology, and plant ecology will work together here. For the period after the birth of Christ, disciplines such as history and place-name research will be included.

Space does not permit me to elaborate on the details of the project, which has now been organized. However, it is important to point out that it involves a combination of overarching questions, macro-studies, and case studies on the micro-level, where the development and testing of methods can be done in connection with concrete investigations. We count on being able to carry out archaeological test excavations and intensive excavations in various contexts. However, the integration of the co-operating disciplines which has been planned is of essential importance for the project. If we are to be able to gain a holistic perspective on settlement patterns, I think that it is necessary to carry out projects of this sort to the greatest possible extent. It is necessary to carry out intensive interdisciplinary analyses of resources and environment in order to in this way gain a concrete basis and better understand components and dynamics in the social system.

Bibliography

Bartholin, T., Berglund, B. E. and Malmer, N., 1981. 'Vegetation and environment in the Gårdlösa Area during the Iron Age'. In Stjernquist 1981: 45–53.

Becker, C. J., 1976. 'Bosaettelsesformer i bronze- og jernalder. Bebyggelsearkaeologi', *Skrifter fra Institut for historie og samfundsvidenskab* 17(Odense Universitet): 70.

Becker, C. J., 1980. 'Bebyggelsesformer i Danmarks yngre bronzealder set i forhold til aeldste, jernalders landsbysamfund. Broncealderbebyggelse i Norden', *Skrifter fra historisk institut* (Odense Universitet, no. 28): 127–41.

Berglund, B. E., 1969. 'Vegetation and human influence in South Scandinavia during Prehistoric time', *Oikos,* suppl. 12, (Copenhagen): 9–28.

Berglund, B. E., 1977. 'Biological/palaeoecological analyses for modern archaeological research', Proceedings of the Nordic Conference on Thermoluminescence Dating and other Archaeometric Methods, Uppsala University, Sweden, 25–26 Nov. 1976 (Risø National Laboratory, Denmark, June 1977).

Björkquist, K-A. and Persson, T., 1977. 'Bonde, by och bygd. Istaby som arkeologiskt projekt', *Blekingeboken:* 13–27.

Gejvall, N-G., 1981. 'Skeletal remains from Gårdlösa, Smedstorp Parish, Scania, Sweden'. In Stjernquist 1981: 59–102.

Hansen, F., 1923. 'De arkeologiska fynden vid Svarte fiskläge', *Fornvännen:* 119–63, 229–48.

Helmfrid, S., 1981. 'The village of Gårdlösa and the Iron Age settlement on the Gårdlösa Ridge. Some reflections based on historical–geographical research'. In Stjernquist 1981: 24–8.

Kristiansen, K., 1979. 'The consumption of wealth in Bronze Age Denmark. A study in the dynamics of economic processes in tribal societies. New directions in

Scandinavian archaeology', *Studies in Scandinavian Prehistory and Early History* (The National Museum of Denmark) *1:* 158–90.

Larsson, L., 1975. 'The Fogdarp find. A hoard from the Late Bronze Age', *Meddelanden från Lunds universitets historiska museum* 1973–74 (Lund): 169–238.

Mikaelsson, J. and Sandgren, P., 1981. 'A geological survey of the Smedstorp area'. In Stjernquist 1981: 38–44.

Olsson, I. U., 1981. 'C^{14} dating of the settlement at Gårdlösa, Smedstorp Parish, Scania, Sweden'. In Stjernquist 1981: 109–13.

Stjernquist, B., 1961. *Simris II. Bronze Age Problems in the Light of the Simris Excavation,* Acta Archaeologica Lundensia, Series in 4°, no. 8 (Lund).

Stjernquist, B., 1969a. *Beiträge zum Studium von bronzezeitlichen Siedlungen,* Acta Archaeologica Lundensia, Series in 8°, no. 8 (Lund).

Stjernquist, B., 1969b. 'En boplats från äldre järnålder i Hötofta, sydvästra Skåne', *Fornvännen:* 161–79.

Stjernquist, B., 1980. 'Bronsåldersbebyggelse på Gårdlösaåsen. Kort presentation. Broncealderbebyggelse i Norden', *Skrifter fra historisk institut, Odense universitet 28:* 67–71.

Stjernquist, B., 1981. *Gårdlösa. An Iron Age Community in its Natural and Social Setting. I. Interdisciplinary Studies* by B. Stjernquist, S. Helmfrid, S. Skansjö, J. Mikaelsson, P. Sandgren, T. S. Bartholin, B. Berglund, N. Malmer, H. Hjelmqvist, N-G. Gejvall, H-A. Nordström, I. U. Olsson, S. Hakansson; Acta Regiae Societatis Humaniorum Litterarum Lundensis LXXV (Lund).

Strömberg, M., 1975a. 'Untersuchungen zur Bronzezeit in Südostschonen. Probleme um die Besiedlung', *Meddelanden från Lunds universitets historiska museum* 1973–74: 101–68.

Strömberg, M., 1975b. *Studien zu einem Gräberfeld in Löderup. Grabsitte – Kontinuität – Sozialstruktur,* Acta Archaeologica Lundensia, Series in 8°, no. 10 (Lund).

Tesch, S., 1980. 'Ett par bronsåldersmiljöer med huslämningar i Skåne och Södermanland. Broncealderbebyggelse i Norden', *Skrifter fra historisk institut, Odense universitet:* 83–101.

Thrane, H., 1975. *Europaeiske forbindelser. Bidrag til studiet af fremmede forbindelser i Danmarks yngre broncealder (period IV–V).* On the external relations of the Danish Late Bronze Age (Mont. per. IV–V). Nationalmuseets skrifter. Arkaeologisk–historisk raekke XVI (Copenhagen).

Thrane, H., 1979. 'Malede vaegge', *Skalk* 1979, no. 3: 10–13.

Thrane, H., 1980. 'Nogle tanker om yngre broncealders bebyggelse på Sydvestfyn. Broncealderbebyggelse i Norden', *Skrifter fra historisk institut, Odense universitet,* no. 28: 165–73.

Welinder, S., 1977. *Ekonomiska processer i förhistorisk expansion,* Acta Archaeologica Lundensia, Series in 8° Minore no. 7 (Lund).

Widholm, D., 1980. 'Problems concerning Bronze Age Settlements in Southern Sweden', *Meddelanden från Lunds universitets historiska museum* 1979–80 (Papers of the Archaeological Institute, University of Lund): 29–46.

Widholm, D., Wihlborg, A. and Tesch, S., 1975. *Forntidens bopålar. Stora Köpinge-bygden under 5000 år,* Riksantikvarieämbetet. Undersökningsverksamheten (Lund).

Index

[*Illustration references are indicated by italic numerals*]

Index

Index